FieldWorking

Reading and Writing Research

FOURTH EDITION

FieldWorking
Reading and Writing Research

Bonnie Stone Sunstein
University of Iowa

Elizabeth Chiseri-Strater
University of North Carolina–Greensboro

Burt —
The date on this edition
marks the 25th year of
your mentorship. (Eeek!
I think it shows.
my thanks for so
much,
Bonnie

BEDFORD/ST. MARTIN'S

Boston ◆ New York

For Bedford/St. Martin's

Senior Developmental Editor: Joelle Hann
Production Editor: Peter Jacoby
Production Supervisor: Samuel Jones
Senior Marketing Manager: Molly Parke
Editorial Assistant: Emily Wunderlich
Copy Editor: Wendy Polhemus-Annibell
Indexer: Melanie Belkin
Photo Researcher: Susan Doheny
Permissions Managers: Kalina Ingham Hintz, Linda Winters
Art Director: Lucy Krikorian
Text Design: Claire Seng-Niemoeller
Cover Design: Donna Dennison
Cover Art: Hundertwasser, Friedensreich (1928–2000) © copyright. *The apartments hang from the underside of the meadows*. Mixed techniques (1970), 44 × 63 cm. Private collection. Photo credit: Erich Lessing/Art Resources, NY.
Composition: Cenveo Publisher Services
Printing and Binding: RR Donnelley and Sons

President: Joan E. Feinberg
Editorial Director: Denise B. Wydra
Editor in Chief: Karen S. Henry
Director of Development: Erica T. Appel
Director of Marketing: Karen R. Soeltz
Director of Production: Susan W. Brown
Associate Director, Editorial Production: Elise S. Kaiser
Managing Editor: Shuli Traub

Library of Congress Control Number: 2011927765

Manufactured in the United States of America.

6   5   4   3   2   1

f   e   d   c   b   a

For information, write: Bedford/St. Martin's, 75 Arlington Street, Boston, MA 02116 (617-399-4000)

ISBN: 978–0–312–62275–6

Acknowledgments

Acknowledgments and copyrights appear at the back of the book on pages 419–20, which constitute an extension of the copyright page.

Implicit in this book is our philosophy of teaching: that teaching is a way of learning. We dedicate this book to all the students who have been our teachers.

Implicit in this book is our philosophy of teaching: that teaching is a way of learning. We dedicate this book to all the students who have been our teachers.

About the Authors

Bonnie Stone Sunstein and Elizabeth Chiseri-Strater have been collaborators and friends for a long time. They hope you'll notice, while reading this book, that they enjoy working together.

(Photo: Wendy Stewart)

During the school year, Bonnie is professor of both English and education at the University of Iowa, where she teaches courses in nonfiction writing, research methods, English education, and folklore. She is the director of undergraduate writing in the English department, coordinates the English Education Program in the Department of Teaching and Learning, and is a faculty member in the Language, Literacy, and Culture PhD program. Elizabeth is professor of English and women and gender studies at the University of North Carolina at Greensboro, where she teaches courses in nonfiction writing, research methods, rhetoric, and composition. She develops programs in writing across the curriculum, and served as director of Freshman Composition.

Bonnie and Elizabeth were each writing teachers long before they met as PhD students at the University of New Hampshire. They discovered that they shared a fascination with ethnographic fieldwork and began their work together on many writing and research processes by taking and teaching courses, designing and giving workshops, and consulting with teachers and students in secondary schools and colleges. They still belong to the same writing group.

Together, they have taught in summer programs at the University of New Hampshire, the Smithsonian Institution, and Northeastern University's Martha's Vineyard Summer Institute. They often present their work together at professional conferences and workshops. They've authored four editions of *FieldWorking* as well as a book for teachers, *What Works: A Practical Guide for Teacher Research* (Heinemann/Boynton Cook, 2006), and several articles and book chapters. Separately, Bonnie and Elizabeth have written chapters and articles about ethnographic writing, portfolio-keeping, and, of course, collaboration. Bonnie's book *Composing a Culture* (Heinemann/Boynton Cook, 1994) and Elizabeth's book *Academic Literacies* (Heinemann/Boynton Cook, 1991) are ethnographic field studies of writing communities.

To the Instructor

When we set out to write this book four editions ago, we wanted *FieldWorking: Reading and Writing Research* to gather together the concepts, readings, and exercises we had each used in the courses we teach. In other words, we wanted to write the book we wished we'd had. We've been proud of the results, and we've learned much from our readers along the way. *FieldWorking* has created communities of students and teachers — not only in writing and research classes, but also in anthropology, sociology, journalism, and folklore courses. We've enjoyed hearing from our readers, and in each new edition, we highlight some of their work on the pages of our book and its companion Web site.

Conducting fieldwork brings the research and writing processes together. It teaches the conventions of writing and rhetoric that students need to master, and introduces them to research strategies that are essential for college writers. But in choosing their own research sites, interacting with others, and documenting their experiences, students also learn to observe, listen, interpret, and analyze the behaviors and language of those around them — and then include these perspectives in their own writing. Research confined to the library or the Internet bring information to life in the same way, just as writing confined to discrete skills doesn't animate students' ideas doesn't necessarily. Doing ethnographic writing and research empowers students to invest in their rhetorical and research skills in a way that more traditional composition work simply can't.

Additionally, students commit more of themselves to the topics they investigate because fieldwork allows them actual contact with people and cultures, often ones different from their own. As a result, students develop a greater understanding of the "self" — their own habits, biases, assumptions — as they reflect on their encounters with the "other." But the most compelling reason for any instructor to use this investigative approach is that through the process of fieldworking, students become better readers, researchers, and writers.

Each chapter in *FieldWorking* introduces specific research concepts and short writing activities ("boxes") that allow students to practice skills that are essential to good fieldwork. The readings, by both professional and student writers, are designed to motivate students and model the skills and strategies they'll need for their own projects. We've put each reading in the chapter where it best serves as an example or expansion of the topic at hand, and we discuss it both before and after we present it.

One way to use the writing activities is to have students create a single, extended fieldwork project that spans the semester. Another way is to assign a number of small units that allow students to master the reading, writing, and research skills of a fieldworker in a few discrete projects.

But in either case, students are interpreting, analyzing, and building a cumulative record of their own research as they learn and practice. Collected into a research portfolio, this work becomes an essential record of their efforts and of the fieldwork they've conducted. And so the research portfolio becomes an essential tool that they (and you) can use for evaluation and future reference.

How Is the Fourth Edition Like Earlier Editions?

- **Activities that emphasize writing, critical thinking, and self-reflection** appear throughout the book in 34 "boxes" that center on specific skills, such as observing, taking notes, interviewing, using archives, and responding to texts. These popular exercises can be used individually or as component parts of a larger research project.

- **Two chapters devoted entirely to college-level writing** help students understand that the rhetorical concepts of purpose, audience, and voice are integral to their research. Chapter 2, "Writing Self, Writing Cultures: Understanding FieldWriting," shows students how to begin writing fieldnotes, and Chapter 8, "FieldWriting: From Down Draft to Up Draft," helps students assemble their data, shape it into a draft, and polish it into a final essay.

- **FieldWriting sections in every chapter** discuss writing strategies related to the chapter's focus, presenting issues of grammar, convention, style, and craft while reminding students that fieldwork is always about writing.

- **Abundant models from professional and student writers** include 20 readings from well-known voices, such as Gloria Naylor, Jamaica Kincaid, Oliver Sacks, and Joan Didion, writing in an array of disciplines and genres—anthropology, folklore, sociology, natural science, education, fiction, nonfiction, and journalism. In addition, nine full student research essays and numerous shorter examples appear throughout the book—with more available on the book's companion Web site.

- **Instruction for keeping a research portfolio** appears in each chapter, showing students how to reflect, interpret, and analyze the data they collect as they share both the processes and the products of their fieldwork.

- **A free and open companion Web site offers more help** with writing, research, and formatting documents; additional examples of professional and student essays; more boxed exercises (including a section on urban folk and fairy tales); and suggestions for further research in other mediums such as art, film, and poetry. Worksheets, consent forms, sample syllabi, and the Instructor's Manual are also downloadable from the site.

- **Coverage that works well with university initiatives that fall outside traditional academic disciplines**. Our selection of projects and student writing samples for *FieldWorking* are appropriate for students engaged in living-learning communities, local outreach projects, and service-learning and study-abroad programs.

What's New in the Fourth Edition?

Over the course of three editions and 15 years, we've collected comments from students and instructors who have used *FieldWorking* both in formal class settings and in independent field projects. We've been lucky to hear from so many people and see some of their work, and we've tried to incorporate their suggestions and meet their needs while developing new ideas of our own as we continue teaching with the book ourselves. We've seen new technologies shift the nature of research and access to materials in ways we never would have imagined when we began teaching. Among the new features in our fourth edition are:

- **Expanded coverage of working with online cultures, communities, and archives**, as well as thorough instruction for evaluating online sources and help for using digital recording devices. A full model student essay in Chapter 3, entitled "Out Patients," demonstrates effective research and documentation of an online community.

- **More writing coverage throughout the book** includes expanded field-writing sections in each chapter, focusing on important topics such as using language effectively, considering an audience, and working with rhetoric. New objectives at the start of each chapter indicate the writing skills covered in the chapter, guiding students to develop essential critical-thinking and rhetorical skills.

- **More examples of student and professional writing**, including four new student essays, eight new professional readings by writers such as H. L. "Bud" Goodall and Ofelia Zepeda, and numerous smaller excerpts throughout the book. Selections cover a range of contemporary topics from urban graffiti and fake disorders to the Ronald Reagan library, cemetery culture, tattoo art, and street pianos, while providing strong models of writing and research.

- **Streamlined for more focused reading and use**, this edition has been redesigned to include new mini-summaries of major skills throughout the book, as well as end-of-chapter activities that guide students through a short, effective exercise before they move on to the next chapter.

More Digital Choices for *FieldWorking*

FieldWorking doesn't stop with a book. Online, you'll find both free resources and affordable premium resources to help students get even more out of the book and your course. You'll also find convenient instructor resources, such as downloadable sample syllabi, classroom activities, and even a nationwide community of teachers. To learn more about or order any of the following products, contact your Bedford/St. Martin's sales representative, e-mail sales support (sales_support@bfwpub.com), or visit the Web site at **bedfordstmartins.com**.

Companion Web site for *FieldWorking*
bedfordstmartins.com/fieldworking

Send students to free and open resources, choose flexible premium resources to supplement your print text, or upgrade to an expanding collection of innovative digital content.

Free and open resources for *FieldWorking* provide students with easy-to-access reference materials, visual tutorials, and support for working with sources.

- Additional student and professional readings, more samples of research portfolios, and extra "box" exercises
- Links to fieldworking resources in media such as film, art, radio, and poetry
- *Research and Documentation Online* by Diana Hacker
- *Bedford Bibliographer*—a tool for collecting source information and making a bibliography in MLA, APA, and *Chicago* styles
- Three free tutorials from *ix visual exercises* by Cheryl Ball and Kristin Arola

VideoCentral is a growing collection of videos for the writing class that captures real-world, academic, and student writers talking about how and why they write. *VideoCentral* can be packaged with *FieldWorking* for free. An activation code is required. To order *VideoCentral* packaged with the print book, use ISBN 978-1-4576-0659-5.

Re:Writing Plus gathers all Bedford/St. Martin's premium digital content for composition into one online collection. It includes hundreds of model documents, the first ever peer review game, and *VideoCentral*. *Re:Writing Plus* can be purchased separately or packaged with the print book at a significant discount. An activation code is required. To order *Re:Writing Plus* packaged with the print book, use ISBN 978-1-4576-0662-5.

E-Book Options
bedfordstmartins.com/Fieldworking/catalog

With Bedford/St. Martin's e-books, students can do more and pay less. For about half the price of a print book, the e-book for *FieldWorking* offers the complete text combined with convenient digital tools, such as highlighting, note-taking, and search. Both online and downloadable options are available. Use ISBN 978-0-312-64408-6.

Instructor Resources

You have a lot to do in your course. Bedford/St. Martin's makes it easy for you to find the support you need—and to get it quickly.

The Instructor's Manual for FieldWorking, available in PDF format, can be downloaded from **bedfordstmartins.com/fieldworking**. In addition to chapter overviews and teaching tips, the manual includes sample syllabi and suggestions for classroom activities.

TeachingCentral (**bedfordstmartins.com/teachingcentral**) offers Bedford/St. Martin's entire list of print and online professional resources in one place. You'll find landmark reference works, sourcebooks on pedagogical issues, award-winning collections, and practical advice for the classroom—all free for instructors.

Bits (**bedfordbits.com**) collects creative ideas for teaching a range of composition topics in an easily searchable blog. A community of teachers—leading scholars, authors, and editors—discuss revision, research, grammar and style, technology, peer review, and much more. Take, use, adapt, and pass the ideas around. Then come back to the site to comment or to share your own suggestions.

Content cartridges for the most common course management systems—Blackboard, WebCT, Angel, and Desire2Learn—allow you to download digital resources for your course. To find the cartridges available for *FieldWorking*, visit the Bedford/St. Martin's online catalog at **bedfordstmartins.com/Fieldworking/catalog**.

How Can You Use *FieldWorking*?

We've designed this book to provide material for a semester-long course. The accompanying Instructor's Manual offers sample syllabi as well as suggestions for different or abbreviated ways to put this course together. Our colleague Jennifer Cook, professor of English at Rhode Island College, is a longtime user of *FieldWorking*, and her additions to the Instructor's Manual for this edition provide imaginative ways to organize your writing course to include *FieldWorking*. You may download the Instructor's Manual from the Bedford/St. Martin's Web site at **bedfordstmartins.com/fieldworking**.

How you use *FieldWorking* will depend on the overall purpose and theme of your course and the other texts you want to include. The text can serve alone in an undergraduate composition/research course. Or you can use it in an ethnographic reading/writing course together with several full-length ethnographies, such as *Mules and Men, Translated Woman*, and *My Freshman Year*, or with a collection of ethnographic essays, such as *Sun after Dark* or *An Anthropologist on Mars*. We've compiled lists of our current favorite options for further reading in Appendix C at the end of the book.

You might have the class start out with Chapters 1–3, which introduce students to the key theories about studying cultures as well as writing and reading strategies. You can then have students move around in the book, depending on the specific focus of your course. For example, Chapter 6, "Researching Language: The Cultural Translator," includes many short readings and exercises focused on language and culture that can serve as a unit of language study within any course. As well, as we mentioned above, service-learning, study-abroad, and university outreach programs provide wonderful opportunities for the kind of student fieldwork this book facilitates.

We believe strong teaching requires the courage to learn alongside your students. It also requires the hope that students will reflect on their own lives through their reading and writing about others. In *FieldWorking*, we invite you and your students to engage in this reflective process together.

About the Cover Art

The cover art for each of the four editions of *FieldWorking* has featured a different work by the Viennese artist Friedensreich Hundertwasser (1928–2000). We find his paintings exciting, colorful, and visually ethnographic, evoking the multiple perspectives of people interacting with their environments.

When we learned more about Hundertwasser's art and architecture, we discovered in his personal writing and philosophy strong statements about his experience painting different habitats and surroundings from the inhabitants' perspectives. Critic Pierre Restany notes that the "extra-lucid power of his analytical sensitivity makes him the perfect decoder of global culture and its guided information." No wonder we find his work so compelling! If you can't make it to Kunst Haus Wien in Vienna, Austria (and so far, we haven't), you can take a virtual tour of the museum (the house Hundertwasser designed and built) and view the galleries that sell his art at www.hundertwasser.at and www.kunsthauswien.com.

Acknowledgments

Effective writing, as we have tried to convey in this book, requires collaboration. It requires a subculture of selected readers—writers' own trusted "insiders"—before it can successfully move to an outside audience. For this book, we shared each reframed idea and each revision with our own subculture of trusted colleagues, whom we wish to acknowledge and thank.

Our thanks go to both our students and our colleagues who have contributed their exercises, short writings, and full essays for use in this edition of *FieldWorking*, helping to keep the book's coverage rich and fascinating: Kathryn Auman, Alan Benson, Beth Campbell, Elise Chu, Moira Collins, Jennifer S. Cook, Cary Cotton, Matt Gilchrist, Zuleyma Gonzalez, Kendra Greene, Deidre Hall, Nancy Hauserman, Janet Ingram, Brett Johnson, Rossina Liu, Sam Mahlstadt, Taurino Marcelino, Amie Ohlmann, William Purcell, Teresa Shorter, Jeannie Banks Thomas, Aidan Vollmer, and Lauren Wallis.

We again thank the students and colleagues who contributed their writings to previous editions of *FieldWorking*: Lori Bateman, Brenda Boleyn, Meg Buzzi, Laura Carroll, Julie Cheville, Karen Downing, Atyia Franklin, Angela Hager, Joelle Hann, Mimi Harvey, Jennifer Hemmingsen, Simone Henkel, David Jakstas, Nick Kowalczyk, Heather Kreiger, Amy Lambert, Yolanda Majors, Cindie Marshall, Maggie McKnight, Donna Niday, Ivana Nikolic, Holly Richardson,

Paul Russ, Katie Ryan, Sam Samuels, Terra Savage, Chinatsu Sazawa, Lia Schultz, David Seitz, Angela Shaffer, Grant Stanojev, Pappi Thomas, Emily Wemmer, and Rick Zollo. Since our first edition in 1997, this book has created a permanent community of fieldworkers.

For giving us their perspectives on the text, we thank our research assistants, Amie Ohlmann and Emily Benton, who read the third edition thoroughly to help us see how we might effectively refresh it for the fourth edition.

Of course, we thank the students and teachers from the courses we have taught with this text: in Iowa, in Greensboro, at the Smithsonian Institution, at the Center for the Humanities at the University of New Hampshire, at the Martha's Vineyard Summer Institute of Northeastern University, and at various other summer cultural studies institutes—the Fife Conference at Utah State University, the Louisiana Voices Institute at the University of Louisiana in Lafayette, Celebrate New Hampshire, and the New England Community Heritage Project at the University of New Hampshire.

We greatly appreciate the thoughtful comments we received from reviewers of the third edition: Kate Adams, Allan Hancock College; Neil P. Baird, Western Illinois University; Linda Burgess, California State University; Nicole Caswell, Kent State University; Stephen Criswell, University of South Carolina at Lancaster; Emily Dotson, University of Kentucky; Stephen M. Fonash, Pennsylvania State University; Shasta Grant, Ball State University; Matthew Hartman, Ball State University; Martha Marinara, University of Central Florida; Cynthia K. Marshall, Wright State University; Margaret A. McLaughlin, Georgia Southern University; Brooke Neely, University of California; Elizabeth J. O'Day, Millersville University; Jane Slama, Allan Hancock College; and Mary C. Tuominem, Denison University.

Both of our universities were generous with fellowships throughout these four editions, providing us with support, time, and research assistance within our academic appointments. We thank the Obermann Center for Advanced Studies at the University of Iowa for two generous grants of time and resources; the Woodrow Wilson Foundation in Princeton, New Jersey, for one of the first Imagining America grants for our forst Web site, www.fieldworking.com; and the National Network for Folk Arts in Education in Washington, D.C., for its recognition and support. Our colleagues' and students' enthusiasm, careful work, and faith allow us to share our confidence about the value of *FieldWorking* with our readers.

Very few textbook authors can claim over 20 years of support from one editor, but we are proud to say that we can: Nancy Perry's vision, judgment, expertise, business acumen, and friendship have guided this book (and us) from one important taxi ride and "What if?" question in 1991 through four editions of this book. Like the finest of teachers, Nancy has allowed us our independence as we've shaped our book. We have learned so much from our collaboration with her. She deserves her reputation as the best in the business among composition book editors. We are proud to know her.

We also wish to mention our remarkable two-edition collaboration with our development editor, Joelle Hann. We've often felt that Joelle is our third author.

Her eye for detail, her continuity, and her overall love for this project have taken it from our very full and comprehensive third edition through to a trimmer but no less comprehensive fourth edition. Joelle's discipline and scheduling have guided our own. As a fieldworker herself, she created the lovely "Travel Journal: Brazil" and photos for the third edition—and we hope you will read it on our Web site as a model of the verbal snapshot. This edition would not exist as it does without Joelle's expertise or the insightful preliminary editing of Sara Eaton Gaunt. We thank project editor Peter Jacoby and copy editor Wendy Polhemus-Annibell, whose combined work refined our understanding of the possibilities of fine-tuning. Thanks also go to editorial assistants Andrew Flynn and Emily Wunderlich for shepherding this project through administrative tasks big and small.

Finally, we thank our now adult children: Tosca Chiseri, Alisha Strater, Amy Sunstein, and Stephen Sunstein. In four different ways, they have grown with us over the writing of four editions of this text. As we wrote this book, they taught us, as our students do, more than we ever thought we could learn.

Bonnie Stone Sunstein
Elizabeth Chiseri-Strater

To the Student

There's both joy and satisfaction in understanding people and situations different from our own. *FieldWorking* gives you special license and formal ways to hang out, observe carefully, and speculate about talk and behavior. This book can show you how to interpret people's lives and surroundings through their eyes, not just your own. And this book also can help you see yourself and your own cultural attitudes more clearly—since any study of an "other" is also a study of a "self."

FieldWorking assumes that you want to *do* fieldwork and not just read about it. Fieldwork is an artistic craft. It showcases the cultures that it represents, just as woodcarving, quilting, and music making showcase the cultures they represent. To understand and present other cultures, you will need to practice the crafts of engaged reading, listening, speaking, and researching—and the art of writing about your findings in clear and engaging prose.

Understanding This Book

There is no single way to use *FieldWorking*, and if you're taking a course, your instructor will surely have ideas about how to use it. Perhaps you need to learn how to do research and writing that will help you throughout your academic career but aren't yet sure what direction you want to take. Or perhaps you plan to focus on cultural studies, anthropology, or education. Wherever you begin and whatever your ultimate goals may be, *FieldWorking* will help you to work with ideas, readings, and assignments that are effective with all new fieldworkers and in courses about fieldwork.

We invite you to make the book work for your own purposes. We know one student, for example, who took our book to Mount Everest and used it to study the culture of the Sherpas and the climbers at the base camp. Other students have used it as a guide for extended fieldwork in India and Ecuador. Many students, of course, have used the book to study more familiar but yet unexplored fieldsites within their own communities. We'd like you to read the entire book, but the way you choose to proceed within it will depend entirely on your own research plans.

Chapter 1 introduces the idea that in all field research you are acting as both participant and observer at the same time. In Chapter 2, we offer some key strategies—for finding and narrowing your topic, taking notes, and writing—that are fundamental to any fieldwork project. We return to writing in Chapter 8 at the end of the book, but you'll notice that we emphasize writing skills throughout each chapter.

Each of the middle chapters is devoted to a different category of collecting data in the fieldworking process. Chapter 3 discusses the fundamental idea that when you set out to study a culture, you "read" it as if it were a text. This chapter includes a section on researching online cultures and communities. Chapter 4 focuses on how to write about a cultural setting (the sense of place that a researcher finds)—both for yourself and for the people who live and work there. If you're interested in examining the behaviors of a person or group, you may want to work first with Chapter 5. You also could go directly to Chapter 6 if your research centers on interviews or language histories. We've devoted Chapter 7 to archives—the "stuff" of a culture, from family letters to Internet resources; if your project involves mostly archival research, you might want to consult this chapter first. Our last chapter, Chapter 8, covers more essential college writing skills—composing a draft, and revising and editing your final study—tying together the threads about writing that we've woven throughout the book.

Understanding *FieldWorking*'s Special Features

With the help of our students, our colleagues, and their students, we've designed some special features for this edition of *FieldWorking*. Although this book may look a little like a traditional textbook, it doesn't act like one. Chapters end with a very practical exercise rather than review questions, and summaries of ideas are presented throughout for quick and easy reference. We trust that you will ask your own questions about the material presented here and will also summarize important concepts as you encounter them. We help you with your fieldwork in a variety of ways, however, each represented in one of the extra features:

- **Box exercises:** Each chapter has several exercises that provide opportunities to practice research skills before you engage in a major project. They provide good ways to practice research habits or change the direction of a project. You may want to explore your research site with each exercise, or you may use the activities to try out a broad range of places or subjects. We hope that the boxes will save you from obstacles or problems you may not have anticipated.

- **Readings:** We hope you'll enjoy reading excerpts from our students' and colleagues' fieldwork—as well as previously published professional pieces, both fiction and nonfiction. In this edition, we sometimes use brief excerpts to illustrate a point and then offer the full text of the selection on our book's companion Web site. These readings (and our responses to them) illustrate the ideas we're describing in each section of text, and we hope that they will give you confidence as you do your own research and write about it.

- **Overview of writing skills:** Each chapter opens with a list of writing skills related to the specific fieldwork skills we cover in the pages that follow. As you move through the chapter, keep these skills in mind. They will guide the development of your fieldwork project—and your college writing.

- **FieldWriting:** Because writing is such an essential part of the research process, we introduce a specific issue of grammar, style, or convention in each chapter. These issues reflect the concerns and frustrations our own students have experienced during the writing involved in their own fieldwork. Some of these ideas will be reminders to you, some will offer old ideas with the new perspective of writing about fieldstudies, and others will be new and, we hope, useful to any writing you do.

- **The Research Portfolio:** A research portfolio is a place for a fieldworker to gather work, review it, and present the process of research to herself, her fellow researchers, and her instructor. It is also a tool that helps the fieldworker decide what she wants to accomplish next. Many of our students have enjoyed using these sections to guide their own portfolio-keeping. To review the entire portfolio process for yourself, try reading all eight Research Portfolio sections together, from first to last. For many, keeping the portfolio is an essential bridge to interpretation and analysis.

- **"Do This" activities:** In this edition, we end each chapter with a short activity that connects with the fieldworking skills we've introduced. Whereas the box exercises are exploratory, the "Do This" activities offer practical, immediate, and hands-on help with jump-starting your work. We urge you to try them out before moving on to a new chapter.

- **Online resources and support:** *FieldWorking*'s companion Web site at **bedfordstmartins.com/fieldworking** offers additional help for developing your research, writing, and fieldworking skills. Here you will find additional writing tips as well as help with documenting sources, formatting papers, and finding resources in other media such as film, art, and poetry. You can also browse through more sample student projects and portfolios for helpful models for your own work, and download worksheets and consent forms. What's more, the site is free and easy to use.

And . . . about Us

The single voice that addresses you in *FieldWorking* is really a double voice. We wrote this book together (many drafts' worth) on a Macintosh Powerbook, and we have shared this project for well over a decade. Colleagues and students who used the three previous editions have contributed continually to its growth, and you'll see much of their work represented here on our pages. We acknowledge the huge role that our students' voices, ideas, and projects play in helping us shape each version of the book.

As you read *FieldWorking*, we hope you'll take what is useful to you and ignore what you can't use. You can skip around—or read the book from beginning to end. But please remember that your field research should be meaningful and valuable to you and to the people you study. We hope that you will find your own voice in your fieldwriting. Work on a project you care about, and you'll make others care about it, too.

Bonnie Stone Sunstein
Elizabeth Chiseri-Strater

Contents

5

Researching People: The Collaborative Listener   219

8 FieldWriting: From Down Draft to Up Draft   351

FieldWorking
Reading and Writing Research

1

Stepping In and Stepping Out: Understanding Cultures

Fieldwork is as much about writing as it is about researching. In this chapter you will:

- develop your writing voice for your fieldwork project
- connect your writing with the research process
- understand what an ethnographic perspective is
- start your research portfolio

Ordinary living involves all the skills of fieldworking—looking, listening, collecting, questioning, and interpreting—even though we are not always conscious of these skills. Many of us enjoy people-watching, checking out how others talk, dress, behave, and interact. We question the significance of someone's wearing gold, hooped earrings or displaying a dragon tattoo. We wonder how a certain couple sitting in a restaurant booth can communicate when they don't look each other in the eye. Fieldworkers question such behaviors in a systematic way.

What is a "field"? And how does a person "work" in it? The word *field* carries a wide range of meanings, but for an anthropologist "working in the field" means talking, listening, recording, observing, participating, and sometimes even living in a particular place. The field is the site for doing research, and fieldworking is the process of doing it.

Close looking and listening skills mark trained fieldworkers who study groups of people in contexts—others' and their own. The job of this book is to help you become more conscious as you observe, participate in, and read and write about your own world and the worlds of others. Although we don't claim to turn you into a professional

Long before I ever heard of anthropology, I was being conditioned for the role of stepping in and out of society. It was part of my growing up process to question the traditional values and norms of the family and to experiment with behavior patterns and ideologies. This is not an uncommon process of finding oneself.... Why should a contented and satisfied person think of standing outside his or any other society and studying it?

—HORTENSE POWDERMAKER

ethnographer, we borrow ethnographic strategies to help you become a field-worker, and we focus on showing you effective ways to write about your process. We'll guide you as you conduct and write up your own fieldwork and as you read about the fieldwork of others. *FieldWorking* will make you consider your everyday experiences in new ways and help you interpret other people's behaviors, languages, and thoughts. But most of all, the fieldwork itself will help you understand why you react and respond in the ways you do. This book will encourage you not only to watch others but also to watch yourself as you watch them.

You've probably spent many hours noticing behavior patterns and questioning routines among the people you've lived with and learned from. In the quotation that introduces this chapter, anthropologist Hortense Powdermaker suggests that as we grow up, we "step out" a bit; we "adopt the **outsider** stance" as we watch the people inside our own group. We also "step in" to unfamiliar groups and examine them closely, which is the fieldworker's "**insider** stance." As insiders, we wonder if there might be a better technique for mincing garlic or cooling pies that is less laborious than our family's method. As outsiders moving to a new school, we might question the ritual cheers aimed against the rival or different rules for submitting papers. When we visit another country, we need to learn new rules for introductions and farewells in order to behave appropriately. When we volunteer as part of a community service program, we need to find a way to conform to the routines we notice rather than challenge them. Fieldworkers study the customs of groups of people in the spaces they inhabit.

Refer to the glossary at the back of this book, or online at **bedfordstmartins.com/ fieldworking,** for help with terms specific to fieldworking.

Inquiry into the behavior patterns of others prepares us for doing fieldwork. Powdermaker also asks why any "satisfied and contented person" would want to research everyday ways of behaving, talking, and interacting. One answer is that fieldworking sharpens our abilities to look closely at surroundings. People, places, languages, and behaviors can be familiar because we've lived with them, but when we move or travel and find ourselves strangers, the very same things can be unfamiliar or uncomfortable. Another answer is that knowing our assumptions and recognizing our stereotypes help develop tolerance and respect for customs and groups different from ours. For example, head coverings—turbans, veils, yarmulkes, ceremonial headdresses, and even baseball caps worn backward—may seem strange to us until we understand their history and significance. Studying and writing about diverse people and cultures does not necessarily make us accept difference, but it can make us aware of our assumptions and sometimes even of our prejudices.

Defining Culture: Fieldwork and Ethnography

Culture is a slippery term. To some people, it implies "high culture"—classical music, etiquette, museum art, or extensive knowledge of Western history. But fieldworkers know that every group has a culture, so there is no useful distinction between "high" and "low" cultures. Anthropologists have tried to define what culture is for as long as they've been thinking about it, and they have developed contrasting definitions.

We define **culture** as an invisible web of behaviors, patterns, rules, and rituals of a group of people who have contact with one another and share a common language. Our definition draws from the work of many anthropologists:

Some Definitions of Culture

- "Culture is local and manmade and hugely variable. It tends also to be integrated. A culture, like an individual, is a more or less consistent pattern of thought and action" (Benedict 46).

- "A society's culture consists of whatever it is one has to know or believe in order to operate in a manner acceptable to its members.... [I]t does not consist of things, people, behavior, or emotions. It is rather an organization of those things" (Goodenough 167).

- "Cultures are, after all, collective, untidy assemblages, authenticated by belief and agreement" (Myerhoff 10).

- "Man is an animal suspended in webs of significance which he himself has created. I take culture to be those webs" (Geertz, *Interpretation of Cultures* 14).

Cultural theorist Raymond Williams writes that *culture* is one of the most difficult words to define, and these anthropologists' definitions illustrate this. As you can see, definitions of culture can be both metaphorical ("webs") and structured (patterns of belief and behavior as well as untidy deviations from those patterns).

In your fieldworking experiences, you will be constantly asking yourself, "Where is the culture?" of the group you are investigating. The goal of fieldworking is to find it. You will find evidence in the language of the group you study, in its cultural **artifacts**, or in its rituals and behaviors. Fieldworkers investigate the cultural landscape, the larger picture of how a culture functions: its rituals, its rules, its traditions, and its behaviors. And they poke around the edges at the stories people tell, the items people collect and value, and the materials people use to go about their daily living. By learning from people in a culture what it is like to be part of their world, fieldworkers discover a culture's way of being, knowing, and understanding.

Fieldworkers who live, observe, and describe the daily life, behaviors, and language of a group of people for long periods of time are called *ethnographers*.

This book draws on the work of a wide range of classic and contemporary anthropologists and folklorists. **Ethnography**, the written product of their work, is a researched study that synthesizes information about the life of a people or group. Researchers in many disciplines rely on ethnographic methods: anthropologists, folklorists, linguists, sociologists, oral historians, and those who study popular culture. Ethnographic researchers conduct fieldwork in an attempt to understand the cultures they study. And as they study the culture of others, they learn patterns that connect with their own lives and traditions.

Fieldworkers historically studied foreign or exotic cultures and occasionally judged these other cultures to be less sophisticated or developed than their own. Fieldworkers of all backgrounds must guard against this attitude of **colonization**. Contemporary fieldworkers no longer restrict their research to non-Western cultures. But all fieldworkers, even those who investigate local cultures and subcultures, risk projecting their own **assumptions** onto the groups they study. They must be ready and willing to unpack their own cultural baggage and embark on a collaborative journey with those they study.

Stepping In: Revealing Our Subcultures

As coauthors of this book, we have ourselves come to our interest in ethnography from membership in a dizzying array of **subcultures**. As collaborators, we share the culture of academia. We are graduates of the same Ph.D. program in which we learned to conduct ethnographic fieldwork. As middle-aged professors, we've both taught in public urban, suburban, and rural schools; directed college writing centers and programs; and taught many college English and education courses. And as mothers of young adults, both of us have spent years navigating the child-centered cultures of nursery school carpools, pediatric waiting rooms, and soccer and Special Olympics teams.

In each of these subcultures, we communicated through special languages with insiders. We knew the ways of behaving and interacting, and we shared belief systems with the others in each group. Yet we held membership in many subcultures at the same time, and we could move among them. As members over the years, we were unaware of those groups as actual cultures, but looking back as fieldworkers, we now understand that we, like you, have always been in a position to research the people around us. And we don't always need to go very far from home to find groups of people whose ways of behaving and communicating are different and interesting, yet unfamiliar to us.

As you begin to think about conducting field research projects, review your own subcultures; you may find that they offer intriguing possibilities for research.

BOX 1

Looking at Subcultures

We consider any self-identified group of people who share language, stories, rituals, behaviors, and values a subculture. Some subcultures define themselves by geography (southerners, Texans, New Yorkers). Others define themselves by ethnicity or language (Mexicano, Irish, Belgian, Filipino, Ghanaian). And others define their interests by shared rituals and behaviors (fraternities, Girl Scouts, Masons, Daughters of the American Revolution, computer hackers). Whether it's your bowling league, your neighborhood pickup basketball team or group of bicycle freestylers, your church, your community government, or your school's ecology club, you simultaneously belong to many different subcultures. With this box, we'd like you to recall your subculture affiliations and share them with others in your class.

ACTION

List some of the subcultures to which you belong. For each subculture you mention, jot down a few key details that distinguish the group—behaviors, insider phrases, rules, rituals, and the specific locations where these behaviors usually occur. You might want to divide your list into a few categories or columns, such as

Group	Rituals	Insider Phrases	Behaviors

Write a paragraph or short essay describing one of these subcultures, either seriously or satirically.

RESPONSE

Some of our students have belonged to these subcultures: computer interest groups, online discussion groups, listservs, deer hunters, gospel singers, specialty book clubs, volleyball teams, science fiction conventioneers, auctiongoers, fly fishermen, billiard players, bull riders, lap swimmers, bluegrass musicians, stock car racers.

Chinatsu Sazawa is a native of Japan, where as a teenager she experienced karaoke quite differently from the way Americans do. Here is what she writes about the subculture of Japanese karaoke participants:

> The Karaoke Box is a small soundproof room with a karaoke machine, a table, and sofas. Customers can reserve it for $5 to $20 an hour and sing as much as they like. This habit is to weekend Karaoke Box warriors as a sports gym is to exercise lovers. We enjoy karaoke and perform extensively to release our stress by singing, shouting, and dancing. The most important thing for weekend Karaoke Box warriors is to be efficient at the Box. Paying by the hour, we do our best to sing as many songs as possible. As we enter the Karaoke Box, we go directly to a remote control and the book listing the available songs. While we take off our jackets and put our bags down, we check "the code" of our opening song and punch in the number on the remote. During the one minute while the machine searches for the song,

BOX**1** continued

we prepare to sing, taking off the sanitary plastic covering on the microphone and connecting it to the machine. We adjust the key of the song by pressing the Key Changer button.

It is an understood rule among us that we take turns and sing only one song each turn. It's also a courtesy to avoid singing too many long songs (songs that would last over five minutes, such as "Hotel California"). While others are singing, instead of listening we constantly flip the pages of the book of available songs and select the songs we will sing in our following turns. It's important to punch in the code numbers before the other people's songs end so that the next song starts immediately without down time. We even press the Stop Performance button just as the song begins its ending.

We talk very little in the Box except to ask questions like "Whose song is that?" or say "That was good!" Seven or eight minutes before our time expires, we receive a phone call from the front desk. That's the cue to punch in the number of our closing songs. We often select closing songs that everyone in the room can sing together. While the last person is singing, the rest of the people clean up the room—pile the books of available songs, place the mikes on the table, throw garbage in the bin—and get ready to leave. When we pass the front desk, we look for discount coupons for our next visit.

Investigating Perspectives: Insider and Outsider

Fieldworkers realize that ordinary events in one culture might seem extraordinary in another. When people say "that's really weird" or "aren't they strange," a fieldworker hears these comments as signals for investigation. When you first ate dinner at someone's home other than yours, you may have felt like an outsider. You stepped out of your own home and stepped in to a set of routines and rituals different from your own. You may have noticed who set the table, passed the food, served, ate first, talked, signaled that the meal was over, cleared off the table, and washed the dishes. Or as an insider among your own relatives, you may have always observed their quirky behaviors. To avoid a head cold, your mother may use crystals and a spiritual chant, but your best friend's mother may depend on echinacea and vitamin C.

Although we would not classify modern families as subcultures, they do have some of the features of a subculture and prepare us to observe outside our own home territory. When you visit another place, you may notice that people move and talk more slowly or quickly, more quietly or noisily, or that they use space differently than you're used to. A fieldworker steps out to adopt an outsider's perspective when investigating unfamiliar (or even familiar) patterns, attempting to unveil the many layers of behaviors and beliefs that make people think as they think and act as they act.

Anthropologist Renato Rosaldo offers a good example of stepping out, using the outsider's detached perspective to look at a familiar routine, the family ritual of making breakfast:

> Every morning, the reigning patriarch, as if in from the hunt, shouts from the kitchen, "How many people would like a poached egg?" Women and children take turns saying yes or no.
>
> In the meantime, the women talk among themselves and designate one among them the toastmaker. As the eggs near readiness, the reigning patriarch calls out to the designated toastmaker, "The eggs are about ready. Is there enough toast?"
>
> "Yes" comes the deferential reply. "The last two pieces are about to pop up." The reigning patriarch then proudly enters, bearing a plate of poached eggs before him. Throughout the course of the meal, the women and children, including the designated toastmaker, perform the obligatory ritual praise song, saying, "These sure are great eggs, Dad." (47)

With his detached language and his careful detailing of their routine, Rosaldo depicts this North American middle-class family as if it were part of a different tribe or culture. He uses his interpretive skills as an ethnographer to create a **parody**—in jest and fun—to allow his family to see themselves as an outsider might describe them.

But fieldworkers do not depend entirely on the detachment or objectivity that comes from stepping out of a culture. They rely on basic human involvement—their gut reactions or subjective responses to cultural practices—as well. In another example from Rosaldo's fieldwork, he shows how his own personal life experience shaped his ability to understand headhunters. As a ritual of revenge and grief over a deceased relative, the Ilongots of the Philippines sever human heads. When Rosaldo and his anthropologist wife, Michelle, lived and studied among the Ilongot people for several years, they were unable to understand the complex emotions surrounding headhunting. But after Michelle died in an accident during fieldwork, Rosaldo began to understand the headhunters' practice of killing for retribution. It was his own experience—rage and grief over his wife's death—that allowed him insight into the cultural practice of the people he was studying. Even though their value systems were different, Rosaldo and the Ilongots shared the basic human response to a loved one's death.

So it is not always **objectivity** or detachment that allows us to study culture, our own or that of others. **Subjectivity**—our inner feelings and belief systems—allows us to uncover some features of culture that are not always apparent. As a fieldworker, you will conduct an internal dialogue between your subjective and objective selves, listening to both, questioning both. You combine the viewpoints of an outsider stepping in and an insider stepping out of the culture you study. And studying culture is as much about the everyday practices of cooking and eating, such as poaching eggs, as it is about the unfamiliar tribal practices of killing as a part of grieving. Detachment and involvement, subjectivity and objectivity, insider and outsider stances are equally coupled in fieldworking.

Stepping Out: Making the Familiar Strange and the Strange Familiar

What is often more difficult to achieve than making the unknown become familiar is making the familiar seem strange. Rosaldo was able to accomplish the outsider view of his family's breakfast-making practices mainly through satire, a technique that distances the reader from the event or practice under consideration. In the following reading written in 1956, "Body Ritual among the Nacirema," anthropologist Horace Miner also depends on satire to depict an ordinary set of daily practices as strange and unfamiliar. As you read this essay, try to figure out what everyday rituals Miner is satirizing.

···

Body Ritual among the Nacirema

Horace Miner

The anthropologist has become so familiar with the diversity of ways in which different peoples behave in similar situations that he is not apt to be surprised by even the most exotic customs. In fact, if all of the logically possible combinations of behavior have not been found somewhere in the world, he is apt to suspect that they must be present in some yet undescribed tribe. This point has, in fact, been expressed with respect to clan organization by Murdock (71). In this light, the magical beliefs and practices of the Nacirema present such unusual aspects that it seems desirable to describe them as an example of the extremes to which human behavior can go.

Professor Linton first brought the ritual of the Nacirema to the attention of anthropologists twenty years ago (326), but the culture of this people is still very poorly understood. They are a North American group living in the territory between the Canadian Cree, the Yaqui and Tarahumare of Mexico, and the Carib and Arawak of the Antilles. Little is known of their origin, although tradition states that they came from the east. According to Nacirema mythology, their nation was originated by a culture hero, Notgnihsaw, who is otherwise known for two great feats of strength—the throwing of a piece of wampum across the river Pa-To-Mac and the chopping down of a cherry tree in which the Spirit of Truth resided.

Nacirema culture is characterized by a highly developed market economy which has evolved in a rich natural habitat. While much of the people's time is devoted to economic pursuits, a large part of the fruits of these labors and a considerable portion of the day are spent in ritual activity. The focus of this activity is the human body, the appearance and health of which loom as a dominant concern in the ethos of the people. While such a concern is certainly not unusual, its ceremonial aspect and associated philosophy are unique.

The fundamental belief underlying the whole system appears to be that the human body is ugly and that its natural tendency is to debility and disease. Incarcerated in such a body, man's only hope is to avert these characteristics through the use of the powerful influences of ritual and ceremony. Every household has one or more shrines devoted to this purpose. The more powerful individuals in the society have several shrines in their houses and, in fact, the opulence of a house is often referred to in terms of the number of such ritual centers it possesses. Most houses are of wattle and daub construction, but the shrine rooms of the more wealthy are walled with stone. Poorer families imitate the rich by applying pottery plaques to their shrine walls.

While each family has at least one such shrine, the rituals associated with it are not family ceremonies but are private and secret. The rites are normally only discussed with children, and then only during the period when they are being initiated into these mysteries. I was able, however, to establish sufficient rapport with the natives to examine these shrines and to have the rituals described to me.

The focal point of the shrine is a box or chest which is built into the wall. In this chest are kept the many charms and magical potions without which no native believes he could live. These preparations are secured from a variety of specialized practitioners. The most powerful of these are the medicine men, whose assistance must be rewarded with substantial gifts. However, the medicine men do not provide the curative potions for their clients, but decide what the ingredients should be and then write them down in an ancient and secret language. This writing is understood only by the medicine men and by the herbalists who, for another gift, provide the required charm.

The charm is not disposed of after it has served its purpose, but is placed in the charm-box of the household shrine. As these magical materials are specific for certain ills, and the real or imagined maladies of the people are many, the charm-box is usually full to overflowing. The magical packets are so numerous that people forget what their purposes were and fear to use them again. While the natives are very vague on this point, we can only assume that the idea in retaining all the old magical materials is that their presence in the charm-box, before which the body rituals are conducted, will in some way protect the worshipper.

Beneath the charm-box is a small font. Each day every member of the family, in succession, enters the shrine room, bows his head before the charm-box, mingles different sorts of holy water in the font, and proceeds with a brief rite of ablution. The holy waters are secured from the Water Temple of the community, where the priests conduct elaborate ceremonies to make the liquid ritually pure.

In the hierarchy of magical practitioners, and below the medicine men in prestige, are specialists whose designation is best translated "holy-mouth-men." The Nacirema have an almost pathological horror of and fascination with the mouth, the condition of which is believed to have a supernatural influence on all social relationships. Were it not for the rituals of the mouth, they believe that their teeth would fall out, their gums bleed, their jaws shrink, their friends desert them, and their lovers reject them. They also believe that a strong relationship exists between oral and moral characteristics. For example, there is a ritual ablution of the mouth for children which is supposed to improve their moral fiber.

The daily body ritual performed by everyone includes a mouth-rite. Despite the fact that these people are so punctilious about care of the mouth, this rite involves a practice which strikes the uninitiated stranger as revolting. It was reported to me that the ritual consists of inserting a small bundle of hog hairs into the mouth, along with certain magical powders, and then moving the bundle in a highly formalized series of gestures.

In addition to the private mouth-rite, the people seek out a holy-mouth-man once or twice a year. These practitioners have an impressive set of paraphernalia, consisting of a variety of augers, awls, probes, and prods. The use of these objects in the exorcism of the evils of the mouth involves almost unbelievable ritual torture of the client. The holy-mouth-man opens the client's mouth and, using the above mentioned tools, enlarges any holes which decay may have created in the teeth. Magical materials are put into these holes. If there are no naturally occurring holes in the teeth, large sections of one or more teeth are gouged out so that the supernatural substance can be applied. In the client's view, the purpose of these ministrations is to arrest decay and to draw friends. The extremely sacred and traditional character of the rite is evident in the fact that the natives return to the holy-mouth-men year after year, despite the fact that their teeth continue to decay.

It is to be hoped that, when a thorough study of the Nacirema is made, there will be careful inquiry into the personality structure of these people. One has but to watch the gleam in the eye of a holy-mouth-man, as he jabs an awl into an exposed nerve, to suspect that a certain amount of sadism is involved. If this can be established, a very interesting pattern emerges, for most of the population shows definite masochistic tendencies. It was to these that Professor Linton referred in discussing a distinctive part of the daily body ritual which is performed only by men. This part of the rite involves scraping and lacerating the surface of the face with a sharp instrument. Special women's rites are performed only four times during each lunar month, but what they lack in frequency is made up in barbarity. As part of this ceremony, women bake their heads in small ovens for about an hour. The theoretically interesting point is that what seems to be a preponderantly masochistic people have developed sadistic specialists.

The medicine men have an imposing temple, or *latipso*, in every community of any size. The more elaborate ceremonies required to treat very sick patients can only be performed at this temple. These ceremonies involve not only the thaumaturge but a permanent group of vestal maidens who move sedately about the temple chambers in distinctive costume and headdress.

The *latipso* ceremonies are so harsh that it is phenomenal that a fair proportion of the really sick natives who enter the temple ever recover. Small children whose indoctrination is still incomplete have been known to resist attempts to take them to the temple because "that is where you go to die." Despite this fact, sick adults are not only willing but eager to undergo the protracted ritual purification, if they can afford to do so. No matter how ill the supplicant or how grave the emergency, the guardians of many temples will not admit a client if he cannot give a rich gift to the custodian. Even after one has gained admission and survived the ceremonies, the guardians will not permit the neophyte to leave until he makes still another gift.

The supplicant entering the temple is first stripped of all his or her clothes. In everyday life the Nacirema avoids exposure of his body and its natural functions. Bathing and excretory acts are performed only in the secrecy of the household shrine, where they are ritualized as part of the body-rites. Psychological shock results from the fact that body secrecy is suddenly lost upon entry into the *latipso*. A man, whose own wife has never seen him in an excretory act, suddenly finds himself naked and assisted by a vestal maiden while he performs his natural functions into a sacred vessel. This sort of ceremonial treatment is necessitated by the fact that the excreta are used by a diviner to ascertain the course and nature of the client's sickness. Female clients, on the other hand, find their naked bodies are subjected to the scrutiny, manipulation, and prodding of the medicine men.

Few supplicants in the temple are well enough to do anything but lie on their hard beds. The daily ceremonies, like the rites of the holy-mouth-men, involve discomfort and torture. With ritual precision, the vestals awaken their miserable charges each dawn and roll them about on their beds of pain while performing ablutions, in the formal movements of which the maidens are highly trained. At other times they insert magic wands in the supplicant's mouth or force him to eat substances which are supposed to be healing. From time to time the medicine men come to their clients and jab magically treated needles into their flesh. The fact that these temple ceremonies may not cure, and may even kill the neophyte, in no way decreases the people's faith in the medicine men.

There remains one other kind of practitioner, known as a "listener." This witch-doctor has the power to exorcise the devils that lodge in the heads of people who have been bewitched. The Nacirema believe that parents bewitch their own children. Mothers are particularly suspected of putting a curse on children while teaching them the secret body rituals. The counter-magic of the witch-doctor is unusual in its lack of ritual. The patient simply tells the "listener" all his troubles and fears, beginning with the earliest difficulties he can remember. The memory displayed by the Nacirema in these exorcism sessions is truly remarkable. It is not uncommon for the patient to bemoan the rejection he felt upon being weaned as a babe, and a few individuals even see their troubles going back to the traumatic effects of their own birth.

In conclusion, mention must be made of certain practices which have their base in native esthetics but which depend upon the pervasive aversion to the natural body and its functions. There are ritual fasts to make fat people thin and ceremonial feasts to make thin people fat. Still other rites are used to make women's breasts larger if they are small, and smaller if they are large. General dissatisfaction with breast shape is symbolized in the fact that the ideal form is virtually outside the range of human variation. A few women afflicted with almost inhuman hypermammary development are so idolized that they make a handsome living by simply going from village to village and permitting the natives to stare at them for a fee.

Reference has already been made to the fact that excretory functions are ritualized, routinized, and relegated to secrecy. Natural reproductive functions are similarly distorted. Intercourse is taboo as a topic and scheduled as an act. Efforts are made to avoid pregnancy by the use of magical materials or by limiting intercourse to certain phases of the moon. Conception is actually very infrequent. When pregnant, women dress so as to hide their condition. Parturition takes place in secret, without friends or relatives to assist, and the majority of women do not nurse their infants.

Our review of the ritual life of the Nacirema has certainly shown them to be a magic-ridden people. It is hard to understand how they have managed to exist so long under the burdens which they have imposed upon themselves. But even such exotic customs as these take on real meaning when they are viewed with the insight provided by Malinowski when he wrote (1948:70):

> Looking from far and above, from our high places of safety in the developed civilization, it is easy to see all the crudity and irrelevance of magic. But without its power and guidance early man could not have mastered his practical difficulties as he has done, nor could man have advanced to the higher stages of civilization.

Works Cited

Linton, Ralph. *The Study of Man*. New York: D. Appleton-Century Co., 1936. Print.
Malinowski, Bronislaw. *Magic, Science, and Religion*. Glencoe, IL: The Free Press, 1948. Print.
Murdock, George P. *Social Structure*. New York: Macmillan, 1949. Print.

· ·

As you read this parody of American (*Nacirema* spelled backward) personal hygiene, you probably noticed how Miner's descriptions of everyday bathroom objects and grooming practices seemed unfamiliar. He describes the medicine chest as a "shrine" that holds magic potions and "charms." The toothbrush is "a small bundle of hog hairs" for the application of "magical powders."

We laugh at Miner's parody because we see ourselves and our American obsession with cleanliness. This reading makes fun of our own cultural attitudes about bathing and cleansing habits; our American belief in dentists, doctors, and therapists; and our reliance on hospitals and diets. Miner de-familiarizes our everyday behaviors so that we can see ourselves as outsiders might describe us: a highly ritualized people who believe in magical customs and potions.

BOX 2

Making the Ordinary Extraordinary

PURPOSE

As the preceding excerpts from Renato Rosaldo (p. 7) and Horace Miner (p. 8) show, shifting oneself from insider to outsider and trying to describe language and behavior from those perspectives are not only the essence of parody but also activities of enormous value when we try to "make the familiar strange and the strange familiar" as fieldworkers must do. This box offers you an opportunity to recognize the value of seeing ourselves as outsiders might describe us.

ACTION

Take something that's familiar to you—an ordinary routine or ritual in your everyday life that would seem extraordinary to someone else in another culture or subculture—and reexamine it as if you were seeing it for the first time. Try something simple—like the way you fix your hair, listen to music, change a tire, take in the mail, or get ready for a sporting event. List the specific behaviors of your routine, and identify what might seem strange or extraordinary to others. Prepare your list to share with others, or write a short paragraph that describes the process.

RESPONSE

Our student Angela Harger wrote this response:

> I pay thousands of dollars a year—dollars I resent giving up but give up anyway. For all this money, I get the privilege of awakening early, long before my body wants to. I groggily get ready and then drive east for half an hour, through rain, snow, or blinding sun. I shell out another extraordinary amount of dollars each day for the privilege of leaving my vehicle. I then subject myself to the weather's elements, trudging off to far-flung buildings so I can sit for hours at a time, always feeling restless. I listen to older people talk and talk, and I write it all down so I can remember it later when I submit myself to stressful testing for days at a time so that these older people can determine whether I've learned anything. For these sessions, I spend exorbitant amounts of time and more dollars for books I will have to force myself to read. But I can't give up this ritual: I have been doing it and perfecting it for more than thirteen years, and I am nowhere close to being finished.

Posing Questions: Ethnographic vs. Journalistic

As a fieldworker, your purpose is to collect and consider multiple sources of information, not facts alone, to convey the perspective of the people in the culture you study. An ethnographer and a journalist may both gather information about the same event but write up their accounts very differently. A standard daily newspaper reporter, for example, conducts research in an attempt to be objective: to give the who, what, where, when, and why of an event for a readership that expects facts without too much interpretation.

The journalist often writes from the outsider perspective, quoting from insiders. The fieldworker asks big, open questions such as "What's going on here?" and "Where is the culture?" as he or she observes, listens, records, interprets, and analyzes. She must combine an outsider's point of view with an insider's perspective. Anthropologists use the term **emic** to mean the insider perspective and **etic** to refer to that of the outsider.

The following piece, "Folk 'Cure' Sold Locally High in Lead," published in Elizabeth's local paper, the *Greensboro News and Record*, provides an example of reportage. But if you read the article with an ethnographer's eye, you'll ask questions that a news writer doesn't usually have the time or the column inches to consider—often because of space and time limitations. To determine an article's complexity, you'll need to uncover many layers of cultural meanings.

. . . .

Folk "Cure" Sold Locally High in Lead

Lorraine Ahearn, Staff Writer

GREENSBORO—When an employee with the Guilford County Department of Public Health walked into the African and Caribbean market to ask for "Nzu," a traditional remedy for morning sickness, it seemed a common request.

The clerk readily produced small, unlabeled bags of what looked like dried clay—Nzu (pronounced new-zoo)—for a few dollars apiece, sold under brand names including Calabash Chalk, Calabar stone, La Craie, Argile and Mabele.

Not so common were lab test results when the health department sent off the samples to be analyzed.

The clay, intended for pregnant women to eat, contained alarmingly high levels of arsenic, a heavy metal that causes cancer and nerve damage. Worse, the tests found lead levels from 60 to 80 times what the FDA considers too high.

Lead has been linked to impaired child development, behavioral problems, brain damage and even death.

Calabash Chalk may be sold as large pellets or in bulk and can resemble balls of clay or mud.

"The biggest concern, especially if you're pregnant, is that lead is going directly to the fetus," said Paula Cox, a senior environmental health specialist for the county. "We could potentially see children born with elevated lead levels."

Cox said the FDA issued a health alert in December, and that inspectors here began investigating in Greensboro and High Point.

There is no word yet on where the product originated, but the Department of Agriculture will trace it as a "food" investigation.

Locally, Nzu was sold not only at the African specialty store, but also was recently stocked at a longtime Asian market. That shop had sold out of the product, said Cox. He said there was little way to determine how long or widespread the use of the contaminated product had been.

Particularly worrisome was the idea that pregnant women used Nzu for nausea. Cox said the concentration of lead would make the consumer sick to her stomach.

Mistaking that for morning sickness, the user might then ingest more of the product, and wind up with an even higher level of lead ingestion.

With help from refugee liaisons at FaithAction International, the health department put out an advisory and also spurred the N.C. Department of Agriculture and Consumer Services to issue a statewide warning Friday.

Because of the large influx of African refugees to Guilford, Cox said it was urgent to get the word to pregnant women and their obstetricians.

With a regimen of prenatal vitamins, doctors can act to bring down affected women's lead levels.

"It's critical that if women are using this product, that they stop immediately and tell their doctor," Cox said. "Otherwise, we can't help until after the baby is born."

Ethnography and journalism differ not only in the writing process but also in the depth of research, the time allotted to it, and, most significantly, the perspective that the researcher adopts. In the example above, journalist Lorraine Ahearn's goal was to gather information about a newsworthy event and to get it out quickly. But as a fieldworker, your responsibility would be to conduct extensive research, to discover knowledge that might take months or even years to complete. The fieldworker's commitment is an emic one—to capture the perspective of the insiders in the culture.

Questions to Consider

A department of public health worker enters an African and Caribbean market and asks for "Nzu." The clerk produces several unlabeled bags of a substance that looks like dirt. A public health agent sends it for testing, and the results show the clay to be too high in lead for American FDA standards. This results in a statewide warning, particularly for pregnant women.

As a fieldworker, you would ask focused questions that differ from the journalist's focus on the who, what, where, when, and why. You would ask questions about this cultural moment:

- Who are the customers at this store? How many of these customers are pregnant women?
- Are they immigrants from African and Caribbean countries who are looking for a familiar product? What languages do they speak?
- What about the Calabash Chalk? Where does it come from? Why are there so many different shapes and forms?
- What are its chemical properties? What does it do for a pregnant woman's morning sickness?
- Why did the public health worker go to the store in the first place? Who sent him?
- How is Nzu used in its country of origin? Who prescribes it? What does it taste like? What other cultures use this cure for morning sickness?

Whether you adapt the perspective of the health worker, the store clerk, a pregnant woman, the owner of the market, a journalist—or all of them—you will offer insiders' perspectives along with your own as you translate your cultural data into ethnographic text for your reader.

When you go to the newspaper's Web site, for example, you'll have an opportunity to see who has commented on the article. You can also investigate the additional background information the newspaper suggests: other places to buy Nzu, where to get free blood-lead tests for children, and the public health agency's contact information. A quick Google search would confirm the health concerns about this product across many countries and the use of the African word "Nzu" in other contexts.

You may sense, for example, the stereotypes associated with eating dirt:

- What's so special about this dirt? Is this a rip-off?
- Who says it's "dirt"? Isn't it clay or chalk? Under how many different brand names is it sold?
- How much money does the African and Caribbean market make from Nzu sales? From where is it imported?
- Who else might have an opinion about the properties of Nzu? Alternative health workers? Mainstream doctors? Women who've used it successfully for their morning sickness? Politicians who advocate for or against ethnic traditions?
- Why does the newspaper's headline use the term "folk," and put "cure" in quotes? Who wrote that headline? Who took the pictures?

Gathering More Information

As a fieldworker investigating all these questions and trying to understand this cultural moment, you would want to collect more information (data) and do more fieldwork. You might, for example, gather artifacts (material objects that belong to and represent a culture): the Calabash Chalk in a bag or in pellets, flyers from markets that advertise the product, the Health Department's reports on Nzu's lead levels, some other African products used for health cures, talismans used by pregnant women in any culture. You might do some research in the library or online about the history of medicinal cures for morning sickness across cultures or Americans' changing attitudes toward alternative cultural medical practices. You might go to the local historical society to find out more about African immigration in Greensboro—and the immigrants' relationships to African Americans. But you would not be able to write your account until you had begun to decipher where the culture is.

One way you could begin would be to locate key **informants** to interview—a few people to help guide you and explain their culture. Such guides represent the "others," those who are different from the researcher. To describe their guides, fieldworkers use the terms *informants*, *consultants*, *subjects*, *natives*, *the other*, or *insiders*. Which term we use is our own decision, but since such descriptions reveal our attitudes toward the people we study, it is a crucial decision to make. Throughout this book, we use anthropology's term *informant* to refer to insiders in a culture. We realize that some readers may associate this term informant with police work (a "snitch," for instance). But we like this term because it emphasizes the knowledge—the *information*—that insiders have. For similar reasons, some fieldworkers like the term *consultant*.

So you would choose key informants in Greensboro to interview, using a translator if necessary, holding conversations in homes and in other community settings like the store. Below is a list of possible informants:

- The clerk at the African and Caribbean market
- The employee of the Guilford County Department of Public Health
- The owner of the market
- The journalist, Lorraine Ahearn, who wrote this article
- Customers who have bought and used Nzu
- Paula Cox, the environmental health specialist
- Refugee volunteers at FaithAction International
- Local obstetricians and prenatal health care givers

Subjective Responses

Throughout the process, you would keep careful fieldnotes describing the details in the places you go and the people you observe as they go about living in those places. You would also record your own subjective responses and feelings and how they affect your data: things that bother you, ideas you don't understand, events or comments that interest you. Looking over all this data, you would begin to formulate hypotheses about what is important in the culture.

BOX**3**

Engaging the Ethnographic Perspective

PURPOSE

Knowing the difference between the insider (**emic**) perspective and the outsider (**etic**) perspective is an important skill for a fieldworker, as it is for a journalist. But for a fieldworker, being sure to represent many perspectives—those of the researcher as well as those of the various people important to the "moment" in a given cultural event—is deeply important to the principles of ethnographic research.

ACTION

Find a news article in your local paper that shows a cultural moment and might challenge a fieldworker to do more research. A cultural moment need not be a major political or social event such as the dismantling of the Berlin Wall or a march on Washington. Local headlines often mark insider culture in smaller places: the opening of an ethnic restaurant, a local hero's action, a community conflict, an institution that's made a major shift. Share the article and your answers to the following questions with your colleagues:

- What cultural information does the article include?
- What kinds of questions might the fieldworker ask to further uncover the culture the article describes?
- How would the fieldworker's questions differ from those of a journalist?
- What information would the fieldworker want to gather to answer the question "What's going on here?"
- What other sources of information might the fieldworker use to penetrate the insider perspective?
- Where would she need to go to find those sources? How might she use the Internet?

RESPONSE

Here are some sample headlines of newspaper articles our students chose: "Amish Community Copes with Rare Murder," "Korean University Professor Develops Education Program in Finland," "Art Teacher Saves Drowning Child in Treacherous River Dam," "Small Business Grant Slashed in Favor of Community Fireworks Display," "Kiwanis Club Donates Funds toward Little Juanita's New Kidney." Note that the headlines are specific, full of cultural details. Our students' analyses were twice as long as the news articles they chose. They asked more questions than they were able to answer as they peeled back layers of information to find out "Where is (or are) the culture(s)?" As an example, our student Lauren Wallis found the following article in her hometown newspaper and wrote the analysis shown on pages 20–22:

Fairfax Residents Become U.S. Citizens: County Government Sponsored a Local Naturalization Ceremony Last Month
Julie O'Donoghue, *Fairfax Connection*

Without a doubt, the most frustrating part about living in the United States without citizenship for Nojan Navab was not being able to vote in elections.

"I will be voting in every election I can after this day," said Navab, who moved to the United States with his family in 1996 at the age of 13.

The Iranian native graduated from Woodson High School, George Mason University and now lives in Fairfax.

"I basically regard this pretty much as my country," says Navab, who has been working toward citizenship for years.

Though his family initially came to the United States seeking political asylum, Navab had to wait nine years before he was granted permanent U.S. residency status. He and other family members got caught in a large backlog of candidates for green cards when the federal government's procedures for applicants changed following the September 11 attacks.

Now that he is a citizen, Navab is also looking forward to traveling more internationally. "I tried to go to Europe in 2006 or 2007 and ended up canceling the trip

BOX 3  continued

because the visa application took so long that I just gave up," he said. With an American passport Navab won't even be required to get a visa before traveling to most countries in Europe.

Navab, the first person in his immediate family to become a citizen, was one of 74 people who became naturalized Americans in the Fairfax County Government Center May 14.

The county government sponsored the citizenship ceremony for the second year in a row in honor of Asian American and Pacific Islander Month.

According to the U.S. Census, approximately 28 percent of Fairfax residents are foreign born and 50 percent of all county residents who are immigrants come from Asia.

"We proudly proclaim ourselves a nation of immigrants but the truth is that our Asian American community had a particularly rocky time," said Fairfax County Board Chairwoman Sharon Bulova (D-At large) who cited several laws from the 19th and 20th centuries aimed at limiting the number of Asian immigrants entering the country.

But Abul Hussam, a George Mason University professor, said the United States offers untapped personal freedom to all our citizens, particularly when it comes to religious thought and political ideology.

The professor and keynote speaker for the ceremony won the federal government's "Outstanding American by Choice" award in 2008 for work he has done to improve the water quality in his native country, Bangladesh.

"I am a Muslim in America, and I am granted more freedom here than in most other countries in the world. When I disagree with American foreign policy, I can still speak my mind about it," said Hussam.

But many of Fairfax's newest U.S. citizens admitted later that their reasons for becoming an American were less lofty than those articulated by Hussam in his speech.

Giovanna Moya, a Bolivian-born Mason student, was primarily motivated to become a U.S. citizen for practical reasons. She wants to work in global affairs and needed citizenship in order to work for the U.S. Department of State this summer.

"I couldn't get the internship without being a citizen. That was the main reason for doing it now," said Moya.

RESPONSE

"Fairfax Residents Become U.S. Citizens: County Government Sponsored a Local Naturalization Ceremony Last Month," *Fairfax Connection,* **June 4, 2010**
Lauren Wallis

In my high school yearbook from Robinson Secondary School in Fairfax, Virginia, the senior pictures are stacked in neat rows, the boys wearing tuxes, the girls wearing a classic black drape that balances on the edge of the shoulders. There was no escaping the tux and the drape: cheerleader, goth, and nerd alike were rounded up, taken to the gym, and forced to cover up their own clothing with the school's choice. As the eye moves across the page, its gaze into the uniformity of the pictures breaks at the appearance of a Muslim girl, wearing a black headdress that covers her head, neck, and shoulders.

Julie O'Donoghue's article from the *Fairfax Connection* also makes visible people with Middle Eastern backgrounds in this affluent Washington, DC, suburb. As O'Donoghue describes a recent ceremony in which 74 immigrants became naturalized American citizens, she centers on the story of Nojan Navab, a young man who emigrated to the United States from Iran, seeking political asylum in 1996, at the age of 13.

The article suggests that there is a sizable immigrant community in Fairfax, and that for Middle Eastern immigrants in particular, gaining citizenship is difficult. The journalist writes that Navab has had a difficult time becoming a citizen: first he waited nine years to become a permanent resident because of increased security measures following September 11, and only now has he been able to become a citizen, 14 years after his arrival.

The article also implies that Navab is a good, nonthreatening citizen. He graduated from high school and college in Fairfax, feels that the United States is "basically" his country, and is excited to vote and travel abroad with more ease as a result of his citizenship. He is pictured smiling on the steps of the government center, wearing a collared shirt and a sports coat with a small American flag in the pocket.

O'Donoghue has a detached journalistic voice and constraints of time and print space. But an ethnographer would be able to give a more nuanced view of the immigrant community in Fairfax. In an ethnographic account, it would be important to understand the Middle Eastern community as a whole and its place in Fairfax, as well as viewpoints of individuals like Navab on their experience as immigrants. The ethnographer might look for statistical data about how many Middle Eastern immigrants live in Fairfax County, when they arrived, and their socioeconomic status since they've been in the United States.

More important, the ethnographer would need to gather extensive, in-depth information from individuals within the community. It might be helpful to start with one individual, such as O'Donoghue did with Navab:

- What were your feelings about leaving Iran and coming to the United States as a child?
- How were you received in school?
- Did anything change about your life after September 11?
- What processes did you have to go through to obtain permanent residency and citizenship?
- What were your feelings about these procedures—as a child and an adult?
- How connected are you to traditional cultural practices?
- How do you feel others perceive your traditional practices (such as style of dress and religious observations)?
- How do you feel the mainstream Fairfax community feels about Middle Eastern people in general?

Since Navab stated that he feels the United States is "basically" his country, it would also be important to ask him how he feels about Iran. Is it no longer really "his country"? The answers to these questions would help provide a more rounded view of Navab, beyond a simplistic portrait of him with an American flag in his pocket.

BOX3 continued

It would also be important to ask Navab (and other informants) about relationships within the Middle Eastern community in Fairfax. An ethnographer might ask how many of his friends are of similar national background—and how many are not. Leads to friends and family members would then help the ethnographer conduct more individual interviews, using similar questions as those listed above. By interviewing many people within the community, the ethnographer might also be able to understand how connected the community is and what causes divisions.

By observing the Middle Eastern community, conducting interviews with people of all ages, and researching statistical facts about immigration and naturalization, the ethnographer could begin to understand the place of the Middle Eastern community in Fairfax. O'Donoghue's article makes the Middle Eastern community in Fairfax visible, like the published senior portraits of young women in headdresses in the Robinson Secondary School yearbook. An ethnographer's account would detail how it feels to be the photo that stops the eye in the midst of hundreds of tuxes and drapes.

Fieldworking with This Book

Researching involves making sense of cultural events. As one of the main goals of your research will be to share what you learn with others, you'll need to organize your research process as you work toward your final written project.

To help you organize, we've arranged this book around four learning strategies: reading, writing, fieldworking, and reflecting. Using these strategies will help you build two projects of your own: a research portfolio and either a fieldwork essay or a series of shorter fieldworking pieces. To help you, we've gathered readings from a variety of genres, academic disciplines, and voices to show how to do fieldwork and how to write about it. Since writing is so integral to fieldworking, we designed exercises to help you develop the fieldwriting skills you'll need. You may do the short exercises on separate topics and collect them in your portfolio. Or you may decide to build these pieces toward one fieldwork essay. In either instance, the writing you do becomes part of your research portfolio. The aim of such a portfolio is to develop insights and reflections on the research process as you go along, not just at the end of your project. Writing is both the means for your thinking and the end result of your fieldwork project. All the writing you do—from brainstorming and keeping fieldnotes to writing reflective memos, designing interview questions, and drafting your final fieldworking project—will become part of your research portfolio.

In this book, you'll read published texts, but you'll also learn to "read" objects as cultural artifacts: buildings, clothing, photographs, and old letters, for example. And you'll learn to read places, events, and people: truck stops, restaurants, bars, mall stores, and horse barns. In the process, you will dig into layers of meaning that lie inside language—in words themselves and in expressions, stories, jokes, proverbs, and legends.

Additionally, this book will initiate you into the gritty part of fieldwork. You will learn to keep researcher's notes, record interviews with informants, collect material culture (research data), develop questions and hunches, and offer interpretations. A pencil and a notebook are your bare necessities, although you might consider other technologies (a camera, a laptop computer, an audio recorder). Far more important than the skills you develop or the equipment you use for controlling your data, however, is the understanding that *you are the main tool for your research*. As a researcher, you'll need to look out at others and back at yourself.

Locating Culture

Locating culture means:

- observing rituals, rules, patterns, and behaviors
- identifying shared language(s)
- making distinctions between groups and communities
- locating differences between cultures/subcultures

An Ethnographic Study: "Friday Night at Iowa 80"

We present here a completed student fieldworking project to give you a sample of the kind of research and writing we hope you'll ultimately do. We want to show you how a fieldworker steps into a culture to investigate it, at the same time stepping out as he maintains the outsider's perspective while he observes. Rick Zollo wrote this study about a truck stop in Iowa as his major paper for a course centered on researching and writing about fieldwork. Though your study will probably be shorter than Rick's, it will share many features of his approach, particularly the emphasis on the self as part of the research process. You'll notice immediately that Rick's study of the truck stop is written as a narrative and reads like a nonfiction article from a magazine.

As a reader new to ethnographic writing, you may not immediately distinguish the features of this study that make it ethnographic research and not journalism. You'll need to attune yourself to what goes into the fieldworking process.

Look for places where Rick interweaves his own feelings, beliefs, and reflections. While reading, ask ethnographic questions:

- What were Rick's sources of data?
- How does he confirm or disconfirm his ideas?
- What interpretations does he offer?
- What is the culture he describes?
- What makes it a culture?
- Does his writing convince you?
- Can you see the places and people he describes?
- Do you understand what it would be like to be an insider in this culture?

You'll need to keep in mind some background knowledge as you read Rick's interesting journey into the culture of truckers. First, it's clear that although Rick writes about a single Friday evening, he's spent many Fridays and other days at the truck stop, Iowa 80, gathering data and working his way into this fieldsite. He writes with the authority of having been there, and he makes us feel that we've been there too.

It's also obvious that Rick has permission from the owner of the truck stop to hang out and interview truckers and staff members and that he has read other articles and books about the trucking culture. He has knowledge about what he expects to see at his fieldsite. Because, like Rick, you will be researching a place you are already interested in and want to know more about, you'll need to admit your possible biases about your topic and look at how other researchers have written about it.

As you read Rick's study, make a list of questions about his research process. In addition, recognize the study's form and content. For example, Rick provides headings to guide you through his study. His form takes the shape of a journalistic essay and his content focuses on the trucker subculture, but most important, Rick describes his fieldworking process within the essay.

· ·

Friday Night at Iowa 80
The Truck Stop as Community and Culture
Rick Zollo

> *Truck stops are the center of trucking culture. "Trucker Villages" . . . offer the driver an equivalent to the cowboys' town at trail's end or the friendly port to sailors.*
> —James Thomas, *The Long Haul*

A Modern Trucking Village

Friday nights are a special time all across America, for big and small towns alike, and it's no different at a "trucker town." Iowa 80 is advertised as "the largest Amoco truck stop in the world" and is located off Interstate 80 at exit 284, outside the small town of Walcott, about 10 miles from downtown Davenport and 40 miles from my Iowa City home.

I arrived at suppertime one fall Friday evening, with the intention of enjoying a meal in the full-service restaurant. But before I could even consider eating, I had to walk the grounds. In my experience, the best way to observe a community is with a walkabout, observing climate and current social interactions.

A huge hole occupied what had most recently been the south-side front parking lot. The hole was filled with a bright blue fuel tank roughly 40 by 60 feet in size and topped by five large green plastic spirals. The operation was a result of another government mandate, concerning leaky fuel storage containers. Delia Moon, company vice president, told me this operation would cost Iowa 80 $180,000 ($40,000 to take out the old tanks and $140,000 for replacements), another example of "government interference." According to Delia, the tanks dug up so far were in good condition.

The truck stop is laid out in the form of a huge rectangle, taking up over 50 acres on the north side of the interstate exit. The first building facing incoming traffic is the main headquarters, which includes a restaurant at the front, video and game room next, a sunken shopping mall, and a stairway leading to second-floor

(Photo: Susan Zollo)

corporate offices, hair salon, laundry room, movie theater (seats 40) and TV room, dental offices, exercise room, and private shower stalls. The last renovations were completed in 1984, about the time I first began noticing the village, but Delia stated that a large building project was planned for 1994.

The evening had yet to begin, and the yard was only a quarter full, without that convoy pattern of trucks coming and going in single file, an orderly parade that in several hours would take on Fellini-like dimensions. I sauntered through the yard (in my usual loping stride), notebook in hand, making eye contact with truckers when they passed, not trying to act like one of them so much as feeling comfortable in their company.

Will Jennings, a former trucker and personal friend, talked about the insularity of the trucker community in Frederick Will's *Big Rig Souls*. "You go in truck stops and they have their own section. . . . Most of them [truckers] could tell from the minute you walk in the door you're not a driver. They hold most people who aren't drivers . . . with a good deal of disdain" (27).

(Photo: Susan Zollo)

(Photo: Susan Zollo)

I had already been spotted by employees of Iowa 80 as "not a driver," and in my many youthful years of hitchhiking around the country, I had been made to feel the outsider whenever I'd stumble into one of these trucking lairs. I had trouble understanding this resentment of outsiders, especially when I was on the road in need of a ride. But familiarity with the culture was bringing what scholar Sherman Paul calls "the sympathetic imagination," and I now felt I was beginning to understand.

On this late afternoon, the lot was rather calm, even though rigs waited in line to diesel up at the Jiffy fuel station, all four bays at the Truckomat truck wash were filled, and service was being rendered at the mechanics' and tire shop. The three buildings stood in a row on the north side of the lot, each about a third the size of the main complex and separated by several truck lanes for traffic.

The truckyard occupied the southern half of the property, with the interstate in its full glory to the south of that. Every time I stood in the middle of this immense yard, with truck traffic in full promenade, I'd experience a thrill. But for now, with walkabout complete, I doubled back to the restaurant. I was hungry.

Truck Stop Restaurant

By 6 p.m., Iowa 80's restaurant was full to capacity. Customers appeared to be divided equally between truckers and four-wheelers. After a short wait, I was led to a small table in the back section, where at an adjacent booth, a young waitress was serving supper to a grizzled veteran. I detected a mild flirtation passing between them.

The night's special was catfish, which I ordered. I ate heartily, fish fried light and crispy, a scoop of potatoes adorned with gravy, cole slaw, and a fresh warm roll. Every book on truckers I've read describes truck stop food as rich, plentiful, and greasy.

(Photo: Susan Zollo)

Ditto!

I sat opposite the veteran and watched him. He ate with gusto, enjoyed a smoke (truck stop restaurants are not smoke-free), and wrote in his logbook. Should I approach him? Why not?

"Excuse me, I'm doing research on truckers and truck stops. Can I talk to you?"

He looked up from his logbook and smiled. "Yeah, sure. I've got time."

I grabbed my gear and joined him. His name was Gordy,* and he drove out of Oklahoma City for Jim Brewer, a company that hauls racks of automobiles to dealerships. Gordy spoke with easy affability, and underneath his three-day growth of beard, I detected once boyish good looks reminiscent of the actor Lee Majors.

Gordy drove all over the country, hauling General Motors vehicles. He stopped at this truck stop often, but only because of the food. He made it a point to let me know that he generally didn't frequent truck stops.

"Your truck have a sleeper?"

"No. Wouldn't drive a truck that had one."

That was a surprise, since I thought that just about all long haulers used sleepers.

Gordy was a veteran, with 22 years of service on the road. "How does driving compare now with twenty years ago?"

"Worse. Things are worse now." So are the truck stops, he said, which are bigger, with more features, but run by national chains with no feeling for the trucker.

---

*The names of all truckers and employees, except those in management, have been changed.

He blamed deregulation for today's problems. Before deregulation, freight rates were controlled, and a trucker knew what he could make from each delivery. Then came deregulation, and "all these fly-by-night companies" flooded the market. The power of the Teamsters was also curtailed, and Gordy, a union man, found his position threatened. "I'm real bitter about it."

He once owned his own truck, was out on the road for long periods of time, and made good money. Today, he drove only four-day runs, for a company that was the highest bidder for his services. He slept in motels and had his choice of destinations.

As for the cursed paperwork that so many truckers complain about: "Hardly got any. Just this logbook. And they're fixin' to do away with that. By '96, they figure it'll all be on computer."

No issue galvanizes a trucker more than the logbook. Any time I wanted to test a trucker's spleen, I'd only have to mention the issue.

"I've been told that most truckers cheat on their logbooks," I said. "If they computerize it, you won't be able to cheat."

Gordy gave me a sly Lee Majors grin. "Oh, there'll be ways."

The Arcade

Fortified by a meal and a successful encounter, I ventured into the arcade area separating restaurant from shopping mall. The area was packed. During my hour with catfish and Gordy, many truckers had pulled off the road, and a handful of them were engaged in pinball games, laser-gun videos, a simulated NBA game, and in front of one large glass case with a miniature pickup shovel, a man and a woman were trying to win a pastel-colored stuffed animal. I stopped to watch. After several tries the man succeeded, and the couple rejoiced. I waited for their enthusiasm to wane and then introduced myself.

The driver's name was Morris, and he wasn't sure he wanted to talk to me. Like Gordy, he was middle-aged and grizzled, but where Gordy's three-day growth covered handsome features, Morris was a buzzard, with a hawk nose, a pointy chin, and a leather motorcycle cap pulled low over his forehead.

I assured him that my questions were for research purposes only, but he looked at me suspiciously, as if I were an authority sent to check on him.

Had he ever been at this truck stop before?

"First time, but I'm coming back. It's got everything."

How long had he been on this particular run? (Gordy was careful to emphasize that he made only four-day hauls.)

"Been home three and a half hours in the past four months."

Did he drive his own truck?

He was a lease operator (leasing his own rig to a company that moves furniture), presently hauling a load from Lafayette, Louisiana, to Cedar Rapids, Iowa.

How long did it take him to drive from Lafayette? (Knowing geography, I tried to calculate the time.) The question of time raised Morris's suspicions again, and instead of answering, he fixed me with a hard gaze. Sensing I had crossed some invisible boundary, I thanked him for his time. Obviously, my question related to logbook procedures, and I made a mental note to avoid that type of inquiry.

Also, I noticed that Morris and the woman for whom he had so gallantly won a prize were not together. Seeking a couple who actually drove in tandem, I walked into the mall area, past the cowboy boot display and chrome section ("the world's largest selection of truck chrome"), and spotted a couple with a baby moseying down the food aisles.

"Excuse me. I'm doing a research paper on truckers and truck stops. Are you a trucker?" I asked, directing my question to the presumed dad in the group.

"No, I'm not," he said emphatically.

Iowa 80 Employees

Truckers, four-wheelers (about 20 percent of the business at Iowa 80), and employees make up the truck stop community. The employees keep the community functioning, like municipal employees without whom towns and cities could not operate.

Two such employees stood at the end of one of the food aisles, stocking shelves. Sally and Maureen knew about me, thanks to a letter that General Manager Noel Neu had sent out a month ago, asking Iowa 80 workers to cooperate with my study. Sally was the shift manager of the merchandise area, and Maureen was one of her staff. I directed most of my questions to Sally.

How long had she been working at Iowa 80?

Eight years. Maureen had been with the company for only a year.

Which was the busiest shift?

"I think it's four to midnight, but if you ask someone on the day shift, they'd probably say their shift."

What did she most like about working four to midnight?

"The people. We get all kinds here. Down-to-earth people . . . crazy people." And she told me about a woman who several weeks ago came into the store ranting and raving, apparently in the throes of paranoid delusions. Authorities were called, and it was determined that "she was on some kind of bad trip—cocaine or something."

Sally mentioned that the police were out in the yard at this moment, making a drug bust. "How'd they know somebody was selling drugs?" I asked.

"A trucker reported it at the fuel center. Heard someone over the CB. We called the cops."

Apparently truckers police themselves. Sally also said that drivers will even turn in shoplifters. "They know if we get too much shoplifting, prices will go up."

I asked Sally about those prices, which I considered reasonable. She replied that they were cheap enough for most truckers, but there were always those who wanted to haggle.

"You're allowed to barter over costs?" I asked.

"Oh, yeah. Not as much as the day manager."

Sally came from a small town north of Walcott, and Maureen was from one of the Quad Cities.* Iowa 80 employed over 225 workers and was one of the largest employers outside of the Quad Cities municipal area.

---

* Bettendorf and Davenport, Iowa, and Moline and Rock Island, Illinois.

"One of the things that most impresses me is how friendly the workers are here," I said.

"We try to be the trucker's second home," said Sally.

Talking to Truckers

Business continued to pick up. As with previous Friday night visits, I found much conversation in the aisles, as if the truckers could afford to be expansive, find community with colleagues, socialize at the end of a workweek. Many of these drivers, though, still had loads to deliver; others were settling in for the weekend, waiting for a Monday morning pickup.

I had hoped to talk to women and minorities. The popular image of the trucker is that of a Caucasian blue-collar male, and for the most part, that group represents the majority of the industry. But more women are entering the field, and from my observations, black men make up 10 to 20 percent of the population. Two black truckers stood behind displays of music tapes, engaged in spirited conversation. I didn't want to interrupt them. Near the cash register, I spotted another black trucker, a beefy 40-something fellow with flannel jacket and flat driving cap. He was reluctant and wary, but he agreed to answer questions.

Ronald was a long hauler from Detroit, making his third stop at Iowa 80. He had been driving for five years, after serving a 12-year hitch in the armed services. He drove all over the country, going out for three to five weeks at a time. He didn't mind sleeping in his rig. For every week on the road, he got a day off. He was presently hauling a load from Omaha to New Jersey, with plenty of time to get there. (I consciously steered my questions away from time lines.)

He wore a forced smile, which served as a shield, and any question that might seem personal made the smile stiffen. He didn't give off the scent of danger I detected from Morris, but he definitely eyed me more as an adversary than as a friendly interlocutor.

Our session was interrupted by a midsized white fellow, probably in his midthirties, sporting an orange pony tail, two diamond studs in his left earlobe, and several menacing facial scars.

"What you up to, man? Who you workin' for?" His voice had a manic edge that reminded me of Gary Busey in one of those action adventures they watched in the movie theater upstairs.

"I'm a researcher from the University of Iowa." I described my project.

"Oh, yeah?" he said, as if he didn't believe me. Then he turned his high-voltage attention on Ronald. They started talking about the rigs they drove.

Cal spoke so fast it was hard to keep up with him. He was telling Ronald that he had bought his own truck and would soon go independent, a status he encouraged Ronald to seek. Ronald's smile by this time had tightened like a band of steel. He was cornered by white guys, one with a notebook, the other a speed rapper with a pony tail. Ronald was clearly on guard.

Cal was from a nearby town, and he mentioned a motorcycle-driving buddy who was writing a book with help from someone in the Iowa Writers' Workshop. I dropped a few names Cal recognized, and he suddenly decided I was OK. When he couldn't convince Ronald to use his method to buy a truck, he ducked away to collar someone else. Ronald kept smiling and muttering, "Man, I don't want my own truck."

Before I could finish questioning Ronald, a well-built 30-something trucker with finely brushed hair and trimmed moustache jumped before me, arms folded, ready to unload his truck.

The atmosphere was getting uncomfortable. Who did these people think I was? I recalled a previous visit, when I was down at the truck wash. A woman named Connie, a road veteran who bragged of living on the highway for years as a hitchhiker, told me, "We thought you were a spotter."

Not knowing what that meant but reckoning that it couldn't be in my favor, I assured her I was only a writer. "What's a spotter?" I asked.

"They go around checking on company drivers, to see that they're not screwing up, taking riders, that kind of stuff."

My new friend's name was Dan, and he was at the truck stop because a trailer he was supposed to pick up at a nearby meat products plant was late being loaded. "Never come down here normally. Know why?" I sure didn't. "No counter in the restaurant. They took out the counter. And the food's greasy." . . .

Town Meeting around the Cash Register

I wandered back downstairs and moved about the merchandise aisles, tired from my talk with Dan. Who did I meet in one of the back aisles but Cal, in the company of a tall, slender woman with a well-used look. He still had that manic glint in his eye. "Man, you're all right. You really are a writer. I thought you were government, but you're not."

My wandering brought me to the cash register, a good place to meet truckers. Drivers were either coming or going and were most receptive to exchange. I found a middle-aged driver paying for a purchase, and we passed pleasantries. No heavy conversations or even probing questions—Dan had exhausted me of that.

The woman working the register and the driver were comparing horror stories about truck stop robberies. I had noticed the woman before. She was one of the friendly employees who liked to talk to drivers. Many of the workers at Iowa 80 had this friendly conversational manner about them, and it always contributed to the atmosphere in the building.

The trucker knew a driver who had been robbed recently at a truck stop in Atlanta, where he was now heading. The woman told of another robbery at a truck stop outside Tampa. Both robberies occurred in the parking lot, and in both cases, the drivers were getting out of their rigs when someone stepped out of the shadows and robbed them at gunpoint.

The trucker left, and I lingered to talk to the woman. Her name was Bea. Her husband had been a trucker until last week, when he was involved in an accident outside Atlanta, caused by a drunk driver three cars ahead of his rig. Nobody was hurt, but there was $8,000 in damage. "Five years without an accident, and they fire him. I sent the guy who fired him a thank-you letter. We got two teenagers at home."

How was her husband taking his dismissal?

"He's broken up about it, but I'm glad."

What's he doing now?

"He's farming with relatives."

I pulled out my notebook and introduced myself. Bea knew about me, again thanks to Noel Neu's letter. She was convinced I had picked a great subject for research. She had been working for Iowa 80 part time, then left for a full-time job in Davenport. "But I came back because I missed it. Took a pay cut, but it's worth it to work here."

I mentioned my interview with Delia Moon and how many Iowa 80 employees seem to love the work atmosphere.

"Isn't Delia wonderful? I love this family." Bea told me a story about Bill Moon, founder of Iowa 80 and an empire builder in the truck stop industry. Years ago, Bea's son had a paper route in downtown Walcott. One morning, her son was stymied by a blizzard. Bill Moon saw the boy struggling to cover his route. The businessman got his car and helped her son finish the job. "That's the kind of guy he was."

Bill Moon died of cancer over a year ago. "You should have seen this place," said Bea. "Everyone was so sad."

Truck Yard at Night

Back outside, three hours after my arrival, I moved through the huge truck yard, filling my lungs with air and trying to catch a second wind. Trucks pulled in and out of the lot in promenade. Diesel fumes filled the air, and the lot was noisy with the sounds of transmissions shifting.

The yard was teeming. Large spotlights mounted on 50-foot poles outlined the scene. Puddles in the middle of the parking lot reflected blue and pink neon from the Jiffy Shop fuel center. A computerized sign facing the interstate spilled a cascade of shifting letters, advertising the night's menu, chrome supplies, free showers with tank of fuel, guaranteed scales to weigh freight.

I loped across the yard, tired but feeling fine, realizing that the more I learned about the trucking community, the more I would never know. I was a four-wheeler, a writer temporarily tangled in all these "webs of significance," an outsider whose sympathies could never connect all the many lives spent in forced but voluntary isolation. Long haulers were sentenced to a solitary voyage, and the truck stop was the oasis where they found temporary community.

Old-Timer at the Fuel Center

Inside the Jiffy Shop: quiet. Iowa 80's fuel center is built like your average convenience store, with fuel and sundries sold at a discount, except that here the fuel is diesel instead of gasoline and the sundries are marketed for truckers' needs.

A young black trucker was buying a sandwich at a back counter. Several of his white comrades were paying for their fuel up front. In one of the two-person booths that line the windows along the west wall sat an older gray-haired gentleman, resplendent in a green polo shirt and reading a trucker magazine.

I sat across from the old-timer in an adjoining booth and, after a few minutes of sizing up the situation, made my introduction. "May I ask you a few questions?"

He looked up from his magazine and admitted to being a trucker but added, "I don't like to get involved."

Fair enough. Still, we talked. Gradually he warmed up, and eventually I opened my notebook and began recording his remarks.

He had been driving trucks for some time but wouldn't say how long. He was at the truck stop getting an oil change for his tractor. He was primarily a short hauler, though he had done long hauls in his time.

I placed his age in the midsixties. Books I had read on over-the-road trucking mention how the long haul prematurely ages the driver. I could understand that this old-timer would change to shorter routes. As he warmed up to me, he revealed more information. He was articulate and had the face of a learned man. Perhaps he had retired from another profession. (More and more truckers were coming from other professions; many were veterans from the armed services.)

He asked me questions as well. His early pose of disinterest belied an avid curiosity. I soon had the impression that he would rather interview me.

He lived in the Quad Cities and had been a trucker all his life, starting at age 17 when he drove for construction outfits in the Fort Dodge area. He let slip that he was 60, an owner-operator of his own rig. Allusions to problems from years gone by hinted at previous financial difficulties.

Dan's populist appeal was still ringing in my ear, so I mentioned the rigors placed on truckers by big business and government. But the old-timer was not buying. True, big business and government put obstacles in the way, but there was a good living out there for anyone willing to put in the time. He told me a story similar to the fable of the tortoise and the hare. He always obeyed speed limits. He was in no hurry. Younger drivers would pass him, impatient with his caution. But the old-timer always got the job done on time. He clearly identified with the tortoise.

I found myself taking a shine to this man. There was something strong-willed and flinty about him, even in his refusal to give me his name. We talked about trucks, and he became a font of information. He pointed to his rig in the yard, a Ford. He would have preferred a Freightliner but couldn't get financing. He made disparaging remarks about Kenworths, called the Rolls-Royces of the profession, and about another highly rated competitor—"Why, I wouldn't even drive a Peterbuilt. Cab's too narrow."

He was presently leasing his truck and services to a company that hauls general merchandise to stores like Pamida, Kmart, and Sam's Warehouse. Earlier in the day, he had hauled 45,000 pounds of popcorn, but at present he had a trailer full of supplies for a Sam's Warehouse in Cedar Rapids. As for his earlier mention of being a short hauler, well, that wasn't quite the truth. He tried to limit his runs to the Midwest—within the radius of Kansas City, Omaha, Fargo, and Youngstown—but sometimes he ventured as far as Atlanta or Dallas.

What about the complaint, first voiced by Gordy, that times were worse now than 20 years ago?

Yes in some instances, no in others. True, the logbook was a joke, especially concerning off-duty time. ("Why, when I hauled steel out of Gary, sometimes they made you wait 12 hours to get your load. That's all your driving time.") Yet the trucks these days were better, and the money was still good. ("I can drive from Kansas City to Des Moines without hardly changing gears. Couldn't do that twenty years ago." And, "I'm not saying I'm not making money. Making more money now than I was three years ago.")

He had to get back to his work, make his Cedar Rapids drop by 11. Otherwise he'd continue the conversation. I could tell he enjoyed our talk, and I had the urge to ask him if I could go out on the road with him. I was sure several weeks of riding with this old-timer would have given me an education.

But we parted as comrades, although when I asked again for his name, he declined to give it.

"I'll just refer to you as 'an esteemed older gentleman in a green shirt,'" I said. He enjoyed that description immensely and left me with a loud, ringing laugh.

Conclusion

My night at Iowa 80 was coming to a close. I had only to walk back through the truck lot and get into my little Japanese-made sedan. I was a four-wheeler, but that didn't stop me from making eye contact with the truckers in the yard, waving a hearty hello before I made my Hi-ho Silver.

What was I to make of this experience? I was exercising what Clifford Geertz calls "an intellectual poaching license" (*Local Knowledge* 12), engaging in what John Van Maanen terms "the peculiar practice of representing the social reality of others through the analysis of [my] own experience in the world of these others" (ix).

But had I truly experienced the community and culture? Had I penetrated the veils of unfamiliarity to become a reliable scribe of trucker life?

I had no doubts on that Friday night, as I returned to my car and drove home. I felt flush. My informants, reluctant at first, had been forthcoming. Employees were friendly, and the truckers, although initially suspicious of my motives, spoke from both head and heart.

My experiences with the culture reflected what I had read by James Thomas and Michael Agar. I sensed a community that felt both proud and put upon, holding to perceived freedoms yet reined in by new regulations and restrictions. Some company drivers, like Gordy and Ronald, felt insulated from variables over which they had no control (fluctuating fuel prices), but others, like Dan, were angry about issues both on the road (DOT and highway patrolmen) and off (time and money constraints involving the unloading of deliveries). The owner-operator, my green-shirted older gentleman, did not feel like an endangered species, and the fact that Cal, however reliable his testimony might have been, was becoming an owner-operator attested to some of the virtues of that status.

The metaphor of the road cowboy certainly has significance. I surveyed the boot and shoe shop and found three varieties of cowboy boots (but not a loafer or a sneaker in sight), ranging from the economical $40 model with nonleather uppers to $150 snakeskin cowboy boots. Not far from the boot section were belts and buckles with a decidedly Western cast and enough cowboy hats to populate a Garth Brooks concert.

But connections to cowboys run deeper than clothes. Thomas writes that the "outstanding characteristics of both the trucker and the cowboy are independence, mobility, power, courage, and masculinity" (7). With all due apologies to the many women now trucking, that definition seems to apply. But it might be more mental than physical since, as my old-timer professed, driving a truck these days is not the physically rigorous activity it once was, and Dan's complaints about loading and unloading aside, truckers are not supposed to touch the product they deliver.

The cowboy element of the culture might seem like romantic accouterment rather than realistic assessment. Yet as Agar has pointed out, even romantic notions of the cowboy were more nonsense than truth, since that species in actuality "wore utilitarian clothes, engaged in long days of hard work, and ate boring and nutritionally deficient food" (*Independents Declared* 10), a description that sounds like trucker life.

I also found some agreement with Agar's assessment of present versus past times. The old-timer had a healthy attitude: "Some things are better, some things are worse." But for the most part, the veteran truckers I talked with see the past as "a better time . . . because regulations were simpler, enforcement was more lax, and fines were lower. Although the technology of trucks and roads has improved, the culturally spun webs of regulation have thickened into a maze" (44).

As for trucker grievances, one thing I found for certain, which Frederick Will documents in *Big Rig Souls*, is that "the trucker is condemned to rapid turnarounds after each load, to physical discomfort, to little or boring leisure, to being forever harried" (29).

I believe I found a community at Iowa 80. Delia Moon described the company's goal as turning the truck stop into a "destination." The dictionary defines *destination* as "the place to which a person or thing travels or is sent." Iowa 80, for all its scope and size, is still a truck stop. But a good many of my trucker informants were regulars, and the ones who were there for the first time were impressed by what they found.

Thomas states that "providing personal services for drivers is not where a truck stop gains most of its profits. The extras . . . are to lure truckers in from the road to the fuel pumps and service area" (17). Delia Moon supported this view. "We're working primarily to satisfy the . . . trucker. That's why you see the movie lounge and so much parking and chrome and everything."

Yet in the process of giving truckers these amenities, as varied as a part-time dentist or a portable chapel for those needing to be born again, Iowa 80 is creating a context, setting up a multiplicity of complex structures that are both conceptual and real. A Friday night at this village is truly an adventure and, for those willing to engage experience as a form of education, an introduction into a dynamic community and culture.

Works Consulted

Agar, Michael. *The Professional Stranger: An Informal Introduction to Ethnography.*
    New York: Academic, 1980. Print.
Agar, Michael. *Independents Declared.* Washington, DC: Smithsonian Inst., 1986. Print.

Geertz, Clifford. *The Interpretation of Cultures*. New York: Basic, 1973. Print.
Geertz, Clifford. *Local Knowledge*. New York: Basic, 1983. Print.
Horwitz, Richard. *The Strip: An American Place*. Lincoln: U Nebraska P, 1985. Print.
Kramer, Jane. *Trucker: Portrait of the Last American Cowboy*. New York: McGraw, 1975. Print.
Moon, Delia. Personal interview. 7 Oct. 1993.
Paul, Sherman. Personal interview. 1993.
Thomas, James. *The Long Haul: Truckers, Truck Stops and Trucking*. Memphis: Memphis State U, 1979. Print.
Van Maanen, John. *Tales of the Field*. Chicago: U Chicago P, 1988. Print.
Will, Frederick. *Big Rig Souls: Truckers in the American Heartland*. West Bloomfield: Altwerger, 1992. Print.
Wyckoff, D. Daryl. *Truck Drivers in America*. Lexington: Lexington, 1979. Print.

Rick Zollo's research study has many features of a fully developed ethnography, which is a book-length study that often takes years to complete. Over the course of one semester, or even a year, neither Rick nor you could expect to write a complete ethnography of a subculture. Rick's study, however, includes most of the parts of a fuller piece of research: library and archival research, cultural artifacts, fieldnotes, photographs, interviews and transcripts, reflective memos, and multiple drafts of his writing. (We will explore these aspects of research in later sections of this book.) In the following pages, we look at the elements of Rick's study to see how they worked—and how he worked with them.

Background Research   In his portfolio, Rick mentions having read Michael Agar's *Independents Declared*, an ethnography about truckers. In his reading at libraries and in private collections, he read Walt Whitman's poem "Song of the Open Road," Jack Kerouac's novel *On the Road*, and Woody Guthrie's road songs. He studied trucker magazines, truck school brochures from a community college, trucker trade journals, truck stop menus, and government regulations about the trucking industry. He also attended a two-day "truckers' jamboree," where he took more notes.

If Rick were doing his project today, he would also visit the Iowa 80 Trucking Museum, in person and online, to gather physical *and* electronic (archival) resources to support his research. Rick might also visit an array of other online trucking archives, such as the Golden Age of Trucking Museum.

Description   In "Friday Night at Iowa 80," Rick begins with descriptions of both the inside and the outside of the truck stop, to establish a full sweep of the landscape. He starts by guiding his reader on a walk around the outside of the truck stop, moving from the huge unfilled hole that marks the uprooted fuel containers to the truck parking lot. Once inside the mall-like complex, Rick shows us around the restaurant, where we watch him eat a meal of catfish and lumpy potatoes. We next accompany him into the arcade of pinball machines and laser-gun videos and then into the aisles of the convenience store, where employees are stocking shelves.

Interviews   In addition to the sense of authority he gains through his thick and rich physical descriptions of Iowa 80, Rick also collects an interesting range of interviews from both truckers and employees at the truck stop. Rick is able to get his informants to talk by hanging out and chatting with them. Sometimes informants don't talk to him because they're suspicious of him, but because he persists and gathers a range of informants—male and female, black and white, trucker and nontrucker—weaving his interviews into the overall narrative, he advances his study toward an analysis of the information he's collected.

Data   The data he relies on come mainly from informant interviews, but within these he sorts through a range of responses to his questions: insider terms, insider knowledge, and insider stories. Some informants supply terminology about the jobs, such as the word *spotter*. Others offer insider knowledge about how truckers do their jobs, answering questions about mileage, speed limits, logbooks, and truck preferences. From still others, he gathers occupational stories by inviting informants both to brag and to complain about their jobs.

Disconfirming and Complicating   After Rick has spent considerable time collecting this data about trucker beliefs and gripes, he introduces an unnamed informant who disconfirms and complicates much of what other drivers have said. Unlike the others, this lifetime driver felt trucking was a solid job and a good way to make a living and had little to complain about. Rather than tossing out this interview data as something that doesn't fit, Rick includes it. Fieldworkers always try to disconfirm and complicate the theories that they are trying out.

Connections   Rick's data analysis leads toward his initial hunch that the truck stop is a kind of community and a subculture for many of the truckers who spend time there. One of the Iowa 80 employees claims that the place is like the truckers' second home—a home away from home—which provides the central metaphor for Rick's paper. By the end of the study, Rick is able to link his own findings with other research that draws on the image of the trucker as cowboy.

Writing Strategies   What makes Rick's study ethnographic, then, is the wide range and depth of description and interview data, the amount of time he spent gathering it, and his commitment to showing the insider's perspective on the trucking culture. As a writer, Rick creates a "slice-of-time" device. He uses one Friday night at Iowa 80 to represent all the days and nights he's collected data there. In actuality, though, he spent weeks and months there. As a researcher, Rick writes himself into the study to show what he's in a position to see and understand, but he also points out what eludes him, who won't talk to him, and who walks away. All along, Rick reads and uses outside sources from other writers to test his own hunches about what trucking life and trucking culture are like. As a writer, Rick makes choices about how he will present his data from a wide range of writing strategies. But as a researcher, Rick conforms to the process of gathering, analyzing, interpreting, and validating his data, which is what *doing* fieldwork is all about.

Doing Research Online

We'd like to pause for a moment to consider the pros and cons of doing research online. It is difficult to imagine doing anything these days without using the Internet. Yet despite the convenience of having so much free information immediately available, we must be able to understand the value of this information. As with any kind of research, it takes skill and knowledge to sift through large amounts of data, decide what is most credible and useful, and link your sources with your project as a whole.

Like the research you do at your actual fieldsite, online research requires patience, attention to detail, selectivity, and analysis. Just as you might spend hours observing at your fieldsite, piecing together information as you find it, you should plan to spend plenty of time reading information on the Web until you know what focus you need, what data seem appropriate, and how the information will fit with the other parts of your research. You may uncover a wealth of information quickly, but you'll need more time to assess it. Keep the following questions in mind as you research online:

- Do your findings supplement any facts or details about people, places, histories, ideas, or artifacts you've already heard about?
- What evidence do you have that the information is reliable? Is it up-to-date? Who authored the text on the Web site?
- How is this Web site connected to other sources? Check out the links and decide if they're useful or distracting to your topic.

Most online searches begin with typing keywords into a search engine, such as Google or Yahoo! These search engines use an algorithm that makes sure the most visited Web sites will appear at the top of the list. But beware: *most visited* does not necessarily mean *most useful*. If you enter a common word or phrase in a search engine (say, "Jos, Nigeria"), the first entry might very well be from Wikipedia, a popular encyclopedia written and edited by volunteers who self-identify as experts in a given field. However, simply because Wikipedia is a highly visited site with a democratic philosophy for sharing knowledge does not make it reliable. Even with thousands of volunteer editors prowling Wikipedia for misleading information, factual inaccuracies abound.

Go to **bedfordstmartins .com/fieldworking** for more help with doing research online.

However, Wikipedia can be a good springboard for further research. How can you tell if a Web site is credible? A good rule of thumb is to consider sites with *.org* (nonprofit), *.edu* (education), or *.gov* (governmental) as more credible than commercial sites with *.com* domains that might have things—or a message—to sell. But even this approach is not infallible. It's better to look for a Web site (in any domain) that has a strong editorial policy. For example, anyone can write a blog on any topic, but a blog published through a reputable media service, such as the *Guardian*, is likely to be reliable. Similarly, the *New York Times* and the *Wall Street*

Journal are examples of news sites that offer in-depth coverage of topics with high levels of editorial control. Sites sponsored by research organizations or universities are also likely to be trustworthy. When you visit any Web site, go to the "About Us" page to gain clues about the site's credibility: editorial policies, guidelines for submission, circulation, authorship, and review standards are all good signs.

Many of the best sources of information you can find on the Web are electronic versions of sources you could also find in a library, like peer-reviewed articles in academic journals. Databases with full-text copies of academic journal articles are easily accessible to students through their college library's Web site. (Nonstudents will likely have to register and/ or pay for access to these same databases.) Searches conducted on general databases such as JSTOR, Project Muse, EBSCOhost, or Lexis-Nexis will yield a wealth of articles related to your topic.

Visit Chapter 3, "Working with Online Communities" (pp. 155–57), for help shaping research projects around online subcultures.

It's critical, though, whenever you do research, but especially when you do it online, to keep careful track of where you've been and where you're going. Bookmark valuable pages so that you don't lose them. Follow the advice in the box below for using the Web as an archive.

Guidelines for Online Research

- *Research well.* Look around and within the electronic world. See who's talking where, in listservs, blogs, discussion groups, social networking sites, and other online forums. Always remember to be a courteous member of the communities you join.

- *Mark your trail.* Make notes about where your online search takes you. You never know when you'll want to return later to check something that at first seemed unimportant.

- *Evaluate your resource.* An electronic resource is only as good as the information it provides. Be a smart researcher. Triangulate a site's information with other kinds of data sources.

- *Document everything you use.* Be responsible. Carefully document, cite, and attribute the text, graphics, and data you use from electronic sources the way you would any published material, both out of respect for the author as well as for your readers' benefit.

FieldWriting: Establishing a Voice

Research writing, like all good writing, has a voice. And this voice should be yours—not that of a faceless third person, as in "it was determined" or "this researcher found." It's preferable, we believe, to use *I* in **fieldwriting**. Contemporary fieldwork doesn't claim to be a totally objective social science. *I* allows you to write with your own **authority** and with the authenticity of your own fieldwork, and it will ensure your credibility.

To create a writing voice, you must invite yourself onto the page. To invite yourself onto the page means to ignore conventions that you've already learned—the formula for an essay, the passive voice, overuse of the third person, or the taboo against the personal pronoun *I*. Your reader needs to know you as the person who has been there.

Taking the Reader with You

Writing research means first "being there"—in the field, as Rick Zollo was at the truck stop, and then on the page, as he is in his ethnographic study. If you've never stopped at Iowa 80, Rick's research will take you there—cruising the parking lot, eating fried catfish and potatoes, hearing the truckers' gripes and recording their lingo, reading their logbooks, and noticing their musical tastes. Rick knew that his major challenge was to make the culture come alive for other people. So he researched his fieldsite and its background, established relationships with insiders, and thought hard about the data piled high on his desk and stuffed into boxes on his living room floor. As a researcher, he temporarily becomes a trucker, and through his writing, you, as his reader, become one too. Here are some of the ways he makes this happen:

1. He begins by writing himself into his fieldnotes.   In this passage from his October journal, Rick contrasts his own mood as a researcher with the surroundings at the truck stop:

> When I hear that Mrs. Moon will be returning from a funeral, I feel uneasy, like perhaps I am partly responsible for this state of affairs, a harbinger of bad times…. That leaves me sauntering across the back lot heading for the Jiffy Stop and trying to shake off my uneasiness. The sun is high in the sky, giving no indication of the coming cold front…. Dark clouds slash in diagonals across the northwest and southeast skies, and I give silent thanks for this bit of good weather…. I am determined to get off my dime and get to work on this project. If it's going to amount to anything, I have to talk to *people*.

2. He writes his interviews as dialogues, capturing both his own voice and that of his informants in his transcripts.   In his interview with Delia Moon, the founder's daughter and company vice president, Rick records some company history. But he also records his own questions as part of the interview. Recording both sides of two conversations helps his readers feel like they took part in it.

RZ: This truck stop was founded by your father?

DM: He worked for Standard Oil, in the engineering department, and when the interstate system was built, Amoco targeted places for stops, and my father would go in and buy the land and set up a dealer. He was responsible for setting up places all over the Midwest.

RZ: So he was a visionary? He had a vision of what truck stops in the future should be? Did he see it coming to this, places like Iowa 80 and Little America?

DM: I'd say it happened over time. Traffic here kept building. He was very... he really liked people, truckers. He'd sit in the restaurant and talk to them. The customers can always tell you how you can be better.

3. He rejects his early drafts because his voice depends too much on other authorities.   In this short excerpt from the beginning of a first draft of "Friday Night at Iowa 80," Rick cites two outside sources and even quotes the roadside sign he recorded in his fieldnotes. Eventually, Rick learns to balance his own voice with the recognized authorities from his reading.

"Truckstops are the center of the trucking culture," writes James Thomas in *The Long Haul*, and the new trucker villages "offer the driver an equivalent to the cowboys' town at trail's end or the friendly port to sailors" (111). One trucking village that exemplifies this roadside oasis is Iowa 80, "the largest Amoco truckstop in the world" (roadside advertisement), located off Interstate 80 in Walcott, Iowa, some dozen miles from Davenport and 40 miles from my Iowa City home.

I spent selected days and evenings at this site during the fall of 1993, with hopes of discovering "those webs of significance" that make up the context of this very particular culture (Geertz, *Interpretation of Cultures* 5). I am interested in trucker life for a variety of reasons and have wanted to write about Iowa 80 since first noting its sprawling growth almost a decade ago. My time there was well spent, "sorting out the structures of signification" that I had to "first grasp and then render" (9–10).

4. He experiments with another genre.   In a fiction-writing class he took while conducting his research, Rick began a novella about trucking that he describes as "pulp fiction." Sometimes fieldworkers discover that writing in another form—fiction, poetry, dramatic dialogue—helps them enter the world-view of their informants. When he later returned to the final draft of his ethnographic essay, Rick felt more confident that he could transform his real-world data into an interesting text for his readers. Though an ethnographic essay is certainly not fiction, it relies on many of the techniques that writers use to craft other genres.

5. He combines some of these techniques in his ethnographic study.   The challenge, as Rick learned, is to create a writer's voice that will engage a reader. Playing with technique, revising, and redrafting helped Rick establish his field-worker's voice for "Friday Night at Iowa 80." In the final draft, his authority comes from combining his personal feelings and observations with those of his informants and of the texts he read.

Developing Your Voice

- Use the first-person *I* to establish your authority as a researcher.
- Recognize that your voice conveys your research process.
- Remember that your reader needs to understand your perspective.

A Community Action Study

The term *community* holds many different meanings in the same way that the terms *culture* and *subculture* do. In fact, the three terms sometimes overlap. A community can be formed around geography, race, class, religion, gender, profession, beliefs, traditions, rituals, shared experiences, or ideals. Communities are everywhere, and some are more obvious than others.

Some colleges and universities have developed programs that join the academy with local communities, recognizing their responsibility to serve their surroundings. They may even require their students to complete a certain number of hours of community service to graduate. Terms such as *service learning, civic engagement, community partnerships,* and *civic action* all refer to programs that link resources between academics and the citizens outside their institutions. When we engage in thoughtful community-outreach projects, we often find that, as volunteers, we gain more insights than we expected to or that the number of hours we volunteered show.

Other college-sponsored activities invite students to become temporary insiders in cultures far more distant than the local community, such as study-abroad programs and various kinds of mission work. Matt Gaumer, for example, a mountain climber and major in recreation and leisure studies, spent a semester in a base camp on Mt. Everest. Although Matt had begun his time assuming he would climb Everest's peak, he became fascinated by the relationships between climbers and their sherpa guides. He found himself stepping in and out of both cultures. To represent the complexity of what he was seeing, he practiced fieldworking skills in his researching and writing.

Whether you're climbing the highest mountain on earth, tutoring a Sudanese student in a local library program, or traveling for a semester to study water supplies in India, understanding this chapter's concepts—stepping in/stepping out, subjectivity/objectivity, insider/outsider—can help you better engage in cultures and subcultures that are not your own.

You can be sure you will be both participant and observer during the course of your fieldwork. How much of your time you spend as a participant and how much you spend as an observer will depend on the culture you choose to study and the relationship you have to it.

"House for the Homeless"

Another student, Ivana Nikolic, studied a homeless shelter during the time she worked as a volunteer there. Ivana acts like a participant-observer since she is part of the life of the homeless shelter during the time she conducts her study. Ivana not only takes notes on the shelter and informally interviews its clients, but she carries out duties as part of a community service volunteer program and gets to know her informants through the ongoing interaction at Ramsey House.

Many students we have worked with have studied subcultures in which they already held roles as community volunteers or workers. Some examples of these subcultures include a children's playroom in a Ronald McDonald house, training sessions and tours for docents at a museum, a consignment dress shop run by Junior League volunteers, and an urban blood donation center. Whether you study a subculture as an outsider as Rick did or become a temporary insider within a community as Ivana did, building sharp fieldworking skills will deepen your understanding of both yourself and the community that you observe and in which you participate.

Read Ivana's full research project at **bedfordstmartins.com/ fieldworking** under Student Essays.

As you read Ivana's study, consider what makes it different from Rick Zollo's. How does each person's stance influence the way she conducts research? How much of their own positions do we, as readers, learn about as the study continues? And, of course, how is their research similar?

House for the Homeless: A Place to Hang Your Hat

Ivana Nikolic

I was only thirteen years old when my parents, my younger brother, and I left our home in Bosnia in the heat of the war. We have lived as refugees for eight years now. During that time we have started our lives from the very beginning twice, with only three travel bags packed with our pictures and belongings reminding us that we led a normal life before. My parents, once well respected and successful, were either unemployed or struggling to get and keep any job that was offered to them. I was brought up in an environment that highly respected education, and soon I realized that school was my only way out. I realized early on that I can lose everything except for what I can carry with myself, and that was knowledge. Since then, I have been a kid on a mission, determined to succeed, never give up, and make the most of the opportunities that were given to me.

Despite everything that happened to us, or maybe because of it, our family bonds grew stronger. We kept each other sane: we supported each other and never allowed each other to fall into despair. There were many times, though, when just as I thought that we hit the bottom, we would sink a little deeper. I learned that helplessness is probably the most difficult position to be in. After all, ever since the war our lives have been nothing but struggle, and we were in no position to change our situation. We were merely political puppets, suspended on the threads of the bloodthirsty puppet-masters dressed as politicians. I tend to think that my personal experiences have made me more responsive and sensitive to the misfortunes of others; however, they have also lowered my tolerance and understanding for those who seem to have given up trying.

When I moved to the United States two and a half years ago, homeless people were among the first to catch my attention. It broke my heart seeing them on the corners of the main roads, inhaling exhaust and the smell of burned rubber. Dirty and tired, they were holding signs offering to work for food and shelter. I knew how insecure, lost, scared, and lonely some of them must feel, since in a way I have been there too. I couldn't understand. How could the same system that brought me here and gave my family a chance when nobody else would fail so many other people? At first I thought that they were unfortunate people, run down by life or the system, who never found a way to blend in with the rest of the society. As the time went by, my perspective changed.

Most of the refugees that come to the United States don't speak English. While I worked as a Bosnian interpreter and case worker for a refugee resettlement organization, I met many Bosnian, Cuban, Somali, Russian, and Vietnamese refugees. The majority of them spoke little or no English, but they all found jobs within a month or two of their arrival in the United States. Therefore, finding a job was not as difficult as I had thought. That made me think that maybe unemployment was not the major problem of the homeless.

I talked to some of my American friends. "Most of them are drug addicts, alcoholics, or both." "They don't like rules and choose to live that life." "They don't want to be helped." That seemed to be the common American public opinion of the homeless. I could not understand, and what was once sympathy grew into fear that stemmed from not understanding. I grew accustomed to seeing homeless people on the corners without paying much attention. Sometimes, when I would run into them on my way back to my car, I would feel uneasy and often scared. It might be because I thought of them as being desperate. I saw them as people who had lost hope and meaning in life. I allowed myself to base my opinions on what I heard from other people, without ever trying to hear the stories of the homeless themselves. Actually, I never even read one book about them. But I felt ashamed. The more I thought about them, the more interested I was to hear some of the stories firsthand. Where are their families? Do they even have families? What did they do before they stepped into the homeless world? If they could, would they even want to get out of that culture? How many of them had had a misfortune or experienced a tragedy that pushed them so far, and how many chose to live that way? I was ready to listen. Thinking that listening to their stories would help me better understand their culture and that better understanding would diminish fear and stigma, I started to volunteer in a homeless shelter.

A Place to Hang Your Hat

It was 6:45 p.m. Wednesday, and, as always, people were standing in a long line waiting for the doors to the Ramsey House to open. The building is located downtown, next to a health care center. I remember taking refugees to this health care center. There were always people standing and hanging around in front of the building and in the parking lot between the health care center and Ramsey House. There were also always people waiting for the bus at the bus stop across the street. This was rare in other parts of the city, since public transportation was everybody's worst nightmare. As I drove into the parking lot, it seemed that nothing had changed. I heard loud hip-hop and rap music coming from a radio on the shoulder of an old and sick-looking man. His hair was gray and braided. He wore a Jamaican-looking hat. Although he looked tired, his appearance projected an illusion of a young spirit. The others were standing in groups, talking and smoking. It was my third day volunteering, and some people recognized me. They greeted me politely as I walked toward the door.

The lobby of the Ramsey House smelled strongly of lemon-scented disinfectant. A large front desk separated the office space from the lobby. The lobby had 30 chairs arranged around a modern, big-screen TV that was the focal point of the room. In one corner there were a couple of tables where some of the homeless sometimes played chess or cards. On one of the walls there was a display of pictures framed in glass. People of all ages and races were smiling and celebrating. I remembered how before I came, I expected to find a place saturated with religion, and the mere thought made me feel slightly uneasy. However, I was pleasantly surprised when I came. The lobby was saturated with hope and support. There were a lot of references to God, faith, and hope in motivational phrases, such as: "Ain't nothin' gonna come up today that me and the Lord can't handle." . . .

Every night after dinner a volunteer minister held a Bible study. Everybody was welcome to join, but nobody was asked to come. There was also a service during the day, a part of the Chaplaincy Program that was oriented toward spiritual counseling, praying, and worship for guests, clients, and staff. There were neither crosses on every wall nor Bibles on every chair. I felt a strong presence of community and faith, but religion was subtle.

It was 7:00 p.m.—time to check in people for dinner. The air conditioning was broken, and the whole place smelled strongly of lemon-scented disinfectant. The kitchen was large. It could seat about 70 people. A wall surrounded one area of the kitchen. This was where the people stood in a line. Lunch is served every day from 10:30 to 12:30 to anybody who stands in the line. However, dinner is served only to those who check in to spend the night. Ramsey House is a year-round shelter for women and men. Guests, as the staff refers to the homeless, have their own beds assigned, and they have to check in through the kitchen every night. Two security guards with metal detectors check everybody before they approach the check-in table.

It was my first time checking in people. I soon realized that this was probably the most diverse-looking group of people I ever saw classified under the same category—homeless. People from all age groups and racial groups were passing me their cards. Some of them were dressed nicer than I was, and I wondered how many times I passed them on the street never knowing where they went to sleep at night. Some were disabled, tired, and dirty; others looked sick. I was helping George, a full-time staff member. As people were checking in, he was joking with them. Most of them had a very high dose of respect for him, but at the same time they were reserved. He had a slightly militaristic tone of voice; you did not want to make him angry.

I asked George about the people who come here. He told me that most of the people had a drug addiction problem. Some of them were "crackheads." Their families couldn't trust them anymore or couldn't withstand the torture of addiction, so they abandoned them. "People here seldom speak of their families, probably because they've lost touch or realized their mistakes and are ashamed to talk about it. Some of them are infected. You know that, right?" asked George. I assumed that they were, although nobody told me that. A lot of the people in the shelter work and use the shelter as a way to save money until they have enough to move away. Their educational backgrounds vary greatly. There are those who can't read, and those who have master's degrees. However, as much as their individual stories differed and although all of them had their own reasons for being here, they all shared the same dream, and that was to move on.

A significant number of the people in the shelter were trying to get jobs, trying to stay clean of drugs, or trying to get their own apartments. I have a great deal of respect for people who have a goal in their lives, even if they are only short-term goals. When you reach the bottom of the social ladder, a goal or a dream might be your most precious possession. That is what kept me going as a refugee. I realized early on that I can feel sorry for myself, or I can set a goal and instead of passively sitting around and complaining I can work on achieving my goals. I found out that when I was busy thinking about the future and working on getting there, even the worst of troubles seemed less significant. I was too busy to think about them. They were just a thorn on my way to the stars. That is how I learned to respect people who have a goal or a dream. On their way to the fulfillment of their dreams, even if they never get there, they will move on.

A Caravan Stop

New people were checking in; others were leaving. There was a constant flux of people through the shelter. Close friendships were rare, and the occasional conversations between the homeless and me were very friendly but not personal. There was no time to be personal: people had to be fed, laundry had to be done. There was always something to keep me busy. I wondered whether the homeless saw the ritualistic nature of their evenings: check in, eat, listen to George read the rules of the shelter, take new linen, get a shower, chit-chat a bit during the cigarette breaks, then lights out. One night, I was helping in the laundry room, and the endless stream of nameless familiar faces coming in and out of the sweaty, stuffy, and stinky room gave a slightly nomadic feel to the place. The shelter was like a caravan stop for these people on a long tiring journey. It was a temporary place of refuge—a place to hide from their vices as well as from the society that chooses to shun them. The fire alarm went off. Calmly, people started to move toward the entrance. Through the mumbling I heard a couple of them joking, "Somebody tried to smoke one again."

All of us were standing outside on the parking lot. It was very loud. The Jamaican man brought down his radio, and a crackling sound mixed with a beat was pounding on asphalt. A young man in his thirties came and sat down next to me. His name was Alejandro. He was about five feet four and rather skinny. The skin on his hands was rough and broken. It was hard to imagine him doing hard labor, but his hands were his witnesses. I had met him earlier in the laundry room. It was difficult to understand his English, and the noise didn't help either. I asked him where he was from. "Mexico," he said. "I came to America twenty years ago." He lived with his mother in California. "I like California," he said. "Everybody speak Spanish there, but they don't pay good in California. Minimum wage four dollars. Here I get six." His eyes got teary when he mentioned his mother. I found out that his mother and all of his friends were still in California. He did not have anybody here. He carried a rolled-up job-search newspaper. He looked tired. The security guards came out and said that we needed to go back in now. I lost Alejandro in the crowd. I never saw him again. I find myself hoping that he found a job.

Going Back into the World

I met Solomon in the lobby another night. His English was proper and sophisticated, but he had a thick foreign accent. "Where are you from?" I asked. "Congo. I came to the U.S. two years ago." He was very calm when he talked. His hands barely moved, and even then it was in a slow, preaching manner. He revealed that back home he was a teacher, but here he doesn't know what he will do. I tried to find out why he came here, but he was very reluctant to talk about his past. "Do you have family back home?" I asked. "My mother is still in Congo. She lives in a polygamous marriage. That is not good. There is too much rivalry. I have brothers in Europe, in Germany. I have not spoken to them in a long time," he said. He got very emotional, and as much as I wanted to find out more about his family and how he came here, I couldn't. He was not interested in talking about it. He was not comfortable with my asking questions about him, his family, or his home. He spoke with a certain dose of mystic philosophy. "I like to observe all the people, women and men. All of them. I can see what a person is like by observing them. What makes one a gentleman and one a bum? If you observe people and their reactions carefully, you can find out what sort of an image you project on the world. You can find out who you would like to behave like—find your role models." He said that he doesn't like to talk. "You can find out more by observing," he said.

The whole conversation was somewhat surreal. Here he was, a young, healthy intellectual, sharing his life philosophy with a stranger in the loud and dirty lobby of a homeless shelter. He was stepping over every stereotype I had of homeless people. "A lot of bizarre things have happened since I decided to come to America. I just want to get my life together now. It will take time though," he said calmly. He stared at me with his large tired eyes. I could feel his eyes dragging around my mind like little spies, trying to decipher what I was thinking.

Solomon had applied for a job as a bank teller and as a substitute teacher. Nobody had called him for an interview yet. I saw a glimpse of frustration in his eyes as he talked about how he would like to work as a bank teller just for a little while. I thought it was strange that he insisted on two very hard-to-get positions. I asked if he had considered any other options for employment, but he did not even want to talk about it. A bank teller, a substitute teacher, or nothing. It sounded like he did not consider any other positions because he used to be a teacher and working in hard labor would be demeaning. He made a choice, but I have to admit that the choice seemed odd to me. My father, who had worked in an office all his life, is now working in maintenance, and as strange as it seems, he says that he is happy. He is happy because that job gave him stability, and therefore he doesn't see it as demeaning. In the light of those experiences, I learned that sometimes one has to choose a small compromise for a greater purpose. I assumed that Solomon had either chosen not to compromise, even if that meant staying in the shelter longer, or he had not yet come to terms with reality. And although I wanted Solomon to succeed, I doubted not his ability to do the job well but rather the ability of society to look past its stereotypes.

At one point he said he liked me. I did not know what to say. An uncomfortable "Thank you" came out of my mouth. Our conversation took a cold shower. "Thank you" was not what he was hoping to hear. I took the first chance I had to excuse myself and go help one of the staff members.

Upstairs in the dorms, I met Hope. She was a young, white 18-year-old girl. I first met her a week ago, during my first night of volunteering. It was her first night in the shelter, too. She was scared and devastated to hear that she couldn't have a night-light. She came from a shelter in another city that closed for the summer due to lack of funding and volunteer support. Hope had epilepsy. She told me she had to drop out of school because of her medical problems. She was on medication so she has not had any seizures in a while. Her doctor had told her that her brain was not fully developed at the time of birth and if she had another seizure she would die. Despite all of this, she was unusually talkative and happy. I wanted to find out how she ended up in a homeless shelter, since I remembered that when she came to the shelter, the first thing she tried to do was to call her mother. We sat down and talked.

She was sad because her best friend had left. She met him in the shelter. "I get along with all the guys. I get along better with guys than with girls. 'Cause guys don't steal your boyfriends or talk about you behind your back." I tutor high-school kids, and for a moment there she was just one of those kids. She was worried about her image and wished for colorful and glittery pens. I was not sure whether she even thought about the fact that she is living in a homeless shelter and that she cannot stay there forever. "My best friend was a guy. Of course. Everybody said I was a 'ho' because I only hang out with guys. But I would still be a virgin if I had not been raped." She told me how one time she had to beat a girl up because she was dating her boyfriend. The girl was pregnant and lost the baby. "I felt really bad. She didn't press charges or anything, 'cause I did not know. If I had known that she was pregnant, I wouldn't have fought her in the first place." She seemed to be too calm talking about all of this. I was more upset just listening to her talk. I couldn't understand how she could be so calm. I found out later that she also had impulse control disorder. This seemed to explain how she could beat up a girl so bad that she lost her baby. Still, she was very calm and relaxed, as if the girl had lost a shoe, not a baby. At that point I started to doubt that she fully understood the consequences of her actions. . . .

I was overwhelmed by Hope's story. My mind was burdened with one question: "How can all this happen to one innocent young human being?" Later, as our conversation continued, I started asking: "Is this really true?" Parts of her story didn't seem to make sense. She told me that her dad bought her a 2000 Eclipse, but she had told me her dad didn't even work and, since she has epilepsy, that she cannot have a driving license until she is 21. I realized that even if she lied about the car, it didn't change anything. She probably needed something to dream about, something to divert her attention from her situation, like the car and going off to college. "I will study journalism," she told me. And as crazy as it seemed to me, she talked about it as if it were nothing. There was not even a slightest doubt in her mind that she might not make it.

I realized early in my study that I came in contact with only a very small number of homeless. The people who were allowed to stay in this shelter had to be clean of alcohol as well as of drugs. Whoever smelled of alcohol or appeared to be high would be kicked out of the shelter. Therefore, I realized that I might have seen only the cream of the crop.

However, I learned that one cannot make generalizations about the homeless. Indeed, the majority of the people in the shelter did have a drug addiction problem and were trying to get rid of the bad habit as well as the bad company. Some of them were more successful than others. They wanted to change and stop the never-ending cycle, or so they said. There, in the shelter, they were offered counseling, support, and programs dealing with drug addiction, and the people who worked there did not judge their character or morality. That is probably why they came there. Some of them, unable or unwilling to escape the vicious circle of addiction, kept coming back. Here, being able to accept your mistakes and face your problems was considered to be a sign of a strong character. Some of the people in the shelter were mentally ill and couldn't help themselves; others were physically disabled, unable to work, living on disability checks or waiting for them to come through. However, all of them—Solomon, Alejandro, Hope, and the others I met—dreamed of and lived for a life outside and after the shelter. For some it will never happen; for some that time will come sooner than they expected. Sitting in the lobby and waiting for their time to come, what keeps them going? What helps them get up in the morning? For most it seemed to be the mere thought that tomorrow they might take their bag, start living, and go home. Maybe the fact that most of the people there appear to be strongly religious explains where this hope that they will make it comes from. Hope was the common thread that I found in this shelter.

As lights were about to go off and I was walking down the stairs, I met one of the older men. He was carrying two large African woven fans and some decorative frames. He was wearing a bright big smile on his face. "Where are you going?" I asked him. "I am moving. I got me a place through Community Village. I am going back into the world. I am going back to living," he said. "Good luck!" I said. "Thank you and good night." That night, in his eyes I saw the biggest flash of hope and happiness ever.

Conclusion

Shortly after the interview, Hope left the shelter. I heard from some of the women that her dad came and took her with him. Unfortunately, George told me that she was kicked out of the shelter. He did not know why, since he was not there that night. I hope that she found a way to live with her dad, mom, or sister. I felt she was too young to be there, anyway. Solomon is still waiting to hear something from the bank or public school system. His frustration seems to grow with every day that passes.

I tried to compare my own experiences to the experiences of the homeless. I shared similar experiences with some of them, and maybe that enabled me to sympathize with them. I learned that "homeless" describes a wide range of people, coming from different cultures, with a wide span of education and a wide variety of reasons for being in the shelter. Like me, most of the people in the shelter had a goal or a dream and hoped that they would succeed and get rid of the need to depend on somebody. I realized that their hope was often rooted in their belief in a higher power. I always believed in myself; however, they have to learn to believe in themselves. But until they do, they put their fate in the hands of their Lord, meanwhile struggling to make it back to the real world.

Reflection as Critique

Both Rick Zollo and Ivana Nikolic composed reflections on their fieldstudies. Rick's came from the notebook he kept throughout the research process, and Ivana composed hers after she'd completed her project. Reflection is a type of critique. Here is Ivana's reflection on studying the homeless shelter—what she learned about herself and her own writing and researching process:

Ivana's Reflection

It was interesting to witness how doing this project helped me form a clearer opinion of the homeless culture and to see how my opinions changed as my research progressed. I was even more surprised to see how much this project helped me look back and reevaluate my experiences as a refugee myself. As much as this research was about the homeless shelter, it was also about me. It helped me see my life in a new light and realize how much I have achieved despite the difficulties I have had. I admit that at times this was disturbing to me, but nonetheless I am grateful because had I not done this project, I may have never had these reflections about my life.

Although ethnographic writing, as with other forms of writing, includes certain kinds of information, it took me some time to realize that fieldwriting is a flexible and fluid form that allows the writer to experiment while trying to find information about the culture. I decided to make my interviews the basis of my project since they provided the best insights into the culture. I must also admit that doing the interviews was the most intimidating part of the whole research project. I was afraid I would ask the wrong questions or open an old wound. I was surprised to find how much people like to talk about themselves. People in a homeless shelter were glad to know that somebody is interested in what they have to say. However, instead of focusing on the interviews so much, I might have written more describing the site, a particular artifact, or something I located from my Web searches. In an ethnographic piece of writing, there is no right or wrong format. The difficult thing is finding the best form for the information. It was painfully difficult for me to come to this revelation, but when I did, it changed my ideas about what fieldwork is really all about — myself in relation to others.

As a writer reflects, she resees her experiences from the multiple perspectives she's gained. Reflection is key in ethnographic work and a good way to end a project because, in the end, every fieldstudy is also about the self.

THE RESEARCH PORTFOLIO:
Definitions and Purpose

Rick's research portfolio, which he kept during the course of his study, housed both the process and the product of his fieldwork. We recommend developing working files for tracking your learning and documenting your work throughout the research process, and we discuss further aspects of portfolio keeping in each of the subsequent chapters of this book.

As you assemble and revise your portfolio, you'll develop a behind-the-scenes account of the story of your research, which you'll want to share with others. Naturally, the research portfolio will include your final ethnographic essay, but your selections will also show artifacts from the thinking process that led to this project. You'll want to represent selections from the reading, writing, and materials you've relied on along the way: writing exercises, fieldnotes, interview questions, charts, methods of analysis, and whatever helped you think your way through the final written report.

To keep track of your project, you'll move back and forth among four key activities: collecting, selecting, reflecting, and projecting. Each time you work on the portfolio, and each time you share it with others, you'll be engaged in these processes.

Collecting   Your portfolio might include such artifacts as maps, sketches, photographs, newsletters, advertisements, brochures, and programs. At first, you might find it strange to *collect* wrinkled scraps of paper, lists on napkins, or snippets of conversation you've overheard, but by gathering them in your portfolio, you'll see how they might fit into your larger project. In fact, the portfolio may look more like a scrapbook to you at first. But over time, you will see that it is a focused, not random, collection of artifacts and writing that lends shape to your fieldwork.

Selecting   Another advantage of a research portfolio is that you can *select* from parts of it for your final ethnographic writing. While your initial fieldnotes may capture something different from the final report, you'll always be able to use some parts of your fieldnotes. If you've studied firefighters, for example, you may have collected pages and pages of fieldnotes describing the fire station even when your final project focuses on the firefighters' language. In your final project, you'll still need to describe the firehouse before describing the words used there because your reader will need to understand the whole context of your fieldsite before looking at specific parts of the culture. The skills of collecting and selecting, as you move between them, are important to your research portfolio.

Reflecting and Projecting   At critical points during the fieldwork process, you will need to take time to *reflect* on the data in your portfolio—to look at your fieldnotes and informant interviews and begin to analyze and synthesize the data that are most important to your work. Every item that you include in the portfolio will require reflective writing on your part, from short fieldnote entries to longer memos to yourself. When you review your data alongside your thinking, you'll find options for further focus and analysis. Reflection is a kind of critique; it helps you analyze as you proceed. When you look over what you've read, thought, said, written, and collected, you will begin to find meanings and patterns across your data that may surprise you and instruct you about where your work is headed. This reflective critique will enable you to *project*—to see your progress and form your goals: where you've been, where you are, and where you'll want to head next.

Keeping a research portfolio makes little sense if it's relegated to the status of end-of-course activity. The major evaluation or assessment ought to be your own. We suggest that you choose a portfolio partner or a small group at the outset of your research and set aside regular times to meet and share your portfolios. At these meetings, you may ask your partner(s) to respond to your descriptions, offer ways of filling gaps in your data, suggest further resources for your research, point out themes or patterns in your data, or help verify your hunches. The process of talking about your data, your hunches, and your research plans and hearing those of others as you look through their portfolios in progress will generate new ideas and strategies for your own fieldwork.

Select a Fieldsite

To prepare for using these concepts as you step into another subculture, try the following activity, which asks you to do some speculating. It's always good to think about your assumptions before you decide on a project. All you need is some time and a piece of paper (or a file on your computer).

FIRST   Make a list of communities, either local or international, that you might study from a fieldworking perspective. While the possibilities might seem endless, the real options are probably close at hand. Bring to mind people, places, events, or subcultures that catch your attention or that you've always been interested in. When something intrigues you, it is probably worth investigating. If you're going to another country, consider whether you are interested in a group of people, a particular location, or an activity practiced there; Matt's interest in mountain climbing led him to study the sherpa guides of Mt. Everest.

SECOND   Pick three or four of these cultures or subcultures to think more about. Where would you like to step in to learn more about a culture's rituals, rules, behaviors, and language? Where might you step out to gain a more distanced perspective on that group's ways of being and operating? Circle your choices, and note how you would step in and step out.

THIRD   Write more about the ethical concerns you might have about such studies. If you wanted, for instance, to study your church's congregation or a Boy Scout troop, what might be the drawbacks? What objections would you face from insiders? If you wanted to investigate street peddlers in Mexico, veiled women in the Middle East, or transnational migrant workers, what problems might you encounter?

FOURTH   As you write, explore the issues that will most likely affect your study. Be specific: What's your place in this culture? Who's in charge? What groups take responsibility for what other groups? Consider, too, what you may be able to give back to a community: Ivana, for example, served as a volunteer to help the homeless people at Ramsey House. What might you actively contribute to your fieldsite?

Early exploratory writing helps you work through your initial assumptions: your feelings, reservations, and passions for researching particular communities. It can also help you identify which features of the fieldsite are alive with cultural detail and worth studying in depth.

2

Writing Self, Writing Cultures: Understanding FieldWriting

Your perspective is important in conducting fieldwork. In this chapter you will:

- explore writing techniques: freewriting, mapping, listing, keeping a notebook
- understand point of view
- develop a rhetorical approach to your fieldwork
- record details from close observation
- learn to take double-entry notes
- organize, interpret, and analyze your fieldnotes

This book is about conducting fieldwork, but it's also very much about field-writing. The writing process of a fieldworker, as anthropologist Margaret Mead describes in the quotation at right, is somewhat like that of a novelist. The fieldworker must "choose, shape, prune, discard...and collect" data, trans-forming words and images into text. Mead reminds us that fieldworkers invent neither informants nor descriptions of their cultural spaces. Rather, as she wrote in 1977, field-workers are "helplessly dependent" on what actually takes place in the field—as we see it and as our informants see it. Yet repre-senting or writing about reality depends on how fieldworkers use language—their own and that of their informants—to describe "what's going on." Today, perhaps more than ever before, fieldworkers pay close atten-tion to how language interactions shape and influence their work.

The fieldworker must choose, shape, prune, discard this and collect finer detail on that, much as a novelist works who finds some minor character is threatening to swallow the major theme, or that the hero is fast talking himself out of his depth. But unlike the novelist . . . the fieldworker is wholly and helplessly dependent on what happens. . . . One must be continually prepared for anything, everything—and perhaps most devastating—for nothing.

—MARGARET MEAD

The Importance of Writing

As in any negotiation, the ability to understand and interpret the point of view and situation of an "other" depends on both participants. It depends on how deeply our informants allow us to enter their worldviews and on how well we participate and listen. The special ethics of writing about fieldwork demand that we respect and represent our informants' voices. At the same time, we must respect and represent ourselves as narrators. Your fieldwork ultimately involves *what* you write as well as *how* you write it.

At the outset of your fieldwork, you may question the importance of writing. Why not just hang out, observe, and listen to others? Why take notes at all? The difference between doing fieldwork and just "hanging out" is the writing. Without writing, the sharp, incisive details about people, places, and cultures are lost to us. The overheard conversation, the aftereffect of an image, or the undertone of an encounter with an informant dissipates unless it is written down. Fieldworkers turn hanging out into a scholarly art form. They begin by choosing from a variety of exploratory writing strategies and developing a dependable system for taking **fieldnotes**.

Constructing Field Experience

Since the days when Margaret Mead did her fieldwork, researchers' thinking has shifted about the writing of fieldnotes. No longer are fieldnotes considered a mirror, or direct reflection, of the research experience; rather, a researcher's fieldnotes are recognized as a **construction** of that field experience. The fieldnotes you gather and record will not be like anyone else's. They will represent your perspective—gathered, recorded, mapped, and written according to your own conscious and unconscious choices about what you see and hear at your fieldsite.

In this chapter, we discuss how writing about the self links with writing about the culture you are investigating. It's critical to understand your personal curiosity or fascination with the subculture you plan to study. To help you start gathering data and taking fieldnotes, we offer you some exploratory writing techniques as well as some examples from both students and professional writers who have used these techniques to write themselves into their topics about subcultures. We hope that by reviewing these you'll find a way into your fieldwork topic as you begin to craft your initial fieldnotes.

Choosing a Subject

Choosing a subculture, an event, or a site you want to learn more about is critical to the success of your project, although we also believe that almost any event, subculture, or site can be fascinating and instructive as long as you keep an open mind. Throughout this book, we will caution you not to choose places or events that are particularly sensational. The culture of a children's playground can be as complex and engaging to write about as the subculture of witch covens or gang warfare.

In the first chapter, we saw how Rick Zollo's fieldnotes helped him construct his stance for looking at the culture of the truck stop. His study shows his fascination with and investment in the subculture of truckers—and from studies our other students have done, we understand this investment. The following is a partial listing of the many interesting studies we have read, and we hope it will help you think about what you might want to study for your own project:

Subcultures

- *People*   martial artists, beekeepers, meatpackers, cloggers, female impersonators, ballroom dancers, blues players, online poker players, gamers, weekend mystery participants, bloggers, shopaholics, protest organizers, soccer parents, street hockey players, ultimate Frisbee teams, and Special Olympics volunteers. Also: a group of quilters who have met once a week for fifty years, and university students who meet weekly in a sports bar to watch *The Simpsons*.

- *Events*   harvest festival, homecoming parade, celebrity's visit to a small town, Weight Watchers meeting, cat lover's book club, ethnic exhibitions, military reenactments, and Renaissance festivals. Also conventions such as: Nancy Drew novel readers, paper makers, and gun collectors. Or events such as: organizing for a cross-country bike trip, and the design, rehearsal, and performance of a ballet.

- *Places*   telemarketing company, law office, sheriff's rounds, tailor shop, barber shop, fish bait shop, farmers' market, old family hotel, fast-food kitchen, animal shelter, high school classroom, alternative high school housed in a trailer, kitchen of a woman with Parkinson's disease, adult book and video store, day-care center, mega-church, traveling circus, movie or music recording studio, flea market, city cemetery, dog kennel, art studio, social network interest groups, specialized discussion groups, popular blogs, fan sites, and dating sites.

The following strategies for exploratory writing—sometimes called prewriting techniques—are good ways to brainstorm ideas for fieldwork projects.

Exploratory Writing

Freewriting

Freewriting belongs to a category of informal writing designed to release your mind from worrying about an audience of readers. A kind of uninhibited doodling with words, freewriting is helpful when you have trouble getting started. Peter Elbow, a scholar of composition, writes extensively about the potential of freewriting as a way of "priming the pump." In his book *Writing without Teachers*, he opens with a chapter about freewriting, excerpts of which we include here.

Freewriting

Peter Elbow

Freewriting is the easiest way to get words on paper and the best all-around practice in writing that I know. To do a freewriting exercise, simply force yourself to write without stopping for ten minutes. Sometimes you will produce good writing, but that's not the goal. Sometimes you will produce garbage, but that's not the goal either. You may stay on one topic, you may flip repeatedly from one to another: it doesn't matter. Sometimes you will produce a good record of your stream of consciousness, but often you can't keep up. Speed is not the goal, though sometimes the process revs you up. If you can't think of anything to write, write about how that feels or repeat over and over "I have nothing to write" or "Nonsense" or "No." If you get stuck in the middle of a sentence or thought, just repeat the last word or phrase till something comes along. The only point is to keep writing.

Or rather, that's the first point. For there are lots of goals of freewriting, but they are best served if, while you are doing it, you accept this single, simple, mechanical goal of simply not stopping. When you produce an exciting piece of writing, it doesn't mean you did it better than the time before when you wrote one sentence over and over for ten minutes. Both times you freewrote perfectly. The goal of freewriting is in the process, not the product....

The Benefits of Freewriting

Freewriting makes writing easier by helping you with the root psychological or existential difficulty in writing: finding words in your head and putting them down on a blank piece of paper. So much writing time and energy is [sic] spent *not* writing: wondering, worrying, crossing out, having second, third, and fourth thoughts. And it's easy to get stopped even in the middle of a piece. (This is why Hemingway made a rule for himself never to end one sheet and start a new one except in the middle of a sentence.) Frequent freewriting exercises help you learn simply to *get on with it* and not be held back by worries about whether these words are good words or the right words.

Thus, freewriting is the best way to learn—in practice, not just in theory—to separate the producing process from the revising process. Freewriting exercises are push-ups in withholding judgment as you produce so that afterwards you can judge better.

Freewriting for ten minutes is a good way to warm up when you sit down to write something. You won't waste so much time getting started when you turn to your real writing task and you won't have to struggle so hard to find words. Writing almost always goes better when you are already started: now you'll be able to start off already started.

Freewriting helps you learn to write when you don't feel like writing. It is practice in setting deadlines for yourself, taking charge of yourself, and learning gradually how to get that special energy that sometimes comes when you work fast under pressure.

Freewriting teaches you to write without thinking about writing. We can usually speak without thinking about speech—without thinking about how to form words in the mouth and pronounce them and the rules of syntax we uncon-sciously obey—and as a result we can give undivided attention to what we say. Not so writing. Or at least most people are considerably distracted from their meaning by considerations of spelling, grammar, rules, errors. Most people experience an awkward and sometimes paralyzing *translating* process in writing: "Let's see, how shall I say this." Freewriting helps you learn to *just say* it. Regular freewriting helps make the writing process *transparent*.

Freewriting is a useful outlet. We have lots in our heads that makes it hard to think straight and write clearly: we are mad at someone, sad about something, depressed about everything. Perhaps even inconveniently happy. "How can I think about this report when I'm so in love?" Freewriting is a quick outlet for these feelings so they don't get so much in your way when you are trying to write about something else. Sometimes your mind is marvelously clear after ten minutes of telling someone on paper everything you need to tell him. (In fact, if your feelings often keep you from functioning well in other areas of your life frequent freewriting can help: not only by providing a good arena for those feelings, but also by helping you understand them better and see them in perspective by seeing them on paper.)

Freewriting helps you to think of topics to write about. Just keep writing, fol-low threads where they lead and you will get to ideas, experiences, feelings, or people that are just asking to be written about.

Finally, and perhaps most important, freewriting improves your writing. It doesn't always produce powerful writing itself, but it leads to powerful writing. The process by which it does so is a mysterious underground one. When people talk about the Zen of this or that I think they are referring to the peculiar increase in power and insight that comes from focusing your energy while at the same time putting aside your conscious controlling self. Freewriting gives practice in this special mode of focusing-but-not-trying; it helps you stand out of the way and let words be chosen by the sequence of the words themselves or the thought, not by the conscious self. In this way freewriting gradually puts a deeper resonance or voice into your writing....

Freewriting can be useful at any stage of the fieldwork process, but it is par-ticularly helpful at the beginning of a research project when you are trying out ideas and thinking about yourself in different research sites and subcultures. One of our students, Aidan Vollmer, did some freewriting when he was consider-ing a study of graffiti artists. Here are three excerpts from his in-class freewrites, written at different times, in which he explores his history with graffiti, antici-pates ethical problems he might have studying this subculture, and expresses his continuing fascination with graffiti:

Freewrite 1.   Graffiti has always fascinated me. I can remember when I was a very young person, perhaps 6 years old, my older cousin (my mother's sister's son), Brian, who I absolutely idolized, telling me he was "learning to tag." I had no clue what it meant to "tag," but I knew I wanted to do it. Through a little more inquiry, I found out that it had to do with graffiti and the beginning of a lifelong interest, bordering on a lifelong obsession, was born. From there I returned home and hit the Internet. I searched and searched, but could find very little on how to tag and how to do graffiti. School came and I became embroiled in everything that was elementary school. . . .

Freewrite 2.   Vandalism or art? Beautification or destruction? What can be classified as graffiti? Does just any scribbling or paint on a wall count as graffiti? Or is there a possible difference between vandalism and graffiti (get definiton of *vandalism/vandal*). Might be interesting to talk about Vandals, the ancient Greek/Roman tribe? When did it start?

Freewrite 3.   (3/27) . . . Another section of graffiti has been painted over. Nothing too impressive; just a few quickly thrown up tags on the cement supports of the train bridge. One of Mario's, and another who writes like him. Mario's piece had already been crossed out and replaced by small indecipherable scribbles. But now the slate is clean again. . . . Strangely, those responsible for the graffiti removal opted to leave the tags on the north and south sides of the bridge side supports.

   (5/28) Update!! . . . Everything has been painted over. The paint crew must have returned during the night to finish the last of the graffiti removal. Found out today that the paint crew was hired or already employed by the railroad company. The owner of the structure that was vandalized is responsible for the removal of the graffiti.

Aidan's freewriting enabled him to brainstorm possible ideas about a fieldproject on the graffiti subculture: his insider-outsider position, the history of graffiti, whom he might interview, and places he might observe. He recalled memories and feelings about graffiti from his childhood. While he might not use all of this writing in his final project, freewriting energized his thinking and released many ways for him to consider graffiti as a subculture.

Mapping

Aidan also used another strategy for unlocking his memories and organizing his ideas. Like many students, he benefited from "mapping," a visual way of inventorying what you know and making plans for a project (see Figure 2-1). To begin mapping, place a keyword in the center of the page, and draw a circle around it. Use the word to free-associate. Words call up words; place these related items in circles around the key phrase. Mapping can be as extensive and complex as you want. Some word-processing programs accommodate this type of visual planning, so you might want to try mapping with your computer.

Figure 2-1 Aidan's mapping

BOX**4**

Exploratory Writing

PURPOSE

Exploratory writing—such as freewriting, brainstorming, list making, mapping, clustering, and outlining—helps you turn off your internal censor, and free your mind. These strategies help you hold conversations with yourself on paper about your interests, your memories, and your curiosities as you consider the pros and cons of possible subcultures or fieldsites to study.

BOX**4** continued

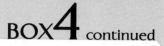

ACTION

Choose one exploratory writing strategy to think about a site or subculture you may want to investigate, and consider some of these questions:

1. What do you already know about this subculture? What insiders do you know?

2. What kinds of connections do you have with the site or subculture now?

3. How easy or difficult would it be to enter this subculture as either an insider or an outsider?

4. In what ways are you either an insider or an outsider already?

5. What do you hope to find out?

RESPONSE

When Terra Savage was considering a study of a tattoo parlor, she freewrote to discover her background knowledge and feeling about tattoos:

> Grunge. Class. No Stress. Responsibility. Lacking education. Overachiever. Artistic. Artistic? Family. Tattoo artisan. Me. At first glance, there seems to be no relationship between my life and this tattoo parlor. But take another look; the more I stare I am not so different.
>
> Men with tattoos ride Harley Davidsons and are running from middle age. Putter putter rev rev. When my stepdad turned fifty, he wanted a Harley I guess to feel masculine and in control; all I could envision was him getting a tattoo. One with "I ♥ MY MAMA" written across his chest. Have you seen it before? Tattoos on teenage kids are a way for them to rebel. My mom would threaten me with my life....
>
> My sister wanted her nose pierced; she chose Harry's Tattoo in order to get the job done. She had to have all the correct documents to prove she was my mom's daughter, an infinite amount of paperwork. Employees must be meticulous with their work....
>
> A girl I graduated high school with worked nights @ the gas station so she could have enough $$$ saved up to apprentice a tattoo artist. She was a good girl who made decent grades in high school. I tend to be very narrowminded when it comes to a traditional education (a typical thought for me, the only reason they're working in the tattoo business, is b/c they can't do anything else)....However, all that aside, as I have matured, I realize that a person who would like to work in a tattoo parlor is just as valid as someone who has 2 bachelors degrees, 3 masters degrees and a Ph.D.
>
> A tattoo artist has a special talent for drawing, but instead of using an easel and paper they choose to use skin. The flesh. Maybe this is one of the most organic forms of art work. I have touched a weak spot—Art. At one time I considered myself an artist, a dancer and choreographer, to be more precise. Have I stumbled on common ground by sheer coincidence? I understand the need to be around your field; I understand the need to be enthused.

FieldWriting: Point of View and Rhetoric

Point of View

You may have encountered the term *point of view* in a literature course in which discussions focus on the angle of vision from which a story is told. Telling a story from inside a character's head, as you know, is significantly different from telling a story through an omniscient third-person narrator. As our colleague Jim Marshall says, "Where you stand is what you see." But as a fieldworker, your job is to stand in several places and see through multiple sets of eyes. We call this an ethnographic perspective.

Ethnographic writing needs to include many different points of view, and that means you'll need to find ways to signal to your reader when you're shifting from one to another. You need to include your own first-person point of view. You also need to include the points of view of your informants as you've gathered them through interviews, as well as a third-person outsider point of view to report on background information and to present events as readers might see them.

It's useful from the outset to take some of your exploratory writing or initial fieldnotes, turn them into short descriptions of people or places, and experiment—for example, try shifting points of view from first-person insider to third-person outsider. Changing point of view can help you locate missing or underdeveloped information about your fieldsite and the informants and, in turn, suggest another round of research you'd want to do.

Here is how Terra Savage moved from the exploratory writing she did about her conflicting feelings as she entered the tattoo parlor (Box 4) to more of a description of the tattoo parlor subculture as she listens to Chance, the tattooist, talk about the artistry of his work. We'll include a few key phrases from her first freewrite:

> Grunge. Class. No Stress. Responsibility. Lacking education. Overachiever. Artistic. Artistic? Family. Tattoo artisan. Me. At first glance, there seems to be no relationship between my life and this tattoo parlor. But take another look; the more I stare I am not so different.
>
> Men with tattoos ride Harley Davidsons and are running from middle age.... Tattoos on teenage kids are a way for them to rebel. My mom would threaten me with my life.

Over several drafts, Terra moves from her early exploratory first-person freewriting to this point of view in her final field study in which she describes Chance and quotes from what he has to say. She is doing the delicate job of giving us both her perspective and Chance's, by using a third-person narrative point of view:

Chance is a tattoo artist at Infinite Arts Tattoo who enjoys what he does. He has a medium build and black hair that he wears in a ponytail. He has quite a few tattoos. The one big one that was visible on his arm is of a dragon. Chance explains, "Getting started in the tattoo business"—he seems to drift back to what may have been a lifetime ago—"spent a long time in kitchens and doing construction work, also doing a lot of drawing, trying to get my name out there. Going to lots of tattoo shops. Pretty much working for minimum wage and trying to find someone to teach me how to tattoo."

Chance gives a picture of a poor starving artisan trying to make his way. Chance goes on, "You can't go to the university and say here's five thousand dollars, give me a trade. You have to find someone who is willing to teach you."

Chance describes how he takes on the role of the customer. He says, "By me being an artist, I still try to let the others have enough artistic freedom without my interfering. There becomes a thin line between a piece of painting that you hang on the wall and a piece of painting that you put on your skin."

Gradually Terra comes back to herself in this fieldstudy, including some of the earlier feelings she wrote about in her exploratory writing:

Can a connoisseur of tattoos tell the difference between one artist and the next by examining your skin? As I began thinking more through the eyes of the tattoo artist, I realized that there were similarities between me and them. I saw them as artists and understood.

Try taking some of your exploratory writing about the subculture you are studying and some of your early fieldnotes to play with point of view. Ask yourself where you can best include your own perspective and where you need to change your angle of vision and include third-person description as well as the actual words of your informants. In ethnographic writing, the more perspectives you include within a study and the more detailed your data, the stronger and more convincing your final essay becomes.

Rhetoric

All writing is rhetorical. You may have heard someone respond to a politician or a magazine advertisement by saying, "Oh, that's just rhetoric." **Rhetoric** is commonly defined as the art of persuasion, but it involves far more than the verbal devices that are often connected with propaganda. It is the shaping of discourses (or simply the uses of language) for different purposes and audiences.

The Greek philosopher Aristotle described the rhetorical event, which can be either oral or written, as having three important elements: ethos (the self), logos (the information), and pathos (sensitivity to an audience). (See Figure 2-2.)

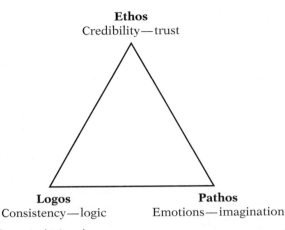

Ethos
Credibility—trust

Logos
Consistency—logic

Pathos
Emotions—imagination

Figure 2-2 The rhetorical triangle

This triadic idea crosses historical periods and academic disciplines. You may have learned, for example, in computer or basic communications courses that the paradigm of sender, message, and receiver describes how people convey ideas to one another. Folklorists and anthropologists see a similar pattern when they study verbal art (like joking, rapping, and story-telling): a three-way interaction among a performer, a performance, and an audience. In contemporary composition, we refer to these three elements as voice, purpose, and audience. As you conduct your fieldwork and then share it with others, you become a rhetorician, making decisions about how to use your own voice (ethos), as well as the voices of your informants and the information from your fieldnotes (logos), and, too, a sense of your audience (pathos).

Writing for an audience can be scary, especially when you're in the initial stages of a project. In Box 4, freewriting is excerpted from Terra Savage's field-working project titled "Much Ta-Too about Nothing." Terra's exploratory free-writing helped her discover what she knew when she wasn't yet ready to think about an audience of readers. In fact, she hadn't yet done field research. We could say that Terra's freewriting helped her develop her voice, which many of these exploratory writing strategies are designed to do. As she gathered more data from more sources, reflected on her ideas, and decided what to use in her drafts, Terra became more confident about all her material. Most important, she began to think about ways to shape her writing away from her writer "self" and toward a reader, an audience of an "other."

Of course, the main audience in a freewrite—exploratory writing—is your-self. But as you write, you begin to envision a potential reader, or what rhetori-cians call your "audience." Exploratory writing helps you understand yourself and your topic, but the more strategies you try out, the more aware you become of potential audiences.

Keeping a Notebook

Many writers find that a personal daybook, journal, or log is useful as a seedbed for ideas. Keeping a notebook, systematically or even sporadically, allows writers to capture observations and emotions that otherwise might dissipate.

Scholars study writers' notebooks because they often reveal the personal source of a writer's ideas. When we return to our recorded notebook scratchings, we also return to those unrecorded circumstances that surrounded the written notes. Like a snapshot or a home video, our jottings trigger a flood of information and remembrance about people and places. Writer Joan Didion reminds us that any types of personal notes will always be unique to the keeper. "Your notebook will never help me, nor mine you." In Didion's famous essay, "On Keeping a Notebook," she meditates on the value of her own personal notebook. It is a way, she writes, of "keeping in touch" with the self.

As you read the following essay, notice how Didion talks about collecting details: cracked crab, a woman in a dirty crepe-de-Chine wrapper, a New York blizzard. When Didion returns to these bits in her notebook, her memory will pull up a version of her original experience.

....

On Keeping a Notebook

Joan Didion

"'That woman Estelle,'" the note reads, "'is partly the reason why George Sharp and I are separated today.' *Dirty crepe-de-Chine wrapper, hotel bar, Wilmington RR, 9:45 a.m. August Monday morning.*"

Since the note is in my notebook, it presumably has some meaning to me. I study it for a long while. At first I have only the most general notion of what I was doing on an August Monday morning in the bar of the hotel across from the Pennsylvania Railroad station in Wilmington, Delaware (waiting for a train? missing one? 1960? 1961? and Wilmington?), but I do remember being there. The woman in the dirty crepe-de-Chine wrapper had come down from her room for a beer, and the bartender had heard before the reason why George Sharp and she were separated today. "Sure," he said, and went on mopping the floor. "You told me." At the other end of the bar is a girl. She is talking, pointedly, not to the man beside her but to a cat lying in the triangle of sunlight cast through the open door. She is wearing a plaid silk dress from Peck & Peck, and the hem is coming down.

Here is what it is: the girl has been on the Eastern Shore, and now she is going back to the city, leaving the man beside her, and all she can see ahead are the viscous summer sidewalks and the 3 a.m. long-distance calls that will make her lie awake and then sleep drugged through all the steaming mornings left in August (1960? 1961?). Because she must go directly from the train to lunch in New York, she wishes that she had a safety pin for the hem of the plaid silk dress, and she also wishes that she could forget about the hem and the lunch and stay in the cool bar that smells of disinfectant and malt and make friends with the woman in the crepe-de-Chine wrapper. She is afflicted by a little self-pity, and she wants to compare Estelles. That is what that was all about.

Why did I write it down? In order to remember, of course, but exactly what was it I wanted to remember? How much of it actually happened? Did any of it? Why do I keep a notebook at all? It is easy to deceive oneself on all those scores. The impulse to write things down is a peculiarly compulsive one, inexplicable to those who do not share it, useful only accidentally, only secondarily, in the way that any compulsion tries to justify itself. I suppose that it begins or does not begin in the cradle. Although I have felt compelled to write things down since I was five years old, I doubt that my daughter ever will, for she is a singularly blessed and accepting child, delighted with life exactly as life presents itself to her, unafraid to go to sleep and unafraid to wake up. Keepers of private notebooks are a different breed altogether, lonely and resistant rearrangers of things, anxious malcontents, children afflicted apparently at birth with some presentiment of loss.

My first notebook was a Big Five tablet, given to me by my mother with the sensible suggestion that I stop whining and learn to amuse myself by writing down my thoughts. She returned the tablet to me a few years ago; the first entry is an account of a woman who believed herself to be freezing to death in the Arctic night, only to find, when day broke, that she had stumbled onto the Sahara Desert, where she would die of the heat before lunch. I have no idea what turn of a five-year-old's mind could have prompted so insistently "ironic" and exotic a story, but it does reveal a certain predilection for the extreme which has dogged me into adult life; perhaps if I were analytically inclined I would find it a truer story than any I might have told about Donald Johnson's birthday party or the day my cousin Brenda put Kitty Litter in the aquarium.

So the point of my keeping a notebook has never been, nor is it now, to have an accurate factual record of what I have been doing or thinking. That would be a different impulse entirely, an instinct for reality which I sometimes envy but do not possess. At no point have I ever been able successfully to keep a diary; my approach to daily life ranges from the grossly negligent to the merely absent, and on those few occasions when I have tried dutifully to record a day's events, boredom has so overcome me that the results are mysterious at best. What is this business about "shopping, typing piece, dinner with E, depressed"? Shopping for what? Typing what piece? Who is E? Was this "E" depressed, or was I depressed? Who cares?

In fact I have abandoned altogether that kind of pointless entry; instead I tell what some would call lies. "That's simply not true," the members of my family frequently tell me when they come up against my memory of a shared event. "The party was *not* for you, the spider was *not* a black widow, *it wasn't that way at all*." Very likely they are right, for not only have I always had trouble distinguishing between what happened and what merely might have happened, but I remain unconvinced that the distinction, for my purposes, matters. The cracked crab that

I recall having for lunch the day my father came home from Detroit in 1945 must certainly be embroidery; worked into the day's pattern to lend verisimilitude; I was ten years old and would not now remember the cracked crab. The day's events did not turn on cracked crab. And yet it is precisely that fictitious crab that makes me see the afternoon all over again, a home movie run all too often, the father bearing gifts, the child weeping, an exercise in family love and guilt. Or that is what it was to me. Similarly, perhaps it never did snow that August in Vermont; perhaps there never were flurries in the night wind, and maybe no one else felt the ground hardening and summer already dead even as we pretended to bask in it, but that was how it felt to me, and it might as well have snowed, could have snowed, did snow.

How it felt to me: that is getting closer to the truth about a notebook. I sometimes delude myself about why I keep a notebook, imagine that some thrifty virtue derives from preserving everything observed. See enough and write it down, I tell myself, and then some morning when the world seems drained of wonder, some day when I am only going through the motions of doing what I am supposed to do, which is write—on that bankrupt morning I will simply open my notebook and there it will all be, a forgotten account with accumulated interest, paid passage back to the world out there: dialogue overheard in hotels and elevators and at the hat-check counter in Pavillon (one middle-aged man shows his hat check to another and says, "That's my old football number"); impressions of Bettina Aptheker and Benjamin Sonnenberg and Teddy ("Mr. Acapulco") Stauffer; careful *aperçus* about tennis bums and failed fashion models and Greek shipping heiresses, one of whom taught me a significant lesson (a lesson I could have learned from F. Scott Fitzgerald, but perhaps we all must meet the very rich for ourselves) by asking, when I arrived to interview her in her orchid-filled sitting room on the second day of a paralyzing New York blizzard, whether it was snowing outside.

I imagine, in other words, that the notebook is about other people. But of course it is not. I have no real business with what one stranger said to another at the hat-check counter in Pavillon; in fact I suspect that the line "That's my old football number" touched not my own imagination at all, but merely some memory of something once read, probably "The Eighty-Yard Run." Nor is my concern with a woman in a dirty crepe-de-Chine wrapper in a Wilmington bar. My stake is always, of course, in the unmentioned girl in the plaid silk dress. *Remember what it was to be me*: that is always the point.

It is a difficult point to admit. We are brought up in the ethic that others, any others, all others, are by definition more interesting than ourselves; taught to be diffident, just this side of self-effacing. ("You're the least important person in the room and don't forget it," Jessica Mitford's governess would hiss in her ear on the advent of any social occasion; I copied that into my notebook because it is only recently that I have been able to enter a room without hearing some such phrase in my inner ear.) Only the very young and the very old may recount their dreams at breakfast, dwell upon self, interrupt with memories of beach picnics and favorite Liberty lawn dresses and the rainbow trout in a creek near Colorado Springs. The rest of us are expected, rightly, to affect absorption in other people's favorite dresses, other people's trout.

And so we do. But our notebooks give us away, for however dutifully we record what we see around us, the common denominator of all we see is always, transparently, shamelessly, the implacable "I." We are not talking here about the kind of notebook that is patently for public consumption, a structural conceit for binding together a series of graceful *pensées*; we are talking about something private, about bits of the mind's string too short to use, an indiscriminate and erratic assemblage with meaning only for its maker.

And sometimes even the maker has difficulty with the meaning. There does not seem to be, for example, any point in my knowing for the rest of my life that, during 1964, 720 tons of soot fell on every square mile of New York City, yet there it is in my notebook, labeled "FACT." Nor do I really need to remember that Ambrose Bierce liked to spell Leland Stanford's name "£eland $tanford" or that "smart women almost always wear black in Cuba," a fashion hint without much potential for practical application. And does not the relevance of these notes seem marginal at best?:

In the basement museum of the Inyo County Courthouse in Independence, California, sign pinned to a mandarin coat: "This MANDARIN COAT was often worn by Mrs. Minnie S. Brooks when giving lectures on her TEAPOT COLLECTION."

Redhead getting out of car in front of Beverly Wilshire Hotel, chinchilla stole, Vuitton bags with tags reading:

MRS LOU FOX
HOTEL SAHARA
VEGAS

Well, perhaps not entirely marginal. As a matter of fact, Mrs. Minnie S. Brooks and her MANDARIN COAT pull me back into my own childhood, for although I never knew Mrs. Brooks and did not visit Inyo County until I was thirty, I grew up in just such a world, in houses cluttered with Indian relics and bits of gold ore and ambergris and the souvenirs my Aunt Mercy Farnsworth brought back from the Orient. It is a long way from that world to Mrs. Lou Fox's world, where we all live now, and is it not just as well to remember that? Might not Mrs. Minnie S. Brooks help me to remember what I am? Might not Mrs. Lou Fox help me to remember what I am not?

· ·

Didion's is a writer's notebook. As a novelist and essayist, she uses the notebook as a playground to toy with ideas she'll later draft into more formal writing. At the beginning of her essay, Didion offers us a few short clips about a hotel bar across from a railroad station in Wilmington, Delaware, during an unspecific year in the early 1960s. For her, these notes signal an imagined scenario that she creates for us in this essay. She might have used the same notes to write a piece of fiction.

On the other hand, a fieldworker researching out of those notes would need to talk to the woman in the crepe-de-Chine wrapper, the bartender, and the woman in the plaid silk dress at the other end of the bar to confirm what they said about what was going on there. A fieldworker's notebook probably won't become an essay or a novel, but it will draw on the same writerly skills of close observation and description. Since fieldnotes eventually shape a research study, a fieldworker has a responsibility to inventory not only what's in the mind but also what's actually at the fieldsite and what informants say.

For writer or fieldworker, keeping a notebook can serve two purposes: it documents a moment and contemplates that moment as well. This double process of recording and being conscious of oneself recording allows for many levels of awareness. As experienced anthropologists and journal writers Barbara Myerhoff and Deena Metzger have noted, this journaling process is "a means for acquiring, not merely recording, knowledge." We think that all exploratory writing, whether it's in a notebook from a fieldsite or a five-minute freewrite in a quiet classroom, carries the potential to generate further writing and more informed thinking.

Aidan's Notebook

Aidan Vollmer kept a notebook while he was researching the world of graffiti artists, which became his study titled "The Need to Spray." Although it was a traditional spiral-bound notebook, his own doodles, drawings, reminders to himself, and other marginalia made it his own, reflecting his interest in outsider art and typography. Following are some excerpts from his notebook.

Aidan writes about himself here:

> Why do I feel the need to spray? Is it the internal drive to express myself outwardly through art coming through? Or is it more related to the physical act of applying paint to a wall? Could I be searching for a rush that comes from an illegal activity, or an act that is generally considered to be socially unacceptable? Whatever mixture of motivations combine to fuel my need to spray, from the first time my finger depressed the cap on a can of red spray paint and I watched it smoothly coat the surface of an already paint-covered wall, I was hooked. That summer when I first discovered the utter joy of taking an afternoon to traverse the rocky path down to the train bridge changed my life. Day after day, I would make that trek, iPod, spray paint, and a blue bandanna (for a makeshift gas mask) all ready with the intent to create. And day after day, I would trudge back home, backpack considerably less full of spray cans and groggy from breathing aerosol fumes, completely content. By the end of the summer, I had claimed every surface with numbed, paint-covered fingertips. I was the king of the bridge.

In this excerpt, he observes details and has one of his first interviews with a graffiti artist:

> I ran into Mario this morning outside the old art building. I asked him about his art and a specific piece of graffiti on a train bridge that runs parallel to the walking bridge. It is a simple piece in only one color that says "Cold." It is in large block letters, each one occupying its own section of the metal bridge, in what looks to be something like "sun yellow" (which is an actual spray paint color). The piece is on the northward-facing side of the bridge, nearly in the middle, out over the river. The reason its location is so important is that it is very nearly impossible to access, especially without being noticed and thus apprehended. In addition, the piece must be created with care, not to lose its artistic credibility while perched in this very risky position. Mario described the very delicate process of perching on a cement support and gripping the bridge with one hand while hanging out over the river and painting the bridge with the other hand.

On the margins of his notebook, Aidan jots down reminders to himself:

> "Make journal writings before and after going to a fieldsite to help see what preconceptions and assumptions I take with me."
>
> "Find the movie and TV series called *Style Wars*, a study of American graffiti, and *Exit through the Gift Shop* about Banksy and street art."
>
> "Maybe make a point to make the reader feel like a graffiti writer is just like them...a regular person."
>
> "Can anyone do it? Or do you have to be special? A thug, outlaw, artist, etc?"

These journal jottings sparked Aidan's ideas for research enough to collect photographs (his own and others); a police record of arrests for graffiti trespassing; magazine and journal articles about children in prehistoric France who left cave markings; British "Graffiti Guerillas"; a local newspaper article about the graffiti he observed; a chart from a paint store and a spray paint Web site about the variety of colors and sizes of spray tips; notes from Eric, his classmate who was his researcher for a week; and lists of movies and books about graffiti. Eventually, much of this "data" found its way into Aidan's final project.

BOX5

Exploratory Notetaking with a Group

PURPOSE

When several people take notes at the same fieldsite, each person's set of notes is unique. In a field research project, especially at the beginning, it can be instructive to share notes among researchers. We often take our new students to a public event for this purpose of taking and sharing notes. We ask students to record as many details, concrete and personal, as they can about what they experience while they're at the site. This activity will encourage you to develop different notetaking formats and share them in class afterward.

ACTION

With a group or in pairs, attend a public event at your school or in a local community—a lecture, symposium, reading, recital, planning board meeting, or business presentation. It's difficult to do this exploratory exercise at a large event with many presenters or performers, so try to stay away from concerts, plays, or sports events. Plan to spend at least an hour taking many pages of notes. Many beginning fieldworkers find that they leave out important details of context—the time frame, the composition of the audience and its response, the conditions of the room, the conversation that surrounds them, and some details of the event itself. After taking notes, compare them with others', and think about and develop an efficient notetaking system that works for you.

RESPONSE

After Bonnie and her students attended an hour-long poetry reading on campus, they reconvened in class and shared their exploratory notes. There were many kinds of notes: some had recorded the ambiance of the auditorium; others focused on the age, gender, and dress of audience members; still others looked at the gestures and behaviors of the poet himself. Some recorded smells, temperature, lighting, and the sound equipment they saw. Most people included their personal responses to being at a poetry reading in a large auditorium at night when they might have been watching television, hanging out with friends, or studying. The class shared both informational and personal responses to this event. Below are some snippets from their exploratory notes:

Informational Notes	**Personal Notes**
"students quiet, cross-legged, leaning, hands clasped, arms crossed, still, chewing gum, baseball caps front and back, French braids, cornrows, pierced eyebrows"	"I don't associate poetry readings with packed auditoriums unless, you know, Jewel is reading"
"a young man in a black tee shirt with his back toward me and the words 'no speed limit' on his shirt"	"Two people are wearing red scarves. I wonder if red scarves have something to do with the poet or poetry reading."

"a man with black glasses and a goatee, carrying a bike helmet and a backpack, enters the auditorium and stands"

"a lot of people are chewing gum"

"there is a lot of motion in this listening audience—coughs and sneezes"

"mustard and white striped ceiling, ceiling tiles like it's a hanging ceiling, square lights and vents, holes around the light fixtures"

"What's the maximum seating by fire code?"

"poet licks his lips as he looks from poetry book to poetry book, telling us he's not organized"

"8:18: poet says, 'Eh, let's see, it's hot in here, I might take off my jacket'"

"there are eleven blonds in the front row"

"the air smells of a mix of musk oil, Liz Claiborne, sweet to spicy oriental scents, dust and mold"

"audience laughs bigtime when poet uses the word 'shit'"

"How do the different generations, genders, and styles of poets present themselves during such public negotiations of identity?"

"How did the popular habit of crossing one's legs begin? Which cultures do this, and what do they have in common? What are the associations with different styles of sitting?"

"My foot is falling asleep. The Velcro of my sandal is sticking to the carpet."

"what a peculiar custom, to position one person before, indeed in the midst of, a crowd, have him speak, to no reply"

"That was too long to stand on an empty stomach. I'm hungry, tired, and bitter. How different would my notes have been? What business do I have 'spying' on people attending the reading?"

"The poet is reading about clocks. How many people have never owned a clock that ticks? What does that say about progress in our society?"

"What is audience etiquette? What function do the long pauses serve?"

"I wonder why more women than men have notebooks."

Getting at the Details

Taking exploratory fieldnotes in a group, as we did in Box 5, allows us to see the differences in how individuals pay attention. But not everyone looks at—or sees—the same things. Rather, we develop our observational skills through practice and careful notetaking. In the following short essay, "Look at Your Fish," Samuel Scudder, a student in the nineteenth century who aspired to study entomology (insects), first learns to observe from his professor Louis Agassiz, whose lessons in natural science are legendary.

Look at Your Fish

Samuel H. Scudder

> Samuel H. Scudder (1837–1911), a naturalist who specialized in the study of insects, wrote this amusing account for a Boston literary journal in 1873. He tells of enrolling at Harvard's Lawrence Scientific School and of his first lesson under the inspired teacher and popularizer of science, Louis Agassiz (1807–1873), then professor of natural history. After hours of detailed but unpatterned observation, Scudder let his problem incubate during an evening away from the laboratory.

It was more than fifteen years ago that I entered the laboratory of Professor Agassiz, and told him I had enrolled my name in the Scientific School as a student of natural history. He asked me a few questions about my object in coming, my antecedents generally, the mode in which I afterwards proposed to use the knowledge I might acquire, and, finally, whether I wished to study any special branch. To the latter I replied that, while I wished to be well grounded in all departments of zoology, I purposed to devote myself especially to insects.

"When do you wish to begin?" he asked.

"Now," I replied.

This seemed to please him, and with an energetic "Very well!" he reached from a shelf a huge jar of specimens in yellow alcohol. "Take this fish," he said, "and look at it; we call it a haemulon; by and by I will ask what you have seen."

With that he left me, but in a moment returned with explicit instructions as to the care of the object entrusted to me.

"No man is fit to be a naturalist," said he, "who does not know how to take care of specimens."

I was to keep the fish before me in a tin tray, and occasionally moisten the surface with alcohol from the jar, always taking care to replace the stopper tightly. Those were not the days of ground-glass stoppers and elegantly shaped exhibition jars; all the old students will recall the huge neckless glass bottles with their leaky, wax-besmeared corks, half eaten by insects, and begrimed with cellar dust. Entomology was a cleaner science than ichthyology, but the example of the Professor, who had unhesitatingly plunged to the bottom of the jar to produce the fish, was infectious; and though this alcohol had a "very ancient and fishlike smell," I really dared not show any aversion within these sacred precincts, and treated the alcohol as though it were pure water. Still I was conscious of a passing feeling of disappointment, for gazing at a fish did not commend itself to an ardent entomologist. My friends at home, too, were annoyed when they discovered that no amount of eau-de-Cologne would drown the perfume which haunted me like a shadow.

In ten minutes I had seen all that could be seen in that fish, and started in search of the Professor—who had, however, left the Museum; and when I returned, after lingering over some of the odd animals stored in the upper apartment, my specimen was dry all over. I dashed the fluid over the fish as if to resuscitate the beast from a fainting fit, and looked with anxiety for a return of the normal sloppy appearance. This little excitement over, nothing was to be done but to return to a steadfast gaze at my mute companion. Half an hour passed— an hour—another hour; the fish began to look loathsome. I turned it over and around; looked it in the face—ghastly; from behind, beneath, above, sideways at a three-quarters' view—just as ghastly. I was in despair; at an early hour I concluded that lunch was necessary; so, with infinite relief, the fish was carefully replaced in the jar, and for an hour I was free.

On my return, I learned that Professor Agassiz had been at the Museum, but had gone, and would not return for several hours. My fellow-students were too busy to be disturbed by continued conversation. Slowly I drew forth that hideous fish, and with a feeling of desperation again looked at it. I might not use a magnifying-glass; instruments of all kinds were interdicted. My two hands, my two eyes, and the fish: it seemed a most limited field. I pushed my finger down its throat to feel how sharp the teeth were. I began to count the scales in the different rows, until I was convinced that that was nonsense. At last a happy thought struck me—I would draw the fish; and now with surprise I began to discover new features in the creature. Just then the Professor returned.

"That is right," said he; "a pencil is one of the best of eyes. I am glad to notice, too, that you keep your specimen wet, and your bottle corked."

With these encouraging words, he added:

"Well, what is it like?"

He listened attentively to my brief rehearsal of the structure of parts whose names were still unknown to me: the fringed gill-arches and movable operculum; the pores of the head, fleshy lips and lidless eyes; the lateral line, the spinous fins and forked tail; the compressed and arched body. When I finished, he waited as if expecting more, and then, with an air of disappointment:

"You have not looked very carefully; why," he continued more earnestly, "you haven't even seen one of the most conspicuous features of the animal, which is as plainly before your eyes as the fish itself; look again, look again!" and he left me to my misery.

I was piqued; I was mortified. Still more of that wretched fish! But now I set myself to my task with a will, and discovered one new thing after another, until I saw how just the Professor's criticism had been. The afternoon passed quickly; and when, towards its close, the Professor inquired:

"Do you see it yet?"

"No," I replied, "I am certain I do not, but I see how little I saw before."

"That is next best," said he, earnestly. "But I won't hear you now; put away your fish and go home; perhaps you will be ready with a better answer in the morning. I will examine you before you look at the fish."

This was disconcerting. Not only must I think of my fish all night, studying, without the object before me, what this unknown but most visible feature might be; but also, without reviewing my discoveries, I must give an exact account of them the next day. I had a bad memory; so I walked home by the Charles River in a distracted state, with my two perplexities.

The cordial greeting from the Professor the next morning was reassuring; here was a man who seemed to be quite as anxious as I that I should see for myself what he saw.

"Do you perhaps mean," I asked, "that the fish has symmetrical sides with paired organs?"

His thoroughly pleased "Of course! Of course!" repaid the wakeful hours of the previous night. After he had discoursed most happily and enthusiastically—as he always did—upon the importance of this point, I ventured to ask what I should do next.

"Oh, look at your fish!" he said, and left me again to my own devices. In a little more than an hour he returned, and heard my new catalogue.

"That is good, that is good!" he repeated; "but that is not all; go on"; and so for three long days he placed that fish before my eyes, forbidding me to look at anything else, or to use any artificial aid. "Look, look, look," was his repeated injunction.

This was the best entomological lesson I ever had—a lesson whose influence has extended to the details of every subsequent study; a legacy the Professor had left to me, as he has left it to many others, of inestimable value, which we could not buy, with which we cannot part.

A year afterward, some of us were amusing ourselves with chalking outlandish beasts on the Museum blackboard. We drew prancing starfishes; frogs in mortal combat; hydra-headed worms; stately crawfishes, standing on their tails, bearing aloft umbrellas; and grotesque fishes with gaping mouths and staring eyes. The Professor came in shortly after, and was as amused as any at our experiments. He looked at the fishes.

"Haemulons, every one of them," he said; "Mr. _____ drew them."

True; and to this day, if I attempt a fish, I can draw nothing but haemulons.

The fourth day, a second fish of the same group was placed beside the first, and I was bidden to point out the resemblances and differences between the two; another and another followed, until the entire family lay before me, and a whole legion of jars covered the table and surrounding shelves; the odor had become a pleasant perfume; and even now, the sight of an old, six-inch, worm-eaten cork brings fragrant memories.

The whole group of haemulons was thus brought in review; and, whether engaged upon the dissection of the internal organs, the preparation and examination of the bony framework, or the description of the various parts, Agassiz's training in the method of observing facts and their orderly arrangement was ever accompanied by the urgent exhortation not to be content with them.

"Facts are stupid things," he would say, "until brought into connection with some general law."

At the end of eight months, it was almost with reluctance that I left these friends and turned to insects; but what I had gained by this outside experience has been of greater value than years of later investigation in my favorite groups.

· ·

Scudder's observational training comes from Agassiz, a natural scientist, but it is equally important for the social scientist. Both researchers learn to gaze beyond the obvious—to look and then to look again. Scudder used many of the same skills that ethnographic researchers rely on—drawing pictures, asking focused questions, and "sleeping on the data."

Scudder faced one of the most humbling experiences a fieldworker can have—to discover how little he actually saw the first time. After looking long and hard, Scudder also realized that the mere recording of data—"facts are stupid things"—is not important unless you connect it with some larger idea. Before you undertake fieldwork in your chosen site, it is good practice to observe an everyday object or event to consider its significance.

Here's what we've imagined that Scudder might have written in his few hours with the fish:

Record	Respond
9–9:10 (first 10 minutes)	
jar—yellow alcohol	does yellow alcohol indicate old?
called a "haemulon"	is that its classification? phylum? kingdom? species?
"keep fish moistened?"	why keep it wet if it's dead? will it crumble? dry out? is it old?
9:30–12:00 (next 2½ hours)	
dries after 10 minutes	how much alcohol can a fish absorb?
all views the same (5 views: under, over, side, ¾, behind)	why does it look ghastly from all positions, perspectives?
throat-teeth sharp	must eat hard things—shells, fish skin?
scales in rows	possible symmetry?
(sketch)	fish looks like a fish, but more complicated than at first

We wrote these notes above to demonstrate another way of keeping fieldnotes, one that we and our students have found most useful. We borrow this notetaking idea from composition theorist Ann Berthoff, who developed this form as a way to encourage her students to look, reflect, and write about natural objects. Like all exploratory writing, **double-entry notes** are designed to make your mind spy on itself and generate further thinking and text. To write double-entry fieldnotes, divide the page vertically, using the left-hand side for direct observations—concrete, verifiable details. The right-hand side is the place to capture your personal reactions, opinions, feelings, and questions about the data on the left side. It's a good idea to number each observation (the left side) and response (the right side) to keep track of your data collection. Like Samuel Scudder, these closely honed notes allow you to "look at your fish." Our students have adapted this phrase as a research mantra. In reading one another's fieldnotes, exchanging early descriptions of fieldsites, we often hear them suggesting to one another, "LOOK AT YOUR FISH!"

Figure 2-3 *Fish Scales* (Anthony Guyther)

Double-Entry Notes

PURPOSE

To practice the art of double-entry notetaking, it's useful at first to focus on something that's not at your fieldsite (where the actions and sensory details can be overwhelming and you know there's a whole project at stake). Instead, try this exercise. Select an ordinary object or event in nature to observe every day for a week. Our students have taken notes on such different things as snow forming and melting on a windshield, coffee grounds accumulating in a trash can, a finch's nesting activities, a cut on a finger as it develops into a scab, and dirt forming in an unattended bathtub.

ACTION

Record your notes over the course of a week in double-entry format, using the left-hand side of the page to list specific details of the changes you observe and the right-hand side of the page to reflect on the meaning of these changes. Your subject must be one that alters in some way within a week's time. At the end of the week, look over the notes carefully, see what's changed and what hasn't, and write a short reflection on what you learned by keeping these fieldnotes. Discuss what surprised you most and what you would do differently if you were to continue with this observation. How might you connect what you have seen with an overall hunch or hypothesis?

Our student Grant Stanojev observed the bathtub he shares with his two roommates and kept a double-entry notebook over the course of six days. These are his recorded notes and reflective responses:

OBSERVATION OF A BATHTUB IN NEED OF A SHOWER

Grant Stanojev

Record	Respond
2/12 White tub around edges with brown crust along the doors. Rings under each shampoo bottle. New bar of Dial soap. The drain drains slowly.	Most of this observation is pretty typical of the apartment. Three guys shower in here once a day and it shows.
2/13 The visible soap has stray hairs plastered to it. One bottle of conditioner is placed upside down. Unused washcloth hangs stiffly on bar.	Not too much going on. The guys had a basketball game last night so the tub got an extra workout. Kind of gross that none of us uses the washcloth.
2/14 Soap is starting to have a slimy film surrounding it. The bottom of the tub is slippery and a little on the beige side. The crust around the edges is particularly dark today. Drain is backing up and is about halfway up the foot as shower proceeds.	The theme of today seems to be film (tub, soap, me). Starting to realize just how big of slobs we really are.
2/15 Bar of soap has dwindled considerably. Water actually covers the feet today and rests around the ankles. Cannot even see through the water.	This is getting disgusting. Went to a concert last night so the soap had to scrub off the layer of smoke and the "legal" stamp on each of our right hands.
2/16 Water is around the ankles again. Washcloth is wet. There is a nasty clump of black hair wadded on top of the drain. More gone from the soap.	Another night out for the guys so same results. A little repulsed by the hair that has accumulated. More repulsed that no one has removed it yet.
2/17 Crust around the edges of everything is a nice golden bronze. Filth lines the bottom of the tub.	Roommates are getting restless at the sight of the bathroom. It even became the subject of conversation. Still no one does anything. I think the end is near though. Everyone is sick of the crust on the tub.

What really struck me was the lack of motivation in our apartment. It was important enough for the guys to play basketball for our health but not to bathe in a sanitary environment. Standing in my own filth is something I would never do if I still lived with my parents. I knew that we were pigs, but I never really documented the decay of our bathing facilities. Bacteria is probably everywhere in our bathroom, and to tell you the truth I am not sure exactly why that is bad. I know it is not sanitary though and it is disgusting to wash yourself in it. I told my roommates that I brought it up in class and Dave cleaned the tub the next day.

Fieldnotes: The Key to Your Project

As a beginning fieldworker, you may be trying so hard to get everything down that your record of details might blur into your feelings about these impressions and vice versa. The reason to develop an organized system is that when you first enter your fieldsite, sensory impressions surround you. You feel as if you'll never get them all down. Taking double-entry fieldnotes as you did in Box 6 provides a clear way to separate your observations from your responses to them.

As you take fieldnotes, you become better at appreciating what you initially took for granted. You start to gather a thick collection of notes, which will serve as a body of data. Later, you'll turn these notes into descriptions of your fieldsite and your informants. You will take far more fieldnotes than you will ever use in your final description. Professional writers publish perhaps a fifth of the writing they do, and movie directors use only about a tenth of the footage they shoot. To become a good fieldworker, you must observe closely and participate intimately, returning to your fieldsite and informants again and again — and still again.

Discovering a System for Notetaking

No matter how you decide to collect your fieldnotes, it is important to find a system that works for you and the project you've chosen. As you create a notetaking system for your particular study, you organize your data to see what's important. There is no one single accepted format for taking fieldnotes. Each fieldstudy demands a different design for notetaking; each fieldworker needs to adapt notetaking strategies a different way. Because the essence of field research is not to duplicate what someone else saw and thought but to describe and interpret data in its particulars, it's not surprising that each study and each researcher's notes are unique.

Your fieldnote system needs to be more organized than the freewrite or the exploratory writing and notetaking we've considered so far. Our experience as researchers has shown us that any fieldnote format that you borrow or design needs to be organized enough so that you can retrieve specific pieces of data easily, even months later.

Fieldnotes actually provide a rhetorical construct: they help a fieldworker begin the movement from self to audience. While your personal observations, opinions, and questions can help form your writerly voice (ethos), the informational notes add to your collection of data (logos), and this combination starts to provide you with the authority to write about your fieldwork for different audiences (pathos). As you shuttle back and forth between your personal reflective observations and your increasing piles of data from fieldnotes and other sources, you'll begin to form theories, see connections, follow hunches, and confirm understandings of the culture you're investigating.

Professionals' Fieldnotes

Professional fieldworkers take their notes in a variety of ways, using codes and systems they've developed themselves. Here, we show two different samples of anthropologists' fieldnotes to give you further ideas about formats. The first example comes from Roger Sanjek's classic 1988 study in Queens, New York. He uses his informants' names—Milagros, Carmela, Phil, Jenny, and Mareya. The second study is from Margery Wolf's 1960 notes taken in a village in Taiwan. She assigns numbers and letters—such as 48 (F 30) and 48I (F 12)—to her informants. Although their coding systems are different and their informants are from different times and places, both excerpts are thick with descriptive detail.

Roger Sanjek's Fieldnotes

7 May 1988—*Carmela George's Cleanup Day**

Milagros and I arrived at 10 am, as Carmela told me, but 97th Street, the deadend, was already cleaned out, and the large garbage pickup truck, with rotating blades that crushed everything, was in the middle of 97th Place. I found Carmela, and met Phil Pirozzi of Sanitation, who had three men working on the cleanup, plus the sweeper that arrived a little later. The men and boys on 97th Place helping to load their garbage into the truck included several Guyanese Indians in their 20s, whom Carmela said have been here 2–3 years ['They're good.']; several families of Hispanics, and Korean and Chinese. They were loading TV sets, shopping carts, wood, old furniture, tree branches and pruning, and bags and boxes of garbage. Most houses had large piles of stuff in front, waiting for the truck. The little boys hanging on and helping were Hispanic, except for one Chinese. They spoke a mixture of Spanish and English together, when painting the LIRR walls.

Margery Wolf's Fieldnotes

March 5, 1960†
Present: 153 (F 54), 154 (F 31), 254 (F 53), 189 (F 50), 230 (F 17)

Yesterday 48 (F 30) was taken by her husband to a mental hospital in Tapu. 48I (F 12) told Wu Chieh that the woman ran out into the field, and her husband had to come to pick her up and take her to the hospital. The women were talking about this today and said that she was sent to a big mental hospital, and that her husband went there to see her but was not allowed to see her because she was tied up. The doctor said there was nothing else he could do with her. Someone told Wu Chieh that something like this had happened to 48 once before, but she was not hospitalized then. The women say that her illness this time came about as the result of her

---

*Part of a page from Roger Sanjek's 1988 Elmhurst-Corona, Queens, New York, fieldnotes, printed from a computer word-processing program. (Size: 8.5 by 11 inches.)

†Part of a page from Margery Wolf's fieldnotes taken in Taiwan. Wu Chieh is her informant/assistant, and Wolf assigns numbers to other informants.

worrying about losing NTS90. She couldn't find the money and asked 49 (her seven-year-old son) about it, and he told her that his father took it to gamble. Her husband said that this was not true. They said that she may have known that she was going to get sick, because the day before she took her baby (3 months) over to her sister's house and asked her to take care of the baby.

Entire books and scholarly articles are devoted to writing and analyzing fieldnotes and explaining researchers' attitudes about their fieldnotes. Anthropologist Jean Jackson, who interviewed field researchers, discovered that many have nightmares about losing their fieldnotes to fires or thieves: "Anxiety about loss of fieldnotes has come up so many times and so dramatically—images of burning appear quite often.... The many legends, apocryphal or not, about lost fieldnotes probably fits [sic] into this category of horrific and yet delicious, forbidden fantasy." Since fieldnotes become the backbone of any fieldstudy, it's no wonder that professional fieldworkers attribute such power and fear to this kind of writing.

Fieldnotes can range from scraps taken furtively on small bits of paper when a researcher wants to be unobtrusive to complex computer programs designed specifically for organizing large amounts of data. The first time you enter your chosen fieldsite, your biggest challenge is figuring out *what* to record. Like free-writing and exploratory notes, fieldnotes include sensory impressions, nascent thoughts, and snippets of conversation. Our own students often feel so overwhelmed by the sheer amount of possible data to record that at first they write very little. As beginning researchers, we both had the same problem.

Elizabeth remembers her first visit to a classroom as a fieldworker. Although she'd spent many years in many classrooms as a teacher, she felt helpless. Should she write down everything or nothing? What was important? After forty-five minutes, she had scribbled very little in her research notebook. She wanted to change her topic and find another fieldsite. But she didn't.

The next day, Elizabeth entered the classroom, turned to a fresh page in her notebook, and began to make lists. First, she wrote down important identifying information: the time, the date, the name of the building, the number on the classroom door. She sketched a small map showing where everyone was sitting, noting windows, doors, and placement of furniture. She developed a code for noting genders, assigning M's and F's, and gave a number to each student. She then made lots of lists—kinds of shoes, colors and sayings on T-shirts, types of bookbags and backpacks. Then she counted things—how many windows were open and how many were closed, who wore nose rings and who wore engagement rings, how many students brought their textbooks to class and how many didn't. She noted specific **underlife** behaviors—who was taking notes and who was asleep, who was whispering and who was putting on makeup. She concentrated on writing down as much dialogue as possible—both the topics and the patterns of what the teacher and students were saying—who spoke and for how long. Although she was not sure what was important or what information would make it into her final study, she trained herself to record more systematically, and over time her fieldnotes became more and more focused. By the end of a month, she knew her study would be about gender and conversation in a college writing classroom.

Organizing Your Fieldnotes

As art historian John Berger writes, "We only see what we look at. To look is an act of choice" (8). In your first trip to the field, details might seem so familiar that you do not lift your pencil to record a single thing. You don't record sounds or smells or textures; you passively wait. You're frustrated. You decide to change field sites. You have not yet learned to look. Seeing—establishing a gaze—requires receptivity, patience, and a willingness to penetrate the outer layer of things.

Our student Karen Downing studied a glamour photography business called Photo Phantasies (which you'll read more about later in this book). Karen took seven pages of fieldnotes on what she saw when she gained entry to Photo Phantasies for the first time. Figure 2-4 on the following page shows two excerpts from her notes (two visits on the same day). Notice that her fieldnotes come from descriptions of the site and interviews with staff and customers.

Read Karen Downing's full project, "Strike a Pose," at **bedfordstmartins.com/ fieldworking** under Student Essays.

You should develop a personal, systematic way of taking fieldnotes. Your system should allow enough room to record details at the site, but it should also allow space to expand your initial impressions away from the site. Fieldnotes are your evidence for confirming theories you make about the observations you record. They are the permanent record of your fieldworking process, and they become part of your research portfolio. Without accurate fieldnotes, you have no project. Although each fieldworker develops his or her own system, any set of fieldnotes needs to include all of the details in an organized way.

Keep Accurate Fieldnotes

Be sure to note:

- Date, time, and place of observation ("Friday, April 6, 11:45 in the store")

- Specific facts, numbers, details ("last appointment at 7 p.m.," "3 customers present," "sign: 'professional makeup artist'")

- Sensory impressions: sights, sounds, textures, smells, tastes ("caramel corn smells, footsteps on tile, children crying, pop music playing fairly loud, gray carpet with muted pink, white walls, black modern furniture, notebook of thank-you notes")

- Personal responses to the act of recording fieldnotes and how others watch you as you watch them ("Giant pictures of Phantasy Phaces. They look pretty darn good. Are these pics taken in this store?")

- Specific words, phrases, summaries of conversations, and insider language ("Girl inquires about modeling special. Asks, 'Do you do it now?' Response: 'Not really, but you really have a nice forehead. You could be a runway model.'")

- Questions about people or behaviors at the site for future investigation ("dressing rooms are small—they don't want you there for long")

- Continuous page-numbering system for future reference ("4/4 studio visit, page 5")

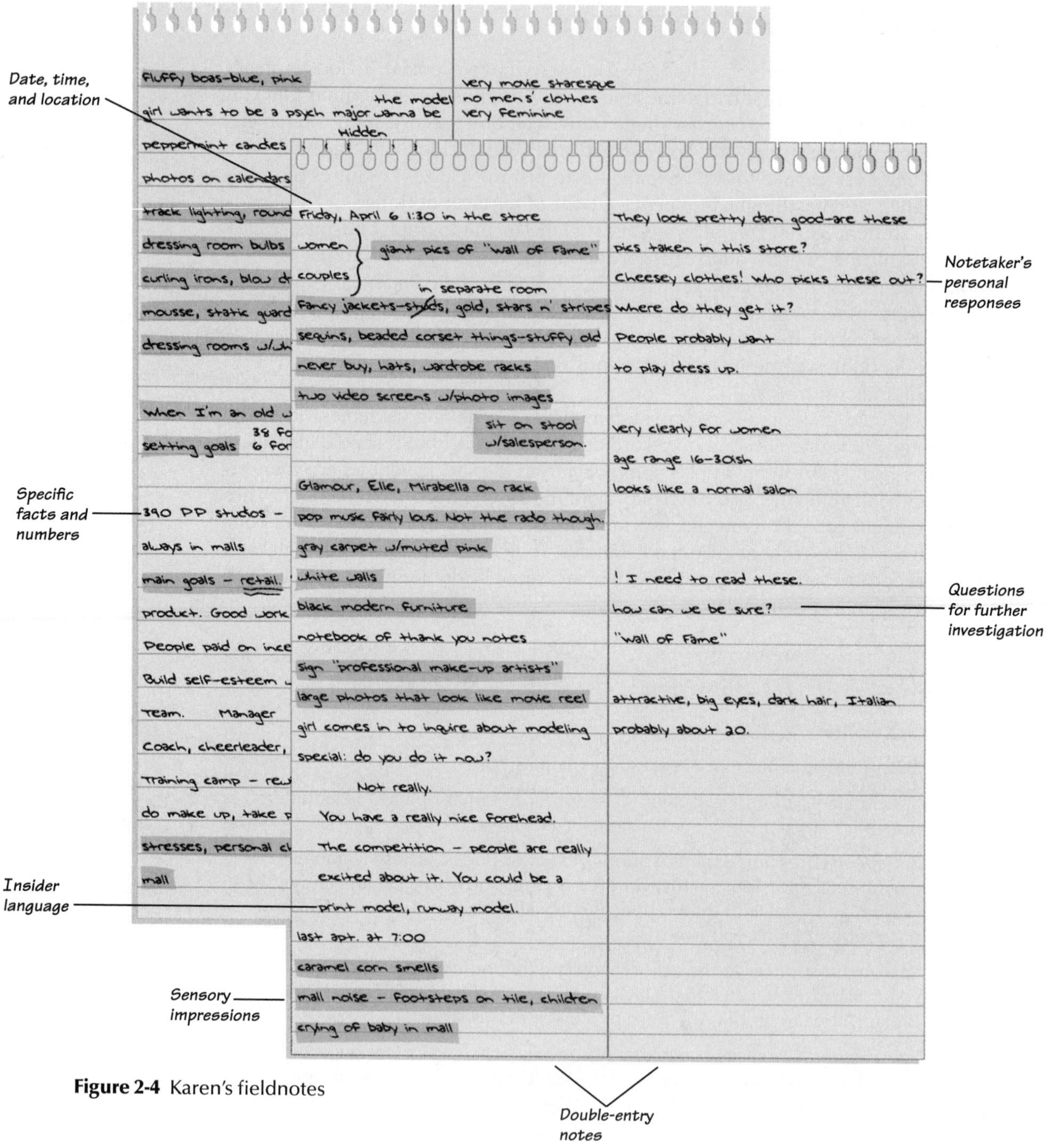

Date, time, and location

fluffy boas—blue, pink

girl wants to be a psych major   the model wanna be   very movie staresque
                                   Hidden   no mens' clothes
peppermint candles   very feminine

photos on calendars

track lighting, round   Friday, April 6 1:30 in the store   They look pretty darn good—are these

dressing room bulbs   women   giant pics of "wall of Fame"   pics taken in this store?

curling irons, blow d   couples   Cheesey clothes! who picks these out?
                              in separate room
mousse, static guard   Fancy jackets—studs, gold, stars n' stripes   where do they get it?

dressing rooms w/h   sequins, beaded corset things—stuffy old   People probably want

                        never buy, hats, wardrobe racks   to play dress up.

                        two video screens w/photo images

when I'm an old   sit on stool   very clearly for women
    38 fo   w/salesperson.   age range 16–30ish
setting goals   6 for

Specific facts and numbers   Glamour, Elle, Mirabella on rack   looks like a normal salon

390 PP studios —   pop music fairly lous. Not the radio though.

always in malls   gray carpet w/muted pink

main goals — retail.   white walls   ! I need to read these.

product. Good work   black modern furniture   how can we be sure?

People paid on ince   notebook of thank you notes   "wall of Fame"

Build self-esteem   sign "professional make-up artists"

Team.   Manager   large photos that look like movie reel   attractive, big eyes, dark hair, Italian

coach, cheerleader,   girl comes in to inquire about modeling   probably about 20.

Training camp — rew   special: do you do it now?

do make up, take   Not really.

stresses, personal c   You have a really nice forehead.

mall   The competition — people are really

                        excited about it. You could be a

                    print model, runway model.

                last apt. at 7:00

                caramel corn smells

Sensory impressions   mall noise — footsteps on tile, children

                crying of baby in mall

Notetaker's personal responses

Questions for further investigation

Insider language

Double-entry notes

Figure 2-4 Karen's fieldnotes

BOX 7

Sharing Your Initial Fieldnotes

PURPOSE

It's a good idea to spend some time at your possible fieldsite making yourself feel at ease there, before you start taking fieldnotes. Once you do begin writing, it's also a good idea to get feedback from one or more colleagues who can help you identify strengths and weaknesses in your initial notes.

ACTION

Take a set of fieldnotes at a site you are considering or at which you have decided on becoming a **participant-observer**. Note important information like time, location, date, weather, and your vantage point. You may also draw a sketch or a map of the space, indicating shapes, objects, focal points, and movement patterns. Listen and look at the people there, and record as much information about them as possible. Create a consistent shorthand or code that you understand to develop a notetaking scheme that you will be able to follow throughout your project. Practice ways to differentiate between verifiable information (12 spotted cows) and your own subjective responses to or reflections on the data ("Yuck. It stinks. It reminds me of my great-uncle's outhouse"). Once you have 10 pages of notes or so, review them, and try to write a short summary of the fieldsite using your best details, so that a research partner will understand them. While you may develop a personal code (as Margery Wolf's or Roger Sanjek's fieldnotes show), at this point, your notes should be clear enough to share with someone else. This is your first step toward shaping your work for an audience.

Bring your fieldnotes and your summary to a research partner for sharing. Here are some questions you and your partner should consider as you read and respond to one another's fieldnotes:

1. Are the notes readable? Are the pages numbered and dated?

2. What background material does someone need to understand the history and location of this place?

3. Does the researcher include information about her subjective feelings as she observes?

4. What other details should she include so that another person could see, hear, and become immersed in the daily routines of this place?

5. What details are most interesting? What would you like the researcher to write more about?

6. What other data do you need to confirm some of the researcher's initial observations about this place?

RESPONSE

In one of our classes, Simone Henkel read Tara Tisue's fieldnotes on the morale captains at an annual university event, the dance marathon. The dance marathon is a charity fundraiser, held in a large auditorium. Students volunteer to dance for hours; the more hours they dance, the more money they raise. The morale captains, whom Tara observes, are

BOX 7  continued

the leaders who keep students' spirits up. After reading Tara's study, Simone responded to the above questions as follows:

1. The notes are neatly printed and numbered and dated. The location of the site is also noted.

2. The background material regarding the history of the dance marathon included where it started, how long it's been happening here at our university. Tara might include the details of what happens at various other sites, since every university will shape this event a bit differently depending on the time of year and the students who choose to participate.

3. I am not sure what feelings Tara brings to her site. This is interesting that she excludes her feelings since Tara has been involved prior to this year. Tara might include how she felt the first year she was a morale captain herself.

4. Tara offers a good picture of what the people are doing, the feeling of being there (smells, sounds, sights, etc.). I can picture the auditorium because I know what it looks like. I think a more detailed description would be helpful, specifically, an expanded description of the auditorium.

5. The most interesting description was of all the water bottles, the soaked red T-shirts, the ponytails flying, the scuffing sounds on the floor, and the specific songs they played over the speakers.

6. I think I'd like to hear more about how the morale captains meet regularly, how long before the event itself, and who trained them. It would also be interesting to know what other students think about the dance marathon through a series of interviews. What about students who won't go? I'd also like to know what they think about the event!

Analyzing Your Fieldnotes

Most fieldworkers write their notes while they're in the field, but some find themselves in situations where they can take only minimal notes on-site. They must return to their desk to flesh out and expand the scanty notes they took while they were in the field. Follow the advice we give our students: before you go back to your busy life with all its distractions, take some time to sit quietly and write in your notebook. Expand your fieldnotes by reading them; by adding details of conversations, sensory impressions, and contextual information; by noting your observations and reflections; and by jotting down possible questions and hunches. Analysis begins with reviewing your notes.

Just as fieldworkers develop many systems for notetaking, they invent, develop, and devise systems for organizing, coding, and retrieving data. Colored folders, highlighters, stick-on (or "sticky") notes, hanging folder boxes, and three-ring binders can be a researcher's best friends. Computers, too, have organizing features that can help you label and find pieces of your fieldnotes when you need them. Accumulating a solid set of fieldnotes is only one step in the process of creating a fieldwork project. You probably know that taking notes in a lecture class does you little good if you try to review them all for the first time the night before a test. Just as periodic review of your lecture notes helps you understand complicated material, your fieldnotes will speak to you if you read them regularly. In reviewing your fieldnotes, you will begin to find recurring themes, images, and metaphors that will form patterns. These patterns will help you form your beginning interpretations. Some fieldworkers write weekly memos culled from their fieldnotes, pulling together pieces of data around an emerging idea.

We have developed a helpful kind of analysis memo that involves three key questions to ask and write about regularly as you review your data. These questions will guide the work we discuss throughout this entire book. While we haven't yet introduced you to some of these concepts in detail, these questions are worth considering even at the beginning of your fieldwork project:

1. What surprised me? (tracking assumptions)   This question helps you keep track of your assumptions throughout the fieldwork process. When you ask yourself this question regularly, you'll articulate your preconceived notions about this project and also record how they change.

2. What intrigued me? (tracking positions)   Asking this question makes you aware of your personal stances in relationship to your research topic. As we've already suggested, you as the fieldworker are the instrument (recorder and presenter) of the research process. So what interests and attracts you about your project will always influence what you record and how you write about it. This question helps you understand the complex idea of positioning, which we discuss in Chapter 3.

3. What disturbed me? (tracking tensions)   This question exposes yourself to yourself. It requires honesty about your blind spots, stereotypes, prejudices, and the things you find upsetting, no matter how small. Focusing on what bothers you about a field project is not always comfortable, but it often leads to important insights.

In time, these three questions should become a kind of mantra for your fieldstudy.

Fieldnotes enhance your ability to step in and step out of the culture you've chosen. From your earliest freewriting as you think about a topic, through the notes you take as you enter your fieldsite, to the reflections you write for yourself as you look back and question what you wrote, fieldnotes offer you the details, language, perspectives, and perceptions that will eventually become your final written product. We hope you'll take fieldnotes with care and patience and treat them as you would any other kind of source material. Although you may not realize it, your fieldnotes create an original source, a primary source that no one else has recorded in the same way you have, at the site you've chosen, and with the people you've studied.

BOX **8**

Questioning Your Fieldnotes

During the course of your research, your assumptions, positions, and tensions will probably change a lot, and looking over your notes will help you see how you learn about your site and your informants as your research progresses. Continually asking the three key questions introduced on page 87 will help you check in on your research and become aware of your own changing attitudes, stances, and even blind spots as you gather new data. You will actually see your knowledge deepen in your researcher's journal.

ACTION

Look over the notes you've taken in your researcher's journal so far. Try for the first time to ask these three key questions:

- **What surprised me?**
- **What intrigued me?**
- **What disturbed me?**

RESPONSE

Holly Richardson is a high school teacher in Alaska who grew up in western New York and worked with us in Massachusetts. To prepare to teach her Alaskan students how to do fieldwork, she practiced by doing a field study of her own. Holly decided to study a bingo game at an American Legion hall:

> Ever since I was a young girl, I have accompanied my mother and a slew of her friends to bingo games at various Veterans of Foreign War posts, Indian reservations, Catholic churches, and volunteer fire stations in Western New York. In my adult life, I have attended bingo games in central Alaska—sometimes just for fun and sometimes to raffle off items or do 50/50 drawings for my student government group. I've always been intrigued by the superstitions and rituals that surface at these games. Although I am not particularly superstitious, I find myself rubbing my neighbor's winnings or coding a particular game by marking an edge with the dabber, hoping that the game will bring me luck. There are mostly women at the games, and usually there is a mix of ages, although the majority are probably over 50. The men seem to accompany the women, not vice versa. Until now, I never actually took notes on what people around me were doing at these games.
>
> *What surprised me?* I went outside before the game started and during the 10-minute break to smoke a cigarette and talk to some of my fellow addicts. As usual, the chitchat was of gas prices, cigarette prices, and our terrible habits. But there was an underlying feeling of camaraderie in this group that didn't seem directly related to bingo, but maybe it was. I realized I was being accepted into their bingo circle merely because we were smoking together. This surprised me; I just haven't thought about it before.
>
> *What intrigued me?* As I began to think about the 10 years I have spent on front porches or in smoking sections, I realized that these strangers whom I meet have shared their life stories with me. I remember and am intrigued by the hundreds of people whose wisdom about life, strengths, and failures have been in my life. I wanted the smoking area to become my central area of focus.

What disturbed me? I went to the bingo game to observe the players, not to focus on the smokers! I was disturbed by my feeling when I was with them. They took me into their lives and shared with me. This has been happening for 10 years, and I am only now realizing it. I wonder if the kindness and closeness I feel with my fellow smokers is part of the addiction I can't seem to kick. I understand why AA meetings can be so important to people. But I'm here to study bingo!

As she reread her fieldnotes and wrote in her journal, Holly realized that she needed to either write more about the bingo games—or focus on the cluster of interesting and talkative people with whom she'd developed a relationship during their smoking breaks. You can see that these three questions helped Holly understand that she had many different ways of researching this site and finding a focus for her study.

A Fieldnotes Study: "Feng-Shui: Reflections on a Sociology Class"

Our colleague Michael Hoberman, a professor and professional anthropologist at Fitchburg State College in Massachusetts, gives an assignment to his beginning fieldworkers. Michael asks them to visit a classroom that is not their own, perhaps the class of a roommate or a friend who majors in a very different discipline. He suggests that his students spend a day or two in the unfamiliar class taking fieldnotes. Of course, they must check ahead to see what permission they might need to attend the class.

Michael's student Amy Lambert visited a sociology class with her friend Jenna. In her double-entry notes, Amy recorded her observations (which she labeled "Record") on the left side and her personal reactions ("Respond") on the right. As an observer—someone who is not a registered student in this class—Amy became highly conscious of the underlife of the class.

Record	Respond
Middle of classroom.	Feeling nervous…pensive…is everyone wondering who I am?
Observing seating arrangements… males and females equally dispersed. I am sitting near my friend Jenna.	Am I in someone's seat?
Someone mumbles from the back of the room. I see people looking at me.	Stop looking at me!
Some students are taking notes. Someone walks out of the class-room…a male with a 'do-rag.	Where's he going? The bathroom? Water fountain?

There are scientific charts in this room.

It must double as a science room as well.

Teacher speaks, "Police suffer from job-related stress."

I think to myself, "Who doesn't?"

The teacher paces while talking and uses hand gestures.

Multicultural class — blacks, whites, Hispanics.

Pages being flipped.

My throat hurts. Obviously, students are not paying attention because pages are being flipped and the teacher isn't referring to the book.

Pen scratching.

Teacher glances at me.

She's curious about what I am writing. I wonder if she'll ask to see my notes before I leave.

Many guys have shaved heads in this class.

Is that like a "criminal justice" thing?

Teacher brings up topic of "evaluation." "Evaluation of any job is difficult — but especially in a bureaucracy."

Does she think I'm evaluating her?

Many people are doodling shapes and geometric figures.

People who doodle geometric figures are more likely to be left-brained, thus, more logical — more logical than me? Probably.

Someone's watch beeps loudly.

Ahh...wakeup call!

Many students carry water bottles.

I'm thirsty. I need a drink. Soda. Yes. Soda.

More questions...no answers.

I know these answers! I want to answer so badly!

There are notes on the board from a previous class.

I think these are for forensics?

I hear people talking down the hallway.

A sign of life!!

Students begin to pack while the teacher is still talking. Zippers zip and people are stretching.

The teacher must be annoyed with the class when they get ready to leave before she is done speaking. She must feel they are not paying attention to her. I'd be pretty mad if I were in her shoes. But I think students do it unconsciously.

Later, Amy freewrites four different times about her visit. Each time, she writes a short paragraph that focuses on a different feature of the class. Here are some excerpts from them:

Freewrite 1.   With heads resting in their hands as a prop to keep them from falling dead asleep right then and there, was one main observation I made. Others just had their arms crossed and looked as if in a daze. Some fiddled with pens — I heard the incessant sound of pens scratching throughout the period. I am tired. I am thirsty. I wouldn't want to die of dehydration. That would be sick.

Freewrite 2.   I remember students doing some intense doodling in class. I glanced at a few people's doodles who were sitting around me and noticed many geometrical figures. I read once that people who draw more geometric figures are more logical than those who doodle freely and organically. 'Organically' would be the art term. I tend to doodle hearts and flowers and squiggles, which I have come to believe represents my artistic personality as well as my free spirit and right-brained mind.

Freewrite 3.   Are you a brown-noser or are you a slacker? Or perhaps you vary between both extremes. While sitting in on a sociology class, I noticed that many of the students seated in the back of the room were out of it. The students in the front row, although half asleep (as were those in the back row), were more attentive....I think it's not only the fact that when you're seated in the front row, the teacher is right there but also because the more adventurous and scholastic students want to be closer, symbolically speaking, to knowledge. If you are sitting straight up with your stomach muscles tightened and a pen in your hand ready to write, you are more alert and ready to learn.

Freewrite 4.   The classroom needed some spunk, some fun charts and posters. I think classrooms need more beauty. They need cute curtains and colorful chalk and bright paint on the walls. I think it would be fun to take notes from colorful chalk. I think even colored blinds if they didn't want to do the curtain thing. That would be very feng-shui.

Amy used her exploratory freewriting and her fieldnotes to assemble a longer, more formal paper in which she interprets her classroom observations. As you read it, notice the places in which she draws directly from both her fieldnotes and her freewrites. During her writing and revising process, Amy looked at both sides of her pages of double-entry notes, the stick-on notes she'd placed on top of them, the four freewriting exercises she'd done, and the comments Jenna and her classmates had made. She was able to return again and again to three questions: "What surprised me?" "What intrigued me?" "What disturbed me?" As she learned more, her interpretations deepened.

Feng-Shui: Reflections on a Sociology Class

Amy Lambert

Have you ever realized how certain aspects of a room can make you feel at home and relaxed or uncomfortable and pensive? A log cabin, for example, appears cozy and safe when shown luminated by a warm, glowing fire. A cold, sterile hospital room can have the opposite effect. Whether or not we realize it, our environment impacts our emotional state. While observing a sociology class on criminal justice, I noticed that the uninterested attitude of the students reflected the boring atmosphere in the classroom. The classroom environment paved the way for the state of the class, the teacher's performance, and student activity.

The first thing I noticed about this classroom was that the walls were bare. White walls remind me of hospitals and asylums. Was this class going to drive me crazy? As I observed the walls, my eyes locked onto two posters. As I got closer, I saw they were scientific charts, and my hope for any interesting decorations faded.

I took a seat next to my friend Jenna, who sat in the center row, second from the front. I feared I was occupying someone else's seat, but Jenna assured me that it was an acceptable place to sit. I watched other people come in. They took their seats with little enthusiasm. Although tired, I was excited to see what a criminal justice class consisted of. Much to my surprise, one of Jenna's friends leaned over and advised me, "I hope you had some caffeine this morning. You'll need it."

"Hmm," I thought to myself. "I wonder if it's going to be that bad." The teacher began speaking in a monotone voice. By the look on Jenna's face, I knew this class would be a long one.

As I sat in my front and center seat, I glanced around slyly to get a feel for the class's composition. It was predominantly white, with a few African American and Hispanic students. Males and females were equally dispersed around the room. The classroom's desks were arranged in rows facing the teacher. I'm not a big fan of rows. I don't think that they create a very good group dynamic. Students hide behind other students so that they can doze off without being noticed. Well, I notice. They are just a little slumped over, supposedly at the task of writing or reading when, in fact, they are sleeping. Trust me, I've seen it before. Perhaps if the teacher had a better view of each and every student, naptime would be delayed until *after* class.

With heads in hands and stares blank, most everyone in the class—with the exception of the three students in the front row—was zoned out. I remember hearing voices outside the classroom down the hallway, and I thought to myself, "A sign of life!" Maybe the room should just be one big front row, and then no one would sleep! I periodically glanced around the room and noticed people doodling geometric shapes. I read that people who doodle squares and other geometric figures are more left-brained than those that doodle organic shapes. Jenna, who was one of the "doodlers," is excellent in math and science. I think the majority of the class was probably left-brained dominant because they are going for a bachelor of science degree. Their future jobs will probably require mathematical and scientific knowledge. They probably like it; I know Jenna does.

My thoughts about doodling were interrupted when a boy dropped his book. THUMP! The loud noise startled everyone, and he blushed. Kids around me were reading their books while the teacher was speaking. I took it that they were doing that evening's homework. When the teacher asked questions, only people in the front row raised their hands. They were into it, and that is admirable. Toward the end of the class, I observed students packing up 10 minutes before class actually ended. They were anxious to go. I couldn't help thinking to myself that this lack of excitement could have been prevented by presenting a warmer, more interactive environment.

If the classroom were painted a different color, other than boring white, and if more interesting charts and posters were up, I believe that the class would be more awake and into the subject matter. Students' imaginations would be sparked, and knowledge would flow freely. The class composition, teacher's performance, and student activity all reflected the dull room. Whether or not we realize it, the environment we are in affects our emotions (mood) and activity.

As Amy looked at both her fieldnotes and her exploratory freewrites, she began to see patterns that showed she'd been generating hunches and recording themes. Her fieldnotes and freewriting held the beginnings of her analysis—much like Samuel Scudder, a century ago, who "looked at his fish" and learned more as he looked further and deeper. Amy's continual observations and writing moved her toward deeper observation. The more she looked, the more she saw. Fieldnotes and exploratory writing alone were the raw data. The patterns, themes, and hunches enabled her to analyze what she saw to write more fully about it.

Double Voiced Fieldnotes

Seeing—establishing a gaze in fieldwork—requires your ability to notice the details of what's happening around you and a willingness to listen to your own inner thoughts. Amy Lambert's study of her sociology class depended on both accurate notetaking and reflective thought. Not only did she train herself to become a better observer of the familiar surroundings of a classroom, she also recorded her subjective feelings and responses in her double-entry notes. Both parts of your double-entry notes will make their way into your final paper based on what we like to call *double voiced fieldnotes*.

Our colleague H. L. "Bud" Goodall, a professor of communication studies, has authored many ethnographic projects about organizations, communications, and culture. Here he writes about how a researcher captures fieldwork in fieldnotes and then in narratives or stories: "ethnography is a story based on the represented, or evoked, experiences of a self, with others, within a context" (83). Your fieldwork story is built out of the everyday life materials that you capture in your notes, as you develop your relationship with others in the field—and then add their perspectives to yours.

Every field study, then, has two stories to tell: one about the culture and what it means to the informants in that culture, and the other about you as a researcher and how you did your research. You always begin your double voiced account with your fieldnotes. In the following excerpt from Goodall's book, *Writing the New Ethnography*, he discusses how he used his fieldnotes to intertwine both his perspective and that of his informants, using the example of his 1989 project, "On Becoming an Organizational Detective."

....

Representing Ethnographic Experiences

H. L. "Bud" Goodall

When I wrote "On Becoming an Organizational Detective" (1989a) I was working from a set of fieldnotes that gradually emerged into a story. The form of the story I chose was the classic detective mystery. I chose this genre because, from my experience, the consultant-as-detective is called into a case, supposedly to investigate one thing—in this case, a "communication problem"—but that one thing usually turns into something else altogether. For me, this is an archetypal account of every consulting job I've ever had. So I decided to write the ethnographic account as a detective story—no formal introduction, theoretical framing, research questions, or anything like that—just as my fieldnotes represented it. Here is the opening, from the finished product:

> His name is Edward R. Seeman.
> "Call me Ed," he commands as we shake hands. We are doing the usual male thing with the squeeze, each one of us applying a little more pressure until it becomes just uncomfortable enough for one of us to release. Because he's paying the tab, I release, although I don't want to. *Call me Ed*, you muse. Call me Ishmael, and his name is Seeman. Where's the whale?
> Equity thus restored I follow him to a table, each of us eyebrow admiring for the benefit of the other the significant nonverbal aspects of the hostess's rearward appearance. In the background is Muzak. It is going to be one of *those* lunches. I knew there were reasons why I got out of this business (1989; pp. 42–43).

Detective stories typically begin this way. The private eye, always a bit of a cultural maverick and usually a loner, meets someone who has a problem. The problem is explained, a fee is worked out, the private eye takes the case. The game is afoot.

In my fieldnotes, I recorded this series of events:

Lunch with Seeman. Decked out in *Esquire* clothes, wears a gold Rolex submariner. Have the feeling that he is not on the level. He mentions the work I did for Phil Davis as if this is an analogous situation. This means he's talked to Davis, which could be good or bad for me. Davis thought I was going to write a different report than the one he received. Turned out okay though. Or maybe Davis recommended me to get even. Hard to say.

Here is how I wrote this episode into the published story:

Ed leans forward, his Rolex catches the light and sparkles. "I saw Phil Davis at the Heritage Club last week," he grins, "and when I told him about my little problem he recommended you."

Thanks, Phil. I try to restrain myself from saying something like "Phil's an ass, which verifies my initial opinion of you," but instead settle for a milder form of insult. "The Heritage Club, huh? Well, my fee just went up."…

About Phil's recommendation I am less certain. Phil Davis hired me a couple of years ago to look into a "communication" problem in an aerospace manufacturing firm that ended up being a cleverly masked excuse for a consultant's report that would blame a particular department for something that wasn't its fault. Phil didn't know this, but he played along as if he knew something, which in a way is worse. I didn't play along, ended up going undercover in the organization to discover the truth, and wrote a very different sort of report. In the end, nobody got hurt, I got paid, and everyone, including Phil, looked good.

But Phil also knew I had done more, and less, than I was asked to do. So this could mean that Phil thinks I will do the same for Ed, or something else entirely. He could be getting even (1989; pp. 43–44).

Notice that in the above excerpt I include a conversation I had with Ed Seeman. I didn't record the details of that conversation in my fieldnotes. Although I recommend that beginning ethnographers write down everything, for some of us who have been at this sort of investigating longer, memory suffices. I *reconstructed* the conversation. Did I leave anything out? Probably. Did I make anything up? Unlikely. One of the rules I use for writing interpretive ethnography is that in the interests of telling a good story it is permissible to omit details that have no bearing on the tale, but it is *not* permissible to make things up.

Sounds good, doesn't it? But what about applying that rule to the line about light catching his Rolex? Did that *actually* happen? Given that there was light in the room and he was wearing the Rolex, it's plausible. But in truth, I thought the line had a certain literary quality to it. I wrote it to make the story *better*.

Now that I've shown that I have rules, but that I also break them, where *do* I draw the ethical line? My answer, which may not be your answer, is admittedly a kind of hedge. All of the good writers I know make productive use of what is commonly referred to as "literary license." I do too. We are *story*tellers. We are creating contexts for interpretation. We write *rhetorically*, which is to say, we try to persuasively adapt our message to our reader's expectations, which means that in the interests of writing a good story, we make use of invention from time to time.

The next entry in my fieldnotes reads:

Followed Seeman back to his office. In the parking lot, I watched him exit his RED Corvette, laughed to myself when I saw him carefully comb his hair before leaving the vehicle. Used some breath spray, too. Then slammed the door. No other car in this lot even comes close to his. He and his vehicle stand out. I snap some photos for the record.

Here is how that fieldnote was translated into the story:

I park my car in the visitor's space and spend a few minutes observing the parking lot. I am big on parking lots as evidence of organizational dramas because in this culture of hypercapitalism and commodity values you are what you drive at least as much as you are what you wear, eat, listen to, or talk about.

This parking lot tells a mundane tale. All the colors are muted and virtually everything has four plain doors and standard-issue tires and wheels. Nothing exotic, no flashy colors, no obvious displays of sensuality or mystique. I am at this point in my musing when Ed pulls in. His vehicle is the clear exception to the rule, a RED, current-generation Corvette.

Very interesting.

He combs his hair before exiting the car, and I get the feeling by the way he slams the door that this is the sort of guy who probably doesn't change his oil regularly or even check its level. A very bad sign. If the guy in charge doesn't pay attention to details, particularly those of a maintenance standard, he is probably the sort of guy who makes up his mind without gathering enough information and then expects others to carry out the work without any new resources (1989, pp. 49–50).

As you can plainly read, much of what was in my fieldnotes was directly trans-ferred to the eventual story. But what is *different* in the story from the account in the fieldnotes? First, I explain my cultural reasoning, actually an enthymeme (that is, a deductive syllogism), about the relationship of parking lots to organi-zational dramas. Clearly that analysis is not in the fieldnotes. It is, however, part of the self-reflection I did while writing the story. Ditto for the association of Ed's door-slamming with his probable managerial style. In both cases, the fieldnotes provided me with the raw materials for my musings. I included the musings in the story because they help readers see things as I do, which, in the conversation we are developing, offers them opportunities to agree or disagree with me. I also included them because they are important to the development of the story. They provide substance within the overall shape of the tale.

For those of you who have read the whole story, you know what happens next. I call a friend of mine who works in Ed's company to see what his account of the issues might be. During the phone call my friend abruptly changes the subject and pretends to be talking to someone else. We agree to speak later. During that conversation I find out that part of the reason Seeman hired me was to help him find a reason to fire my friend. I write, in the story, these lines:

> I decide, at that moment, to take the case. Sometimes you take the case for money, and sometimes you take the case because you think you can do some good in the world, and sometimes you take the case because you don't know any better, This time it was all three, although at the time I didn't know that (1989; p. 51).

Clearly this is a bit of invention on my part. It is also designed to evoke from readers a sense of the kind of attitude and style found in Raymond Chandler detective mysteries. In truth, at this point in my fieldwork, I don't recall having any such thoughts. I decided to take the consulting gig because it seemed interesting and the money was good. It was only later, toward the end of the gig, when I realized that my motives for getting involved became part of the problem I would eventually have to face. I thought I was in control of a situation that was far more complex than I realized at the time. So I wrote that paragraph after the fact, not during the fieldwork. Again, it seemed to me that the storyline allowed it.

The rest of the story includes a lot of the ordinary practices that comprise the activities I perform as a communication consultant: phone calls, interviews with employees, collaboration with a partner on the meaning of the data we were collecting in the company. Most of the material in these scenes is drawn directly from my fieldnotes. Then, in the story, a climactic meeting takes place with Seeman. During this pivotal encounter, he informs my partner and me that we have been duped. He couldn't care less about what we "find " with our "data"; the point of hiring us was to appease his employees. He doesn't even believe there *is* a "communication problem." Furthermore, if we don't write the report in a way that is favorable to him, he'll just hire another consultant who will write the report he wants.

These events happened pretty much as they are given in the story. At the time it was hard news to receive, and the implications were personally and professionally devastating. But the larger meaning of this scene came in the writing of the story. Up until this moment all of the scenes, the episodes of phone calls, interviews, and the like, were staged as components in the "rising action" of the overall drama. This pivotal scene was positioned as the dramatic climax: the place in a drama, or in a detective story, where the original conflict is revealed and ultimately resolved.

As it turned out, this was *not* the end of the case *nor* of the story. A mysterious woman, who had played a supporting role to the character of the detective earlier in the tale, reemerges as the power figure behind Ed Seeman. Her motives for having him hire me, and for requiring me to write a consultant's report that made Seeman out to be a scapegoat instead of the cause of the company's problems, reveal several lessons—*moral* lessons—in the story. First, no matter how much we may believe we are in charge of a situation, and think that we are using free will to make informed choices, chances are good that our part is but a small one in a much larger, more complex, human drama. Second, finding the truth does not always equal acquiring power, nor does knowing the truth necessarily change things for the better. The relationship between communication and truth, for consultants and for researchers alike, is complex and problematic. In real life, as in detective stories, the virtuous are not always rewarded and the wicked are not always punished, or even found guilty. Third, the telling of the story in a detective genre shows how we, as researchers but like detectives, become part of what we are studying by assigning meanings to clues and by interjecting into our accounts our views on the nature of persons and things. We are never detached, neutral observers any more than we are detached, neutral consultants, or detached, neutral writers. Along those same lines, we—researchers and consultants—must be held accountable for whatever it is we help bring about: for ideas, like actions and consulting reports, have consequences.

At the end of "The Consultant as Organizational Detective" I am confronted with these moral lessons, and learn from them. The detective/consultant believes he has done some good in the world and has gotten paid for it; he certainly has discovered some powerful truths and gained some moral lessons. But all of these events have come to him at a precious cost to his worldview, with additional damage done to his professional ethics. Seeman gets a better job in another state, and Stella Mims, the mysterious and powerful woman behind the action, remains as mysterious and powerful as ever. The story ends, rounded off by the hard moral and rhetorical dictates of the genre.

At the end of my fieldnotes about this episode in my consulting life, there was less closure, not more. All of the lessons I learned took longer to understand and to deal with than they did in the story. When I wrote the story, over a year after it happened, I was still smarting from it. I wrote it, in part, to heal myself, to gain narrative control over an experience that would otherwise remain underexamined. Through the writing I created two stories—one about the culture of consulting, another about a journey of self-discovery—that were intricately and experientially intertwined.

In writing, as in speaking, we sometimes come *to know*.

Work Cited

Goodall, H. L., Jr. "On Becoming an Organizational Detective: The Role of Context Sensitivity and Intuitive Logics in Communication Consulting." *Southern Communication Journal* 55.1 (1989): 42–54. Print.

....

Like Goodall, we believe that writing is a way of knowing. Oftentimes we do not fully understand what we know—or what we're seeing—until we write it down and then reflect on it. As Goodall reminds us, good ethnographic writing borrows rhetorical strategies from other genres, especially those that lean on skillful narration. In fiction writing as well as creative nonfiction and journalism, the story is key. The story is what keeps the reader engaged, and helps reader and writer make sense of the experience, be it fact or fiction. However, there is an important difference between fieldwriting and fiction writing: in fieldwriting, researchers must be accountable for the information they present about their informants and the cultures they study. Your accountability is based on the data you gather. Because of this, you must record your notes with accuracy and reflect on them thoughtfully. This double voiced recording process allows you to capture your informants' perspectives alongside of your own. Your goal as a fieldworker is to weave many perspectives together into your fieldstudy.

THE RESEARCH PORTFOLIO:
Reflecting on Your Fieldnotes

In Chapter 1, we called the research portfolio a "behind-the-scenes account of the story of your research" and mentioned four key activities of portfolio keeping: collecting materials, selecting according to your emerging focus, reflecting on the overall data and themes, and projecting as you look forward toward further progress and continue to form your plans. Collecting and selecting are activities that come with the abundance of data you gather and sort. Projecting, as we use it here, is a sophisticated kind of goal setting that naturally emerges as you work with your fieldsite and recognize what more you need to learn.

Reflecting, as we see it, is a skill with which most people need particular practice and strategies. To reflect is to think about your own thinking, to monitor the evidence of your mind's work. Gathering pages and pages of fieldnotes won't help you unless you take the time to reread them and reflect about what they mean. Try writing one- or two-line summaries on stick-on notes or index cards explaining what's important about certain pieces of data and then affix them to your fieldnotes. While you're doing this, you'll begin to understand more about your project and your position in relationship to it. Then you'll get better at choosing material for your research portfolio that's a representation of your work.

As you collect fieldnotes, pictures, and artifacts, data will accumulate quickly. Stick-on notes are particularly useful tools because their small size forces you to summarize succinctly and they're easy to replace as your insights change over the course of your project. Once you have your fieldnotes captioned with a stick-on note, you can lay out the array of data to see what kinds of larger themes emerge.

Writing teachers refer to this type of thinking about thinking as **metacognition**. Metacognitive work, such as periodically taking notes on your notes, helps you with analysis, the complex thinking you'll need to do about what all this data might mean. By monitoring your thinking as your data and research material accumulate and testing your ideas with captions or summaries on stick-on notes, you will begin the process of analysis.

Question Your Notes

FIRST   Choose any of the writing you've already done, based on either the fieldnotes you've already taken or the writing you did in Chapter 1 about your potential project.

SECOND   Choose any of the writing strategies from this chapter's boxes: freewriting, exploratory fieldnotes, expanded notes, clusters or diagrams, or double-entry notes. Now, transform your notes into one of the other formats. You might be surprised by the patterns that emerge. If you turn a freewrite into double-entry notes, for example, you might find a conflict between your feelings and your observations. A diagram of your fieldsite might reveal details you've left out of your notes. The more time you work with your fieldnotes, the more you will learn about your site and yourself.

THIRD   Ask yourself the three questions we introduced in Box 8 (pp. 88—89): What surprises you? What intrigues you? What disturbs you? See what kinds of responses you have to these questions. Keep them as a record. You'll want to consult them later.

By repeating these last three questions continually throughout your participation in a community, you will have a record of how your interpretations and analyses change as you learn more about the place you are exploring.

3

Reading Self, Reading Cultures: Understanding Texts

Your ability to "read" involves texts, but also artifacts, cultures, and yourself. In this chapter you will:

- react and respond to readings
- explore your positions as they relate to a topic
- describe and interpret cultural artifacts
- integrate source material
- learn to work with online communities

We all read differently. Literary theorist Louise Rosenblatt suggests that a reader's main instrument for making meaning is one's self. And meaning is an intertwining of our past reading experiences, current tastes, attitudes about genres and forms, and history of teachers, mentors, friends, and relatives. No one reads exactly as you do because no one has exactly the same experiences.

We also read differently because we have different needs as readers, and we read differently at different times in our lives. You may have a different reaction to a book like *Charlotte's Web*, for example, when you reread it as an adult. When Bonnie read *Little Women* to her daughter, she felt connected with the character of the mother "Marmee," although as a 10-year-old reading *Little Women*, she hadn't noticed the mother at all. We bring our current lives into the reading we do.

The reader performs the poem or the novel, as the violinist performs the sonata. But the instrument on which the reader plays, and from which he evokes the work, is—himself.

—LOUISE ROSENBLATT

As a reader, you have formed tastes and predispositions from your many past experiences. What are your attitudes toward reading? Are you a reluctant reader? Do you like to whip through a book quickly, or do you luxuriate in how an author uses words? Do you read novels differently than textbooks? Poetry differently than magazines and newspapers? Online magazines and Web sites differently than print versions? Do you like to mark your own comments in the margins of a book? Do you respond to your reading in a journal? Do you like to talk with friends in a book club about what you read?

Reading as Negotiation

Meaning itself is a process of negotiation among the reader, the text, and the writer. This negotiation takes place both on and off the page. *On the page* of your mystery novel you may find yourself rereading for clues to the murder as you are reaching the conclusion of the book. But negotiation *off the page* is a less visible process. When you read a poem or hear a song, for example, the words on the page may have little meaning without your off-the-page experience. Sometimes it is through talk with others that you discover new meanings. At other times, knowing about the writer's background helps you negotiate meaning. Your understanding may come entirely through an emotional response. If no other person reads exactly like you do, it follows that no text has the same meaning for another reader. Meaning is a subjective experience.

Reading Cultures as Text and Texts as Culture

Fieldworkers research cultures in the same way as readers approach novels. As you read the following excerpt from the opening of Gloria Naylor's *Mama Day*, we'd like you to "read yourself" into this text. This bestseller about the fictional sea island of Willow Springs invites you into an entire culture—one that you may approach by "stepping out" or one that you may already know by having "stepped in." You may know something about the novel's setting, the Georgia–South Carolina sea islands. You may have vacationed there with your family or worked at one of the hotels. You may have read about or seen a movie set there. In other words, how do you situate yourself as a reader?

You probably approach any text with expectations based on your membership in different subcultures, including your readership preferences, which represent subcultures in themselves. For example, all readers of a particular mystery science fiction writer belong to a subculture, whether they know one another or not. Gloria Naylor is an African American female novelist. What other writers does Naylor remind you of? Does she make you think of other African American women writers, such as Alice Walker or Toni Morrison? If you're male, how will you approach a novel about a black matriarch? Do you think your ethnicity and gender affect the way you read, or are they irrelevant?

We chose this excerpt from a novel because it depicts a fieldworker researching his culture. Reema's boy, though fictional, represents the novice fieldworker—a position you'll take when you enter your fieldsite. He puzzles over an unfamiliar term he hears, "18 & 23," and tries to make sense of it. Notice both what he does as he researches this culture—in which he once lived—and what he forgets to do. As you read, use your subjective experiences to negotiate meaning—your personal background and your history as a reader. Add your response to that of the text. Take notes, pose questions, and write about your process of reading.

Mama Day

Gloria Naylor

Willow Springs. Everybody knows but nobody talks about the legend of Sapphira Wade. A true conjure woman: satin black, biscuit cream, red as Georgia clay: depending upon which of us takes a mind to her. She could walk through a lightning storm without being touched; grab a bolt of lightning in the palm of her hand; use the heat of lightning to start the kindling going under her medicine pot: depending upon which of us takes a mind to her. She turned the moon into salve, the stars into a swaddling cloth, and healed the wounds of every creature walking up on two or down on four. It ain't about right or wrong, truth or lies; it's about a slave woman who brought a whole new meaning to both them words, soon as you cross over here from beyond the bridge. And somehow, some way, it happened in 1823: she smothered Bascombe Wade in his very bed and lived to tell the story for a thousand days. 1823: married Bascombe Wade, bore him seven sons in just a thousand days, to put a dagger through his kidney and escape the hangman's noose, laughing in a burst of flames. 1823: persuaded Bascombe Wade in a thousand days to deed all his slaves every inch of land in Willow

Springs, poisoned him for his trouble, to go on and bear seven sons—by person or persons unknown. Mixing it all together and keeping everything that done shifted down through the holes of time, you end up with the death of Bascombe Wade (there's his tombstone right out of Chevy's Pass), the deeds to our land (all marked back to the very year), and seven sons (ain't Miss Abigail and Mama Day the granddaughters of that seventh boy?). The wild card in all this is the thousand days, and we guess if we put our heads together we'd come up with something—which ain't possible since Sapphira Wade don't live in the part of our memory we can use to form words.

But ain't a soul in Willow Springs don't know that little dark girls, hair all braided up with colored twine, got their "18 & 23's coming down" when they lean too long over them back yard fences, laughing at the antics of little dark boys who got the nerve to be "breathing 18 & 23" with mother's milk still on their tongues. And if she leans there just a mite too long or grins a bit too wide, it's gonna bring a holler straight through the dusty screen door. "Get your bow-legged self 'way from my fence, Johnny Blue. Won't be no 'early 18 & 23's' coming here for me to rock. I'm still raising her." Yes, the *name* Sapphira Wade is never breathed out of a single mouth in Willow Springs. But who don't know that old twisted-lip manager at the Sheraton Hotel beyond the bridge, offering Winky Browne only twelve dollars for his whole boatload of crawdaddies—"tried to 18 & 23 him," if he tried to do a thing? We all sitting here, a hop, skip, and one Christmas left before the year 2000, and ain't nobody told him niggers can read now? Like the menus in his restaurant don't say a handful of crawdaddies sprinkled over a little bowl of crushed ice is almost twelve dollars? Call it shrimp cocktail, or whatever he want—we can count, too. And the price of everything that swims, crawls, or lays at the bottom of The Sound went up in 1985, during the season we had that "18 & 23 summer" and the bridge blew down. Folks didn't take their lives in their hands out there in that treacherous water just to be doing it—ain't that much 18 & 23 in the world.

But that old hotel manager don't make no never mind. He's the least of what we done had to deal with here in Willow Springs. Malaria. Union soldiers. Sandy soil. Two big depressions. Hurricanes. Not to mention these new real estate developers who think we gonna sell our shore land just because we ain't fool enough to live there. Started coming over here in the early '90s, talking "vacation paradise," talking "pic-ture-ess." Like Winky said, we'd have to pick their ass out the bottom of the marsh first hurricane blow through here again. See, they just thinking about building where they ain't got no state taxes—never been and never will be, 'cause Willow Springs ain't in no state. Georgia and South Carolina done tried, though—been trying since right after the Civil War to prove that Willow Springs belong to one or the other of them. Look on any of them old maps they hurried and drew up soon as the Union soldiers pulled out and you can see that the only thing connects us to the mainland is a bridge—and even that gotta be rebuilt after every big storm. (They was talking about steel and concrete way back, but since Georgia and South Carolina couldn't claim the taxes, nobody wanted to shell out for the work. So we rebuild it ourselves when need be, and build it how we need it—strong enough to last till the next big wind. Only need a steel and concrete bridge once every seventy years or so. Wood and pitch is a tenth of the cost and serves us a good sixty-nine years—matter of simple arithmetic.) But anyways, all forty-nine square miles curves like a bow, stretching toward Georgia on the south end and South Carolina on the north, and right smack in the middle where each foot of our bridge sits is the dividing line between them two states.

So who it belong to? It belongs to us—clean and simple. And it belonged to our daddies, and our daddies before them, and them too—what at one time all belonged to Bascombe Wade. And when they tried to trace him and how he got it, found out he wasn't even American. Was Norway-born or something, and the land had been sitting in his family over there in Europe since it got explored and claimed by the Vikings—imagine that. So thanks to the conjuring of Sapphira Wade we got it from Norway or theres about, and if taxes owed, it's owed to them. But ain't no Vikings or anybody else from over in Europe come to us with the foolishness that them folks out of Columbia and Atlanta come with—we was being un-American. And the way we saw it, America ain't entered the question at all when it come to our land: Sapphira was African-born, Bascombe Wade was from Norway, and it was the 18 & 23'ing that went down between them two put deeds in our hands. And we wasn't even Americans when we got it—was slaves. And the laws about slaves not owning nothing in Georgia and South Carolina don't apply, 'cause the land wasn't then—and isn't now—in either of them places. When there was lots of cotton here, and we baled it up and sold it beyond the bridge, we paid our taxes to the U.S. of A. And we keeps account of all the fishing that's done and sold beyond the bridge, all the little truck farming. And later when we had to go over there to work or our children went, we paid taxes out of them earnings. We pays taxes on the telephone lines and electrical wires run over The Sound. Ain't nobody here about breaking the law. But Georgia and South Carolina ain't seeing the shine off a penny for our land, our homes, our roads, or our bridge. Well, they fought each other up to the Supreme Court about the whole matter, and it came to a draw. We guess they got so tired out from that, they decided to leave us be—until them developers started swarming over here like sand flies at a Sunday picnic.

Sure, we coulda used the money and weren't using the land. But like Mama Day told 'em (we knew to send 'em straight over there to her and Miss Abigail), they didn't come huffing and sweating all this way in them dark gaberdine suits if they didn't think our land could make them a bundle of money, and the way we saw it, there was enough land—shoreline, that is—to make us all pretty comfortable. And calculating on the basis of all them fancy plans they had in mind, a million an acre wasn't asking too much. Flap, flap, flap—Lord, didn't them jaws and silk ties move in the wind. The land wouldn't be worth that if they couldn't *build* on it. Yes, suh, she told 'em, and they couldn't build on it unless we *sold* it. So we get ours now, and they get theirs later. You shoulda seen them coattails flapping back across The Sound with all their lies about "community uplift" and "better jobs." 'Cause it weren't about no them now and us later—was them now and us never. Hadn't we seen it happen back in the '80s on St. Helena, Daufuskie, and St. John's? And before that in the '60s on Hilton Head? Got them

folks' land, built fences around it first thing, and then brought in all the build-
ers and high-paid managers from mainside—ain't nobody on them islands
benefited. And the only dark faces you see now in them "vacation paradises" is
the ones cleaning the toilets and cutting the grass. On their own land, mind you,
their own land. Weren't gonna happen in Willow Springs. 'Cause if Mama Day
say no, everybody say no. There's 18 & 23, and there's 18 & 23—and nobody was
gonna trifle with Mama Day's, 'cause she know how to use it—her being a direct
descendant of Sapphira Wade, piled on the fact of springing from the seventh
son of a seventh son—uh, uh. Mama Day say no, everybody say no. No point in
making a pile of money to be guaranteed the new moon will see you scratching at fleas you don't have, or rolling in the marsh like a mud turtle. And if some
was waiting for her to die, they had a long wait. She says she ain't gonna. And
when you think about it, to show up in one century, make it all the way through
the next, and have a toe inching into the one approaching is about as close to
eternity anybody can come.

Well, them developers upped the price and changed the plans, changed
the plans and upped the price, till it got to be a game with us. Winky bought
a motorboat with what they offered him back in 1987, turned it in for a cabin
cruiser two years later, and says he expects to be able to afford a yacht with the
news that's waiting in the mail this year. Parris went from a new shingle roof to
a split-level ranch and is making his way toward adding a swimming pool and
greenhouse. But when all the laughing's done, it's the principle that remains.
And we done learned that anything coming from beyond the bridge gotta be
viewed real, real careful. Look what happened when Reema's boy—the one with
the pear-shaped head—came hauling himself back from one of those fancy colleges mainside, dragging his notebooks and tape recorder and a funny way of
curling up his lip and clicking his teeth, all excited and determined to put Willow
Springs on the map.

We was polite enough—Reema always was a little addle-brained—so you
couldn't blame the boy for not remembering that part of Willow Springs's problems was that it got put on some maps right after the War Between the States.
And then when he went around asking us about 18 & 23, there weren't nothing
to do but take pity on him as he rattled on about "ethnography," "unique speech
patterns," "cultural preservation," and whatever else he seemed to be getting
so much pleasure out of while talking into his little gray machine. He was all
over the place—What 18 & 23 mean? What 18 & 23 mean? And we all told him
the God-honest truth: it was just our way of saying something. Winky was awful,
though, he even spit tobacco juice for him. Sat on his porch all day, chewing
up the boy's Red Devil premium and spitting so the machine could pick it up.
There was enough fun in that to take us through the fall and winter when he
had hauled himself back over The Sound to wherever he was getting what was
supposed to be passing for an education. And he sent everybody he'd talked
to copies of the book he wrote, bound all nice with our name and his signed
on the first page. We couldn't hold Reema down, she was so proud. It's a good
thing she didn't read it. None of us made it much through the introduction,

but that said it all: you see, he had come to the conclusion after "extensive field work" (ain't never picked a boll of cotton or head of lettuce in his life—Reema spoiled him silly), but he done still made it to the conclusion that 18 & 23 wasn't 18 & 23 at all—was really 81 & 32, which just so happened to be the lines of longitude and latitude marking off where Willow Springs sits on the map. And we were just so damned dumb that we turned the whole thing around.

Not that he called it being dumb, mind you, called it "asserting our cultural identity," "inverting hostile social and political parameters." 'Cause, see, being we was brought here as slaves, we had no choice but to look at everything upside-down. And then being that we was isolated off here on this island, everybody else in the country went on learning good English and calling things what they really was—in the dictionary and all that—while we kept on calling things ass-backwards. And he thought that was just so wonderful and marvelous, etcetera, etcetera . . . Well, after that crate of books came here, if anybody had any doubts about what them developers was up to, if there was just a tinge of seriousness behind them jokes about the motorboats and swimming pools that could be gotten from selling a piece of land, them books squashed it. The people who ran the type of schools that could turn our children into raving lunatics—and then put his picture on the back of the book so we couldn't even deny it was him—didn't mean us a speck of good.

If the boy wanted to know what 18 & 23 meant, why didn't he just ask? When he was running around sticking that machine in everybody's face, we was sitting right here—every one of us—and him being one of Reema's, we woulda obliged him. He coulda asked Cloris about the curve in her spine that came from the planting season when their mule broke its leg, and she took up the reins and kept pulling the plow with her own back. Winky woulda told him about the hot tar that took out the corner of his right eye the summer we had only seven days to rebuild the bridge so the few crops we had left after the storm could be gotten over before rot sat in. Anybody woulda carried him through the fields we had to stop farming back in the '80s to take outside jobs—washing cars, carrying groceries, cleaning house—anything—'cause it was leave the land or lose it during the Silent Depression. Had more folks sleeping in city streets and banks foreclosing on farms than in the Great Depression before that.

Naw, he didn't really want to know what 18 & 23 meant, or he woulda asked. He woulda asked right off where Miss Abigail Day was staying, so we coulda sent him down the main road to that little yellow house where she used to live. And she woulda given him a tall glass of ice water or some cinnamon tea as he heard about Peace dying young, then Hope and Peace again. But there was the child of Grace— the grandchild, a girl who went mainside, like him, and did real well. Was living outside of Charleston now with her husband and two boys. So she visits a lot more often than she did when she was up in New York. And she probably woulda pulled out that old photo album, so he coulda seen some pictures of her grandchild, Cocoa, and then Cocoa's mama, Grace. And Miss Abigail flips right through to the beautiful one of Grace resting in her satin-lined coffin. And as she walks him back out to the front porch and points him across the road to a silver trailer where her sister, Miranda, lives, she tells him to grab up and chew a few sprigs of mint grow-ing at the foot of the steps—it'll help kill his thirst in the hot sun. And if he'd known enough to do just that, thirsty or not, he'd know when he got to that silver trailer to stand back a distance calling *Mama, Mama Day*, to wait for her to come out and beckon him near.

He'da told her he been sent by Miss Abigail and so, more likely than not, she lets him in. And he hears again about the child of Grace, her grandniece, who went mainside, like him, and did real well. Was living outside of Charleston now with her husband and two boys. So he visits a lot more often than she did when she was up in New York. Cocoa is like her very own, Mama Day tells him, since she never had no children.

And with him carrying that whiff of mint on his breath, she surely woulda walked him out to the side yard, facing that patch of dogwood, to say she has to end the visit a little short 'cause she has some gardening to do in the other place. And if he'd had the sense to offer to follow her just a bit of the way—then and only then—he hears about that summer fourteen years ago when Cocoa came visiting from New York with her first husband. Yes, she tells him, there was a first husband—a stone city boy. How his name was George. But how Cocoa left, and he stayed. How it was the year of the last big storm that blew her pecan trees down and even caved in the roof of the other place. And she woulda stopped him from walking just by a patch of oak: she reaches up, takes a bit of moss for him to put in them closed leather shoes—they're probably sweating his feet something terrible, she tells him. And he's to sit on the ground, right there, to untie his shoes and stick in the moss. And then he'd see through the low bush that old graveyard just down the slope. And when he looks back up, she woulda disappeared through the trees; but he's to keep pushing the moss in them shoes and go on down to that graveyard where he'll find buried Grace, Hope, Peace, and Peace again. Then a little ways off a grouping of seven old graves, and a little ways off seven older again. All circled by them live oaks and hanging moss, over a rise from the tip of The Sound.

Everything he needed to know coulda been heard from that yellow house to that silver trailer to that graveyard. Be too late for him to go that route now, since Miss Abigail's been dead for over nine years. Still, there's an easier way. He could just watch Cocoa any one of these times she comes in from Charles-ton. She goes straight to Miss Abigail's to air out the rooms and unpack her bags, then she's across the road to call out at Mama Day, who's gonna come to the door of the trailer and wave as Cocoa heads on through the patch of dogwoods to that oak grove. She stops and puts a bit of moss in her open-toe sandals, then goes on past those graves to a spot just down the rise toward The Sound, a little bit south of that circle of oaks. And if he was patient and stayed off a little ways, he'd realize she was there to meet up with her first husband so they could talk about that summer fourteen years ago when she left, but he stayed. And as her and George are there together for a good two hours or so—neither one saying a word—Reema's boy coulda heard from them everything there was to tell about 18 & 23.

But on second thought, someone who didn't know how to ask wouldn't know how to listen. And he coulda listened to them the way you been listening to us right now. Think about it: ain't nobody really talking to you. We're sitting here in Willow Springs, and you're God-knows-where. It's August 1999—ain't but a slim chance it's the same season where you are. Uh, huh, listen. Really listen this time: the only voice is your own. But you done just heard about the legend of Sapphira Wade, though nobody here breathes her name. You done heard it the way we know it, sitting on our porches and shelling June peas, quieting the midnight cough of a baby, taking apart the engine of a car—you done heard it without a single living soul really saying a word. Pity, though, Reema's boy couldn't listen, like you, to Cocoa and George down by them oaks—or he woulda left here with quite a story.

BOX**9**

Responding to Text

PURPOSE

We hope you found yourself reading the excerpt from *Mama Day* more than once. We did. When each of us first read it, we realized we needed to read it again. Bonnie's interest in the character of the bumbling young researcher, Reema's boy, focused her reading so that she excluded other characters. Elizabeth found herself looking at Naylor's map, imagining how close it might be to where she lives in North Carolina. As Elizabeth read the code word "18 & 23," she found herself trying to substitute other words each time she encountered it. But as we reread the text together for the purpose of writing this book, we talked about it and found ourselves discovering much more. We began to read the text in two ways: one as a parody of fieldworking and the other as a rich fictional account of a cultural group with its own codes, behaviors, stories, and rituals.

ACTION

Describe your own process of reading and rereading *Mama Day* in a page or two. If you're keeping a journal or a process log, you might want to use these questions to guide your response:

- What assumptions did you bring to this text? About this region's geography? This group of sea islanders? Rural families and their belief systems and values?

- What other books have you read or movies have you seen that this excerpt reminds you of? In what ways?

- How do your previous reading experiences affect the way you appreciate Naylor's writing? How would you describe Naylor's style?

- What was hard for you to understand in this text? Which words, phrases, or paragraphs made you stop and reread? How did you solve this problem?

- What stood out for you? Where in the text did you find yourself entertained? Immersed? Confused?

- What information was helpful as you read the first time? In your second reading, what did you discover that you missed the first time?

- Which of the characters interested you most, and why? Cocoa? Mama Day? Reema's boy? Sapphira Wade? The narrator?

- What details of the setting involved your imagination? When you share your response with your colleagues, notice how they might have read differently.

RESPONSE

Our student Janet Ingram responded to this reading in her journal:

I immediately remembered a road trip my family took to Hilton Head when I was in high school. Even though my dad had a meeting there, my family couldn't afford a hotel, so we all stayed at a nearby Day's Inn. The "southern hospitality" was awesome. Since this was our family's first trip to the South, we expected to hear deep accents and were surprised that not everybody had one, but we still had trouble understanding some people. My sister and I took a tour of the Sea Islands, which reminded me of the movie *Daughters of the Dust*, the story of the Gullahs in the early twentieth century. The tour guide told us about the Gullahs having had their property stolen from them so Hilton Head could develop as it now is. I had known about that from some National Public Radio programs I heard a few years back. We heard samples of the Gullah language when we stopped at a museum. The movie and programs and the boat ride on this trip influenced my visualization of the events in *Mama Day*.

But it was still hard for me to see what Gloria Naylor was doing with the 18 & 23 code in this reading. I found it both distracting and annoying. I was so confused that I completely missed the story until I read it a second time, and then a third time, which cleared some things up for me. Sapphira Wade was my favorite character because she is larger than real life. Somehow, she smothers a man and then marries him, bears him seven sons, and puts a dagger through his kidney. She must have been quite a woman to have killed the same man so many times.

As a reader, I felt sorry for Reema's boy since all of his relatives and former acquaintances in Willow Springs withheld information from him, which then made him look foolish. He was just trying to be a good researcher, taking notes and asking questions and all that. I guess he wasn't a very good listener and that seems to be the reason why we read this piece in the first place. I hope to do better with my own research project.

The kinds of questions that we list in Box 9 can be asked of any text you read. Reading any complex text can also involve reading a culture. In the excerpt from *Mama Day*, we see culture's ordinary life in dailiness that fieldworkers always try to penetrate—catching crawdaddies, chewing tobacco, truck farming. But we also see this culture's uniqueness through Naylor's specific characters and setting.

With the character of Reema's pear-headed nameless boy, Naylor offers us a parody of a field researcher. He is an insider, born on the island, but his college education had so shaped him that he was unable, even as an insider, to do what fieldworkers need to do: listen, observe, and participate in the life of the people he studied. Even the residents of Willow Springs knew more about how to do his fieldwork than he did: "If the boy wanted to know what 18 & 23 meant, why didn't he just ask?" The narrator concludes that a researcher who doesn't know how to form questions would never be in a position to understand answers.

You'll need to think about how your background can affect what you see in another culture just as it does when you read a written text. What you see is affected by who you are. Your education, geography, family history, personal experiences, race, gender, or nationality can influence the way you do research. Learning to read a culture like a text is similar to learning to read a text like a culture.

Positioning: Reading and Writing about Yourself

As we conduct our fieldwork, we must be conscious of ourselves as the key instruments of the research process. When you begin to research a site, you will need to "read" yourself in the same way that you have deciphered texts, and you will want to write that perspective into your study. Had Reema's boy thought or written about his insider status, education and field training, family history, and geography, he might have asked different questions and gotten different answers. Instead of leaving out personal, subjective information, fieldworkers should write it in.

In fieldwork, **positioning** includes all the subjective responses that affect how the researcher sees data. Readers of ethnography sometimes wonder how this kind of research could be considered social "science" if the researcher is not offering "objective" data. In fact, fieldworkers achieve a type of objectivity through **intersubjectivity**, the method of connecting as many different perspectives on the same data as possible. These multiple sources encourage the fieldworker to interpret patterns and interrelationships among various accounts alongside the researcher's own account and to leave other interpretations open as well.

Being the researcher so influences your fieldwork that it would be deceptive *not* to include relevant background information about yourself in your study. From our own experiences as fieldworkers, we believe that as a researcher you position or situate yourself in relationship to your study in at least three ways: fixed, subjective, and textual.

Fixed Positions

Fixed positions are the personal facts that might influence how you see your data—your age, gender, class, nationality, race—factors that do not change during the course of the study but are often taken for granted and unexamined in the research process. Does it matter that you are middle-aged and studying adolescents? Or that you grew up on a kibbutz in Israel? Does being a middle-class African American affect the way you interpret the lives of homeless African Americans?

Our word *fixed* is problematic; nothing is truly "fixed." Sometimes fixed factors are subjected to change during the research process, and then that, too, demands the researcher's attention. If, for example, a male researcher looking at the play behaviors of preschool children becomes the father of a girl during his study, he may find himself looking at his fieldsite data through a different lens. If what originally seemed a fixed influence in the researcher's position becomes more fluid, then that process of changed perspectives would become part of the researcher's data.

Subjective Positions

Subjective positions such as life history and personal experiences may also affect your research. Someone who grew up in a large extended or blended family will see the eating, sleeping, and conversation patterns of groups differently than someone from a small nuclear family. Many people who grew up in large families confess that they learned to eat quickly at family meals because they wanted to get their fair share before the food disappeared.

Textual Positions

Textual positions—the language choices you make to represent what you see—affect the writing of both fieldnotes and the final ethnographic report. The way that you position yourself in the field with respect to the people you study—how close or how far away you focus your research lens—determines the kind of data you'll gather, the voice you'll create in your finished text, and to some extent your credibility as a researcher.

BOX 10

Positioning Yourself

PURPOSE

This activity will help you uncover the assumptions, preconceptions, personal experiences, and feelings that influence you as a fieldworker by writing about them throughout your research process. In this way, you will become conscious of your positioning as a researcher.

ACTION

Writing short commentaries regularly will help you understand how fixed, subjective, and textual positions affect your continuing research process. You can do the following exercise while considering a site or subculture you might want to research, or at any stage of the research process.

Ask yourself: What are your reasons for choosing this particular subculture? Which of your own "fixed positions" may affect what you see? What "subjective positions" do you carry into your site? Then, write a short commentary describing how your positions might affect what you'll see at your fieldsite.

RESPONSE

Cary Cotton studied an after-school program for Spanish-speaking public school students called Latino Impact for his undergraduate senior honors project. His writing allows him to discover that his fixed and subjective positions might affect the textual position he will take as he writes. As you read Cary's response, notice how he blends these positions while thinking about his fieldsite:

> I am a white, 22-year-old male from an upper-middle-class family in the Washington, DC, suburbs. I spent the first 17 years of my life in the city, and moved southward to North Carolina thereafter. I am finishing an undergraduate degree in English and intend to matriculate into medical school. I have mostly lived in the medium-sized city-towns that characterize much of North Carolina. My parents grew up in very rural parts of Kentucky, so I've been out of the metropolis regularly throughout my life. I am culturally of the mainstream, which may explain my attempt to speak the dominant discourse of middle-class English within these programs. I grew up watching *I Love Lucy* and the Discovery Channel. I played soccer in my suburban neighborhood and watched MTV.
>
> My subjects are Latino students at a middle school in North Carolina. They belong to an afterschool program called Latino Impact designed to keep Latino youth from going astray during their teen years. It is encompassed by a greater community program that offers service to Latinos that would mostly be useful to new immigrants who don't speak English (document translation, free health and legal services, interfacing with insurance companies and landlords). The students are almost entirely the children of families who use services of the community group. So, my subjects mostly come from families that have very limited resources and do

BOX**10** continued

not speak English but have developed a community support system. I assumed my subjects would share the demographics I had observed in the greater Latino community group. This turned out to be the case, although it was not obvious from the way they spoke and dressed. They would be hard to pick out of a lineup of regular middle school students.

I'm very concerned about being rejected. I worry that this fear will prevent me from reaching out. At least, I think I will tiptoe into the lives of my subjects instead of diving in. I think young people like me are more able to cross social boundaries. I don't know why this is, but maybe it's because we are all exposed to the same things. For example, my subjects and I have played the same video games, we watch the same things on TV, and we experience the same public school curriculum. We both know what Snookie and Lady Gaga are up to. As a young person interacting with young subjects, I hope this works in my favor, but it could also leave me more exposed and the integrity of my intentions open for judgment. Though we are from different places, I thought we would share membership in a common culture. This preconception was affirmed in some ways. We were exposed to the same media and played the same video games (some students played them in class). However, there were differences as well. My subjects were seven or eight years younger than me and for that reason, and because of our different cultural backgrounds, watch different TV programs than I do. One central subject in my study mostly watched TV shows with Latino characters and was particularly apt to quote George Lopez. Despite our interest in different programs, we found a strange resonance in the fact that I also obsessed over an old sitcom when I was his age.

I presume that we have different experiences in the values and practices of our families. I have never ventured out of the United States but I do speak Spanish, although rather poorly. I can understand others speaking in Spanish almost completely, though. My education, while it makes an effort at being culturally inclusive, is limited to American high schools and universities. I didn't work in high school and only worked a little in college, whereas some of my subjects spend more time supporting their family than they do at school. While we both attended public schools, my subjects attend a semirural school with a median family income beneath the national average. I attended a relatively wealthy suburban high school. Most of my family attended college, but many of my subjects are the children of first-generation immigrants who did not attend college in this country. My assumption was that this would strongly influence the values of my subjects. I found some divergence in this as well. One subject was very interested in higher education and this interest was instilled by her parents. Another subject had to work many hours outside of school at a family business. He felt that school was a distraction from work and his family at least partly agreed. While my expectations that the very different family history of my subjects would shape their values were correct, I found it very difficult to predict the individual manifestations of this cultural difference.

My political opinions, like those of the university, are relatively left-leaning. My ideas about social justice and educational equality certainly permeate this study just as they do the theory and research on which it is constructed. However, sometimes

I worry that they are presumptuous or paternalistic. For this reason, I feel a little queasy about speaking Spanish with my subjects, especially bad Spanish. If speaking is a way of culturally identifying oneself, it seems to say, "I am able to mimic your way of talking and being but haven't made the effort to actually become or embrace it." If I were asked why I chose to speak Spanish when my subjects speak perfect English, I don't know how I would answer. If I'm doing it to be a part of his or her culture, was I invited? My concern that I would be seen as an impostor was mostly shattered. The kids readily accepted me as a friend. However, I felt that the other Latino volunteers my age were less accepting of me and were very guarded and distrusting throughout the study.

Understanding Positioning: Checking In on Yourself

Throughout the process of conducting your fieldstudy, you'll need to continue to ask how who you are affects how you understand yourself and your fieldwork. In Chapter 2, we offered you three questions to help you monitor your assumptions, stances, and blind spots:

- What surprised me?
- What intrigued me?
- What disturbed me?

These questions help provide ways of "checking in" on yourself as well as ways of interrogating the different features of your positions as you bring them to your study. This kind of monitoring will eventually help you see how your fixed and subjective positions contribute to the textual voice you'll develop as you write about your topic. Even more important, checking in will heighten your awareness of the extent to which the instrument of your data gathering is not statistical information or a computer program or an experiment but *you*—with all of your assumptions, preconceptions, past experiences, and complex feelings.

A humorous essay by Laura Bohannan about her fieldwork experience in West Africa, "Shakespeare in the Bush," illustrates the importance of checking in on yourself—on your assumptions, expectations, and feelings—throughout your research experiences. In "Shakespeare in the Bush," Bohannan, an anthropologist, exposes how she tried to import the "universal" message of *Hamlet* to the Tiv tribe she was studying in Africa.

At one point in the essay, Bohannan decides to skip summarizing the famous "To be or not to be" speech because she feels her listeners would misinterpret it. They have already approved of Claudius quickly marrying Hamlet's mother soon after her husband's murder—something Western audiences usually condemn. Bohannan then proceeds to try to explain Hamlet's father's "ghost" to her audience. She finds herself interrupted at every turn in the telling of what she had previously thought to be a "universal" and "transcultural" story:

> I decided to skip the soliloquy. Even if Claudius was here thought quite right to marry his brother's widow, there remained the poison motif, and I knew they would disapprove of fratricide. More hopefully I resumed, "That night Hamlet kept watch with the three who had seen his dead father. The dead chief again appeared, and although the others were afraid, Hamlet followed his dead father off to one side. When they were alone, Hamlet's dead father spoke."
>
> "Omens can't talk!" The old man was emphatic.
>
> "Hamlet's dead father wasn't an omen. Seeing him might have been an omen, but he was not." My audience looked as confused as I sounded. "It *was* Hamlet's dead father. It was a thing we call a 'ghost.'" I had to use the English word, for unlike many of the neighboring tribes, these people didn't believe in the survival after death of any individuating part of the personality.
>
> "What is a 'ghost'? An omen?"
>
> "No, a 'ghost' is someone who is dead but who walks around and can talk, and people can hear him and see him but not touch him."
>
> They objected. "One can touch zombis."
>
> "No, no! It was not a dead body the witches had animated to sacrifice and eat. No one else made Hamlet's dead father walk. He did it himself."
>
> "Dead men can't walk," protested my audience as one man.
>
> I was quite willing to compromise. "A 'ghost' is a dead man's shadow."
>
> But again they objected. "Dead men cast no shadows."
>
> "They do in my country," I snapped.

To appreciate the full scope of Bohannan's mistaken assumptions, read her complete essay online. As you read, you'll want to notice the ways the author monitors herself as she relates the story of Hamlet to the audience of informants she is trying to win over through her storytelling.

Bohannan's essay also raises the many ethical issues she faced in the field. Should she drink beer in the morning with her informants? Should she try to change parts of *Hamlet* to make the story more culturally relevant to her audience? Should she defend the way her own culture thinks of family relationships when clearly her audience thinks differently? Although Bohannan constructs herself textually as a bewildered fieldworker in "Shakespeare in the Bush," she also makes it clear that the ethical issues she faced are serious ones, worthy of lengthier consideration than she was able to give them in this essay.

The mental checking Bohannan does in this reading is what we are suggesting you do as well, seeing yourself as outsiders like the Tiv might see you. Try to think, as Bohannan did, about your own cultural assumptions as you encounter others in the fieldstudy.

BOX**11**

Unlearning Our Privilege

MIMI HARVEY, SHORELINE COMMUNITY COLLEGE, SEATTLE, WASHINGTON

Mimi Harvey designed the following exercise for her students based on the fieldwork she did as a student herself. Mimi wrote this reflection when she was on a fellowship in Korea.

PURPOSE

To discover and reflect on the forces of privilege and power that position you as researcher and your participants as coresearchers in your research.

ACTION

Make a list of all the privileges you have. Include those that you enjoy through your own efforts (for example, an educational scholarship that you have thanks to your hard work and good grades). Also include privileges that require no effort on your part. Think, for example, about being born into a middle-class family or of having American citizenship. How might these privileges affect your field research? Some areas to think and write reflectively about are

- Age
- Nationality
- Gender
- Skin color, race, or ethnicity
- Education level or opportunities
- Social and/or financial support
- Freedom of religion or of speech or freedom to travel
- Socioeconomic status

By thinking about your own privileges, you will think about the privilege and power that your participants possess—or don't.

BOX11 continued

I spent a year with Indonesian migrant workers in Korea, sorting through issues of power and privilege. Korea has the money to employ laborers from other countries, and these workers were the focus of my study. I reflected on my identity as a white, Western, educated researcher.

I am, in certain ways, a "comrade"—introduced by the migrant workers as "someone who supports our struggle for legalization and for human and labor rights. She has accompanied us on all our rallies and struggle activities."

These are two sides of the same coin. My whiteness, socioeconomic status, and education create borders and boundaries, ones I cannot and would not want to cross. It is clear to me that there are certain ways my status is not open to change: *"Mimi, sebagai seorang Barat, lebih peka, lebih sensitive"* ("Mimi is a Westerner and therefore more refined, more sensitive"), Boedhi says to Samsul to explain why he must call me more often and be more polite and attentive to me.

I ask myself, "Am I a true border crosser? A Borderlands dweller?" I must always be aware of the possibilities and limits of such a position.

My dilemmas are directly tied to my ethical beliefs and commitment to the migrant workers I have marched beside. I am in solidarity with them in their struggle to force the government to give them legal status and to honor their internationally recognized human and labor rights. I cannot be neutral in this research. I am not neutral. I care. I am committed.

How can I give back to my participants beyond what I have done so far? Translating, urging of solidarity, witnessing and hearing the stories of the workers, a few treats, food occasionally. I regularly offer to teach English at shelters, churches, and the Myongdong tent city. But it is difficult for the migrant workers to find the time and the motivation to come to a class when they are working 14 to 18 hours, six or even seven days and nights a week.

Approaching fieldwork from this perspective demands a constant awareness of realities—power and privileges—for both the researcher and the informants. If I am working at the "hyphens"—at the Borderlands in Korea—I must be conscious of my multiple, overlapping, and contradictory identities. I cannot make the migrant workers into the "other." I will, indeed, only ever have a partial perspective. I will never be able to see the whole picture.

These issues and concerns stuck to me like cockleburs throughout my year of fieldwork in Indonesia and South Korea. They cling to me still at my desk here in the Western world. At least once a week, I get a phone call from one or another of the Indonesian migrant workers who shared their lives with me. When our talk of manhunts, deportations, and crackdowns becomes too depressing, they ask me about my life in *surga dunia* (earthly heaven)—their imagined picture of Canada and the United States. I try to tell them honestly that, while "heavenly" in some respects, it is certainly not perfect here. There is growing fear and suspicion of "illegal aliens" and legal immigrants here, too. Each time I weave their stories with mine, these words echo: we must always be "unlearning our privilege."

Getting Permission

When you enter a fieldsite and make yourself known, you must follow many courtesies to make yourself and the people you're observing feel comfortable. All places in which you are a participant-observer involve an official process for "negotiating entry." As a beginning researcher, don't enter a site where you feel at risk in the subculture. For the kinds of projects this book suggests, you will not have adequate time to gain entry or insider status in an intimidating group. One of our students, for example, wanted to research a group of campus skinheads. They permitted Jake to hang out on the edges of their subculture, even allowing him to read their "code of honor," which included these statements:

- Be discreet about new recruits; check them out thoroughly.
- For prospects, we must have at least a 90-day contact period in which we can attest to your character. A probationary period and productivity report will be given.
- Outsiders need no knowledge of what goes on or is said in our meetings.
- No racial exceptions whatsoever! All members must be 100 percent white!

Early on, Jake began to realize that his research position was unworkable, that he was stuck. While the skinheads had let him into their subculture as a potential recruit, he could never fully enter their subculture or worldview. Their code of honor, which excluded minority groups, stood against his personal ethics. In an early portfolio reflection, Jake wrote, "I never hung out with them in public. I never went to an organizational meeting. I realized I was an outsider to this subculture."

Jake's negotiation experience was so dramatic that he was unable to gain full access, and so he was unable to collect the data he wanted. No matter how interested in and enthusiastic we are about a possible fieldsite, we must be conscious of our own comfort levels and even potential dangers in investigating certain groups or places.

Harvey DuMarce, another of our students, experienced difficulty negotiating entry into a fieldsite owing mainly to his own assumption that it would be easy for him to do so. He is a Native American, a Sioux, who wanted to research a gambling casino on another tribe's reservation. Because of his heritage, he assumed that he would be welcomed. But he wasn't. He had enormous difficulty finding people who were willing to talk to him, and he never really knew whether it was because of his Sioux background or because he was perceived as a student. Eventually, he had a conversation with the woman who ran the gift shop at the casino, and she introduced him to others. As his informant, she helped him gain an insider status in a place where he had assumed he already had it.

Any fieldsite you enter requires that you be conscious of your own personal assumptions and how they reflect your ethics, but you must also be respectful of the people whose lives you are watching. It is common courtesy for research-ers to acknowledge time spent with informants with gestures as small as writ-ing thank-you notes or as large as exchanging time (tutoring or babysitting, for example) or obtaining grant-funded stipends to pay them. As you work your way through the process of getting permission or "negotiating entry," be sure to follow the guidelines in the box below.

Guidelines for Negotiating Entry

- Explain your project clearly to the people you will study, and obtain the requisite permission from those in charge.

- Let your informants understand what part of the study you'll share with them.

- Think about what you can give back to the fieldsite in exchange for your time there.

Some sites may require official documentation, as in the case of two of our students who collaborated on a study of a day-care center. The center required them to have an interview, submit a proposal describing their project, and sign a document attesting that they had reviewed all of the center's rules and proce-dures. Entry might be simple, laborious, or even impossible. For this reason, don't wait too long to make yourself visible to the insiders you study. One stu-dent we worked with spent over a month in the field observing a Disney store. When she attempted to get official permission to write about this store, however, she was denied entry and could not continue her project.

Once you finalize your site, you might want to check with your instructor to find out your university's policy with respect to research on human subjects. For long-term projects, the university's **human subjects review board** usually requires that you file a proposal and submit permission forms from your infor-mants. They are called "**informed consent** forms," and on the facing page we present a sample of one of our own forms as a model. Universities usually have less formal procedures for the kind of short-term fieldwork that you might do for a one-semester course, and often have no requirements for filing permis-sions. Fieldworkers, no matter what size their projects, are ethically respon-sible for accurately showing the voices of their informants on the page. We feel strongly that you should receive permission from all the informants whose work you audio or video record as well as from any official person at your fieldsite.

The Ethics of Fieldwork: A Brief History

Whether you're conducting a long-term project with formal permission or a classroom-based study with a short informed consent from each informant, it's important to understand a bit of the history of human subjects review for research. In 1974, the National Research Act established the National Commission for the Protection of Human Subjects of Biomedical and Behavioral Research. Members of the Commission came from diverse disciplines, including medicine, law, religion, and bioethics, and their job was to identify the basic ethical principles that should underlie research with human subjects. Prior to this time, there had been far too many cases of research that harmed its subjects. In 1979, five years after their first meeting, the Commission published

---

Mary Smith
Dormitory Hall
State University
City, State
Telephone number

I give my permission to Mary Smith to use my written and spoken words in her research project written for "Composition/English 102" at State University. I understand that I may read and approve the final draft of the material she uses about me in her project.

Signature: _____ Date: _____

Address: _____

_____

Telephone number: _____

I prefer to use this pseudonym: _____

Informed consent form

what's commonly called "the Belmont Report," which identifies three basic principles relevant to the ethics of research involving human subjects:

1. Respect for Persons   Informants should participate in research studies voluntarily and have enough information to make a decision about their participation. If you expect to interview a nurse, for example, and follow her throughout her clinical day or even meet her at home, you would need to inform her of your plan and see if she is willing and available to give you that much of her time.

2. Beneficence   Researchers should protect informants against risk from harm and also from the loss of any substantial benefit that might be gained from research. Let's say, for instance, you're working with a punk rock band that has fallen on hard times. You write an exciting essay about their ups and downs. You sell it to a magazine. In this instance, you are profiting from their story. As an ethical researcher, you should either share the profits or not sell the story.

3. Justice   We need to select our informants fairly, without creating undue pressure, especially for people who already experience burdens. In this country, for example, in the 1940s, the Tuskegee syphilis study used disadvantaged, rural black men to study the untreated course of a disease that is by no means confined to that population.

These three principles from the Belmont Report cover the ethics of research in the United States in all disciplines across research communities. Whether you're working in a lab on stem-cell research, studying the behavior of penguins, working in a soup kitchen, or writing about a punk rock band, the basic ethics are the same—respect for persons, beneficence, and justice.

BOX12

From Ethos to Ethics

JULIE CHEVILLE, ILLINOIS STATE UNIVERSITY, NORMAL, ILLINOIS

PURPOSE

"Ethos" in speakers' or writers' texts implies their ethics, and it emerges in writing or speech as their credibility: When my students and I read *Mama Day*, many of us sympathize with Reema's boy. The tactical errors of a college student turned fieldworker hit close to home. And they raise imposing questions. How do we enter a cultural space and earn the trust of insiders? And how, as outsiders just stepping in, do we recognize the essence of identities and relationships?

I like to read this selection from *Mama Day* to students so we can concentrate less on processing language than on listening to the rich images of character and culture. I ask groups of students to notice particular "informants" so that when we finish the story, we can interpret the lives Naylor writes about without obsessing first on the question of "18 & 23." Rather than attend to the single and most obvious question, as Reema's boy does, we focus on informants' habits of mind, language, and body—all features of cultural life that answer the question implicitly.

While notetaking and recording are essential field techniques, they can become liabilities and get a fieldworker into trouble. For Reema's boy, these tools are a means to his particular end—the "truth" about "18 & 23." But in the same way that Sapphira Wade "ain't about truth or lies," the culture that memorializes her resists a single interpretation. When Reema's boy contrives his own interpretation, the residents resist him. For the descendants of Sapphira Wade, "18 & 23" represents the totality of the unsaid.

From the experiences of Reema's boy, we understand that entering the field is not about exerting oneself on others but about emerging into delicate relationships with those who guide us where they choose. In this way, our credibility, or "ethos," arises from our receptiveness to what and to whom we're introduced.

So how do fieldworkers position themselves without overriding informants' identities, relationships, and histories? This is where this excerpt from *Mama Day* invites a discussion of ethics. As you'll learn in this book, fieldworkers by profession rely on written ethical principles to monitor their interactions. These principles ensure that research involving human subjects protects the welfare of all involved. In this activity, you will research many of the professional codes that govern fieldworkers in a variety of disciplines.

ACTION

In small groups, analyze the online ethics statements of some of the professional organizations that monitor fieldwork. Here are a few of them:

American Anthropological Association

Association of Internet Researchers

American Folklore Society

American Psychological Association

American Sociological Association

Museum Ethnographers Group

The Society of Professional Journalists

Each group can study a single statement for principles that might have helped Reema's boy to make more sensitive choices. As a class, talk about the strengths of each association's code. From this discussion, you may either come to consensus about the code that seems most relevant to your work or create a code of your own. During fieldwork, as you encounter particular dilemmas, you will be able to use the guidelines to identify options and obligations.

BOX 12 continued

RESPONSE

Here is the preamble the students in one of my classes wrote:

Preamble

We have created this code of ethics to guide our behavior as we enter fieldwork. Because our subcultures are not the same, we will face different ethical questions. This code of ethics will help us to remember our responsibilities to informants and to their perspectives and histories. As researchers, we understand the importance of the following:

1. Before fieldwork begins, we should explain the process and purposes of our project to members of the subculture. This should be done in such a way that allows informants an opportunity to ask questions. We should avoid using technical language that informants might not understand, and we should listen and respond to each question they ask.

2. Before fieldwork begins, we should understand that the purpose of our research is not to put a subculture "on the map." We must focus on accurate portraits of those we observe and interview. Final products should be shared with informants before they are due. This should be done either orally or in writing, in whatever form our informants choose.

3. During fieldwork, we should protect the anonymity of informants at all times. Whenever possible, we should offer our services and support as a way of compensating for the help our informants provide us.

4. We should develop interview questions that reflect not just what we don't understand but, most important, what informants say and do. As much as possible, we should take part in rituals of the subculture so that our questions arise from the actual behaviors and objects that are important to members. We should never let notetaking or audio-recording become the most important ritual.

5. We should make conclusions about a subculture based on beliefs that are shared across several informants. We should realize that the emphasis in field research is not on discovering the truth but on discovering how informants perceive their subculture.

Reading an Object: The Cultural Artifact

As you enter the field, you should train yourself to notice material objects—**artifacts**—that represent the culture of that site. Objects are readable texts. As you read an object, your position as researcher affects your reading just as it affects the way you read a fieldsite. You can investigate the surface details of an object, research its history, or learn about people's rules and rituals for using and making the object. Researchers—folklorists and anthropologists—use the term **material culture** to refer to those personal artifacts loaded with meaning and history that people mark as special: tools, musical instruments, foods, toys, jewelry, ceremonial objects, and clothes.

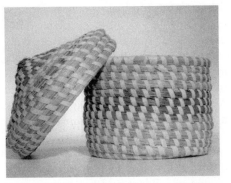

(Photos: Bruce Drummond)

South Carolina Low Country coil basket

As you look at the photographs of the basket above, think about the kinds of questions you might want to ask the owner or the basketmaker. How is it made? How old is it? What is it used for?

On the surface, it is a woven basket with a lid. But the basket holds a coiled history, a collection of stories that belongs to its makers, its sellers, and its owners. The basket itself is an artifact produced by several interconnected cultures. It is made by African American women on the coast of South Carolina, near the city of Charleston, not far from Gloria Naylor's fictional Willow Springs. The basketmakers use natural materials (coastal sweetgrass, palmetto fronds, and pine needles) found on the southeastern coast of the United States, much like the plants their ancestors knew on the western coast of Africa. These baskets come out of a strong craft tradition of using available materials to make everyday objects. It is a tradition that daughters learn from mothers, who learned it from their mothers, who learned it from their mothers. The basketmaking technique represents a long chain of informal instruction over many generations of craftswomen. And each generation—in fact, each basketmaker herself—adds her own technique and her own circumstances to what she has learned. During their years of American slavery, for example, African American women modified kitchen implements, such as spoons, to create the tools they needed to continue making baskets according to their traditional designs.

But knowing the history of this craft and even holding the basket in your hand does not speak about the object the way the maker does. When Bonnie interviewed a basketmaker in the Charleston marketplace, a middle-aged woman named Wilma, she learned more than the observable and historical details we described here. Bonnie was already positioned by knowing the history of this craft from reading about the tradition and having heard her mentor, folklorist Burt Feintuch, lecture on exactly this topic. So when she visited Charleston, she was eager to find a basketmaker who would talk about her craft. Bonnie wanted to buy one of Wilma's baskets, one with a beautifully tight-fitting top. As they examined it together, Wilma explained the challenge of pulling the fresh sweetgrass, weaving in palmetto fronds, and keeping the pine needles fresh enough to bend. After the basket is finished, Wilma said, it is important to coil it all carefully and work it with an awl-like tool made from a spoon. Bonnie complimented her on the top.

"Oh, I didn't make this," Wilma answered as she stroked the top that fit so well. "My cousin is the only person in the family who can make a tight top. My tops just float around. She's good at making tops. I'm good at selling them." This conversation contained important firsthand information about the stories that lie inside cultural objects. The information from Wilma—about the awl-like tool made from a spoon, and the separate roles she and her cousin took—explained that the craft of basketmaking, like much folk art, is a collective endeavor that involves not only a long history of instruction but also a family of craftspeople who establish rules, determine roles, and invent new methods to carry on an old tradition. Bonnie's subjective positioning from her knowledge of folklore and her history as a basket collector affected the way she "read" Wilma's basket. And Wilma's story of her family's craft unpacked another layer of meaning and cultural knowledge.

BOX 13

Reading an Artifact

BETH CAMPBELL, MARSHALL UNIVERSITY, SOUTH CHARLESTON, WEST VIRGINIA

PURPOSE

The everyday objects people use inside a culture are often so utilitarian and taken for granted that the members of the culture don't recognize them as being important or symbolic of their history. An outsider is more likely to notice them and wonder where the objects come from, what they're used for, who makes them, and why they're made the way they are. All of these facts become clues to the traditions, rituals, values, rules, and behavior of a cultural group.

Our colleague and friend, Beth Campbell, shares an exercise she developed for her class, using the "inscribed artifact" of the tattoo. Tattoos, while they're now almost mainstream in our culture, have a long history of cultural meanings. Beth writes:

We often think of artifacts as connected with archaeology: potsherds, for example, or projectile points and stone tools. But things that are *inscribed* are artifacts too: cave paintings, hieroglyphics, and philosophical texts are all things made by human hands that carry significance. Some kinds of artifacts, in fact, have been with us for thousands of years. Like tattoos.

Tattoos are a kind of written, or *graphic*, artifact. Some tattoos signify status; some signify affiliation with particular groups. Others call up memories; still others express the aesthetic preferences of the wearer. Some call up all of these meanings and more.

For many years in the West, tattoos signified marginal lives. Sailors and soldiers had tattoos, as did prisoners, bikers, prostitutes, and equally "dangerous" others.

But tattoos have clearly lost their outlaw edge; they have moved from the margins to the mainstream. Today, one in three people under thirty has at least one tattoo.

Those numbers are even higher for those between the ages of eighteen and twenty-five. If you are reading this book as part of a typical, twenty-five student writing class, it's likely that at least ten of your classmates have tattoos.

ACTION

1. Break into small groups and pick one tattoo you'll all write about. It could belong to someone in your group, or you might also find images of tattoos on the Web.

2. Write a physical description of the tattoo. Focus on the material artifact itself and get as much detail into your description as you can. Describe the graphic or the figure itself, of course, but also describe the color, the placement, and the shading. Challenge yourself to write words that paint a picture.

3. Once you've finished, compare your description with others in your group. What did some of you catch that others missed? What did some of your group members describe really well? Pick a few of those passages and read them out loud. Talk about why they work as well as they do.

4. Now, focus on what you think these artifacts signify. Write about what you think this tattoo might mean to the person who has it. Where do you think the image comes from? What is it related to? What is she trying to do or say with this tattoo? Why do you think he got it? When you've finished that, write a little more about what this tattoo means to you. What does it bring to your mind? What would it mean if it was on your body?

5. Come back together as a group and compare the meanings you created with the meanings made by others. If you were all writing about the same tattoo, how similar were your attributions of meaning? How different? Compare some of the most interesting similarities and differences. How can people who look at the same thing in the same setting at the same time see and interpret things so differently?

RESPONSE

Taurino Marcelino and Zuleyma Gonzalez, students at Kirkwood Community College, worked together on this box assignment. They browsed Web sites of tattoos on the Internet and came upon this example from the Māori, an indigenous people in New Zealand. Together, they studied the tattoo and researched its history and cultural meanings. Then, they wrote this summary:

> *Tā moko* is the name for the incredible tattoo markings of the Māori, indigenous people of New Zealand. Usually, the tattoos appeared on men and women's faces, thighs, and even buttocks. Instead of ink punctured into the skin, the tattoo is carved into the skin, applied by a chisel called a *uhi* which leaves actual grooves. Here, the tattoo covers the man's face with dark spirals and lines. The lines are long and many of them connect between the eyes right above the nose.
>
> Spirals on this man's tattoos are done on the nose, chin, and temples. The colors look dark, like black pigment. His forehead and nose-to-jaw line have long lines close together with some spirals. These unique designs become more concentrated here than on the rest of the face.
>
> The *tā moko* face markings created order and distinguished people among their peers. Men would typically get *tā moko* on their, face, buttocks, thighs, back,

BOX **13** continued

stomach, and calves. Women would mark their lips, chin, forehead, buttocks, thighs, neck, and back. *Tā moko* is not commonly performed anymore. The Māori brought this custom to New Zealand from Polynesia and used traditional Polynesian methods.

Lots of cultures have coming-of-age parties, whether it's a sweet 16, a bar mitzvah, or a quinceañera. The *tā moko* tattoo was a coming-of-age ritual in Māori culture. They also used these tattoos for status identification. A person could tell another's importance by his or her tattoo. High-ranking people in society received *tā moko*, and those who were less fortunate—people of a lower social status—did not. So the tattoo was a big player. It denoted power.

Although Taurino and Zuleyma chose this tattoo together and learned similar information about its history and meaning, they also wrote and compared their separate responses to it:

Taurino wrote: "To me these tattoos are beautiful. They are worn with pride and with dignity. We may find it taboo to walk around with a tattoo on our faces, but who are we to judge? This tattoo has a lot of importance to the Māori people. It is what distinguishes them in their world. The appearances of the tattoos are tribal, maybe even warrior-like, which adds to the fascinating design and meaning to it. The *uhi* makes the process overwhelmingly painful, because of the way the Māori apply these incredible tattoos. They aren't like any normal tattoos. They take a longer time to imprint, and in my opinion they are a lot more painful. Just the thought of getting a tattoo with a chisel utensil makes my stomach drop. But to me this tattoo is absolutely beautiful, its intercut designs and its jagged feel are what make me consider this tattoo artwork. If I were Māori, I would wear those spirals with much pride."

Zuleyma observed: "A tattoo has great cultural meaning. It defines who you are, and brings social identity to the person who has it. If I were part of this culture today, I would get a small tattoo on my back, not on my face or any other visible place. Tattoos are still taboo there in New Zealand, and are sometimes associated with gangs or crime (although this is not necessarily true)."

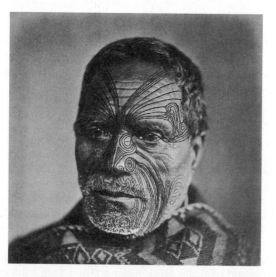

The Uses of Cultural Artifacts

Your fieldsite and your informants will, of course, be the keepers of many important cultural artifacts that will offer you information and insight into their world. As a researcher, you'll want to sketch, photograph, record, or actually acquire as many artifacts as you can. As you gather them into your portfolio and begin to write about them, you'll find the ways they represent the group or place you're studying.

We love the following short story "Everyday Use," by Alice Walker, for its analysis of cultural artifacts. Even though it's fiction, it reveals the significance of objects—a quilt, butter churn, clothing, other household objects—that define a culture that one daughter has discarded and another has embraced. Dee, the daughter of the narrator, places value on her family's artifacts without recognizing their cultural meanings or functions. Here are some questions to think about while you read the story:

- What are the different values the characters place on the cultural artifacts in the story? The butter churn and its dasher? The table benches? The food? The quilts?

- How are different characters positioned to value the cultural artifacts? What subjective history affects their positioning? How do the fixed positions of age, race, and gender affect the way they see these artifacts?

- Where are the indications of the interaction between tradition and creativity? Dee's old and new names, for example? The quilts?

- How does the narrator position herself in relationship to each of her daughters? What scenes show this?

- In what kind of culture do Maggie and her mother live? What everyday details stand out for you as they would for a fieldworker? The mother's outdoor work? The role of the church in the community? The use of snuff?

....

Everyday Use

Alice Walker

for your grandmama

I will wait for her in the yard that Maggie and I made so clean and wavy yesterday afternoon. A yard like this is more comfortable than most people know. It is not just a yard. It is like an extended living room. When the hard clay is swept clean as a floor and the fine sand around the edges lined with tiny, irregular grooves, any- one can come and sit and look up into the elm tree and wait for the breezes that never come inside the house.

Maggie will be nervous until after her sister goes: she will stand hopelessly in corners, homely and ashamed of the burn scars down her arms and legs, eying her sister with a mixture of envy and awe. She thinks her sister has held life always in the palm of one hand, that "no" is a word the world never learned to say to her.

You've no doubt seen those TV shows where the child who has "made it" is confronted, as a surprise, by her own mother and father, tottering in weakly from backstage. (A pleasant surprise, of course: What would they do if parent and child came on the show only to curse out and insult each other?) On TV mother and child embrace and smile into each other's faces. Sometimes the mother and father weep, the child wraps them in her arms and leans across the table to tell how she would not have made it without their help. I have seen these programs.

Sometimes I dream a dream in which Dee and I are suddenly brought together on a TV program of this sort. Out of a dark and soft-seated limousine I am ushered into a bright room filled with many people. There I meet a smiling, gray, sporty man like Johnny Carson who shakes my hand and tells me what a fine girl I have. Then we are on the stage and Dee is embracing me with tears in her eyes. She pins on my dress a large orchid, even though she has told me once that she thinks orchids are tacky flowers.

In real life I am a large, big-boned woman with rough, man-working hands. In the winter I wear flannel nightgowns to bed and overalls during the day. I can kill and clean a hog as mercilessly as a man. My fat keeps me hot in zero weather. I can work outside all day, breaking ice to get water for washing; I can eat pork liver cooked over the open fire minutes after it comes steaming from the hog. One winter I knocked a bull calf straight in the brain between the eyes with a sledge hammer and had the meat hung up to chill before nightfall. But of course all this does not show on television. I am the way my daughter would want me to be: a hundred pounds lighter, my skin like an uncooked barley pancake. My hair glistens in the hot bright lights. Johnny Carson has much to do to keep up with my quick and witty tongue.

But that is a mistake. I know even before I wake up. Who ever knew a Johnson with a quick tongue? Who can even imagine me looking a strange white man in the eye? It seems to me I have talked to them always with one foot raised in flight, with my head turned in whichever way is farthest from them. Dee, though. She would always look anyone in the eye. Hesitation was no part of her nature.

"How do I look, Mama?" Maggie says, showing just enough of her thin body enveloped in pink skirt and red blouse for me to know she's there, almost hidden by the door.

"Come out into the yard," I say.

Have you ever seen a lame animal, perhaps a dog run over by some careless person rich enough to own a car, sidle up to someone who is ignorant enough to be kind to him? That is the way my Maggie walks. She has been like this, chin on chest, eyes on ground, feet in shuffle, ever since the fire that burned the other house to the ground.

Dee is lighter than Maggie, with nicer hair and a fuller figure. She's a woman now, though sometimes I forget. How long ago was it that the other house burned? Ten, twelve years? Sometimes I can still hear the flames and feel Maggie's arms sticking to me, her hair smoking and her dress falling off her in little black papery flakes. Her eyes seemed stretched open, blazed open by the flames reflected in them. And Dee. I see her standing off under the sweet gum tree she used to dig gum out of; a look of concentration on her face as she watched the last dingy gray board of the house fall in toward the red-hot brick chimney. Why don't you do a dance around the ashes? I'd wanted to ask her. She had hated the house that much.

I used to think she hated Maggie, too. But that was before we raised the money, the church and me, to send her to Augusta to school. She used to read to us without pity; forcing words, lies, other folks' habits, whole lives upon us two, sitting trapped and ignorant underneath her voice. She washed us in a river of make-believe, burned us with a lot of knowledge we didn't necessarily need to know. Pressed us to her with the serious way she read, to shove us away at just the moment, like dimwits, we seemed about to understand.

Dee wanted nice things. A yellow organdy dress to wear to her graduation from high school; black pumps to match a green suit she'd made from an old suit somebody gave me. She was determined to stare down any disaster in her efforts. Her eyelids would not flicker for minutes at a time. Often I fought off the temptation to shake her. At sixteen she had a style of her own: and knew what style was.

I never had an education myself. After second grade the school was closed down. Don't ask me why: in 1927 colored asked fewer questions than they do now. Sometimes Maggie reads to me. She stumbles along good-naturedly but can't see well. She knows she is not bright. Like good looks and money, quickness passed her by. She will marry John Thomas (who has mossy teeth in an earnest face) and then I'll be free to sit here and I guess just sing church songs to myself. Although I never was a good singer. Never could carry a tune. I was always better at a man's job. I used to love to milk till I was hooked in the side in '49. Cows are soothing and slow and don't bother you, unless you try to milk them the wrong way.

I have deliberately turned my back on the house. It is three rooms, just like the one that burned, except the roof is tin; they don't make shingle roofs any more. There are no real windows, just some holes cut in the sides, like portholes in a ship, but not round and not square, with rawhide holding the shutters up on the outside. This house is in a pasture, too, like the other one. No doubt when Dee sees it she will want to tear it down. She wrote me once that no matter where we "choose" to live, she will manage to come see us. But she will never bring her friends. Maggie and I thought about this and Maggie asked me, "Mama, when did Dee ever *have* any friends?"

She had a few. Furtive boys in pink shirts hanging about on washday after school. Nervous girls who never laughed. Impressed with her they worshiped the well-turned phrase, the cute shape, the scalding humor that erupted like bubbles in lye. She read to them.

When she was courting Jimmy T she didn't have much time to pay to us, but turned all her faultfinding power on him. He *flew* to marry a cheap city girl from a family of ignorant flashy people. She hardly had time to recompose herself.

When she comes I will meet — but there they are!

Maggie attempts to make a dash for the house, in her shuffling way, but I stay her with my hand. "Come back here," I say. And she stops and tries to dig a well in the sand with her toe.

It is hard to see them clearly through the strong sun. But even the first glimpse of leg out of the car tells me it is Dee. Her feet were always neat-looking, as if God himself had shaped them with a certain style. From the other side of the car comes a short, stocky man. Hair is all over his head a foot long and hanging from his chin like a kinky mule tail. I hear Maggie suck in her breath. "Uhnnnh," is what it sounds like. Like when you see the wriggling end of a snake just in front of your foot on the road. "Uhnnnh."

Dee next. A dress down to the ground, in this hot weather. A dress so loud it hurts my eyes. There are yellows and oranges enough to throw back the light of the sun. I feel my whole face warming from the heat waves it throws out. Earrings gold, too, and hanging down to her shoulders. Bracelets dangling and making noises when she moves her arm up to shake the folds of the dress out of her armpits. The dress is loose and flows, and as she walks closer, I like it. I hear Maggie go "Uhnnnh" again. It is her sister's hair. It stands straight up like the wool on a sheep. It is black as night and around the edges are two long pigtails that rope about like small lizards disappearing behind her ears.

"Wa-su-zo-Tean-o!" she says, coming on in that gliding way the dress makes her move. The short stocky fellow with the hair to his navel is all grinning and he follows up with "Asalamalakim, my mother and sister!" He moves to hug Maggie but she falls back, right up against the back of my chair. I feel her trembling there and when I look up I see the perspiration falling off her chin.

"Don't get up," says Dee. Since I am stout it takes something of a push. You can see me trying to move a second or two before I make it. She turns, showing white heels through her sandals, and goes back to the car. Out she peeks next with a Polaroid. She stoops down quickly and lines up picture after picture of me sitting there in front of the house with Maggie cowering behind me. She never takes a shot without making sure the house is included. When a cow comes nibbling around the edge of the yard she snaps it and me and Maggie and the house. Then she puts the Polaroid in the back seat of the car, and comes up and kisses me on the forehead.

Meanwhile Asalamalakim is going through motions with Maggie's hand. Maggie's hand is as limp as a fish, and probably as cold, despite the sweat, and she keeps trying to pull it back. It looks like Asalamalakim wants to shake hands but wants to do it fancy. Or maybe he don't know how people shake hands. Anyhow, he soon gives up on Maggie.

"Well," I say. "Dee."

"No, Mama," she says. "Not 'Dee,' Wangero Leewanika Kemanjo!"

"What happened to 'Dee'?" I wanted to know.

"She's dead," Wangero said. "I couldn't bear it any longer, being named after the people who oppress me."

"You know as well as me you was named after your aunt Dicie," I said. Dicie is my sister. She named Dee. We called her "Big Dee" after Dee was born.

"But who was *she* named after?" asked Wangero.

"I guess after Grandma Dee," I said.

"And who was she named after?" asked Wangero.

"Her mother," I said, and saw Wangero was getting tired. "That's about as far back as I can trace it," I said. Though, in fact, I probably could have carried it back beyond the Civil War through the branches.

"Well," said Asalamalakim, "there you are."

"Uhnnnh," I heard Maggie say.

"There I was not," I said, "before 'Dicie' cropped up in our family, so why should I try to trace it that far back?"

He just stood there grinning, looking down on me like somebody inspecting a Model A car. Every once in a while he and Wangero sent eye signals over my head.

"How do you pronounce this name?" I asked.

"You don't have to call me by it if you don't want to," said Wangero.

"Why shouldn't I?" I asked. "If that's what you want us to call you, we'll call you."

"I know it might sound awkward at first," said Wangero.

"I'll get used to it," I said. "Ream it out again."

Well, soon we got the name out of the way. Asalamalakim had a name twice as long and three times as hard. After I tripped over it two or three times he told me to just call him Hakim-a-barber. I wanted to ask him was he a barber, but I didn't really think he was, so I didn't ask.

"You must belong to those beef-cattle peoples down the road," I said. They said "Asalamalakim" when they met you, too, but they didn't shake hands. Always too busy: feeding the cattle, fixing the fences, putting up salt-lick shelters, throwing down hay. When the white folks poisoned some of the herd the men stayed up all night with rifles in their hands. I walked a mile and a half just to see the sight.

Hakim-a-barber said, "I accept some of their doctrines, but farming and raising cattle is not my style." (They didn't tell me, and I didn't ask, whether Wangero (Dee) had really gone and married him.)

We sat down to eat and right away he said he didn't eat collards and pork was unclean. Wangero, though, went on through the chitlins and corn bread, the greens and everything else. She talked a blue streak over the sweet potatoes. Everything delighted her. Even the fact that we still used the benches her daddy made for the table when we couldn't afford to buy chairs.

"Oh, Mama!" she cried. Then turned to Hakim-a-barber. "I never knew how lovely these benches are. You can feel the rump prints," she said, running her hands underneath her and along the bench. Then she gave a sigh and her hand closed over Grandma Dee's butter dish. "That's it!" she said. "I knew there was something I wanted to ask you if I could have." She jumped up from the table and went over in the corner where the churn stood, the milk in it clabber by now. She looked at the churn and looked at it.

"This churn top is what I need," she said. "Didn't Uncle Buddy whittle it out of a tree you all used to have?"

"Yes," I said.

"Uh huh," she said happily. "And I want the dasher, too."

"Uncle Buddy whittle that, too?" asked the barber.

Dee (Wangero) looked up at me.

"Aunt Dee's first husband whittled the dash," said Maggie so low you almost couldn't hear her. "His name was Henry, but they called him Stash."

"Maggie's brain is like an elephant's," Wangero said, laughing. "I can use the churn top as a centerpiece for the alcove table," she said, sliding a plate over the churn, "and I'll think of something artistic to do with the dasher."

When she finished wrapping the dasher the handle stuck out. I took it for a moment in my hands. You didn't even have to look close to see where hands pushing the dasher up and down to make butter had left a kind of sink in the wood. In fact, there were a lot of small sinks; you could see where thumbs and fingers had sunk into the wood. It was beautiful light yellow wood, from a tree that grew in the yard where Big Dee and Stash had lived.

After dinner Dee (Wangero) went to the trunk at the foot of my bed and started rifling through it. Maggie hung back in the kitchen over the dishpan. Out came Wangero with two quilts. They had been pieced by Grandma Dee and then Big Dee and we had hung them on the quilt frames on the front porch and quilted them. One was in the Lone Star pattern. The other was Walk Around the Mountain. In both of them were scraps of dresses Grandma Dee had worn fifty and more years ago. Bits and pieces of Grandpa Jarrell's paisley shirts. And one teeny faded blue piece, about the size of a penny matchbox, that was from Great Grandpa Ezra's uniform that he wore in the Civil War.

"Mama," Wangero said sweet as a bird. "Can I have these old quilts?"

I heard something fall in the kitchen, and a minute later the kitchen door slammed.

"Why don't you take one or two of the others?" I asked. "These old things was just done by me and Big Dee from some tops your grandma pieced before she died."

"No," said Wangero. "I don't want those. They are stitched around the borders by machine."

"That'll make them last better," I said.

"That's not the point," said Wangero. "These are all pieces of dresses Grandma used to wear. She did all this stitching by hand. Imagine!" She held the quilts securely in her arms, stroking them.

"Some of the pieces, like those lavender ones, come from old clothes her mother handed down to her," I said, moving up to touch the quilts. Dee (Wangero) moved back just enough so that I couldn't reach the quilts. They already belonged to her.

"Imagine!" she breathed again, clutching them closely to her bosom.

"The truth is," I said, "I promised to give them quilts to Maggie, for when she marries John Thomas."

She gasped like a bee had stung her.

"Maggie can't appreciate these quilts!" she said. "She'd probably be backward enough to put them to everyday use."

"I reckon she would," I said. "God knows I been saving 'em for long enough with nobody using 'em. I hope she will!" I didn't want to bring up how I had offered Dee (Wangero) a quilt when she went away to college. Then she had told me they were old-fashioned, out of style.

"But they're *priceless*!" she was saying now, furiously; for she has a temper. "Maggie would put them on the bed and in five years they'd be in rags. Less than that!"

"She can always make some more," I said. "Maggie knows how to quilt."

Dee (Wangero) looked at me with hatred. "You just will not understand. The point is these quilts, *these* quilts!"

"Well," I said, stumped. "What would you do with them?"

"Hang them," she said. As if that was the only thing you *could* do with quilts.

Maggie by now was standing in the door. I could almost hear the sound her feet made as they scraped over each other.

"She can have them, Mama," she said, like somebody used to never winning anything, or having anything reserved for her. "I can 'member Grandma Dee without the quilts."

I looked at her hard. She had filled her bottom lip with checkerberry snuff and it gave her face a kind of dopey, hangdog look. It was Grandma Dee and Big Dee who taught her how to quilt herself. She stood there with her scarred hands hidden in the folds of her skirt. She looked at her sister with something like fear but she wasn't mad at her. This was Maggie's portion. This was the way she knew God to work.

When I looked at her like that something hit me in the top of my head and ran down to the soles of my feet. Just like when I'm in church and the spirit of God touches me and I get happy and shout. I did something I never had done before: hugged Maggie to me, then dragged her on into the room, snatched the quilts out of Miss Wangero's hands and dumped them into Maggie's lap. Maggie just sat there on my bed with her mouth open.

"Take one or two of the others," I said to Dee.

But she turned without a word and went out to Hakim-a-barber.

"You just don't understand," she said, as Maggie and I came out to the car.

"What don't I understand?" I wanted to know.

"Your heritage," she said. And then she turned to Maggie, kissed her, and said, "You ought to try to make something of yourself, too, Maggie. It's really a new day for us. But from the way you and Mama still live you'd never know it."

She put on some sunglasses that hid everything above the tip of her nose and her chin.

Maggie smiled; maybe at the sunglasses. But a real smile, not scared. After we watched the car dust settle I asked Maggie to bring me a dip of snuff. And then the two of us sat there just enjoying, until it was time to go in the house and go to bed.

In Walker's story, you may have noticed that Dee seeks to remove the cultural artifacts from the site as she leaves her culture behind. Reema's boy saw himself as a fieldworker in training, and Dee considers herself a sophisticated collector of valuable folk art. Neither is successful at listening or looking at the language, the rituals, or the artifacts of their home culture.

These stories provide us with a contrast between "stepping in" and "stepping out." Dee and Reema's boy serve as both insiders and outsiders. Their histories and kinships mark them as insiders. Yet they have each left their home cultures and returned, no longer able to read the culture or its artifacts in the same way as the people who continue to live there.

Both Gloria Naylor and Alice Walker illustrate culture as everyday lived experience that is not easily understood by outsiders. They show culture as more than kinship, geography, language, or ways of behaving and instead as a combination of all of these. And with these pieces of fiction, we've drawn on your strengths as a reader, the same kinds of strengths you will need while you are reading and researching in the field.

Responding to Reading

Reading is the essence of almost all college work. In this chapter, we've encouraged you to read cultures and artifacts, but we can't forget the importance of knowing and understanding what kinds of readers we are of texts. Fast readers are not necessarily good readers. Good reading means personal interaction with the text: taking notes, underlining, scribbling thoughts in margins, highlighting with purpose and discrimination. Good reading also means rereading, since each subsequent reading offers new insights and information that you may not have noticed at first. Just as we revisit our favorite movies to see new things and to remember lines and scenes, rereading gives us deeper access to texts.

Louise Rosenblatt, a teacher and scholar whose words open this chapter, suggests that we read across a spectrum that spans what she calls aesthetic and efferent responses. Aesthetic reading, for example, involves paying attention to the ways an author puts words together. It means envisioning sensory details, such as the image of a logging camp in a John Irving novel. It also means noticing the rhythm of words in a rap song or the play of puns in a Shakespeare play. In its extreme, a student focuses so much on metaphor, description, and language use that she misses the information necessary to answer a test question.

Efferent, meaning "to carry away," refers to a reader's ability to carry meaning away from a text. In an effective efferent reading, then, you are interpreting directions on an aspirin bottle, navigating a trip using MapQuest, or underlining important points in your biology textbook. In its extreme, a student focuses so much on the information at hand that she misses the way the item looks, feels, and sounds.

When you're a student, it's important to determine how much aesthetic reading and how much efferent reading each text requires. They are all different, as are our readings of them. We think the same is true of reading cultures. In any cultural moment, material artifact, community conversation, or ritual or language behavior, we need to notice how we slide along this spectrum of reading between efferent and aesthetic.

Aesthetic vs. Efferent Reading

- To read *aesthetically* means to read for language use.
- To read *efferently* means to read for practical information.

One way to understand how to write fieldwork is to read it. The essays in this book, ethnographic in nature and method, were done over a semester or a year but are not full ethnographies. Most studies that can claim themselves as "ethnographies" are done over long periods of time. We realize, however, that it can be difficult to read more than one study during a semester in which you're conducting your own fieldwork. One way to sample many approaches to doing fieldwork is to form book clubs within a class and have each small group read an ethnographic study or an ethnographic novel. In Box 14, our colleague Katie Ryan shares her process for forming book clubs in a first-year writing course devoted to fieldwork.

BOX**14**

Fieldworking Book Clubs

KATHLEEN RYAN, UNIVERSITY OF MONTANA, MISSOULA, MONTANA

PURPOSE

The point of fieldwork is to tell the story of your reading of a culture, and the point of a fieldworking book club is to figure out the story of the book you are reading. This project shows you how doing fieldwork, like reading, is about acts of interpretation. In other words, the abilities you use for fieldworking translate into the abilities you use for reading, and, of course, the opposite is also true.

In a fieldworking book club, you will read an ethnography, an oral history, or an ethnographic fiction work with four or five of your classmates. The point of this book club is to collectively figure out what your book can teach you about being a fieldworker and

BOX **14** continued

what being a fieldworker can teach you about your book. The five phases of the project include choosing a book, writing in a reading journal, meeting regularly in class for book club discussions, presenting your book to the class with your book club at the end of the semester or year, and finally, individually reflecting on the entire project.

ACTION

1. Choose a Book

    When my students did fieldworking book clubs, each club chose one of these three books: *The Mole People*, an ethnography by Jennifer Toth about the homeless communities who live beneath the streets in New York City; *Mules and Men*, a historical study by Zora Neale Hurston of African American stories from Florida and hoodoo practices in Louisiana; and *The Handmaid's Tale*, novelist Margaret Atwood's futuristic fiction written from the viewpoint of Offred, a vital participant and outsider in a post–nuclear war society. I call this book ethnographic fiction because Offred writes from the perspective of a participant-observer in her culture and the text asks readers to read as fieldworkers. My students grouped themselves according to the book they chose.

2. Keep a Reading Journal

    Once you have a book and a club, you are ready to begin writing and talking together. You'll write regularly in a reading journal as you read. Bring at least a two-page journal entry and your book to each book club meeting. The reading journal serves as a place that documents your process of reading, a starting point for your club discussions, and a place for you to write about the text on your own. Here are some sample questions to ask of your reading:

    - What's the book about? How do I know?
    - How does the field researcher/narrator position himself or herself?
    - What choices do you imagine the author made in writing the book?
    - How do authorial choices in detail and style affect your reading?
    - How does reading with a club affect your reading?
    - How does the organization of the book help you think about the arrangement of your own research?
    - What do you bring to your book as a fieldworker? What do you bring to your book as a reader?

    Here is an excerpt from my student Matt Furbish's reading journal on *The Mole People*: "If Toth had not positioned herself in the story, she could not have shown exactly how much underground life changes a person. At the beginning of the book, she's just a sweet, innocent graduate student from Columbia. At the end, however, she comes to find a part of herself she never knew existed: her animal side."

3. Have Regular Book Club Meetings

    In my class, fieldworking book clubs meet once every two weeks. Students bring their book and most recent journal entry to each meeting. As a book club, their assignment is to explore reading and fieldworking by talking about this book. Each group is responsible for determining a reading schedule and an agenda of discussions aimed at fulfilling the assignments and the general goals of the fieldworking book club. Since they know they will be writing evaluations of the books and offering them to the others, their readings and discussions need to move in that direction. Here are some tips to help book club meetings run smoothly:

- Exchange e-mail addresses and phone numbers to reach other members.
- Give clear book club assignments for each meeting.
- Do long-range planning by creating a reading schedule and preparing for the group review and presentation.
- Be sure someone takes notes during class discussions.
- Plan discussions around recurring questions, interests, and ideas that come up in journals.
- Plan ahead for assignments.

4. Write a Group Paper, and Give a Presentation
    Each fieldworking book club writes a collaborative review of the book according to its qualities as ethnography, oral history, or ethnographic fiction, answering the question "How did this work contribute to your understanding of fieldworking and reading?" This review also becomes the content material for a creative and informative 20-minute class presentation.

5. Write an Individual Reflection
    Each club member also writes a one- or two-page summary reflection on the entire book club project. Students reread their journals, reread their group notes, and answer these questions:

- What did you notice about the way you made sense out of the book as you read?
- How did reading and talking about the book with others shape or change your thinking? Your reading?
- What did you learn about the process of fieldworking?
- What did you learn about your own project?
- How does this book relate to your life in this class as a fieldworker and your life beyond this class as a writer and reader of books and culture?

RESPONSE

One of my former students, Kelli Frazier, describes how her book club read *Mules and Men* by applying their growing knowledge of oral histories to their reading:

As I look back over the semester, I see that our group really made a lot of progress. I must admit that during the first few weeks of class, I was discouraged about the way our group discussions were going. We seemed unable to get past the fact that we were not enjoying the book and spent all of our time reiterating just how much

BOX 14 continued

we disliked it. Finally, I think everyone realized that we were not getting anywhere with the attitudes we had and the way we were handling the assignment. From that point on, we were able to start to look at the book from a different perspective, and we gained a new appreciation for it and the author's purpose in writing it. I was really proud of us because we made a huge change as we began to focus on it as an oral history. Once we began to evaluate it on that basis, we really discovered a lot of things to discuss: Hurston's method of transcribing in the 1930s by candlelight at night, the old male storytellers who were part of her own past as they sat on the porch in the evening, etc. By that point our book group conversations were becoming really interesting as each of us brought different ideas to the group but no longer in a negative way.

FieldWriting: Published and Unpublished Written Sources

Fieldwriting depends far more on oral source material than on written sources. Your informants, along with your fieldnotes, will contribute the most important data to your fieldprojects. When fieldworkers write up their research, they treat informants' words in the same way that library researchers cite textual references. (See Chapter 5 for information on recording, transcribing, and presenting oral language on the page.)

But you'll still need to refer to written texts from both published and unpublished library and archival sources, as well as documents you've collected at your fieldsite, to support your fieldwork's oral sources. As all research writers know, the basic role of documentation is to attribute ideas that are not your own to their original source. For example, when we use the phrase "stepping in and stepping out" in this book, we put quotation marks around it to indicate that it is not our original idea. We do this because we want to attribute this term to Hortense Powdermaker, whose quote from *Stranger and Friend* opens our book and whose idea has given us a new way to explain the insider-outsider researcher stance.

One exception to information that requires documentation is common knowledge. Common knowledge refers to information that everyone might be expected to know, such as the presidents or the population of the United States. Sometimes it's difficult to determine, however, what common knowledge particular readers will have. Writers who are unsure of their own readers' common knowledge should include contextual information, which itself often comes from published written sources.

When you use documentation (published or unpublished) to support your fieldwork, you should refer to a more complete handbook or research manual, such as the Modern Language Association's *MLA Handbook for Writers of Research Papers*, used in the humanities. In other subject areas, your instructors may guide you toward other research manuals, such as the *Publication Manual of the American Psychological Association*, used in psychology and education; *The Chicago Manual of Style*, used in history; or one of the many other manuals of style specific to other disciplines, such as law, mathematics, science, medicine, linguistics, or engineering.

Following these examples and consulting a handbook will help you avoid inadvertent plagiarism. **Plagiarism** means using the words and ideas of others without giving them credit. Whether you intend to plagiarize or not, you are committing a serious offense to the academic community. Using appropriate citation conventions helps you avoid plagiarism.

The current convention for documenting any source—informant or text, published or unpublished—is to give as much information about the source as possible within your actual written text. This is called *intertextual citation*. Intertextual (or in-text) citation might include the author or informant's name and the book or document title, depending on how you introduce the material into your writing. Your first citation must always refer to the original source. For published sources, this would be the page number (for example, "Naylor 7" or "*Mama Day* 7"). For unpublished written sources, how you cite depends on the type of material you have collected. When you cite a written source intertextually, you must provide information that allows a reader to find the complete citation in your "Works Cited" section—or "References," "Bibliography," or "Fieldreading"—at the end. Intertextual documentation provides helpful context without interrupting the flow of your text and cluttering it with information that readers can find elsewhere. Another way of including outside source material without interrupting the flow of the text is to use a system of endnotes and footnotes, as Elise Wu does in the study on page 143. For more information on incorporating published and unpublished sources into your text, consult a handbook or research manual.

Visit **bedfordstmartins .com/fieldworking** for more help working with sources.

Reading Electronic Communities

Most of the time we think of a fieldsite as being a physical place you can enter—a place where you can talk with people face-to-face. But with the advances of electronic technologies, the idea of place has widened to include listservs, blogs, microblogs, message boards, social networking sites, and other sites of interaction. Some people find a virtual conversation more comfortable than an actual one. Participating in electronic communities brings you a wealth of information that is relevant to your fieldworking study. Insider sources of data are available, and you can step in yourself, learning how a community operates from the inside and, in a sense, doing virtual fieldwork as you read the culture electronically.

Not all cultures exist in the electronic world as completely as others, but you probably will find something related to your fieldsite on the Internet. You may turn up nothing of value, or you may discover a host of insiders conversing as if they were meeting face-to-face.

It's important to read the electronic media with the same ideas we've been discussing about conventional print texts. Interactive participation is a skill our electronic culture requires of us as readers. Take a look at Web sites you know about, survey online discussions about your topic, or search for sites by using keywords. If your fieldsite's subculture engages in electronic conversations, you can develop your skills in reading that community.

Do some analysis offline, thinking about the data as well as the interactions you've witnessed and taken part in. Make notes on all the topics that suggest data you might explore further and potentially **triangulate** for your study. Think about how the members of the community you've joined interact with one another. How do they address one another, for instance? What names have they given themselves in the virtual world? What tone does each conversation take? How do informants seem to conceive of themselves as a community or culture? And don't forget that the people you meet online are potentially valuable resources to you to contact later for your study.

Fieldwork in a Changing Field

For her project on a little-known medical condition called *factitious disorder*, Elise Wu, a graduate student in a nonfiction writing program, did much of her research online. Because the disorder is complicated, misunderstood, and sometimes embarrassing, Elise (who also suffered from it seven years before she did her research) looked for primary sources on the Internet, where she had a hunch that people would be able to discuss their condition anonymously. These included people who shared the disorder, their relatives, and professionals who treated the patients.

As she suspected, Elise found that Web sites provided her with key sources. But the ever-changing nature of online information wasn't reliable enough to allow her to explore the disorder fully. As a result, she supported her Internet research with interviews and print sources from medical libraries, as well as her own memories. She writes: "Web pages can be launched or shuttered; user profiles can be modified; postings can be edited or deleted—all with just a few clicks of a mouse. For a researcher trying to observe communities that exist in this medium, data can play pretty frustrating tricks: now you see it, now you don't."

Elise's study, called "Out Patients," also provides an excellent example of using primary and secondary sources to create a broader view of her subject. Notice how she uses footnotes to provide background information that doesn't fit easily into the flow of the main narrative, as well as a Works Cited list at the end of the essay that meets the requirements of MLA documentation.

Out Patients

Elise Wu

"Elise?[1] Elise, talk to me," the man in purple scrubs says, concern rising in his voice.

I stay silent, close my eyes once, wait a beat, then reopen them, fixed, as if I'm trying desperately to speak through intense pain. I've come to the emergency room with what looks like a textbook case of appendicitis.

"You're really sick, aren't you," he says softly and rests a hand on my shoulder, his gaze full of compassion.

I close my eyes again and let his gentle words wash over my body, curled on a narrow gurney. I'm tingling everywhere, senses hyper-heightened.

When the moment is over, I'm left aching for more at the same time that I'm flooded with shame and fear. *Yes*, I think, once my mind is capable of language again, almost wishing he could hear me. *I am sick. But not in the way you believe.*

In the most acute years of the near decade I spent faking illness, I thought I was simply a terrible person. Belly pain was my specialty when this began just before I turned 16, and it was what got me my last hospital admission at 21. After that, fresh out of college with limited health insurance, I forced myself to stop, only exaggerating symptoms when I had real but minor illnesses (respiratory infections and the like) to stave off the desire to do more.

It's an understatement to say that the intensity of my hunger for this specific sort of care frightened me. Why did I need this bizarre kind of attention? And where had I learned how to perform in this manipulative way?

I was case zero, I was sure of it, and utterly alone.

That is, until I discovered I wasn't.

Five years after my last night in the ER, still wracked by guilt and fear and harboring dangerous desires, I turned to the Internet in a last-ditch appeal for answers. "Faking illness," I typed, or some such simple search string, expecting most of my hits to be for Web sites with advice for parents on how to handle kids trying to get out of school. Imagine my shock when within the first ten links, there was a reference to a diagnosable condition for my exact compulsion: something called *factitious disorder.*

The medical community defines factitious disorder (FD) within a spectrum of conditions that involve psychological problems manifested as physical ones. Someone with FD deliberately creates physical or psychological symptoms simply to take on the role of the patient. There are no other motivations (that is, seeking external gains such as financial benefits or excuse from legal responsibilities) (Feldman, Hamilton, and Deemer 133). While the creation of false illnesses has been recognized in medical literature since the nineteenth century (131), the most severe form of this behavior was not given a

---

[1] I've changed my name to protect my identity.

name—Munchausen[2] syndrome—until 1951 (150). Patients with Munchausen, who constitute 10 percent of those with FD, are "singularly dedicated to playing the sick role" and "manipulate their bodies to simulate or induce physical illness or injury" (135)—which can go so far as to involve causing actual infection or other bodily harm (138).[3] Those with Munchausen may present with "maladies . . . so esoteric that most physicians have little familiarity with them" (135)—and when the truth of their role in causing their illnesses becomes known to their caregivers, they tend to relocate to other medical care facilities where they can perform for fresh audiences (135).

While I was admitted to more than four different ERs between the ages of 15 and 22, I never deliberately induced real illnesses—which was about all the comfort I could draw from these descriptions, as I scrolled through the information on the Web that morning. I was most certainly *not* someone so far entrenched in the need to be "sick" that I would qualify as a Munchausen patient, I decided. But, still reeling from the discovery that I fit into a classification at all, I closed my browser and didn't return to research FD for another two years.

It wasn't fear of what more I would learn that halted me. It was the grim prognosis: the Web page I found that day belonged to a Dr. Marc Feldman, who claims in his online biography to be "an international expert in Munchausen syndrome" with book titles under his name that include *Patient or Pretender: Inside the Strange World of Factitious Disorders* and *Playing Sick: Untangling the Web of Factitious Disorder, Munchausen Syndrome, Munchausen by Proxy, and Malingering.* From his site, I found link after link to case studies and FAQs about FD. One FAQ said that although someone with FD "actively seeks treatment for the various disorders he or she invents, the person often is unwilling to admit to and seek treatment for the syndrome itself. This makes treating [him or her] very challenging, and the outlook for recovery poor" (Cleveland Clinic Foundation). It went on. "In most cases . . . the disorder is a chronic, or long-term, condition that can be very difficult to treat. . . . Even with treatment, it is more realistic to work toward managing the disorder rather than to try curing it."

So, I thought, *I'm screwed.*

There is a dilemma to getting treatment. It's not just that someone with FD wants to avoid being found out; those who have been manipulated by that person—family and friends as well as members of the medical community—tend to react with justified anger when they find out they've been deceived.

---

[2] After Baron von Munchausen, a fictional character originating in an eighteenth-century narrative series (Munchausen Library). He was known for his self-aggrandizing fabrications about his life experiences (Cleveland Clinic Foundation).

[3] There are some ailments FD patients produce with greater frequency than others, including "infection, impaired wound healing, hypoglycemia, anemia, bleeding, rashes, neurologic symptoms such as seizures or dizziness, vomiting, diarrhea, pain or fever of undetermined origin, and symptoms of autoimmune or connective tissue disease" (Feldman, Hamilton, and Deemer 137–38).

This idea lingered in my mind during the months I refused to look further into FD. What was the point of seeking treatment? Only to "manage" the disorder? Why be subjected to rejection more painful than the guilt I already carried? FD, I realized, wasn't a disorder controlled only by the whims of FDers (my name for those of us who have engaged in FD behaviors). What about those affected by our acts? Did they help fuel the disorder somehow? Not that I am trying to lay blame; I only want to establish the way innocent bystanders can feel like obstacles to FDers who want to get treatment.

My FD was no longer active, but the weight of the secret and the unresolved desire to slip back into the old behaviors made me want a better recovery. If I was going to have a fighting chance at disentangling myself from the deceit I had created, I was going to need to examine the way FD's subcultures, the actors and their audiences, interacted. I would have to look at what happened once the scrim of illness was removed and the performers behind it were free to communicate directly. Enter the Internet.

Of course, because FDers face a catch-22 in "coming out," I was sure I'd never find a space in which FDers and their audiences could be physically observable, at least not in public.[4] Faked illness is not so much a scrim but a fourth wall, and even though both the actors and audience may know it is there, neither group has a script that explains how to break it. But given the anonymity that chat rooms, discussion forums, and other such virtual spaces could offer, I had a hunch I'd find others on the Web who could speak to their experience.

The first place I return, on a morning two years later in mid-February, is Dr. Feldman's Web page. I return there with some trepidation—his headshot is mounted within the banner at the top, and the "expert's smile" he wears puts me off.... The whole thing feels more commercial than service-oriented. I can't help looking at myself as the sort of curiosity that would have made it into a nineteenth-century traveling circus freak show, and the diagonal stripes in the background of Dr. Feldman's site aren't helping my Big Top associations: if I'm going to be a freak, I don't want to feel like someone else is making money by sensationalizing my misfortune, self-induced or otherwise.

I venture toward the list of links to other sources on FD, trying to set my misgivings aside. The second item catches my eye: "A virtual discussion group for people interested in factitious disorder, Munchausen syndrome, and—to a lesser extent—MBP and malingering."[5] Will this be a group of therapists swapping stories about patients? Or people who have FD or Munchausen? Either

---

[4] Support group meetings for alcohol and/or drug addiction might constitute such an environment.

[5] Munchausen by proxy (MBP) and malingering, which bear behaviors similar to those of FD, are characterized by different motivations. A person with MBP seeks fulfillment of some internal desire by feigning or inducing illness in another person (Nadelson 10); a malingerer seeks external benefits (such as financial gains or access to medication) from playing sick (14).

way, this is what I think I'm looking for. "I do not moderate nor necessarily endorse the comments made on the site," Dr. Feldman notes in a prominent parenthetical placed next to the link. Good. I draw a breath and let my cursor take me forward.

The stripes on my screen dissolve into a soft, sea-green background: "Factitious Disorder, Munchausen Syndrome, Munchausen Syndrome by Proxy, and Malingering Discussion and Survivor's Forum" welcomes me in dark gray. *Well, that's a mouthful,* I think—*but then again, if this is for FDers, when would we ever be in a situation where we'd have to say the name out loud?*

I recognize the message-board format, posts sorted by threads. I jump to the oldest message, dated not even a month after I first found out about FD's existence. A counter at the bottom of the page tells me there have been just over 7,700 visitors[6] since the counter was activated. Twenty-one months, a little under 400 hits per month or 100 hits per week, if the counter was started when the forum was opened—seems like steady traffic, though not a lot. It's impossible to tell whether the same people keep coming back or if the counter distinguishes new IP addresses from old ones. But the fact that there *is* such traffic quickens my pulse. I'm strangely jittery, hyped up on the discovery of what I think are the footprints of compatriots in this weird hinterland I've entered: that state of limbo between being "out" to myself but not to the world at large. There's pain, too, a certain grief that there are so many others who have a reason to come here—I've already assumed they're mostly FDers from the forum's name.

A quick scan of the post titles, though, tells me otherwise about the primary visitors. "Ready to give up on a friend," says one thread. "What hope for the future of our marriage?" says another. And "Is it factitious disorder or manipulation?"

Ouch. These aren't FDers—they're the people we've played for.

During each of the episodes that landed me in an ER, I always wondered if my caretakers—roommates who called the ambulances, doctors who examined me, my parents—suspected that my physical pain was not real. If they did, they certainly never let on to me. But one vivid memory makes me wonder: After a night of fitful sleep, I wake up to a line of medical students filing into my room. A young doctor, probably in his early 30s, comes to my right side while the rest of the group takes position around the bed in their white coats. I notice that the doctor isn't wearing one; he has on a dark green sweater that zips at the neck.

"This is a 21-year-old female with abdominal pain," he says and runs through the diagnostics that have already been done, along with their results—all negative for anything specific, as the chart notes. "There is no evidence of appendicitis yet, but we'll continue to watch and wait. Sometimes these things take longer to

---

[6] As of February 18, 2009. But note that counters do not necessarily indicate the number of visitors from the creation of a Web page, since these tracking devices can be added long after a site first comes into existence.

develop; sometimes they go away over time without explanation," he says, giving me a reassuring smile at these last words.

This is part of an accepted approach to handling FDers: providing a non-confrontational face-saving "out" that encourages recovery (Eisendrath and Feder 199).Even though I'm unaware of this as a documented strategy at the time, I don't miss the option the doctor has revealed to me. *Sometimes these things take longer to develop; sometimes they go away over time without explanation*. I have no idea, as I watch the eyes of everyone watching me, if they know that I'm feigning my discomfort, but I've definitely never heard of abdominal pain—the kind severe enough to land someone in the hospital—that just vanishes.

"Remember, if your pain gets worse then disappears suddenly, let us know right away—you might feel better after that happens, but it could mean that the appendix has ruptured," the doctor says to me. "Otherwise, just take it easy."

I nod meekly, and the group files out, I assume, to move on to their next case. But a few feet down the hall, they stop, just visible to me around the edge of the doorframe. The doctor seems to address the group again—I can't quite make out his words—and I notice at least one head turns toward the entrance to my room.

They know. Oh God, they know.

This memory comes lurching back to me out of the fog surrounding the rest of that hospital stay as I stare at the queries on the FD forum seven years later. Even if the doctor who gave me the "out" never intended for it to be one, my panicked brain saw the perceived exit and ran for it: within a day, I was reporting reduced pain and trying the clear liquid diet I'd been put on.

So I'm dismayed, then, as I read through the posts on the Web site. One of the main subjects is *confrontation*—and sometimes, even worse, abandonment. I see a pattern emerging: many posters open with the back story on the "illnesses" and behaviors of a family member or friend; they explain how that has impacted the poster (and, as relevant, other family), express in some form that the poster has reached his or her capacity to handle the situation, and finally ask for support or advice about how to address the suspected FDer directly or cut ties. "Sometimes you can only save yourself," writes someone who calls herself Odette[7, 8] in response to another user's post describing his mother, even though that user never asks for advice on how to respond. "Do I…let [my mother] continue to manipulate me or do I continue on not talking with her?" Hil[9] asks. And, "It's all

---

[7] The forum allows users to post using whatever handle they wish.

[8] October 11, 2007. (Individual messages do not have distinct URLs on this forum. For reference purposes, provide dates of the messages, which can be used to search this forum.)

[9] November 20, 2007.

crap and I am done," AC[10] writes after describing her mother's numerous "hard to detect" conditions (AC's words), asking, "How do you convince someone with FD to get help?"

The response to this last post makes me pause. It's from Dr. Feldman himself:

> Unfortunately, the prognosis is poor. At this point, the behaviors are very well-entrenched and unlikely to change, unless your mother agrees to psychiatric treatment, which is unlikely. Instead, you have to decide on how you yourself are going to respond to the continual crises. Do you rush to her side each time, or do you keep firm boundaries? That is the challenge, particularly because your mother may escalate her complaints to try to get you back on board. Note, though, that I've never met anyone involved and so my comments are merely provisional.[11]

I wince at his opening sentences. They remind me of the information I've linked to before from his Web site. The idea of establishing firm boundaries does make sense to me and strikes me as good advice, as much as I also feel for the mother who might see her daughter as cold or uncaring.

But several weeks later, when I read the article edited by the same Dr. Feldman on the good outcomes of face-saving "outs" physicians can offer patients with FD,[12] I wonder: *Why isn't he telling people about this approach?* Just to be certain, I check the date of publication of the article against the date of the post. He has to know of this at the time of his response. He does. In fact, he even refers in his own writing to some of the same studies from that article (Feldman, Hamilton, and Deemer 153–54).

What Dr. Feldman *is* forthcoming about in his posts are his most recent book and Web page—that is, he frequently plugs them as references for those who visit this other site. I'm not the only one who seems to have picked up on this; eventually, users begin mentioning in their questions to Dr. Feldman that they *have* read his book, perhaps in hopes of receiving more information than just the simple, repeated referral he makes. To a user named stacey, who believes her sister's urinary problems (kidney stones, infections) are factitious, he writes, "Much more about urinary FD can be found in my book, *Playing Sick.*"[13] To northerngirl [sic], author of the post entitled "Is it factitious disorder or manipulation?"[14] which describes her ex-husband's posing as their daughter on the Internet to announce that he's had a heart attack: "This is probably both [FD and manipulation].... Thanks for the inquiry. You might want to check out my website for more

---

[10] October 21, 2007.

[11] October 24, 2007.

[12] In "Management of Factitious Disorders," *The Spectrum of Factitious Disorders*, edited by Drs. Marc D. Feldman and Stuart J. Eisendrath.

[13] February 11, 2008.

[14] June 9, 2008.

information."[15] To Emily, who wonders if her brother's wife has Munchausen and Munchausen by proxy: "I would recommend that you get ahold [sic] of my book.... I think you will find it very helpful in determining what steps to take."[16] To Julie Bellar, who asks if intervention of the kind used for other addictions might work on her sister and where to obtain professional help: "I know only of anecdotal reports in which an 'intervention' worked, but it may be worth a try.... I do think you would profit from reading my book...and perhaps sharing it with other members of the family. There is a chapter on the toll on family members, and a chapter on intervention and management."[17] And to Desere' [sic], who asks specifically if others think she herself has Munchausen after listing numerous behaviors: "I would strongly encourage you to read my book... (available at Amazon at a discount) because it has a tremendous amount of information that will help you."[18, 19]

Only a handful of posters to this forum seek help for themselves. It doesn't surprise me, as the majority of the users are there to seek support from others dealing with FDers, not the compulsions of FD itself. While forum participants of the former type tend to converse with one another actively, leaving responses to questions and offering sympathy, responses to FDers are notably thin if not absent. This doesn't rule out the possibility that Dr. Feldman contacts each FDer privately, but my hope for an example of direct conversation between FDers and their audiences begins to fade a month after I find this forum and watch it for such interactions.

To Desere', though, Dr. Feldman leaves this message in addition to his book plug: "You might also want to join a group for Munchausen sufferers at http://groups.yahoo.com/group/cravin4care.... You can post there and get feedback, hopefully."

Bingo.

And so I go there. The Web site looks almost like my e-mail inbox, except instead of folders on the left of the page and messages in the center, there's a list of "Members Only" links to posts, files, photos, and member information in the former location and a brief description of the group's purpose in the latter. "Support group for those who suffer from Factitious disorders (Munchausen Syndrome or Munchausen by Proxy) to find comfort and support in their recovery. Our aim is to assist each other in dealing with the reality of our thirst for concern from others," the description reads. Hence the group name, "cravin4care."

---

[15] June 10, 2008.

[16] June 25, 2008.

[17] August 16, 2008.

[18] March 19, 2009.

[19] On the cravin4care discussion group, where Dr. Feldman also responds unofficially to queries about FD and Munchausen syndrome, a user calls Dr. Feldman out (albeit gently) by expressing her hope that he is on the forum "not just to promote your book." Dr. Feldman responds that he "will never make money off of my book (alas)—I spent a fortune doing the research and taking time off from work to write it."

Unlike the forum referenced by Dr. Feldman's Web page, to access any of the messages, I have to subscribe to the list, so I click on the bright blue button on the upper right of the page that invites me to "Join This Group!" The member list will make my membership (and e-mail address) public knowledge to anyone else who joins, so I create an alias with an entirely separate e-mail account. *How many others like me have found themselves here, going through the same steps to obscure their identities,* I wonder.

Being at this virtual portal feels suddenly more significant than my wanderings among the threads on the previous forum because I've had to manufacture another persona in order to enter this space. It's paradoxical, this act of protection that allows the people who perform it to reveal themselves even as they hide.

The stats for the group, which I examine as soon as I'm logged in, are encouraging: more than 160 members since the group's founding,[20] with just over 3,400 messages.[21] I realize that I may end up facing an opposite problem from the one on the other forum—only FDers talking, no audience members piping up—but at least I'll have the conversations *about* FD *by* FDers, which is part of the post-disclosure dialogue I'm seeking.

That reversal I'm expecting does seem to characterize what I see at first. In fact, even the pattern to people's introductory posts in this discussion group bears a mirror-image quality to those on the other forum: there's the back story on the "illnesses" and behaviors (this time of the person posting), an explanation of how they have impacted the poster (and, as relevant, other family and friends), an expression in some form that the poster has reached his or her capacity to handle the situation, and a request for support or advice in curbing FD behaviors.

But unlike the posters on the other forum, who tend to be mostly transient (submitting queries and then vanishing once they receive answers), the members of this group return over and over, develop friendships, and maintain day-to-day contact that extends for several years. Once the initial introductions are out of the way, the next most prevalent topic of conversation is the decision to "come out"— to therapists, doctors, family members, and friends.

Many members in the group admit they've already done this, which surprises me during my initial reading. Despite my hope that gathering others' revelations will give me the vocabulary to speak too, I can't imagine attempting a confession yet, especially to the people I've deceived. "I started very small and sort of tested the waters," writes one woman who gives her first name as Carolyn. "I told one

---

[20] The founder, who goes by the handle livinondawildside [sic], indicates in a post from January 3, 2002, that she "was trying to start a group because I wanted to meet more people who suffer from Munchausens [sic] syndrome." Ironically, she stops participating in the group not long afterward for reasons unknown. Her current status, as of May 13, 2009, on the member list is "bouncing"—that is, her e-mail address no longer accepts messages.

[21] At the time I joined the group (March 24, 2009). The roster as of May 13, 2009, lists 176 members, 3,467 messages.

shrink about one episode where I lied for attention. . . . So then I told my regular shrink about one or two instances where I lied for attention. He said he was 'proud of me' for telling him. Then I burst into tears and spilled my guts." She goes on about her eventual confession to her husband and her family doctor, both of whom responded positively, she says.

Others in the group post that they're on the brink of confessing to someone, usually a therapist. A woman who calls herself Jenny writes, "Have arranged to see a counsellor [sic] next week and this time [I]'m going to tell him everything in the first session so that [I] can't avoid the topic and talk about other random things."

Then there are those who want to confess but have no idea how to go about it or cannot bear to lose the "support" they feel they receive from the relationship dynamic FD creates. "I am soooo scared of being rejected, treated like slime. It sounds like some of the therapists around don't want to deal with us," a woman who goes by Caroline writes. "And do you have to tell your family?"

Sin, whose full handle is sinandshame, first says "I want to get help . . . but I know that I never will be able to face the very people most able to help me with the truth." A day later, Sin adds, "[I] can't do it. [I] can't tell the truth. [I] just can't. [I] wish [I] could but [I] can't . . . the nurturing [I] get from my therapist is something [I] cannot jeopardize."

The anecdotes from different members and the familiar emotions they give voice to overwhelm me at first. My own history flashes like a TV hospital drama as I recognize again and again the language of desire and repulsion these FDers use to describe their attention-seeking episodes. "I used to fantasize about [doctors] saving me, and EMT technicians bringing me back from the edge," writes Caroline, who when describing her behaviors, says she "indulged" in them. *Yes, exactly*, I think, *it's very much a form of pleasure, as much as it feels like a depraved one.* At the same time, she says, "I feel so bad about myself at the moment" and "I keep thinking over and over again about what I did, and I can't get it out of my head."

I find myself following the initial few members—Carolyn, Caroline, Jenny, another woman who goes by the handle Lapis, and a few others who join later on. Each of their histories comes out over a period of about three years. But as the group grows, I find myself growing oddly numb to the pattern of the later stories from newer members. Is it that my capacity for empathy is being drained, just as FDers' audiences become tired out?

This idea gives me pause. Here I am, an FDer in recovery myself, but what does that really mean if to be recovered means to take a place among the people who are no longer able to care, in a sense, for the FDers' plight? *I don't know where I belong within these two subcultures anymore.*

My shift in perspective and the discomfort that goes with it linger for several days, and I stop reading the messages on the forum. I had intended to "come out" myself within one of the forums so I might document what happens to me as a true participant in the post-disclosure world. But neither venue feels right. For obvious reasons, the first one I visited doesn't present an optimal environment for my first outing. The second doesn't appeal to me either, as the members whose stories I feel most invested in are now much less active.

So outing myself on cravin4care right then looks to be nothing like outing myself would have been seven years prior when the group was founded. There isn't much at stake for me in revealing to the forum my qualifications for what Carolyn calls "the least desired club on the [I]nternet." After all, the anonymity, as well as the fact that I've never tried to manipulate any of the users, already neutralizes any disease I might have in coming out there. Part of recovery, I realize, requires me to go through some form of confession where there *is* something at stake, which seems to be what each person's "coming out story" in the cravin4care forum points to.

The option that presents itself, one I've known about for months but have been too skittish to consider until this moment, is contacting my own therapist, under whose care I remained for two of the most acute years of my experience with FD. I met this doctor in the fall of my freshman year after several episodes of "unexplained physical symptoms," as the intake records note. The director of mental health services, who assigned me to this doctor, writes in a memo added to the file, "the Dean filled me in on the fact that [Elise has] been very demanding of her roommates and has some physical complaint almost daily. We have not discovered any underlying medical cause for her problems. At this point it appears that her symptoms are stress related...." This, along with a note six months later written by the doctor himself with reference to "undifferentiated somatoform disorder," is the closest any documentation comes to the possibility of FD. I find it compelling that we never addressed somatoform disorder directly in therapy, at least not to my knowledge. Did we talk about the ways psychological pain can manifest itself in the body? Maybe once, and I'm sure if we made a move in that direction, I diverted it.

Perhaps this is why the doctor's name emerges first in the line of people I might contact at this juncture in my research. Perhaps, because he was so close to being right about my diagnosis, he will be understanding when I finally tell him the truth. When we parted ways at the end of two years, he was leaving the university to start his own practice, and I didn't have insurance. So even though I would have liked to continue with him, it wasn't possible. And a year later, I was back in the ER.

I find him easily through the Internet. Dial, several rings, voicemail. I leave my name and number, explaining that I'm one of his former patients interested in consulting him on "some research"—vague seems the best way to go until I've had the chance to feel him out. Two days later, he calls me back.

His voice is still the same, and he tells me he recognizes mine. His low tenor tones still carry the warmth I remember, soothing but not in a creepy, hypnotic way. "It's good to connect person to person again," he says and means it. I'm grateful that he's not using the therapist's warm-fuzzy, "you-have-to-let-yourself-feel-your-emotions" manner of speaking that just ends up being smug. I hate the therapists that cosset at the same time that they condescend.

He only has a few minutes between appointments, so we schedule an official phone consultation. Our chat is over, almost before I can believe I've actually done it—set the wheels in motion for this conversation with someone I've lied to, if not outright, then by my omission, in our previous talks.

When we begin on the phone two weeks later, I'm hopeful. He says he's tried to access the records from our time working together. The fact that he's gone after them to prepare for this conversation tells me he's still the same person, attentive to detail, invested in whatever time we have. I tell him that I have the records, which surprises him for a moment. It's my opening, though, so I plunge ahead before he can say anything more: "You mentioned somatization disorder in your notes," I say.

"I was just trying to sort out—is this a manifestation of unacknowledged feelings…or something you were participating in," he says, as if to explain.

I'm sure now that we never gave a name to my symptoms out loud, and his words are the perfect lead-in to what I've called to tell him. Can't put it off any longer. "I'm in recovery for factitious disorder. Does that make sense?" I ask. I want no mistake, no ambiguity.

A pause. "Oh, yeah." He doesn't sound surprised but I can't read his tone. Certainly not angry. Perhaps it's intellectual? Like he's being consulted (which he is).

I feel strangely calm. He segues back to the record, referring back to needing to rule out previous possible disorders. "I have to take on faith what people's report of their experience is," he says. Is he going to get defensive? Is he making sure I don't blame him for not "fixing" me? I want to ask him why he didn't tell me his suspicions as they're noted in the record, but he's still talking and I don't want to interrupt.

We go through the history of when the faking really started, and as the truth comes out, the tone of his reactions changes to one of empathy. "It must have been hell," he says. At this point, I know we're on solid ground.

We talk about my plan for continuing to move forward. "Trust your instincts," he says. "It's the same advice I give to anyone who's coming out. This is partially a process for you; you want to pay careful attention."

Yes, I think. *I am.*

Works Cited

"Biography." *Dr. Marc Feldman's Munchausen Syndrome, Malingering, Factitious Disorder, & Munchausen by Proxy Page*. Ed. Marc D. Feldman. 2004–2007. Web. 12 May 2009.

Caroline. "New-comer." *cravin4care*. Online posting. 19 Jul. 2004. Web. 12 May 2009.

———. "Very Scared About Talking to a Therapist." *cravin4care*. Online posting. 19 Jul. 2004. Web. 12 May 2009.

cravin4care. Home page. Web. 12 May 2009.

Eisendrath, Stuart J., and Adriana Feder. "Management of Factitious Disorders." *The Spectrum of Factitious Disorders*. Ed. Marc D. Feldman and Stuart J. Eisendrath. Washington, DC: American Psychiatric Press, 1996. 195–213. Print.

"Elise Wu" (anonymous). Medical Center Emergency Department Nursing Record. 8 Apr. 2002. Print.

Factitious Disorder, Munchausen Syndrome, Munchausen Syndrome by Proxy, and Malingering Discussion and Survivor's Forum. Home page. Web. 12 May 2009.

Feldman, Marc D. "Going Public." Online posting. *cravin4care*. 30 May 2004. Web. 12 May 2009.

Feldman, Marc D., James C. Hamilton, and Holly N. Deemer. "Factitious Disorder." *Somatoform and Factitious Disorders.* Ed. Katharine A. Phillips. Washington, DC: American Psychiatric Publishing, 2001. 129–166. Print.

Henderson, Carolyn. "Re: [Cravin4Care] Hi, New." Online posting. *cravin4care*. 6 Feb. 2004. Web. 12 May 2009.

———. "Re: I will start being more active here…" Online posting. *cravin4care*. 15 Mar. 2002. Web. 12 May 2009.

Holder-Perkins, Vicenzio, and Thomas N. Wise. "Somatization Disorder.*" Somatoform and Factitious Disorders.* Ed. Katharine A. Phillips. Washington, DC: American Psychiatric Publishing, 2001. 1–26. Print.

Jenny. "Hi, New." Online posting. *cravin4care*. 5 Feb. 2004. Web. 12 May 2009.

Lapham, Douglas. "Elise Wu." 25 Oct. 1999. University Health Services, anonymous university. Print.

Lapis1402. "Re: Going Public." Online posting. *cravin4care*. 29 May 2004. Web. 12 May 2009.

"Links." *Dr. Marc Feldman's Munchausen Syndrome, Malingering, Factitious Disorder, & Munchausen by Proxy Page.* Ed. Marc D. Feldman. 2004–2007. Web. 12 May 2009.

Lombard, Eric. "Clinic Notes: 52482 MH." 9 June 2000. University Health Services, anonymous university. Print.

———. "Intake for Elise Wu." n.d. University Health Services, anonymous university. Print.

———. Telephone interview. 10 Apr. 2009.

———. Telephone interview. 24 Apr. 2009.

"Munchausen." *Munchausen-Library*. Ed. Bernhard Wiebel. Feb. 2008. Web. 12 May 2009.

"Munchausen Syndrome." *Cleveland Clinic*. 1995–2009. Web. 12 May 2009.

Nadelson, Theodore. "Historical Perspectives on the Spectrum of Sickness: From 'Crock' to 'Crook.'" *The Spectrum of Factitious Disorders.* Ed. Marc D. Feldman and Stuart J. Eisendrath. Washington, DC: American Psychiatric Press, 1996. 1–20. Print.

Sin. "[S]orry." Online posting. *cravin4care*. 4 Nov. 2005. Web. 12 May 2009.

———. "[T]hanks Cathy." Online posting. *cravin4care*. 3 Nov. 2005. Web. 12 May 2009.

Elise's essay shows rigorous attention to detail as she explores the discussions she found about factitious disorder—from the patients, their family members, and their doctors. She is especially careful to archive the postings, noting times and dates. In addition, she tried to see what others had known when they posted their comments. She later wrote,

I needed to be especially careful about how I kept track of the information I gathered while "in" the field and how I presented it. I wanted anyone reading my work to be able to retrace my footsteps—rather, mouse clicks—through the same spaces, so that the path I'd taken was at least plottable, if not completely replicable—hence, the need for not only precise Web addresses but also timestamps to indicate exactly when I'd been where. Providing that information protects you and gives you credibility. Even if someone else goes to the page you claimed you visited and doesn't find the data you insisted was there, your documentation can back you up.

Elise used her other sources offline to triangulate the data she gathered from the two FD Web sites. On the phone, she interviewed a doctor with whom she'd spent time during college. She obtained her student health service records by mail to compare them with what she remembered and to study those events from the perspectives of her caregivers. In libraries and medical journals, she read medical accounts of FD and related disorders. She changed names for anonymity; her purpose was to learn about FD, not to expose any of the people who had supported or treated her. Of course, in her position as a former patient, she wrote much about her own personal experiences; later on, she talked with her family, friends, and other doctors about their memories of her at the time while continuing to keep track of all of her research. Her "Works Cited" page is an inventory of her careful documentation en route through her project and as she crafted a much longer essay, the online part of which you've just read.

For more help doing research online and citing electronic sources, visit **bedfordstmartins.com/ fieldworking.**

Working with Online Communities

Working in online communities challenges us differently than working in physical fieldsites. As you saw in Elise's study, online informants are often anonymous as they interact. Your own online experiences have probably taught you that online communities are fluid, ever-changing, and sometimes unidentifiable. There are no rules for online research, but we think guidelines are important to have. We asked our former student, Alan Benson, who studied online communities, to think about guidelines and share them with you in this section.

Online communities share many characteristics with their face-to-face counterparts. Participants interact with one another over a long period of time (decades, in some cases), they spend a lot of time "together" online (even though they may be physically far apart), they engage with each other using insider language, and they see themselves as a coherent group. While not every online meeting place is home to a community, many can serve as excellent fieldsites to begin a study.

Your first task is to identify that the online group is a real community since not every collection of people in the online world will be one, just as not every group of people in the physical world is. One key feature of an online group is shared language, so look for the use of their specific terms and rhetoric and record this information as part of your data.

Online communities can take shape around message boards or Web forums. These sites support the interactions in which a coherent group can flourish and may be focused on a particular theme (for example, the *Anime Forum*) or they may be wide open (*The WELL*). Some boards began life as an offshoot of another cultural project (for example, *The Straight Dope Message Board* started as a place to discuss the newspaper column called "The Straight Dope"). Message boards are handy because they log the language that takes place in the community, providing a record of the participants' words. This helps you focus your fieldnotes on the interactions, interpret common themes, and collect impressions about members and the sources they suggest in their talk.

Virtual environments such as *Second Life* or *Active Worlds* also allow for people to interact online. Visiting one of these worlds is akin to diving into a digital world where everything—bodies, objects, physical spaces—can be reshaped. But unless you already use it, or have a lead on a community you want to study, it can take a long time to master the software. Online games, such as *World of Warcraft*, are popular to study, and the comments sections of well-traveled Web sites, such as *Amazon* or *Internet Movie Database*, have developed into small communities. However, these sites are better as supporting data for a larger study, because by themselves they are difficult to manage.

You will want to consider the coherence of the community. Social networking sites, such as Facebook or MySpace, allow people to forge links, but a simple link to another person does not make a community. Similarly, the tech fans who read and post on *Slashdot* may all identify as "*Slashdot* readers," but this definition may not translate to a coherent community identity. Facebook's fan pages are closer to communities, since they allow people who share a particular interest (a band, an activity, or a cause) to interact. When looking at online communities, keep an eye out for ones that share a similar culture (they are all interested in the same topics), have a high level of engagement (people post actively), and have very visible cultural elements (behaviors, rules, and rituals).

Once you've chosen your community, get a feel for its shape and size. Is the site dedicated to discussion? Do interactions take place alongside other content (news stories, products on sale, or essays)? Does it require people to sign up, or can anyone participate without registering? Are there any limits on the names people use? Can users select avatars or user pictures to represent themselves?

As an online researcher, be sensitive to the forces shaping people's word choices. Create a glossary of the frequent terms. What's the group's rhetoric? Do members rely upon *logos* (information, such as links to news sites), *pathos* (tone for the audience, such as humor, criticism, enthusiasm), or *ethos* (profile of the community, such as their reputation or how people view them)?

Next, look at who participates. How many active users are there? What does it mean to be active? Are there moderators or administrators? If so, how active are they? If not, how does the community deal with disruptive members? Are there ranks or levels of usership that mark more senior, helpful, or humorous members? Try to identify the powerbrokers, who are often frequent posters or senior members. How do they shape the community's discourse? Do they police other users or lead by example? Watch these members interact with others. Note how they construct their messages, address other members, and react to one another. Powerbrokers can be useful as you research your site and understand its community.

Finally, to understand how a community works, you might find a way to "step in." That is, you may want to get involved in the community. You don't have to dominate discussion, and you might spend time just lurking before engaging in conversation. Whatever way you get involved, the community's interactions will become part of your data.

How to Work with Online Communities

1. Identify what kind of online community you're studying. In what ways is it a community? For how long have its members been interacting? Do they see themselves as a coherent group? Look at the site's design and interactive features. Who are the leaders?

2. Identify insider language. Make a glossary of terms and identify the group members' rhetoric. How do they address each other? How do the leaders use the language you've noticed?

3. Identify participants and community organization. What are the rules for interacting? Who participates? Who administers the site and makes the rules? What kinds of behavior do you notice?

4. Get involved with the community. How do the people talk to you? What do you need to know in order to communicate well with them?

5. Check with offline sources for triangulation. What library resources could you consult? Where offline might you go to understand more about what the community discusses?

Among many online communities, our students have studied online recycling, Craigslist, foodie blogs, rock star fan clubs, cartoon collectors, and more. Working online allows you access to archived information and conversations as well as current ones, giving you rich material for your fieldnotes. Whether you use an electronic community as support data for a study—or as a cultural site in itself—you use the same approaches to fieldwork in any culture or subculture, whether it's virtual or actual.

BOX 15

Locating Online Cultures

PURPOSE

Can we consider an electronic community a "culture"? Are all electronic communities "cultures"? If not, why? If we study people interacting on the Internet, the most public of spaces, can we call it "fieldwork"? Certainly, some sites are temporary communities but not cultures.

Students in Bonnie's graduate class on ethnographic methods, theories, and texts wanted to test out this question. Each person chose a site and analyzed it for its cultural features. Students asked whether a fieldworker could make it the focus of an ethnographic research project involving data from many other sources. Marie Gernes studied A Practical Wedding, a site begun and managed by a woman who wanted other "smart and funny women, to figure out how to be a bride and a wife on our own terms," but it stays in business because of the wedding vendors who sponsor it. Amelia Carl found Oh No They Didn't! Creepy, or ONTD, a community of people who love "creepy" events, which amassed over 7,000 members and over 250,000 comments in a short eight months. After a few weeks, Bonnie's class agreed that what an online community needed to be a culture was a common language, a clear organizational pattern, shared behaviors and rituals, and members' consistent engagement.

ACTION

Choose a Web site connected to an interest of yours—or choose one that supplements an aspect of your ongoing fieldwork project. Look carefully at its features: design, membership, comments, links, history, related source material, and so on.

Follow a conversation and note who's speaking. Try to find the place where the site states its rules. Try to determine if this is a subculture. Does it have "insider" language? Does it invent special words or use words in specific ways? Can you create a list of insider terms?

Check whether there are "gatekeepers"—monitors who allow or disallow participation, people who ensure that the site meets its purpose. What are their reasons for rejecting a poster's comments? How can you detect rituals or rules of behavior? Can you determine what the group shares as goals or interests? Why would someone join or quit the group?

Then expand your research to triangulate your data. If you wanted to study this site as a culture, where else might you go to gather important data? With whom would you talk? What offline locations does it represent? Where are they? What print or media sources would you consult to explore further information?

RESPONSE

Outside of his work as an assistant writing center director, and his life as a husband and father, Matt Gilchrist loves to bake bread. He chose to study a site for amateur bread bakers:

> I point my browser to www.thefreshloaf.com, and it commands my attention to three large photos at the center of the page, above which are the words "Chia Sourdough," "Leinsamenbrot," and "Pain Aux Cereales." They're three seed-covered loaves, two

cut to display cross-sections of wide air pockets of the inner loaves. Each is positioned artistically and placed against a contrasting backdrop for its close-up. Each is today's image for The Fresh Loaf (TFL), a site that claims it's a "community for amateur artisan bakers and bread enthusiasts."

About two years ago, I started baking bread after the gift of a secondhand food processor inspired me to bake a loaf for the first time. The results were tasty enough to be worth my effort, and I began playing around with recipes and ingredients. I turned to the Internet for guidance and found this site, where user forums, blogs by bakers, recipes, and discussions are all about bread bakers' attempts, failures, and successes. Videos and links enrich the content. The site gives five lessons for the first-time baker, a handbook, and "a distillation of the baking wisdom of the Fresh Loaf community."

The homepage contains summaries of content areas and links: recent forum posts and comments, baker blogs recently updated, advanced and professional topics, latest news from the bread world, favorite site recipes, and "highest rated stories."

Does this site represent a culture? I think so. One marker of a culture is language used in a culture-specific way, so I scan the homepage to see if I find evidence of cultural language. One forum post is titled "This is how I finally have open crumb and ear without pouring water or using high heat (500F)." It draws many comments from users. Others write about soaking bran, stretching and folding, starters, hydration. There are bakers' posts titled "2 Stage Liquid Levain Sourdough Boules" and "Another Convert for Mini's Favorite 100% Rye." Highest rated is "Maintaining a 100% Hydration White Flour Starter." In the advanced topics section is a post called "dough percentage pros and cons."

The homepage digests contain evidence of 60 different users who have posted to the site recently, most within the last day. I want to learn if they share any rituals, so I go to the Artisan Baking forum and look at a post titled "ISO [in search of] Easy and Great Recipe for Hamburger Buns."

The hamburger bun post is by a user named GSnyde, who refers to himself as Glenn. He says he's a novice who has only baked twice, and asks for advice for an

BOX 15 continued

easy hamburger bun that will give him "some substance, not so heavy-crusted as a sourdough roll, but maybe the texture of a Kaiser Roll." Glenn asks for advice, specifically from "David" or "Brother David." His time stamp indicates 7:48 Tuesday evening. David posts a reply at 10:47, with links to his favorite roll recipe posts on TFL, and he includes a picture of a "double-knotted" roll sliced and made into a leftover turkey sandwich with lettuce and mayo on a plate with cranberry sauce and pepperoncini. Other users weigh in with advice and links for Glenn. Some answer his questions about adapting a recipe and about hand-mixing a dough that most might use a machine mixer to make. One user (SylviaH) links to her own bun recipe post, in which she adds "made it to the front page photo recipe post." David and Sylvia reassure—and teach—Glenn, the newest baker of the three, in a long discussion back and forth. David cites a recipe that contains "diastatic barley malt powder" and Glenn asks where he could find it. "A homebrew supply store, maybe?" David answers, and explains the ingredient.

Some activities in this post might suggest rituals, too. One user asks a question and shares an idea; others offer their insights or questions, and veteran users refer to older content by citing links and including photos of bread they've baked. Veteran users seem to take on the mentoring roles. They act as tradition-bearers. I'm fascinated as I think of these activities as rituals, so I turn to posts from other days, searching for questions from newer bakers. Yes, those posts contain similar interactions. I see more rituals as I look through the site: photos of bread-baking successes with comments of admiration in response, and photos of bread-baking failures or imperfections with comments of support and suggestions for improvement.

It strikes me that a subculture might, in addition to rituals and shared language, have a kind of mythology and history. The Fresh Loaf has both. Users refer to posts that were made years ago (history); the site owner selects and displays classic posts; the handbook compiles and celebrates the site's combined historical knowledge. The bakers at TFL refer to classic texts (offline), notable chefs, impossible loaves, unattainable perfection. They certainly seem to build a mythology this way.

This culture enforces rules, too, both formal (stated) rules and implicit ones. One rule is that serious bakers use metric measures of weight rather than volumetric measures like cups, teaspoons, etc. To make a post with a recipe that is written in grams associates a user with the most respected and envied bakers on the site. This is one of the ways they establish power. Some users challenge the gram-standard, and thus challenge the power structure, as people in other cultures tend to do. I wish I had time to study TFL more. There's enough at this site to fill a book about the online culture of bread baking.

THE RESEARCH PORTFOLIO:
An Option for Rereading

We suggest that you reread and review your portfolio periodically as it develops during the course of your project. Our classes have shared their work in progress with many combinations of partnerships: students work together throughout a whole semester (or year), small collaborative groups of students report back to one another, and (what we like best of all) the "weekly research assistant" puts the research efforts of an entire class at the disposal of one student and her project. All of these support systems help you see your data from perspectives other than your own. In other words, even an informed "other" can help you reread and reorganize the data as it accumulates.

Rereading the Artifacts   In Chapter 1, Rick Zollo wrote several short reflections about his positioning as he researched Iowa 80. In them, he was able to explore how his own personal history linked with his research and affected his work in the fieldsite. His portfolio included artifacts from the truck stop as well as his related reading and writing: a menu, a few brochures about trucking regulations, photocopies of articles he'd read about truckers, a trucker magazine, photographs he had taken at the truck stop, five writing exercises describing his fieldsite, and a **transcript** of an interview with one of his informants. Each time he reviewed his portfolio, he wrote a short commentary about where he found himself in the research process.

Researching another culture can be both messy and confusing, but if you reflect on the process, you'll find yourself sorting out the mess and clarifying much of the confusion. We believe that the process of reflecting is just as important as the final end product of an ethnographic study. For this reason, we want you to take time to think and write about what you've actually learned from each exercise you do at different stages of your research process. Get together with your portfolio partner, and share your work. Have your partner ask questions about your project, and include those questions and responses in your portfolio as well:

- How does your own personal history affect what you've chosen?
- What does each artifact represent about a growing theme in your research?
- How do the artifacts connect to one another?

Rereading Your Reading   For your portfolio, you'll want to review each of the short readings you did and reflect on them: Gloria Naylor's introduction to her novel *Mama Day*, the excerpt from Laura Bohannan's essay "Shakespeare in the Bush," and Alice Walker's short story "Everyday Use."

Look through your portfolio for the books, pamphlets, articles, and other print materials you've collected from magazines, journals, and the Web. Review what you have, and try to explain it to a partner: describe which information relates directly to the questions you're asking about your topic, which information might take you in a different direction, which information gave you background material that you might now discard. Apply a stick-on note with a short summary to each written artifact, and take some time to show your partner—or your group—how you think it connects to the whole project. Our students find this a great way to begin organizing data thematically.

- What categories could you use to tell the story of your project so far?
- What written source offers a historical backdrop or an important understanding about the culture you're studying?
- Which written sources represent—or come directly from—the culture itself? If you don't have a piece of writing from or about your culture, where might you locate one?

Rereading Your Sources of Support   The multiple perspectives in your study can come from your classmates as well as your informants. One simple way to do this is bring a friend, relative, or classmate to your fieldsite to take notes, and then reciprocate by visiting that person's site.

As you work with the materials in your portfolio, you'll notice that you've had lots of assistance from others, and it's always useful to acknowledge your sources of support: who helped you gain access to the culture, who suggested key informants, who found an article about your topic. Who worked with you in organizing your data? Who asked an insightful question? Who went with you to your fieldsite? Of course, one strategy for enriching your data is to assign someone as your research partner for the whole course of your project.

Our favorite strategy is the "weekly research assistant." Everyone in the class becomes your research assistant for a week, including your teacher. You design their assignments (three people, for example, read articles and write reports for you, three people go with you to your fieldsite on one day, two people do Web searches on your topic, four people try out a cultural practice and report in writing about how it worked). A week later, you have accumulated much new data for your portfolio and lots of new insights on your project. Aidan Vollmer, who you may recall studied the graffiti culture, tried this approach with his class. Bonnie was his teacher, and she took notes on a film called *Style Wars*, a documentary by linguistic sociologist and scholar Dwight Conquergood. Bonnie recorded quotes from the movie that reflected the graffiti artists' insider language, which in turn helped Aidan see the perspectives artists took on their own work. Aidan's classmate, Eric Landuyt, went out into the local college town and recorded and described all the graffiti he could find, some of which Aidan hadn't seen. Eric categorized his long list of observations into "Current Graffiti," "Past Graffiti," and "Future Graffiti Locations"—both pro and con. Aidan kept this list in his portfolio because it gave him ideas about how to categorize the graffiti he'd already seen.

Rereading Your Writing   If you've worked on the boxes in this chapter, you may have already

- written about your positionality (the assumptions you carry into your fieldsite)
- written about an everyday object or event using the double-entry format
- kept notes for a book club
- considered the process of negotiating entry and worked with ethics statements
- selected and "read" a cultural artifact

 ## Read Your Fieldsite

Learning to read levels of explicit and implicit behaviors, rules, languages, and codes can take time. Use this exercise to practice how to read your fieldsite and to move from outsider to insider without disturbing the culture.

FIRST   Try to identify the codes or behaviors you're unfamiliar with in your site. In what situations must you act with care? Learn new rules of politeness? Wait to be told what to do? What behaviors do you need to observe quietly to master? In what ways do the people in that culture expect you to behave like them? Excuse you for doing things your own way?

Read Your Fieldsite

SECOND Make a list of questions you would like to ask an insider in this culture. For example, how do insiders know when a meal begins and ends, and what are the codes of behavior for eating? If you are studying abroad where English is not the primary spoken language, identify what you are unsure of: how to make a phone call, how to greet someone or ask directions, or how to locate a bathroom.

THIRD Choose a single code or behavior you've identified. Describe in a detailed paragraph the rules an outsider would need to know to fit into the culture. As Paulo Freire would say, what "words" do you have to "read" to understand the "world" in which you are participating?

4

Researching Place: The Spatial Gaze

· ·

What you see is based on how you look. In this chapter you will:

- understand and describe your own personal geography
- recognize ways to depict a cultural landscape
- provide focus by selecting details
- find and document tension at a fieldsite

· ·

The word *fieldworking* implies place. When researchers venture "into the field," they enter the surroundings of the "other." Researchers step out of familiar territory and into unfamiliar landscapes. But no matter where they conduct their research, they take their **perspectives** along. When you return to a place where you spent time in your early years, like your grandmother's apartment or a childhood playground, you're probably surprised that the place seems different, maybe smaller or larger than you imagined. And if you visit a kindergarten room, you notice that the scale is designed for small people: you bend down to look at the gerbils in their cages; you stuff yourself into a tiny plastic chair or fold your legs to your chin during rug time. Your spatial memory and your spatial assumptions depend on your past experiences and your present situation.

"Gaze" is the act of seeing; it is an act of selective perception. Much of what we see is shaped by our experiences, and our "gaze" has a direct bearing on what we think. And what we see and think, to take the process one step further, has a bearing upon what we say and what and how we write.

—PAUL STOLLER

As anthropologist Paul Stoller implies in the quotation above, what we see depends on how we filter or select what we see. What we see also depends on *how* we look—how we open ourselves to the acts of seeing. Just as we all read differently at different times in our lives, we also perceive differently. As a child, you may not have realized that the reasons for rug time in kindergarten often had more to do with the teacher's desire to establish community than with the fun you had leaving your desk. Stoller's expression "the spatial gaze" represents the fieldworker's stance and worldview. Anthropologists use the term *worldview* to encompass an informant's entire cultural perspective. Of course, how we understand an informant's worldview is dependent on our own.

This chapter is about researching place: remembering your personal geography, learning how to look at your fieldsite, detailing and mapping space, finding unity and tension within a place, and locating a **focal point**. We are always part of the places we study. Whether they are familiar or unfamiliar, we always stand in relationship to those places. No matter how far outside or how close inside we may situate ourselves, there can be no place description without an author. And authoring a place description requires personal involvement. You must always decide on an angle of vision when you take a picture; describing a place is much the same as choosing the perspective from which to shoot.

You may have selected a fieldsite by now and spent some time learning how to "read" it and some of its cultural materials. Researching place takes a long time; this chapter extends many of the skills of reading a cultural site that you may have tried in Chapter 3. Understanding how informants use the space in a fieldsite constitutes the researcher's data. For this reason, fieldworkers train themselves to look through the eyes of both the insider (**emic** perspective) and the outsider (**etic** perspective) at once to locate their own perspectives.

Personal Geography

Each of us has a sense of place, whether we've moved great distances or stayed within the same spaces all our lives. That sense of place evokes a kind of loyalty linked to a familiar landscape that comforts us, even when it is not beautiful or particularly comfortable. Even in a new place, something can evoke past sensations, uncovering a geographical memory and bringing with it a sudden surge of images. Our personal geographies influence our spatial gaze; they influence how we look. In fact, sometimes our memories of home—or other places where we have felt comfortable—obscure our abilities to understand other perspectives. Political, economic, and social influences often shape a place in ways that are not always visible to its inhabitants.

Jamaica Kincaid's nonfiction essay, "On Seeing England for the First Time," shows that people sometimes grow up unaware that their personal geography can be shaped by invisible forces. As a child growing up on the Caribbean island of Antigua, Kincaid did not realize that England's cultural values dominated her island life. Notice in the following excerpt how many of her childhood practices and values are shaped by a culture an ocean away.

On Seeing England for the First Time

Jamaica Kincaid

When I saw England for the first time, I was a child in school sitting at a desk. The England I was looking at was laid out on a map gently, beautifully, delicately, a very special jewel; it lay on a bed of sky blue—the background of the map—its yellow form mysterious, because though it looked like a leg of mutton, it could not really look like anything so familiar as a leg of mutton because it was England—with shadings of pink and green, unlike any shadings of pink and green I had seen before, squiggly veins of red running in every direction. England was a special jewel all right, and only special people got to wear it. The people who got to wear England were English people. They wore it well and they wore it everywhere: in jungles, in deserts, on plains, on top of the highest mountains, on all the oceans, on all the seas. When my teacher had pinned this map up on the blackboard, she said, "This is England"—and she said it with authority, seriousness, and adoration, and we all sat up. It was as if she had said, "This is Jerusalem, the place you will go to when you die but only if you have been good." We understood then—we were meant to understand then—that England was to be our source of myth and the source from which we got our sense of reality, our sense of what was meaningful, our sense of what was meaningless—and much about our own lives and much about the very idea of us headed that last list.

At the time I was a child sitting at my desk seeing England for the first time, I was already very familiar with the greatness of it. Each morning before I left for school, I ate a breakfast of half a grapefruit, an egg, bread and butter and a slice of cheese, and a cup of cocoa; or half a grapefruit, a bowl of oat porridge, bread and butter and a slice of cheese, and a cup of cocoa. The can of cocoa was often left on the table in front of me. It had written on it the name of the company, the year the company was established, and the words "Made in England." Those words, "Made in England," were written on the box the oats came in too. They would also have been written on the box the shoes I was wearing came in; the bolt of gray linen cloth lying on the shelf of a store from which my mother had bought three yards to make the uniform that I was wearing had written along its edge those three words. The shoes I wore were made in England, so were my socks and cotton undergarments and the satin ribbons I wore tied at the end of two plaits of my hair. My father, who might have sat next to me at breakfast, was a carpenter and cabinetmaker. The shoes he wore to work would have been made in England, as were his khaki shirt and trousers, his underpants and undershirt, his socks and brown felt hat. Felt was not the proper material from which a hat that was expected to provide shade from the hot sun should have been made, but my father must have seen and admired a picture of an Englishman wearing such a hat in England, and this picture that he saw must have been so compelling that it caused him to wear the wrong hat for a hot climate most of his long life. And this hat—a brown felt hat—became so central to his character that it was the first thing he put on in the morning as he stepped out of bed and the last thing he took off before he stepped back into bed at night. As we sat at breakfast, a car might go by. The car, a Hillman or a Zephyr, was made in England. The very idea of the meal itself, breakfast, and its substantial quality and quantity, was an idea from England; we somehow knew that in England they began the day with this meal called breakfast, and a proper breakfast was a big breakfast. No one I knew liked eating so much food so early in the day; it made us feel sleepy, tired. But this breakfast business was "Made in England" like almost everything else that surrounded us, the exceptions being the sea, the sky, and the air we breathed....

Read Kincaid's full essay at **bedfordstmartins .com/fieldworking**, under Professional Essays.

Kincaid depicts herself as someone who leaves her childhood land and grows to understand the enormous influence of English culture on her worldview. The British controlled these Caribbean islanders' government, economics, and political practices, as well as their personal geography, their everyday cultural practices, and even their spatial gaze—the way they viewed their surrounding landscape.

The British spatial gaze had been instilled in Kincaid as a child. She grew up feeling a tension between what she actually saw and what she was told to see. Her internal landscape was based on her everyday experiences living on Antigua, but the landscape she read about, sang about, and learned about was based on a more powerful island in an entirely different geography. Islanders, for example, felt sleepy from eating "so much food" early in the hot morning, and she instinctively knew that her father's brown felt hat, which he had selected from a picture of an Englishman wearing one, should have been a hat more suited to the Caribbean climate. All these practices, she suggests, were "'Made in England' like almost everything else that surrounded us."

Kincaid evokes a sense of place and brings us into that childhood landscape, making us as readers feel as she did, perhaps a little shocked. She selects sensory details of time, place, weather, color, smells, textures, sounds, tastes, and sights, creating verbal snapshots of both Antigua and England, real and imagined. Through her descriptive language, we learn to map the space that she has mapped as a child.

BOX16

Recalling a Sense of Place

PURPOSE

We carry our sense of place, our personal geography, into our fieldwork. To research place, it is important to retrieve and record our own internal landscape and make it explicit to ourselves. What images do we remember from particular landscapes? What details do we recall about places we've visited? Why do these sensations return to us at particular moments in time? Why those images, details, and sensations—and not others?

Writer Barry Lopez suggests in his essay "Losing Our Sense of Place" that the intimate link between landscape and memory comes through the act of writing and "through the power of observation, the gifts of eye and ear, of tongue and nose and finger, that a place first rises up in our mind; afterward, it is memory that carries the place, that allows it to grow in depth and complexity. For as long as our records go back, we have held these two things dear, landscape and memory" (p. 38).

ACTION

Choose a spot that brings back a rush of sensory details—sights, sounds, smells, textures, and tastes. It doesn't need to be an enormous natural wonder like the Grand Canyon. Try describing a private spot—a certain tree in your backyard, a basketball court, a relative's dining room, the corner of a city lot, the interior of a closet, or a window seat that catches the sunlight. As you think about the specifics of this place—its details and sensations— you'll probably remember a dominant impression, a cluster of images, or a person connected to the place. These are all part of your internal landscape. Write a few short descriptive paragraphs with as many details as you can to share with your writing partner.

RESPONSE

Maggie McKnight grew up in Northern California, worked as a baker in a restaurant there, and landed temporarily at a university in the Midwest. In this excerpt from a longer essay, "Cookies and Complaints: A Foodie Deals with Displacement," she views her new landscape through the lens of her background as both a Californian and a "foodie," trying to come to terms with the contrasts between her personal sense of place and the new landscape.

> I've spent the last several months watching the angle of the sun change as it shines through the window onto my dining table, and I am bracing myself for the long ordeal of my first midwestern winter. It's a cold December morning and I'm sitting in my dining room drinking Peet's English Breakfast tea, having just finished a poached egg with prosciutto on garlic toast. Until four months ago, I'd lived all my life spoiled by northern California's beauty and mild weather, so I have some adjusting to do. But even worse than the climatic shock—which I first experienced in the steamy heat of August—is the gastronomic shock.
>
> So here I am in the heartland. The heart of America's farmland. Over ninety percent of the state is cultivated farmland, but the landscape around here reveals none of the small family-owned organic farms that I came to rely on in the Bay Area. Nope, haven't seen any of those yet. What you see here, if you head south on the main street out of town, are endless eighty-acre plots of two things: corn and soybeans. Once, when I was riding my bicycle through the fields of corn and beans (there's only one kind of beans here, making soy redundant), I came across a hog farm—two long buildings with divided pens. I peeked into a chicken-wire window, and the hogs squealed in surprise, climbing over each other in their tight quarters to get away from the sudden invasion by a strange helmeted being. I breathed a sigh of relief— finally, something I could eat.
>
> For even though I enjoy corn, and beans, too, these corn and beans aren't grown for people to eat. Most of this farmland is owned by corporate "farmers" and is

BOX**16** continued

cultivated for one purpose: livestock feed. Small farmers compete with these corporations and most often lose. Though many of my fellow students come from rural areas, few of them come from farming families. Those few speak of the increasing struggle to survive as a small farmer—often, their parents have had to take on second jobs, as if farming itself isn't already more than a full-time job.

Back in California, I worked at one of the finest restaurants in the entire U.S. Even in my own kitchen, I only ate organic, locally grown food, preferably the day it was picked. I also grew up eating fresh food grown and preserved by my parents and had, to my dismay upon arriving here, developed a refined taste for only the very best produce. Sure, there's industrial agriculture in California—plenty of it. But it's easy to forget, given the success of the smaller organic farms and the constant availability of locally grown fruits and vegetables.

So what's a food snob to do here in the Midwest? It wasn't just the food itself that I missed; it was the particular food culture. It was knowing that when I asked "where was it grown?" others would understand that I meant what farmer, not what state (or hemisphere for that matter). It was the comfort of not having to explain why I chose the more expensive, organic yogurt at the market. It was the very existence of such a thing as a market—more than just competing chains of supermarkets. I could also choose from various grocery stores, where the manager recognized me, where if I was a dollar short my check-out clerk would tell me to just bring it the next time I came in.

Selective Perception

Your own spatial gaze influences your observation process, and understanding how it does this is critical to understanding insiders' perceptions of their own landscapes. Folklorist Henry Glassie's *Passing the Time in Ballymenone: Culture and History of an Ulster Community* is a full-length ethnographic study (10 years, 852 pages) of storytelling, conversation, and music making in a small community in Northern Ireland. In this short excerpt, which introduces a *ceili* (fireside session) at the Flanagans', Glassie begins with a verbal snapshot of the landscape, a wide-angle sweep of the hillside, and ends with a close-up of the neighbors as they gather around the hearth:

> The house cattle should have been onto the hillsides early in April, but summer came lashing wet winds down the brown hedges and through bleak fields. Across the bog and over the hills, air lay bone cold. Some of the cows, they say, starved in their byres, dying on beds of sodden rushes, and into the minds of men waiting for the sun blew years when black frost shriveled the spuds on the ridges, years when turf lay on the spread through the summer, and winter closed down without food for the belly

or fuel for the hearth. The bright, warm days expected in May and June never came. In running gray skies, in the dank sloughs of the gaps, summer broke, damp, chilled.

Now it is calm. Fat cattle move slowly in the blue harvest evening. Lush grasslands swell and fold in the haze. Some of last year's potatoes and turf and hay remain, heaped into pits on the moss ground, thatched in lumps on the bog, piled in haysheds, built into rotund pecks along the lanes. Old defenses against hard times, displays of industry cover the land.

A month ago summer ended in a blaze of sunshine and a frenzy of work. Hay was rooked, turf was clamped. Sun and warm winds drove out the wet. Once built into rounded conical rooks, and clamps the shape of ancient oratories, hay and turf are considered won. That is their word for victory in the cyclical war fought with the hand-tools they call weapons: the pitchfork and the spade.

Now it is quiet, an interlude in work and worry. The main crop potatoes are not yet ready to dig, nor is it time to transplant winter cabbage, shear the corn, or drive the cattle onto the sweet aftergrass of the meadows. Work slows but does not stop. It is a time for gathering in the spoils of war, drawing turf and hay home, and it is time to hack back hedges with bill-hooks and cart broken turf to gardens built on barren land. Gently, the next campaign begins.

Turf and hay are won. For a month the new potatoes, the Epicures, have been boiled for dinner. It is a time, too, for mild extravagance. This year's potatoes are boiled in lavish numbers, fires built of this year's turf are unnecessarily hearty. Winter's word is bitter. In its depths, when winds pound at the walls of home, potatoes will be sparingly spent and the fire will be stretched with gathered sticks, but today victory expands in little luxuries.

Joe Flanagan turns from the sack of turf next to the open front door. Damp green and blue melt behind him. He cradles an armload. Peter lifts a violin from its case in the corner and settles on a stool by the hearth. Dinner is done, the hens are fed, empty teacups sit on the floor. Joe tongs live coals from the fire, lines them in front of the hearthstone, and sweeps the ashes off to his side with a besom of heather bound round with twine. (95–96)

In this short passage, Glassie writes from the stance of the Ballymenone residents, capturing the lilting rhythms of their language, seeing what they would see, using words they would use to describe the setting. His description focuses on the features of the landscape that the villagers themselves would notice: bog, rushes, spuds, turf and hay, cattle. His eye rests on the things their eyes would rest on.

Glassie's description begins with a large but detailed sweep of the landscape—fattened cattle moving on lush grasslands in a hazy blue harvest evening—and continues into a small space—here, the Flanagan hearthstone with empty teacups sitting on the floor. His spatial gaze moves from outside to inside, creating a mood and a setting for the ceili (storytelling session). Though Glassie writes using the third-person point of view, this description is not objective. In fact, some scholars believe that Glassie romanticizes the Irish culture in descriptions such as this. Like all of us, Glassie operates with a spatial gaze framed by his own biases, assumptions, and cultural baggage. He might ask himself questions about his descriptions, as all of us should about our fieldsites.

Questions to Ask about Descriptions

- Why do I focus on this element of the landscape and not that?
- What is my reason for narrowing my gaze to any specific place?
- What spaces have I rejected as I've narrowed my gaze?
- Why do I use the metaphors and descriptions I do?
- Which metaphors and descriptions did I abandon as inappropriate?
- Where in my fieldnotes do I find evidence for this description?
- What have I rejected, and why?

Spatial details are an important part of the fieldworker's data. All fieldworkers describe their informants in a setting, working from an abundance of evidence: fieldnotes, photos, maps, and background history gathered over time. Researchers cannot lean entirely on visual details; the ethnographic "eye" should also record sounds, textures, tastes, and smells. Important details also come from noticing and documenting, as Glassie does, conditions of color, weather, light, shape, time, season, atmosphere, and ambiance. Choosing details is an act of selective perception. As we write, we revise our worldviews. The point of doing fieldwork is to learn to see not just the other but ourselves as well. The spatial gaze demands that we look—and then look back again at ourselves.

FieldWriting: The Grammar of Observation

Fieldwriting places special demands on us as writers. We write by drawing on our collected data—our fieldnotes, expanded versions of them, and reflections about them. When we assemble and draft our final researched account, we revise it many times because fieldwriting, like all writing, is a recursive process. But fieldwriters must return often to their evidence—fieldnotes, transcripts, artifacts, reflections—to verify the account. Throughout our drafts, we must be aware of the words we choose. The special demand of fieldwriting is that descriptive material must have corresponding verification in the data. That's why it's called field research.

Over the years, as we and our students have conducted research, we've developed some strategies specific to fieldwriting, what we call the "grammar of observation." Here are a few ways we help our students revise their field-projects, based on working with four elementary parts of speech.

Nouns

Fieldwriters draw on an abundance of detail by making lists in their fieldnotes of actual people, places, and things that both they and their informants observe. Sometimes these lists appear in a final text.

But more often, fieldwriters review their lists and look for strong nouns that organize a description or provide a focal point like Glassie on the hearth or Kincaid on her English breakfast. A focal point is often a noun—a concrete object in the informants' space that represents even more than it actually is. A focal point can serve as a metaphor, a frame to set off more complex cultural themes. Glassie's hearth was a space for storytelling and music-making among neighbors. An effective fieldwriter searches through fieldnotes to identify important nouns that hold cultural meanings in those spaces and uses them to write up the research study.

Verbs

Strong verbs assist all writers because they bring action to the page. A strong verb can capture motion in one word. The words *walk, saunter, lumber, dart, toddle, slither, sneak, clomp, traipse, schlep, dawdle,* and *pace* all refer to a similar action. *Walk* is the weakest word in the list, but it is the one that would most readily come to mind. Forcing yourself to find the right verb makes you look more closely at the action in your fieldsite so that you can describe it. Finding the right verb makes you a more accurate fieldwriter. But finding the right verb may not happen until you've drafted and redrafted.

Try what we call a "verb pass." Scan through your text, and highlight or circle the tired, flabby, and overused verbs that flatten prose. Most often, these are forms of the verb *to be* or passive voice constructions. Excise these with no remorse. Substitute more precise and more interesting verbs to describe the actions you've observed. Haul the action forward with active, not passive, verbs. Locate focal points, metaphors, and cultural themes in your data to get ideas for new verb choices.

Adjectives and Adverbs

Cultural assumptions can hide inside the adjectives and adverbs you use. When you write "The dinner table was arranged *beautifully*" or "The *perky* dog greeted me with a *frenzied* lick" or "The *sultry* atmosphere was *warm and friendly*" or "The *dull, dirty* apartment was crammed with *cheap blue* pottery," the qualifying words convey value judgments that are not verifiable because they belong to you. As a fieldwriter, let your reader make the judgment from the material you present. And let your informants and your other data contribute that material.

Karen Downing, whose notes you saw in Chapter 2 (p. 84), learned to reserve her assumptions and value judgments for portions of the paper devoted to discussing them. With her permission, we have altered a portion of her study, in which she describes Ginny James's office, by stuffing adjectives and adverbs into her clean sentences. We loaded up these paragraphs to show how a writer can bury attitudes under adjectives and adverbs. To see how qualifiers impose a researcher's value judgments and hide cultural assumptions, compare our versions of her description with Karen's online at this book's companion Web site.

Read Karen's project at **bedfordstmartins.com/ fieldworking**, under Student Essays.

Version 1

Underneath Ginny's untidy desk, there are five bulging purses of varying sizes, from sleek, expensive leather clutches to cheap plastic bags. I gather from this backstage mess that the disorganized people who mechanically work here also need to use Ginny's sleazy office for their unprofessional belongings. On the top of Ginny's trashy desk, there are sloppy stacks of paper and torn notebooks and curled Post-it notes and a noisy, out-of-date, obsolete fax machine. She has her own ridiculously posed Photo Phantasies photograph, taken hurriedly, with her wearing a yellowed straw hat and a faded denim jacket with garish sunflowers embroidered haphazardly on the collar. Right beside this tacky photograph is a picture of an old haggy witch complete with bent broom and a wicked scraggly black cat.

Version 2

Underneath Ginny's meticulous desk, there are five neatly arranged purses of varying sizes, organized carefully from large to small. I gather that the efficient, tidy people who cheerfully work here need to use Ginny's neat office for their modest personal belongings too. On the top of Ginny's antique cherry desk, there are straight stacks of brightly colored paper and well-organized matching burgundy notebooks and recently purchased Post-it notes and a quiet, understated fax machine. She has her own sedately posed Photo Phantasies photograph, taken carefully with her wearing a jaunty straw hat and an imported denim jacket with delicate sunflowers hand-embroidered on the dainty collar. Right beside this elegant photograph is a picture of a spiritual witch, complete with handcrafted broom and a sleek, assured black cat.

The grammar of observation is really just the grammar of good writing: strong specific nouns, accurate active verbs, and adjectives and adverbs that add texture without masquerading cultural bias. All writers face a responsibility to bring their observations—as they see them—to the page. But fieldwriters face a double ethical challenge: to translate their informants' voices and perspectives for their readers yet still acknowledge their own presence in the text. This challenge requires careful observation, focused selection and verification of detail, and a deep awareness of the role of the self in writing about the other.

Using the Grammar of Observation

- Use active verbs. Avoid the passive voice. Double-check your work by conducting a "verb pass" on your draft. (*Active voice*: "I did a verb pass on this draft." *Passive voice*: "A verb pass was done on this draft.")

- Use specific nouns, particularly those that represent meaning for insiders in the culture.

- Avoid adjectives and adverbs that contain assumptions or stereotypes about people, places, or things. What might seem tacky, disheveled, odd, beautiful, or exciting to you may not be to your informants.

- Separate your perspective from your informants' by using their language, their quotations, and their insider terms.

BOX 17

Writing a Verbal Snapshot

PURPOSE

Your fieldnotes are a rich source of data from which you can select key details to begin to create verbal snapshots for your project. Choose a small portion of your fieldsite to describe for this exercise. Whether you have recorded your data as a list, double-entry fieldnotes, or a narrative, read and review those fieldnotes, and underline, tag, or highlight five to 10 details that stand out for you at your fieldsite.

Writing a place description involves more than making an inventory or listing details. Your description needs to suggest the overall sense of place you are trying to understand and should mirror your informants' perspective as well. Sometimes one small detail from your data can expand into a rich image that reflects a dominant theme within the culture. For example, Glassie (see p. 170) gives us the image of Joe sweeping the hearth with a "besom of heather bound round with twine," which evokes the poetic and domestic sides of Irish culture. It would have been a quite different description had he written, "Joe swept the floor with a homemade broom." Such a sentence would imply more of an outsider's perspective than an insider's, and one of the goals of fieldworking is to include your informants' worldview.

BOX 17 continued

ACTION

Comb through your data to determine categories of sights, sounds, smells, textures, and tastes; weather, atmospheric conditions, colors, light, shapes. Categorizing will help you write your description, and it will also help you fill in the missing data in your fieldwork. Noticing the gaps helps you determine where, or in what ways, your data might be incomplete. "Do I need different sensory details? More about the setting at different times of day? Do I want to focus on a certain spot in this place where important activity is going on? What details do I need more of? What did I forget to take in?" Asking these questions will help you decide if you want to return to your fieldsite to gather more evidence.

After writing a short description based on your notes about setting details, share a page or two with a colleague to see if you've successfully created a sense of place and to discuss what you might research further. As you respond to your partner, point out your most telling details. Which details evoke larger images? Which details uncover cultural information about the place? Which details seem to represent the informant's perspective? Do any specific words seem like insider language?

RESPONSE

When the editor of our book, Joelle Hann, visited Brazil, she became interested in how the fieldworking process provides a lens for everyday life. She decided to take pictures and fieldnotes on her trip from a focused perspective—as a new fieldworker, not just as a traveler. Here is an excerpt from her extensive notes, as well as photographs. Notice how Joelle captures the sights and sounds of Brazil from an outsider's point of view as she crafts a verbal snapshot.

For another example response to this box, go to **bedfordstmartins.com/ fieldworking** and click on Writing a Verbal Snapshot.

One of the first things tourists see when they step from the airport in Salvador da Bahia, Brazil, is a taxi driver. At the feet of these hardworking men, the hesitant tourist lays her plans—concocted far away with the help of foreign books, maps, and Web sites. *Take care of me*, she thinks, *take care of my dream*. First glimpses—of palm trees and bamboo forest, food stands, white sand dunes, the crumbling city, and the glorious sun—are viewed through the tinted windows of a taxi.

Every taxi in Salvador is painted the same way: white with parallel blue and red racing stripes along the sides. Most are compact cars made in Brazil: my driver Cacique's taxi is a four-door miniwagon that comfortably holds five adults and carries, in the far back, a natural-gas tank and whatever luggage its passengers might have.

Cacique's taxi has seen better days. Off-white putty stains on the hood and body show where scratches have been patched recently. It stalls while idling. Below 20 degrees Celsius, the car has trouble starting because the natural gas is slow to move. He's preparing the car for sale as he waits for his new one to arrive from São Paulo on a car carrier. Bought with money borrowed from banks and local businesses, the new taxi is due to arrive Monday of next week—June 27 (but doesn't actually arrive until the end of July).

Cacique in his taxi, Salvador da Bahia

For the seven years he's owned his current taxi, Cacique has done many of the repairs himself. His hands are thick and scarred. As a young man, he dreamed of going to Rio—the most perfect city, he calls it—to be a mechanic. But instead he settled into married life in Salvador, first working in an auto shop and then as a taxi driver.

When he's on duty, Cacique puts his taxi sign on the roof, where it draws juice from the engine. A magnetic foot keeps it in place. When he's off duty, which isn't often, Cacique stores the taxi sign under his seat.

Inside the cab, over the rear-view mirror, a laminated taxi-driver's license shows a photo of Cacique looking younger and healthier than he does today. His full name is listed as Jubíraci Martins da Silva (Zhoo-BIR-a-see Mar-CHEENs da SEEW-va). But no one calls him Jubíraci; they call him Cacique (ka-SEE-kee), which means "little Indian chief"—a boyhood nickname he earned for the way his hair used to stand on end....

Around the rear-view mirror of the taxi flow streams of *fitas* (ribbons) from Salvador's famous church, *Igreja do Bonfim* (Church of the Good End). Each one is stamped with the words *Lembrança do Senhor do Bonfim da Bahia* (in remembrance of Jesus Christ), and though they come in many colors—yellow, red, pink, blue, green—all of Cacique's *fitas* are white. When I asked him about this, he explained

BOX**17** continued

that white is a Bahian color: all *candomblé* priestesses, for example, wear white since they are devotees of the *Orixás*, the *candomblé* deities. More practically, white is also cool in the tropical sun and looks elegant against dark skin. Women's traditional Bahian costume—a fashion that seems more of a leftover from the eighteenth century—consists of a white head cap, a white hooped skirt, and a white bodice. Often, the staff at *pousadas* (inns) wear white....

The *fitas* in Cacique's taxi flutter in the tropical breeze that wafts in the car window. Among them, hung on a chain and twirling with the motion of the car, is a dark brown *figa*, a small wood carving of a hand that shows a thumb poking out between the index and middle finger. The *figa* is a charm used to ward off the evil eye and a fertility symbol worn by young girls hoping to one day have children.

(Photo: Joelle Hann)

Fitas from *O Senhor do Bonfim*

Joelle's fieldnotes create a verbal snapshot, capturing the broad sensory details of this Brazilian city but also focusing on artifacts. The accompanying photographs reveal information that the researcher might simply not see. Photographs provide a different perspective on the space a fieldworker is trying to understand, whether the space is as small as the inside of a cab or as large as a country's landscape. Joelle's photographs show details of Cacique, his taxi, and the *fitas* hanging around his rearview mirror. Pictures you gather from a fieldsite will provide you with specifics about your generalized impressions and give you finely grained data for your study, and studying your photos can help you identify other data that you might yet need to obtain.

Read the full project at **bedfordstmartins.com/ fieldworking**, under Professional Essays.

Deepening Description through Research

Jeannie Banks Thomas is a professor at Utah State University whose expertise is in the history of cemeteries and supernatural legends. In the following essay, she writes about her research in Salem, Massachusetts, one of the sites of the famous Salem Witch Trials in colonial America. In her rich descriptions of Salem's past and present, Thomas overlays her own knowledge of European cemeteries and their cultural history to show how contemporary Salem functions as a public gathering place, much like ancient European cemeteries used to be. As you read this excerpt from her larger project, note the places in which Thomas's use of sensory details evoke a sense of "being there."

The Cemetery as Marketplace in Salem, Massachusetts
Jeannie Banks Thomas

On an October day in Salem, Massachusetts, I stopped to watch a street performance on the downtown pedestrian mall. A man who appeared to be an unhappy cross between Fagan and the Marlboro cowboy positioned his large boom box and yelled at some teenagers walking by, "Hey, don't worry! It's just a phase you're going through!" An older couple passed by; they got: "We'll do bingo—later!"

My "Marlboro Fagan" was the impresario for a troupe of skinny street performers consisting of two young women in spandex and a young, well-muscled, blonde contortionist with what I guessed was either an Australian or a New Zealand accent. Fagan managed the sound, while the youthful, charismatic Heath Ledger lookalike twisted into painful, Picasso-esque positions. The two underaged-looking girls, awkward in their Lycra, did their best to serve as Vanna Whites to the young Heath. One of the girls lacked an arm, so when both stood behind him and held up their arms to accent his impossible positions and tricks, the effect was asymmetrical and distracting. A crowd formed in response to Fagan's calls. The young acrobat bounded around, juggling, contorting, and reminding the crowd, "I need money to go home! If I don't get enough money, I'll stay and marry one of your daughters—or worse, one of your sons!"

Despite the nuptial threats, the crowd metastasized and blocked much of the brick walkway. The tall glass windows of the town's grande dame of a museum, the Peabody Essex, loomed above the bright, spandex figures on the street. A small crowd gathered inside the museum to look down on the street antics, sporting white hair and finely tailored clothes. "Don't try this at home, kids! Try it at school!"

Welcome to "Haunted Happenings," which is billed on the Web as "America's premiere Halloween festival" (HauntedHappenings.org). Events vary each year, but often include street fairs and performers, a parade, a blessing of the animals by a local psychic, themed functions (Harry Potter and Quidditch on Salem Common one year, for example), a fun run, ghost tours, and vampire tours. Another event, the Festival of the Dead, initiated by Salem witch Christian Day, boasts a witches' ball, a vampires' ball, a "retro zombies" ball, a psychic fair on the downtown mall, and a workshop for little witches that includes an ice cream buffet and tips on how to make magic wands and banish nightmares.

The same day that I watched Heath Ledger's doppelganger contort on the downtown mall, I had a conversation with Christian Day, Festival of the Dead architect, who is also a psychic and the founder of a local voter registration drive called "Witches Vote!" He was dressed in a purple shirt, a long black jacket, and black pants with a white stripe tucked into high boots with pointed toes. His top hat and a ring on every finger finished the look. In the course of our discussion, Christian mentioned that he was a Brandeis University alum, that he liked the controversial downtown *Bewitched* statue, and that he thought Jesus was a "historical personage who did some pretty witchy things." His Festival of the Dead, he told me, explores all sides of death. Salem, he said, wants to be more respectable, and it sometimes tries to ignore the identity that it already has. He says, "We already have an identity—and witchcraft is it." (For an extended portrait of Day, see Wicker 2005.)

Salem's Haunted Happenings and its Festival of the Dead were inspired—if that's the right word—by Salem's association with the Essex County Witch Trials of 1692. In the span of a few fearful months in the seventeenth century, 20 people were executed as witches and several others died in jail. In the middle of the twentieth century, "Witch City," as it calls itself, began promoting its history to draw tourists. And the tourist experience that emerges from this dark past forms a kind of contemporary *danse macabre* as it parades down Salem's main streets year round. The *danse macabre* is the late medieval motif of skeletal figures dancing with people from all walks of life, "an eternal round in which the dead alternate with the living. The dead lead the dance....Death holds out its hand to the living person whom it will draw along with it....The moral purpose was to remind the viewer both of the uncertainty of the hour of death and of the equality of all people in the face of death" (Ariès 1981: 116). The images served, too, as a reminder of the vanity of life. The earliest known artistic example, dating to 1424–25, was the painting of a chain of 30 figures, each dancing with death, on the walls of the Paris Cemetery of the Innocents. The motif is also found in the woodcuts of Holbein the Younger in the early sixteenth century. Scholars say the motif may have emerged from beliefs about the activities of the dead in cemeteries. But it's also possible that it was fueled by early beliefs associated with the ominous fairy folk, especially the connection

Danse macabre

between dancing and death—specifically, the seductive dance of the fairies who lured mortals to their doom.

I use *danse macabre* in relation to these contemporary American scenes in a larger way; it is not meant to refer to only a single image. When I talk about the *danse macabre* in Salem, I'm referring to the considered playfulness that the town associates with its tragic history. Not far from the downtown pedestrian mall in Salem, a somewhat controversial statue of Samantha Stevens from the 1960s *Bewitched* television series presides perkily from her broomstick perch over a street corner. The local site rumored to be the Gallow's Hill where those accused of witchcraft in 1692 were hanged, today boasts a park and a playground. Both locals and scholars note how these kinds of playful sites and tourist attractions contrast with the actual tragic history of the Witch Trials of 1692.

One place that addresses the dark history of Salem in a more somber way is the Salem Trials Witch Memorial. Established in 1992, it is a serious interpretation of those trials and executions. A shaded green space, surrounded by a New England stone wall, holds 20 benches that memorialize those who were killed as witches. On the ground are stones with words taken from the surviving court

Statue of Samantha from *Bewitched*, Salem, Massachusetts

documents, protestations of innocence from the victims. The memorial abuts the Old Burying Point Cemetery, a fragile site dating to 1637—where Nathaniel Hawthorne's infamous forebearer, the witch judge John Hathorne, rests.

But each fall the grass at that memorial site gets trampled into mud, and the slim cemetery is overtaken for purposes of October profit by ghost tours. One year I snapped a picture of a large sign at the cemetery gates that read "Candle Lit Ghostly Tours," flanked by a plywood and tent village that sold "gobbler" (turkey) sandwiches, root beer floats, fried dough, soup in a bun, coffee, footlong hot dogs, ice cream, clam chowder, sodas, hot chocolate, chili, and French fries. A few feet across from this vending village, a patchwork of temporary tarp walls hid the sides of the colonial brick buildings in the area. Small-time entrepreneurs had erected sidewalk-scale haunted houses with such names as the "Witching Hour."

As I watched this plastic plaza flapping in the rain that afternoon, a swarm of high school kids on a field trip staggered en masse into the small, historic cemetery. I wanted to take off, but instead I took photos—and worried about the historic cemetery being trampled into sweet-sticky little mounds of slate with a hot dog here and there for punctuation.

Now…stop. Hold that image of food, commerce, an overabundance of life forms, and the cemetery in your mind. Return with me to the not-so-hygienic days of yesteryear: medieval and early modern yesteryear and the city of Paris, France,

Cemetery in Salem, Massachusetts

to be exact. Drawing on the descriptions by Philippe Ariès (1981), Ragon (1983), and Cerf and Babinet (1994), journey with me to the Cemetery of the Innocents, home of that early *danse macabre* mural.

In that cemetery, overcrowded and overburdened with smells from the living and dead, I'd want to run, not dance. As many as 1,500 bodies of the poor would lie before me in a large, and often open, burial pit. At best, they would be blanketed with a thin layer of dirt. Dogs and cats would dine on the remains strewn about, and I'd watch children playing ball with a cranium (Ariès 1981: 56).

Like the teenagers in contemporary Salem, I'd have been able to actually purchase commodities near and in this French cemetery. In fact, my range of consumer choices would be even better: cookies, bread (often cooked in onsite ovens), fish, chicken, beer, wine, cloth, and books. Theatrical troops, dancers, mummers, jugglers, and musicians would entertain me. I could gamble, practice military drills, make love, look for work, bid during a public auction, defecate, finish a pilgrimage, practice prostitution, and be tried and imprisoned for a variety of crimes—all in the cemetery. Such commerce and festivity existed in churchyard cemeteries throughout Europe and the British Isles.

In short, as Auguste Bernard says, the cemetery was "the noisiest, busiest, *most* boisterous, and most commercial place" in the community (Ariès 1981: 64).

Life danced with death, festivity, and commercialism in these old cemeteries. The rhythms of life and death literally ran together in the graveyards. The mundane but vibrant activities that took place in the cemetery were themselves a kind of *danse macabre*. Given the behaviors and customs associated with the historical cemetery, it's not too surprising that images of the dead mingling with the living appeared on the walls of European cemeteries and churches.

Now, back to twenty-first-century Salem. At first I was troubled, like many scholars and residents, by the marriage of festive tourism with the deaths of the innocent. But Salem's swirl of death, pleasure, commerce, and the cemetery is bland compared with those earlier, historic versions of death and revelry. And so it makes some sense that the teenagers I saw in the cemetery of today—who are, after all, the descendents of those long-ago buried in the festive, European cemeteries—might still dance some of the old dance.

When I first saw Salem's dark festive side, I thought, like others, that Salem is only a manifestation of the capitalistic and consumerist excesses inherent in our time. And don't misunderstand me—those forces are entirely present in the tourism of twenty-first-century Salem. As Bridget Marshall says, Salem's commercialism is offensive in the way it trades on and distorts the misery and death of historical individuals (2004: 244). Those who live in Salem have rightly complained about callousness, excessiveness, and obnoxiousness, not to mention parking difficulties.

But as a folklorist attuned to history, I'd say Salem's indulgences are tepid when we compare them to the Cemetery of the Innocents and her sister cemeteries in previous centuries. Our era did not invent consumerism mixed with death. Salem's charismatic, young contortionist (without his boom box) could've just as easily shouted matrimonial threats involving the daughters and sons of sixteenth-century Paris. What happens in Salem is not a new degradation. Rather, Salem has actually reverted to an old tradition.

Salem has lost some historical fidelity to the tragic story of the accused witches while it's probably unknowingly reenacting the history associated with cemeteries, death, and festivity. Its painful, hard local history has paved the way for pleasure and the seasonal exchange of money and goods in and around a Salem cemetery. Contemporary Salem gives us witches, "retro zombies," haunted houses, Hawthorne, abundant MSG, and an intriguing question: Why does its historical rupture also lead to a surprising historical connection with the old traditions surrounding cemeteries?

It's more than coincidence; it has to do with a human response to a particular set of circumstances. With the cemeteries and the spaces near them, both Paris and Salem provide open spaces that invite commerce. In early modern Paris, the cemetery was one of the few open spaces in town, and the laws and customs associated with the sanctuary the cemetery offered were conducive to the marketplace. Salem's cemetery is also a public gathering place that is linked with tourism, which in turn is tied to commerce. Other public places haven't claimed the witch story and history. Think of Salem's downtown mall and the most prominent building on it—the Peabody Essex Museum. The PEM is a major not-for-profit museum, and it is a public gathering place; it holds a significant collection of documents and artifacts related to the witch trials. However, it doesn't present the witch story as one of its major themes, nor does it make its witch collection easily accessible to the public. It focuses on "culture," and "art," not witches. So, many for-profit organizations have sprung up to fill the void caused by the lack of a major, visible, not-for-profit entity claiming the story of the witch trials. These businesses claim anything and anyone who are even a little bit related to Salem merely by the virtue of spookiness.

Edgar Allan Poe and Lizzie Borden had no significant historical ties to Salem, but for some Salem entrepreneurs, that doesn't matter because "scary" sells. When the PEM didn't claim the witch story, it forced it to the streets and other public spaces (such as the cemetery), and it left the door open to the locals to narrate the story. And tell the story they do—for profit and from a mom-and-pop-who-got-laid-off-when-local-industry-went-bust perspective. This is the people's approach to two things that are important to them: local history *and* profit making. Those who take over the story often don't have the budget, grants, or donations that a glossy, well-heeled, not-for-profit can command. Their enterprises are low-budget, low-overhead, and fluid, like the "ghost tour" businesses or the storefront "haunted houses" that dot the downtown. They don't have much capital to invest; they must conjure profit to exist. And so they turn to tourism; local stories; and a tried, true, and very old pairing of revelry and darkness. And thus, in this contemporary American city, death once again waltzes, romances, and brings a smile to the lips of the living.

Works Cited

Ariès, Philippe. *The Hour of Our Death*. New York: Vintage, 1981. Print.

Cerf, Delhine, and David Babinet. *Les Catacombes de Paris*. Meudon: Éditions Moulenq, 1994. Print.

"Discover the Magic of Halloween in Salem." *HauntedHappenings.org*. HauntedHappenings .org, 2010. Web. 24 Oct. 2010.

Marshall, Bridget. "Salem's Ghosts and the Cultural Capital of Witches." *Spectral America: Phantoms and the National Imagination*. Ed. Jeffrey A. Weinstock. Madison: University of Wisconsin Press, 2004. 244–64. Print.

Ragon, Michel. *The Space of Death*. Charlottesville: University Press of Virginia, 1983. Print.

Wicker, Christine. *Not in Kansas Anymore: A Curious Tale of How Magic Is Transforming America*. New York: HarperOne, 2005. Print.

The author wishes to thank Nancy Banks for her French translations.

. . . .

Thomas's study of contemporary Salem emerged from her interest in the history of cemeteries during her visit as a tourist in this East Coast town. Her "spatial gaze" was unique because she herself had that combination of interest, knowledge, and personal experience—and then she chose to write an essay about it. As we write to you about describing a sense of place, we want to emphasize what Thomas's writing brings to our chapter. As she strolls along Salem Common and the pedestrian mall on one October day, she notices food, sounds, smells, games, outfits, and signs, and she talks to a few people to get their perspectives on that space. But then she overlays her images of this particular place with her knowledge of history: the unusual story of the witch trials in Massachusetts as well as the traditions of centuries-old European cemeteries. Even though she's an expert, she needed to do research to write this essay. That's what the citations are for: to help you understand those extra minds, the printed perspectives she consulted in order to bring you this essay. She looked up *danse macabre* to be sure to define it appropriately for what she saw. She checked her sources carefully, and rechecked books and articles she already had about cemeteries. She collected tourist brochures, maps, and Web sites describing Salem, the Peabody Essex Museum, and other points of interest she tells us about. She took hundreds of pictures. Of course, we don't see her research process—or the time she put in to make her choices for her final draft. What we do see is a very detailed description of a place through one person's perspective, enhanced with names, dates, colors, textures, dialogue, and the stories of her encounters there. Thomas's research gives us the sense of place we need to understand her deeper message: that the phenomenon of cemeteries as public spaces for play, commerce, and culture is not unique to contemporary America. As Kincaid's essay about her personal experience at school on a colonized Caribbean island teaches us about the politics of colonization, Thomas's focused essay on her trip to Salem teaches us about history and human traditions related to both death and life. The writer deepens her understanding of a place with carefully chosen details and research that help bring the place to life.

Learning How to Look: Mapping Space

As a researcher, you'll teach yourself how to look and how to "read" a space. Make lists of sensory details at your site, interior and exterior, paying attention to more than just visual impressions. Track who goes in and out of the fieldsite at different times of day and how they use different areas. Draw actual maps or diagrams, which give you information that would be difficult to get merely through observation. Research the space further by talking to informants or by studying documents that describe it. As you take notes, record your assumptions about how the space is used. As you follow up on these initial notes, you will discover surprising information about the place. Through recording, listing, mapping, and researching, you'll learn about how the people you're studying use their space.

Fieldworkers who study cultures for long periods of time make extensive inventories of household goods and cultural artifacts; study kinship patterns, genealogies, and family records; sketch and photograph buildings, implements, and topography; categorize local flora and fauna; and conduct surveys among the locals. Sometimes a culture's archives can assist the fieldworker in developing a sense of place.

For more on archives, see Chapter 7, page 311.

BOX18

Mapping Space

PURPOSE

Creating a map or a diagram of a space that shows how people use it can capture details of a culture you otherwise might not see. We and our students have charted many spaces—marching-band musicians practicing on a field, Indian dancers giving an exhibition at a community college auditorium, two people making dinner in one private kitchen. Understanding how people create patterns and movements over time and space can teach us a lot about a subculture. Alone or with a partner, map or diagram a situation over time. You might invite someone to go with you to your own fieldsite to take notes and then offer to go with your partner to her site. Another approach is to find a place to chart—like a coffeehouse, a playground, a cemetery, or a subway station—just to see what's there and how people choose to interact in that setting.

ACTION

Here are some features to consider when you map or diagram a site. Not all are relevant to every fieldsite, but these are good strategies to try as you detail people in the cultural spaces they use:

1. *Obtain access.* Choose a site in which at least two people are engaged in the routine of using that space (a kitchen, a practice field, or a shop, for example). Choose people who are willing to be watched, as this exercise demands close observation by you and possibly by a partner. Be sure to offer something in return.

2. *Record your assumptions.* Before you go, speculate on what you think you'll see. What do you already know about how people use this space? What skills does a person need to have to use this space? What would an insider know? An outsider not know?

3. *Take notes on the overall setting.* What details of the whole place seem relevant or irrelevant? How does this space fit into an overall plan for its purpose? Is it casual or formal? Governed by whose rules? Be specific with details: in a kitchen, for instance, note "eight hand-painted Delft plates" rather than "pile of plates," or in a music studio note "six sound mixing boards, eight monitors, two computers" rather than "a slew of electronic equipment."

4. *Map the space.* Draw a diagram of the place in which people are interacting, and use it to show where your informants move within the space. Colored pencils, arrows, or markers can be handy to designate each person's movements.

5. *Describe the activities.* Develop a system for recording the movements. Pay attention to what's going on. What interruptions take place? What utensils, objects, or artifacts do your informants use in this space? How do they use them? Make a time line, noting how long each activity takes.

BOX 18 continued

6. *Record the conversation.* Either by electronic recording or by hand notes, document what people say inside that space. How much of the talk is related to their purpose in the space? What power relationships can you discern in the conversation? Who initiates the talk? Who leads and who follows? Who is silent? Who interrupts? Are there differences in talk related to age, gender, or other differences between the people?

7. *Talk with your research partner.* Expand your fieldnotes with your research partner, discuss your findings, and speculate on what your conclusions or interpretations might be. What do you agree on? What do you see differently?

8. *Write up the data.* In two or three pages, try to write a narrative description of what you've seen and thought.

RESPONSE

As well as being a college student, Emily Wemmer is a barn manager and a riding instructor who is certified with the North American Riding for the Handicapped Association and with the Certified Horsemanship Association. It's not surprising that Emily chose to study a horse auction.

Emily visited the site of this horse auction many times over a semester. Often, she went with Diane, a friend, research partner, and fellow horse lover. Emily took photographs to remind herself of the details of the horses, the people, and the activities she saw. In the excerpt from her final draft (p. 190), she includes all of the eight mapping actions we described above. As you read her work, you may want to try to identify each of the corresponding points that might have come from her notes.

Over the course of her study, Emily used maps to think out both the large and small features of the horse-auction situation. She includes in her study a map of the horse industry, in which she illustrates her own location within it, showing her own changing position from horse lover to horse professional. "My classmate Jeff," she writes later in her portfolio, "suggested during an in-class workshop that I use maps, rather than narrative, to position myself metaphorically and physically in the auction setting, and this turned out to be the most helpful advice I got all semester! This is a map that I drew up on the computer to represent the different but overlapping areas of the horse industry. I used it to show myself how I related to other people in my study." Looking at this map on the facing page, we can see where her interests intersect within the larger features of the subculture of the horse industry.

For her own research purposes, Emily decided to draw a simplified map of the large barn in which she conducted her study. (See Figure 2, on p. 190.) The map allowed her to see how space gets used in the barn—by owners, sellers, buyers, tourists, and horses. First, she used this map to understand the fieldsite itself. Later, in her final essay, Emily offered her map as a visual aid for her reader.

The map helped Emily understand her fieldsite, but in her essay, she brings the barn to life with a description. Without her attention to the space and her detailed mapping,

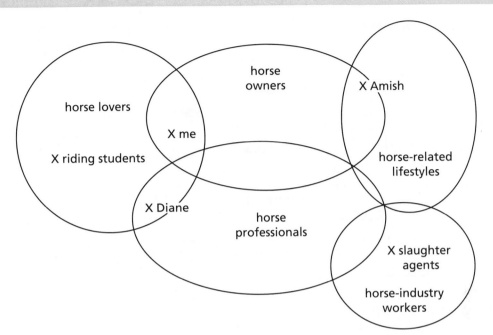

Figure 1 The horse industry involves many different people with vastly different motivations, values, and perspectives on horsemanship.

Emily would not have created such a detailed verbal image of this place. Her data and careful documentation create a spatial gaze for us as readers:

> Out-of-towners drive into Carver on Highway 5, an undulating stretch of road that runs through cornfields and pasture lands dotted with livestock and bales of hay. Laundry dries behind farmhouses and Amish top buggies are silhouetted on the horizon. The Carver Sales Barn is a few blocks away from a row of antique stores, just south of the Carver Historical Village, where a man riding a horse on the sidewalk somehow seems natural. The heart of the Carver Sales Barn is its kitchen: a brigade of Mennonite women in bonnets and Nikes keep the food coming non-stop all day long. By 8 a.m. the heavy smell of frying potatoes and sausages and eggs drapes itself over the entire barn; by noon, it's hamburgers and macaroni salad; by 4 p.m. the stands are lined with pie plates. "You are only as happy as you allow yourself to be," reads a handmade sign on the kitchen's ice cream freezer, and customers perched around the diner-style counter generally take it at its word. On auction day, the kitchen is full of middle-aged farmer types who exchange smiles with the waitresses and nods with each other.

Emily offers her readers some important background information about her past experiences and more details about the specifics of the Carver Sales Barn, and then she brings the space to life this way:

BOX**18** continued

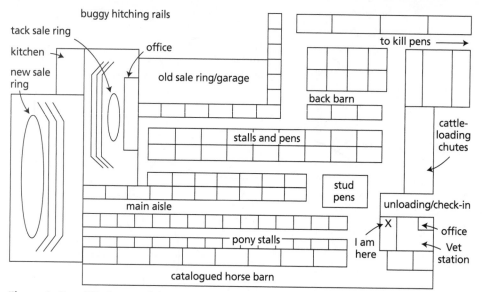

Figure 2 Simplified map of the Carver Sales Barn

It's early, just before 7:30 a.m., with a few hours to go before the horse auction begins, but Diane and I already have our favorites.

Mine is a hairy, chocolate-colored pony who pokes his head over a fence and sizes me up for treats. He's right. I pull a mini-carrot out of my sweatshirt pouch; his little lips pucker up and, quivering, snatch it out of my hand.

"Number 422," Diane reads off of the pony's haunch. "What a cutie!"

It bothers me that he doesn't have a name. It makes him seem somehow less alive. When I was a horse-crazy little girl getting an annual Breyer model horse for Christmas, the first thing I would do was name it. I would snip it out of its wrapping and turn it over a few times, running my hands over its smooth, cool body, tracing the permanent waves in its mane and tail with one finger. I'd look down into its dark, deep eyes and let it tell me what name it wanted.…

"Tony," I tell Diane. "I think his name is Tony, and I think he'll fit into my living room." Diane, a riding instructor, trainer, and barn manager, laughs and pulls me away. She knows I'm a sucker for little ponies with expressive eyes. She knows I fall in love too quickly.

I'm not here to buy a horse today, but I can't resist looking, window shopping. Diane and I have already registered for bidding numbers in the Sales Barn's central office, and mine is burning a tempting hole in my back pocket. At the Sales Barn, it all seems so simple, so easy. Just my name, address, phone number, and bank name on a little white card and I, Number 116, am qualified to buy a horse.

Diane and I make our way through the Sales Barn's main stable area, an enormous structure subdivided into a labyrinth of stalls and pens and corridors. As always, I am impressed by two things: the barn's size and its accessibility. There are no "No Trespassing" signs in here, no locked gates or blocked doors. Everything in the barn is wood, old wood, chewed wood rubbed smooth by the teeth of thousands of nervous horses. The barn is nothing fancy: dirt floors, rusting metal gates, and 60-year-old cobwebs. The pens have no real bedding, just concrete and dirt, so manure sits and dries naturally and dark red urine trickles out of the pens and into the aisle. It's gross, sure, but it's a barn. There's no such thing as a pristine working barn. I know that from back-aching, pitchfork-wielding experience. Above our heads, men in blue coats shake down clouds of hay chaff as they wander along the catwalk, chewing the fat and munching on cinnamon rolls.

There is one main aisle in this barn, lined on either side with numbered horses in pens of various sizes and occupancies. Some of the horses are loose, single or in groups; some are tied to the fence; some have saddles; some are bare. Each horse has a white number stuck on its hindquarters, but there doesn't seem to be any rhyme or reason to their order, except that horses in the same pens tend to have similar numbers, as if they arrived at the same time. From pen to pen, however, the numbers skip from 305 to 216 to 423—and to make things even more confusing, each pen also has a number in faded white paint that does not seem to correspond to the numbers on the horses' rumps. One side of this main aisle has stalls labeled 200, 210, 220, but the other side has the 400s. A couple pens are labeled with handwritten cards: "J. Smith, 4 head," or "Mare, open, 1996," often with a photocopy of some registration papers. I can only assume these are advertisements for the horses, promoting either a popular seller or a valuable characteristic, but they strike me in a silly way less like classified ads and more like personal listings, vague and loaded codes that say to the insider everything important—and to me absolutely nothing at all.

At the end of the aisle is the unloading area, where sellers often consign their horses. It's a busy place before the sale; the air vibrates with diesel-engined trucks waiting for their turn to pull up and empty their trailers. The unloading area is a good place to evaluate horses, Diana tells me, because it may be the only chance we have to see them interacting with their owners. It may be our only opportunity to figure out their histories. We slip through the dusty gate and press ourselves to the wall, trying to be inconspicuous. As usual, though, I attract attention. There aren't many young women with brand new shoes at the Sales Barn. But no one asks us to leave.

Mapping helped Emily create not only significant place descriptions but a deeper understanding that led to her much larger field study, "Deconstructing the Horse: An Ethnographic Study of a Sales Barn." Throughout her longer essay, Emily handles the provocative ethical themes surrounding the selling and using of horses.

Read Emily's full essay and reflections at **bedfordstmartins.com/ fieldworking**, under Student Essays.

Learning How to Look: Finding a Focal Point

By looking at how space is used, fieldworkers come to understand the field-site—what it looks like and how their informants inhabit it. Mapping helps researchers lay out masses of data that might otherwise be overwhelming. Studying fieldsite maps alongside other information about the culture and its informants can help you find a focal point within data. A *focal point* is a spot, an area, or a place where the insiders' activities cluster. Because of Emily's careful data collection, observation, diagramming, and mapping, she is able to offer us the sales barn's main stable area as an ironic focal point in her study: horses with numbers instead of names, with owners and trucks on the periphery. Researchers often comb their data looking for focal points in their fieldsites.

In anthropologist Barbara Myerhoff's full-length ethnography *Number Our Days*, she studies elderly Jews, many of them Holocaust survivors, who spend their days at the Aliyah Senior Citizens' Center in Venice, California, but live independently in apartments. Myerhoff follows them around the community, tracking their daily routines to and from the center and into their homes. From the data that Myerhoff collected, she selected the Senior Center and its external extensions—a set of benches near the beach and the boardwalk—as her focal points.

While most of her study's data revolves around the activities inside the Senior Center, Myerhoff pulls her reader toward her other focal point—the benches outside, which face both the ocean and the boardwalk. She uses these benches as her vantage point, as her informants do, to survey the surrounding cultural scene. Myerhoff observes that the benches serve as a village plaza, a public place for social interaction. In the following description, she analyzes the seniors' bench behavior—and what the behavior represents—as an outside extension of the Center:

> As the morning wears on, the benches fill. Benches are attached back to back, one side facing the ocean, one side the boardwalk. The people on the ocean side swivel around to face their friends, the boardwalk, and the Center.
>
> Bench behavior is highly stylized. The half-dozen or so benches immediately to the north and south of the Center are the territory of the members, segregated by sex and conversation topic. The men's benches are devoted to abstract, ideological concerns—philosophical debate, politics, religion, and economics. The women's benches are given more to talk about immediate, personal matters—children, food, health, neighbors, love affairs, scandals, and "managing." Men and women talk about Israel and its welfare, and about being a Jew and about Center politics. On the benches, reputations are made and broken, controversies explored, leaders selected, factions formed and dissolved. Here is the outdoor dimension of Center life, like a village plaza, a focus of protracted, intense sociability. (4–5)

In these paragraphs, Myerhoff observes her informants enacting their gender and cultural roles within the setting. She documents months of recorded conversation by noting men's and women's separate interests but also the topics—critical to their cultural history—that they share. Myerhoff sees these cultural roles acted against the backdrop of the benches as part of the boardwalk's staged setting outside the Center.

Not only does she gaze outward at the landscape, but she also looks inward with a reflexive gaze at her own internal landscape to examine how she is affected by the place she studies. As a Jewish woman of a younger generation and a former social worker, perched on the benches that define the boundaries between inside and outside, she acknowledges her role as researcher within this social drama. Myerhoff uses the benches to meditate on her own relationship with the seniors; she uses the benches as her informants do:

> I sat on the benches outside the Center and thought about how strange it was to be back in the neighborhood where sixteen years before I had lived and for a time had been a social worker with elderly citizens on public relief. Then the area was known as "Oshini Beach." The word *shini* still made me cringe. As a child I had been taunted with it. Like many second-generation Americans, I wasn't sure what being a Jew meant. When I was a child our family had avoided the words *Jew* and *Yid*. (11)

BOX19

Finding a Focal Point

PURPOSE

In this box, we'd like you to review the data you've collected about your fieldsite: fieldnotes, descriptive paragraphs, cultural artifacts, archival documents, and maps. As you read through your material and reflect on what you have gathered, look for the focal points of your site, either from your vantage point or that of your informants. Are there any contradictions?

ACTION

Write a description of one focal point you find in your setting. Consider whether there are any ways in which your own perspective influences you to see what you do see in this site. Share a draft of your focal point description with a colleague to see if it creates the image you're after.

BOX 19 continued

RESPONSE

Karen Downing, as she studies the glamour photography business Photo Phantasies, finds a contradiction when she matches her fieldnotes with the map of the space and the cultural artifacts she gathered. This contradiction is in the image of its "hostesses," who stand outside the door greeting customers with compliments but are trained in hard-sell tactics for roping customers into the store. In her fieldnotes, she describes the "horse," a sitting area and display table that is used to promote the Photo Phantasies business and to solicit customers. In Karen's reflective fieldnotes, she suggests that the horse serves "to take 'em for a ride," admitting her cynicism and her feminist perspective toward the beauty culture. After viewing a training video that outlines the company's customer service policies, she summarizes the purpose of the "horse":

> A Photo Phantasies hostess should man the horse, the brochure stand outside the store, at all times, particularly when the mall is busy. The hostess should greet the people in the mall as they pass and tell them about the professional makeup salon and photo studio. She should show them the "Look Book" with the before and after pictures of previous customers, give them a brochure, take them on a tour of the store, explain the Photo Phantasies process, and work to get an appointment set up on the spot. "Yes or no" questions should be avoided—the focus is on selling the concept.

The "horse" is a place detail that illuminates the values of the beauty culture; the illusion of beauty can be sold to any customer. A salesperson posts herself at the "horse," ready to rope in her customer and tie up the transaction with the biggest package of photos she can sell.

Learning How to Look: Identifying Unity and Tension

Karen Downing's description of the "horse" and the "hostesses" who "man" the sales table (see Box 19) serves to confirm other details she's already accumulated about her Photo Phantasies fieldsite and the beauty business it represents. Her interview with Ginny the manager, her description and map of the store's space, and her viewing of training videos unify Karen's growing skepticism.

To write about the culture you've researched, you must look, as Karen did, for a unifying perspective. Much of fieldwork involves confirming unity—unity of themes and patterns that hang together in the data. Disparate data sources—maps, interviews, observations, and reflections—accumulate to form a coherent whole. Looking for unity in masses of data is much like Samuel Scudder looking at the fish, as we discuss in Chapter 2. At first, you'll see very little, but over time and with close study, important unifying details will come together.

But it is equally important for a researcher to locate disconfirming data, discontinuity, and tensions. Tensions show up in data at moments of contradiction when multiple or opposing perspectives collide. For Karen, the first tension in her study arises when she realizes that not all people share her attitude toward having beauty pictures taken. She begins to recognize the discontinuities between her own values and those of others. In a way, this moment serves as a disconfirming source of data. Whenever a researcher senses tension, she needs to recognize and record it.

....

Strike a Pose

Karen Downing

"God, these are beautiful. How much?" The woman on the other side of the counter smiles as she picks up my flowers and brings them close to her face. I have been checking out movies here for 10 years, and she has never asked me anything other than perfunctory information.

"Uh, ten dollars, I think. Aren't they great? And not really all that expensive. I bought them as a treat." I grin at her with my lips pressed together.

"Are there any left? I just may get some. A treat, like you said. It's either flowers or Photo Phantasies. I've been wanting to do that for so…"

"Photo Phantasies?" I raise my eyebrows at this notion.

"God, yes." As she turns to retrieve my movie, I see her name tag reads "Darlene." "I mean, what could be a better treat? I wanna go in there, have 'em do up my hair and my makeup, put on all those cool clothes, take a whole bunch of pictures, and then go out on the town lookin' so hot! I'd leave my kids with my mother and stay out as late as I wanted. Hopefully, plenty of men would be willin' to buy me drinks."

"Yeah. Hmmm." I don't know how to respond to this because Darlene's version of a treat or an indulgence is not mine. I hate the idea of having my picture taken. Period. And having my picture taken in clothes and hair and makeup that turn me into someone I'm not? Never! I know the feminist rhetoric—a woman's body is hers to do with as she pleases. And I think I believe this feminist rhetoric, or I would like to think I do. But a Photo Phantasies makeover? What a waste of money for something that won't last.

"We'll see. Maybe someday." As Darlene says this, she pushes up the sleeves of her white uniform and sighs. Her two-inch red nails with chipped polish click the price of my movie into the cash register. I am on the verge of suggesting that Darlene get a massage instead of a makeover when I stop short. I see a smudged blue pen mark on her cheek and the trace of dark circles under her eyes.

"No, not someday. Now. Why wait?" Suddenly, I want Darlene to leave the grocery store this instant and drive straight to Forum West [Mall]. I am surprised by my encouragement, but I empathize with her, despite our different ideas of indulgence. "This is weird, but here, look what I just happen to have." I reach into my coat pocket and take out the Photo Phantasies brochure. "I was just at the mall. They gave me this. Here. You can have it. I think they're doing some kind of model search. You should go. Give it a try." It did not escape me that I sounded just like Bettie from the Photo Phantasies store....

"A model search? Wow. No way. That's so cool! I can have this? Really? Cool! Thanks. I just may go. I just may." Darlene tucks the hot pink brochure into the front pocket of her white uniform and hands me the movie.

"Do it!" I say, smiling. "And remember me when you get discovered."

Darlene smiles, showing the white of her teeth. "Maybe when you come back, I'll have pictures to show you." I think about her comment while I wait in the checkout line to pay for my $10 flowers, which I know won't last a week. I buy them anyway.

* * *

It is this conversation with Darlene that causes Karen to unpack the personal "baggage" about beauty photography that she brings to her project and to examine her assumptions. Her encounter at the checkout is a moment of insight in which Karen sees Photo Phantasies through the eye of the "other." This tension helps her recognize that she's guided her study with her own values, not those of the "other." She realizes she must now research Photo Phantasies from the insider's position.

If Karen had continued to look only for unity by just interviewing customers who shared her perspective, she might have discarded her encounter with Darlene as data. After interviewing customers who were, in fact, proud and satisfied with their beauty photographs, she understood the value of beauty photography through their eyes, not just her own. In spite of her own resistances throughout the project, Karen reaches a dramatic and ironic conclusion about the sub-culture of Photo Phantasies. At the end of her paper, she writes, "Sometimes things are not what they seem."

Read Karen's full study at **bedfordstmartins.com/ fieldworking**, under Student Essays.

We recommend that you read Karen's entire study, "Strike a Pose," which is available online at this book's companion Web site. You will find her complete portfolio at the end of this chapter (pp. 204–14).

Karen's study shows us that researchers can impose their own values on the places they study unless they are reflective about the process of their own fieldwork. As educated middle-class American women, Karen and her informants exercised personal choices about ways to join or not join the mainstream American beauty culture. To indulge herself, Karen chooses Reeboks, exercise clothes, and health clubs over beauty photos, and she admits this in her writing. All researchers need to explain—to themselves and to their readers—the differences between their values and those of others they study, separating their attitudes and assumptions both on and off the page.

Fieldworkers look for the tension in the way informants inhabit their spaces because sometimes informants inhabit spaces not of their own choosing. The Photo Phantasies photographer, for example, may prefer to be outside shooting pictures of the natural landscape rather than the artificial images he is paid to create for customers. The woman with the baby on her lap at the employee sales meeting might prefer to stay at home with her child rather than work in a cramped store at the mall. If Karen had researched even further some of the employees she observed, she might have found that they, too, feel tensions in their everyday jobs of creating glamour.

Learning How to Look: Colonized Spaces

When people inhabit spaces over which they have no control, we consider them to be *colonized*. In particular, when a dominant or powerful culture forces itself on a less powerful group, assuming control over its territories and people, this constitutes **colonization**. Researchers must recognize the vantage point of their own dominant culture and guard against describing others in terms that belong solely to their own culture's values and belief systems. Colonization can involve imposing your own culture's sense of time, place, religion, food, rituals, hygiene, education, morals, and even story structures. Descriptive words about other places and people—like *quaint, picturesque, simple, primitive, native,* or *backward*—imply cultural value judgments. When researchers write about cultures other than their own, they must try to separate their belief systems from those they study. This is a difficult—and sometimes impossible—task.

For example, about a century ago, anthropologists who studied religion in cultures that practiced witchcraft and sorcery needed to acknowledge how their own Judeo-Christian backgrounds influenced what they saw, as well as how they wrote about it. Many did not. Contemporary fieldworkers who study **marginalized** groups such as the homeless, gang members, immigrants, or the elderly must be careful not to let their value systems dominate their fieldwork. One way they guard against **ethnocentrism** is to write about their personal reactions and their belief systems throughout the research process, sometimes in their journals, sometimes in double-entry fieldnotes, and sometimes in letters to their colleagues. Writing about it doesn't solve the problem of colonization, but writing can expose it.

Colonization can take place both in the field and in the writing process. In the field, it happens when researchers don't adopt the informants' perspective. Karen Downing, for example, had to recognize that her own value system made her prefer Reeboks and irises over a Photo Phantasies package. In the writing process, colonization happens when we use our own language rather than allow our informants' language to describe their spaces. Henry Glassie's description of the broom as a "besom of heather bound round with twine" is the phrasing of his Northern Irish informants, not his own.

We don't need to be living in a colonized country to experience colonization. Within our own dominant American culture, many subgroups unconsciously colonize others. What's important about researching place is to understand how we acquire our spatial gaze, how that gaze informs our look at others, and what's behind the gaze of others who look back at us.

Jennifer Hemmingsen is a practicing journalist who conducted her first fieldstudy in Oregon. Her focal point was the Pendleton Round-Up, an annual September rodeo that draws visitors from across the United States and that also hosts the Happy Canyon Pageant, a historic pageant that is put on by Pendleton's white settlers and members of its indigenous tribes. The history of this pageant, Jennifer finds, suggests the shifts in attitudes between settlers (cowpunchers, wheat growers, and wool makers) and the local Indians who perform at the pageant. Its complex story involves colonization, politics, strong opinions, and changing contemporary understandings about who owns the land, who conserves the water, whose traditions should be performed, which stereotypes can remain, and which should go.

Jennifer's essay is a fine example of ethnographic journalism and place description that shows the multiple perspectives that are involved when people practice—or think about—colonization in the spaces they call home. As you read this excerpt from the beginning of her essay, you may want to ask yourself some questions: Who is colonizing whom, and what political and personal issues come to the surface through Jennifer's data? Like a good fieldworker, Jennifer provides us with data about the settlers, the Cayuse, the Umatilla, the Walla Walla, and her own role in the fieldstudy so that we as readers can make up our own minds about the Happy Canyon Pageant. In this excerpt, she brings to life for us the pageant and the rodeo within the specific geography of the interior Pacific Northwest.

Read Jennifer's full study at **bedfordstmartins .com/fieldworking**, under Student Essays.

The Happy Canyon

Jennifer Hemmingsen

It's a few days before Round-Up in the eastern Oregon town of Pendleton. There's no hotel room to be had for miles. All the camping spots—marked out on school playgrounds, baseball fields, front yards, and road ditches—are taken. Those Pendletonians who are tired of the weeklong drunken cowboy party are packing up and heading for the coast or for Portland. They want to be anywhere but here, where very soon tens of thousands of rodeo fans from all over North America will swarm to watch sinewy cowboys ride Brahma bulls to AC/DC songs. It's 97 degrees outside and dusty. The sun glares down from the sky and is reflected back from every surface.

I came to the Pendleton Round-Up in 2003 because the town and nearby Indian reservation are at a crossroads in their struggle over this place and who belongs here. The conflict started two hundred years ago when white settlers started to travel along the Oregon Trail—right through the backyard of the Cayuse, Umatilla, and Walla Walla. It continued through wars, land scams, and the boom-and-bust years of the interior West.

"They enticed us with beads and blankets, with tires and gasoline for our cars, hay for our horses," says tribal treasurer Les Minthorn, age 72. "Maybe we should have known better, but they had the advantage."

Pendleton (population 16,000) and the Confederated Tribes of the Umatilla Indian Reservation are close neighbors. In fact, the federal government has had to redraw reservation boundaries where white squatters "accidentally" built part of the town on reservation land....

The history between Pendleton and the tribes is complex. The town passed segregation laws, and some residents conducted scams to rob Indians of their land, but there were also intermarriages and legitimate business deals. White people crowded the reservation for horse races and parties. Indian people bought wool blankets from the Bishop family mill. Over time, the two communities settled into an uneasy peace.

The town, known internationally for the Pendleton Woolen Mill, cruised its way through most of the twentieth century as an outpost of the old West. But all that was disputed a decade ago when the tribes built the Wildhorse Resort and Casino, which pumps some $24 million into their economy each year. Since then, the tribes have used gaming revenues and their strengthened administrative structure to take control of many essential town services—like police, fire, housing, and health. They've been able to provide hundreds of jobs for tribal members and hundreds more for other people in Umatilla County. In fact, the tribes have become the county's second-largest employer—second only to the state of Oregon....

Still, many people of Pendleton find it difficult to see the tribes as anything other than the unemployed, uneducated losers of American history. Some power brokers worry the tribes will use their increasing economic and political muscle for revenge—to buy back the land that they lost 150 years ago. Others, who grew up on John Wayne movies and family stories about taming the frontier, are jealous and resentful that it now seems more popular to be an Indian than a cowboy.

A sociologist might look at drug abuse and teen pregnancy rates to study the changes between Pendleton and the tribes. An educator might look at test scores and participation in activities. But the best time to see the changes between these two proud communities is every September during the Happy Canyon Pageant.

During the Happy Canyon Pageant, the people of Pendleton and the Confederated Tribes play cowboys and Indians for some of the 50,000 tourists who visit the Round-Up. The pageant was written in 1914 by one of Pendleton's founding white fathers and depends in no small part on the cooperation of the indigenous area residents, commonly called "our Indian friends" by the white promoters. The pageant has always reflected the complex, tense, and unequal relationship between Pendleton and the tribes. Now that those relationships are changing, the tribes are starting to have some creative control over the pageant. But local history isn't something you can tinker with. For Pendleton and the Confederated Tribes, every stroll down memory lane can turn into a minefield, and in the middle is the Happy Canyon.

"If you want to have this town burned up, it could happen very easily," Minthorn says. "There's a lot of uneasiness between the communities."

Our Indian Friends

The Round-Up began in 1910.... Inspired by the county fair and a similar event 950 miles east in Cheyenne, Wyoming, a young Pendleton lawyer by the name of J. Roy Raley and some of his friends decided to hold an exhibition with parades, cowboy skills tests, and entertainment. To add to the spectacle, Round-Up organizers paid local Indians to camp on the rodeo grounds, to dance, and to show off their intricately beaded regalia....

From the start, the Round-Up was a bigger success than Raley could have possibly imagined. Raley had arranged for special trains to bring tourists from Portland, Seattle, and Spokane. Closer to home, the towns of Hermiston and Echo closed their stores and schools and chartered their own trains. On opening day, the event sold 7,000 tickets and had to turn away hundreds of would-be spectators. That night, crews built seating for another 3,000 fans. Those seats were filled the next day.

Emboldened by their success, Round-Up directors bought 17 acres to build a permanent rodeo grounds. In 1912, they sold out the 21,000 bleacher seats—more than four times the town's population—and overfilled the stands by thousands more. By 1913, correspondents from eastern magazines like *Harper's, Leslie's Weekly*, and *Judge* were covering the event. *New Yorker* writer and adventurer Charles W. Furlong of Boston wrote a book about the Round-Up, titled *Let 'er Buck*, giving the Round-Up and its slogan nationwide recognition.

In 1915, Raley added a nightly pageant to the Round-Up. It was based on stories his father told about traveling the Oregon Trail in 1862 and about life on the frontier. Originally burdened with the moniker "The Pageant of the West—an Outdoor Dramatic Production, Symbolizing the History and Development of the Great West," the show was advertised as "first-class entertainment" for the nighttime crowds. In fact, the pageant—which was followed by drinking, dancing, and gambling—was intended to lure drunks away from downtown, where they had been vexing local business owners.

Raley paid local Indians to circle wagons, die in reenacted battle scenes, and slink offstage in a scene titled "Passing of Race"—to make room for singing pioneers, can-can-dancing saloon girls, and fat-cat cattle barons. The Indians' job was to fill the roles as written to add local color to visitors' pulp-fiction images of the West.

"It was disturbing, but we just went along with it," says Marie Dick, 67, a tribal member who has acted in the show for 48 years. "It was just like Hollywood to me, you know? They'd stereotype us, and we just went ahead and did it."...

Indians who dressed up and danced for the Round-Up received a small payment for their participation. They could watch the rodeo for free from a fenced-off

(Photo: Jennifer Hemmingsen)

Cigar store Indian outside a curio shop, Pendleton, Oregon

area known as the Indian section. They were given food by white ranchers and merchants.

Despite the paternalism, many Indian people looked forward to each September. The idea of a rodeo fit in with the Plateau culture: Cayuses, Umatillas, and Walla Wallas had been roping and riding horses for 300 years. They had been getting together with other Indians from the Columbia River Plateau for celebrations for thousands more.

"A lot of our traditional people, they still had close ties with their culture," Luke said. "They did things together all the time. That was all important to the people, to their religion. That was just the way that they thought."

Circling wagons was fun ("I would have done that for free," says Marie's husband Louie Dick, 68). And between scripted elements, almost in spite of the hokey Hollywood portrayals, the show did give the Cayuses, Umatillas, and Walla Wallas a chance to show white audiences a little about themselves. The pageant gave Indians a reason to bring out elk-tooth dresses that had been in families for generations. Onstage, Indian grandmothers showed children how to bake bread or grind roots. A traditional marriage ceremony was performed. Tribal cultural preservationists say some of those skills, like the Owl Dance, would have been lost in the culturally tumultuous first half of the twentieth century if it weren't for their annual portrayal in the Happy Canyon Pageant....

Like the visiting crowds, most white Pendleton residents, even those who went to the public school or played on football teams with reservation kids, didn't know much about Indian culture, says Cliff Bracher, 52, an Umatilla County wheat farmer and former Happy Canyon Pageant show director. They just came to watch the "colorful Indians," as he put it.

"All those people that came here, that lived here all their life, they didn't know what the Indians were," Bracher says. "They think that their folks were cowboys that came in and kicked their asses and moved them out of here."...

Immigrants

I moved to Pendleton in 2001 to work as a reporter for the *East Oregonian*, a family-owned newspaper that had been publishing in Pendleton for more than 125 years. Pendleton was my chance to survive on my own merits, far from any place or anything I had ever known. It was a chance to experience an alien world. Very pioneerish, really. I came west for all the reasons Americans have done so for a century....

Growing up in the Midwest, I was accustomed to a landscape that meets the eye in manageable chunks—parallel rows of crops, large squares of fields, and farmsteads. Where Minnesota was lush, Umatilla County was stark. In eastern Oregon, there were no groves of trees to hide dump heaps of old refrigerators and farm machinery, no neat frame houses and red-painted barns....

When people think of Oregon, they think of Mount Hood, Cascade Locks, and Pacific rainforest. But there's a dry side, too, in the rain shadow of the Cascade Mountains, a semiarid highland that's all dryland wheat farming and irrigated veg-etable fields. For the longest time, the only white people who stayed in Umatilla County were traders and missionaries. When Americans started moving westward in the 1850s, most passed through on their way to the more forgiving climate on the other side of the Dalles. In their journals, they described eastern Oregon as forlorn, a "deep wild place."...

Like those early settlers, my understanding of the interior West was minimal. I had read about Manifest Destiny in elementary school and had read a series of books called *Wagons West!* in junior high. But that was about it. It was a romantic landscape that Frederick Jackson Turner could have painted—absent the plunder-ing by railroads and logging companies and lacking the racism, land scams, and water wars that characterized the history of the real West....

It wasn't long after I began to settle into daily life in Pendleton that coworkers and acquaintances started to fill me in on the local Indians. Their families were messed up. The kids were delinquents and given special treatment because of affirmative action rules. They got paid by the federal government just for being Indians. They were lazy; they were drunks. They wanted it both ways: to be Indian and part of a tribe distinct from white Pendleton but also to have jeans, cars, fast food, and cable TV.

In twenty-first-century Pendleton, intolerance isn't as easy to spot as a whites-only bathroom. It surfaces in small groups in casual conversation, like the time I was talking to a county commissioner about the Wanapa tribal energy project. He was upset that the tribes partnered with another city without ever approaching the county. He was suspicious that the county would have to pay for infrastructure and services that would be required by the plant. He was worried that the plant would pollute the county airshed. But what he said to me was this: "I just don't like Indians."

Not everyone in Pendleton felt this way. Former *East Oregonian* editor Richard Hensley defended the town, saying that while Pendleton had its share of bigots, it was no more or less racist than any other place he has lived. But in my experience, few residents, myself included, confronted people who made bigoted statements. Mostly, we just acted embarrassed and oblivious, as if we had caught the offender with his zipper down. Pendleton is a conservative place, and political correctness is a sort of running joke. Nowhere is this more evident than at Round-Up, a celebration of cowboy toughness and independence.

. . . .

When you're an outsider living or working in another culture in another landscape, you need to identify the things that influence your own spatial gaze. Jennifer Hemmingsen was an outsider to the cultures she studied. Being sensitive to her own internal geography as she looked at this new place helped her to record how insiders saw their geography—from many of their own perspectives.

Let's say you're in a study-abroad program and living for a semester in a culture far away from your own. Understanding the new landscape in relationship to your internal one may help you learn far more about your host culture than you can imagine. Whether or not you conduct a formal research study, by observing, mapping space, taking fieldnotes, and writing about your own personal geography, you create an important souvenir document of your experience.

Whether you're involved in a service-learning or study-abroad program or are taking a semester on your own somewhere, recording your observations, impressions, images, and reactions will provide you with data. Begin with your first impressions and continue to ask the questions that will help you confirm your hunches, analyze the main themes of your experience, and see the landscape from both your own and insiders' perspectives. The data you record will enrich your understanding of your spatial gaze—what makes you see things the way you do. Imagine, for example, how U.S. soldiers abroad must feel when they see anti-American graffiti. You could discover, like Jamaica Kincaid did, that your own past landscapes have been colonized by your education, your travel experiences, your prior reading, your family, or your patriotism.

....

THE RESEARCH PORTFOLIO:
Learning from Your Data

....

Many people think that portfolios are meant primarily for display or that they are summaries of accomplishments. Artists submit their portfolios to juries for art shows. Financial advisors present portfolios to their clients to explain investment possibilities and potentials. Students often assemble portfolios to fulfill course requirements or institutional evaluations.

But your research portfolio can serve a very different purpose. It can become a tool for documenting your learning and analyzing your research process. Think of your portfolio as a cultural site—in this case, your personal fieldsite. The artifacts you choose to place in your portfolio are the data that teach you about your own fieldworking process. The readers of your portfolio (who, of course, include you) need to know why you collected and selected the cultural artifacts you display. Your portfolio might also include a representation of what data you've rejected, what data you've left out, or what data you might collect more of in the future. Your own reflections on your portfolio artifacts need to accompany the selections to document your learning process. By writing reflections about each artifact, you'll learn about your unifying themes and be able to find tensions and notice gaps in your data.

As the researcher, you are an intimate part of your data, and yet you can learn from it. In Chapter 3's portfolio suggestions, you reflected on how you read and write and how you select and position yourself in the field. In this chapter, we'd like you to think about what you can learn from laying out your data. Look at the range and depth of artifacts and information from the field and from your background research from maps, archives, documents, and books.

Karen Downing's portfolio contained 12 artifacts, her complete study, and a reflective essay based on her analysis of her process. She presented each arti-

Read Karen's full project with portfolio at **bedfordstmartins.com/ fieldworking**, under Student Essays.

fact in a plastic slipcover and wrote a reflection about it on a stick-on note attached to each. On the following pages, we reproduce nine of Karen's artifacts from the list below, along with the reflective essay Karen wrote after her study's completion. She used reflective notes she had written throughout her fieldproject as a basis for the essay.

Karen Downing's Portfolio

Artifacts

1. A typed page, labeled "Assumptions" (p. 206).

2. A map of the store (p. 207).

3. A promotional flyer for Photo Phantasies (not pictured): "This came in the mail in a mailing of coupons and real estate options. On the back of this is an ad for 'Long John Silver's Big Fish Deals, $3.99 for

combination platter #4.' Both ads prey on getting a good deal for a small price. The text of the PP ad indicates the model theme prevalent in PP rhetoric."

4. A bright pink promotional checklist for customers to pick up in the store (p. 208).

5. A three-page business statement for employees, printed on fax paper (p. 209).

6. A copy of a poem that Ginny James had posted in her office (p. 210).

7. A list of guiding questions for interviewing informants (p. 211).

8. The transcript of a conversation with Mrs. Conway, a customer (p. 212).

9. Pages from Karen's fieldnotes torn out of a stenographer's notebook (p. 213).

10. A collage of fashion words (p. 214).

11. The cover of the bestselling book *Backlash: The Undeclared War against Women* by Susan Faludi (not pictured).

12. A photo of Karen, her friend Amy, and Amy's husband (not pictured).

FieldStudy

Read Karen's full essay online at **bedfordstmartins.com/fieldworking**, under Student Essays, or see the excerpt on pages 195–96.

Portfolio Reflection

Read Karen's portfolio reflection, "A Pose on 'Strike a Pose,'" on pages 215–16, immediately following her project portfolio that begins on the next page.

PORTFOLIO

Assumptions

I should start first with the whole mall culture. I spent many weekend hours circling that place with Carolyn. We would poke around the stores, fingering the clothes, knowing we would rarely make a purchase. We would then go downstairs and each order a piece of pizza and a Coke at Scottos or whatever it was called. We had no P.P.--that hadn't made its way to __ yet. I doubt very much that I would have been going to it even if it were in the mall. I could picture certain girls--Jill Jacobs, Sundi Geisler, Nikki Hampton--going for the big photo shoot and then bringing the pictures into school to pass around or making up a cute little gift package for their boyfriends. Maybe since I never had a serious boyfriend, I had no compelling reason to go.

Ok, now I'm on to something here. I associate P.P. with a certain kind of woman, of which I am not one. It's not even necessary that this imaginary woman be beautiful, but she would be someone who has her bedroom done in matching patterns, believes in window treatments, has coordinating clothes for workouts, and lives in a new apartment. I see these women in the making in some of my students, the ones that bring in their P.P. pictures to school and ask me which one is my favorite. The other students in the class will flock around and ooh and ahhh and say how wonderful this girl looks as I stand by and wonder just what the heck all this attention means.

There is something quite overwhelming to me about getting my picture taken. I cried for five years straight growing up each time my parents assembled us in August to pose for the annual Christmas card wearing our coordinating wool sweaters with our white dog. My parents were out of town during my senior pictures, and to this day my mother still laments how bad the shots are because she didn't get to pick out my outfit or advise me on hair and make-up. What I remember about sorority pictures is pretty limited, although I was one of the few girls that only had one half-way decent proof to choose from. My tongue always poked out between my lips and my smile had a way of sloping quite unattractively. My hair was always a crap shoot--would or wouldn't the curls cooperate at that particular moment.

So for me to hear the woman behind the pharmacy counter tell me that she's thinking of going to treat herself, I don't quite get it. It was my bunch of irises that spurred her into sharing this with me. "I just want to do it, w[...] those pictures. I want to find a babysitter, have everything pos[...] then go out for the evening and have a great time. God, what[...] myself encouraging this woman to do just that, giving her [...] short line" and all that other Hallmarky stuff. As I wal[...] had a feminist dilemma on my hands. Part of me knew it w[...] the physical appearance bit. Maybe I should have told he[...] white grocery store uniform--that she would look just gre[...] she believed it. But the other part of me thought, right[...] and treat yourself. And if make-up and hairstyling and p[...] gosh darn, you go right ahead. Inspires a muddle of thin[...] strong emotions. I'd love to say that looking good doesn[...] but it does. I choose to shape my look through exercise [...] that's me. Where do I get off being holier than thou? Bu[...] That combines two things that I can't stand.

> My assumptions, written before I began the research process. I "discovered" this on my disk late last week—interesting that I "forgot" about this. My dilemma about PP is evident here.

A typed page from Karen Downing's portfolio

desk

Filing
cabinet

Photo
Studio

Dressing rooms

Ginny's Office

racks of
clothes & hats

bath | washer | microwave
room | dryer

mirror with
rounded lights
thank you note
book/ look book

Video monitors
and stools

chair

makeup and hair product co

the three
stations or lines

magazine
rack

chair

cash register

Front desk/receptionist position

Video
monitor

the "horse"

A map of the PP store (very
much not in scale!). What my
drawing doesn't show is just how
small the store actually is.
The layout reflects the theme
of efficiency: greater sales.
Everything moves in a progressive
way, from one step to the next,
like a well-orchestrated dance.

A map of the Photo Phantasies store

CHECKLIST

HIGH FASHION PHOTOGRAPHY

HAVE YOU THOUGHT OF EVERYONE?

- *Husband* ☐
- *Wife* ☐
- *Mom* ☐
- *Dad* ☐
- *Grandparents* ☐
- *Children* ☐
- *Uncle* ☐
- *Aunt* ☐
- *Brother/Sister* ☐
- *Cousin* ☐
- *Friend* ☐
- *Boyfriend/Girlfriend* ☐
- *Wedding Attendants* ☐
- *Classmates* ☐
- *In-laws* ☐
- *You* ☐

REMEMBER THESE PHOTOGRAPH GIVING OCCASION

- *Birthdays*
- *Valentir*
- *Chr*
- *Anni*
- *We*
- *Grad*
- *Mother's Da*
- *Secret*
- *Tha*
- *Engagem*
- *E*
- *Su*
- *Housewarming*

A "needs" sheet from PP. The purpose is to have the customer begin thinking about buying photos right when she comes in for her appointment. "Suggestion selling in pretty pink." (A Ginny James quote.)

A promotional checklist from Photo Phantasies

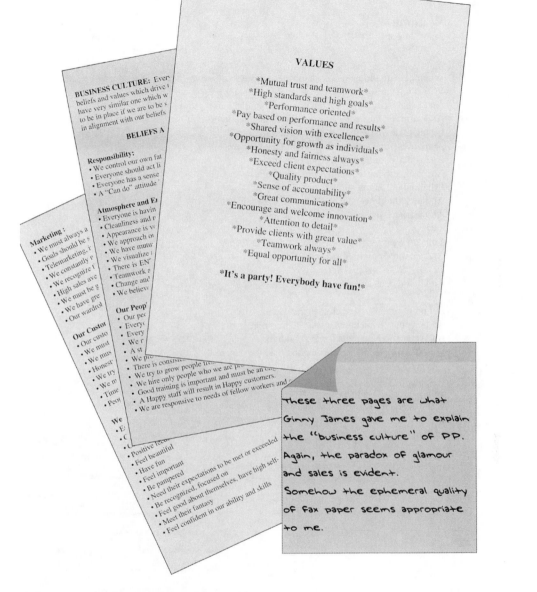

VALUES

Mutual trust and teamwork
High standards and high goals
Performance oriented
Pay based on performance and results
Shared vision with excellence
Opportunity for growth as individuals
Honesty and fairness always
Exceed client expectations
Quality product
Sense of accountability
Great communications
Encourage and welcome innovation
Attention to detail
Provide clients with great value
Teamwork always
Equal opportunity for all

It's a party! Everybody have fun!

BUSINESS CULTURE: Ever
beliefs and values which drive
have very similar one which w
to be in place if we are to be s
in alignment with our beliefs

BELIEFS A

Responsibility:
• We control our own fat
• Everyone should act li
• Everyone has a sense
• A "Can do" attitude

Atmosphere and E
• Everyone is havin
• Cleanliness and r
• Appearance is vo
• We approach or
• We have mutu
• We visualize
• There is EN
• Teamwork
• Change and
• We believe

Our Peop
• Our pec
• Every
• Every
• We r
• A st
• We pro
There is consist
• We try to grow people fi
• We hire only people who we are jo
• Good training is important and must be an o
• A Happy staff will result in Happy customers.
• We are responsive to needs of fellow workers and

Marketing :
• We must always a
• Goals should be s
• Telemarketing, t
• We constantly r
• We recognize t
• High sales ave
• We must be g
• We have gre
• Our wardrol

Our Custor
• Our custo
• We must
• We mus
• Honest
• We try
• We m
• Time
• Peol

We
• E
• C
• Positive recc
• Feel beautiful
• Have fun
• Feel important
• Be pampered
• Need their expectations to be met or exceeded
• Be recognized, focused on
• Feel good about themselves, have high self-
• Meet their fantasy
• Feel confident in our ability and skills

These three pages are what
Ginny James gave me to explain
the "business culture" of PP.
Again, the paradox of glamour
and sales is evident.
Somehow the ephemeral quality
of fax paper seems appropriate
to me.

A three-page business statement for employees

Warning
Jenny Joseph

When I am an old woman I shall wear purple
With a red hat which doesn't go, and doesn't suit me.
And I shall spend my pension on brandy and summer gloves
And satin sandals, and say we've no money for butter.
I shall sit down on the pavement when I'm tired
And gobble up samples in shops and press alarm bells
And run my stick along the public railings
And make up for the sobriety of my youth.
I shall go out in my slippers in the rain
And pick the flowers in other people's gardens
And learn to spit.

You can wear terrible shirts and grow more fat
And eat three pounds of sausages at a go
Or only bread and pickle for a week
And hoard pens and pencils and beermats and things in boxes.

But now we must have clothes that keep us dry
And pay our rent and not swear in the street
And set a good example for the children.
We must have friends to dinner and read the papers.

But maybe I ought to practise a little now?
So people who knew me are not too shocked and surprised
When suddenly I am old, and start to wear purple.

A copy of a poem Ginny James
had in her office. She had it
next to her witch picture and
her PP photo. The sentiment
expressed in the poem seems
so contrary to the PP
philosophy. This is just one of
the many paradoxes
I encountered there.

A poem posted in Ginny James's office

Questions for informants who have been to Photo Phantasies

1. How did you decide to go?

2. Who went with you?

3. How did you feel before the appointment?

4. Tell me about the process in the store—what parts did you like, dislike?

5. What did you talk about with the stylists?

6. What clothes did you pick out?

7. What was it like to have your picture taken?

8. Watching the video images, did you feel any pressure to make a purchase? Did you feel pressure before that?

9. Did you like the pictures?

10. How have you used the photos?

11. Would you go again?

The two interviews I did with informants who had been to PP gave me a feeling of control over the material. While I did ask all of these questions, the conversations with these two women really opened up and quickly became centered on much larger issues, like marriage and family.

Questions to guide interviews with informants

PORTFOLIO

transcription of a conversation with Mrs. Conway
place--her house on the east side of town
date and time--April 24, 1995 2:00 on Monday afternoon

I have never met Mrs. Conway before, but I know her daughter-in-law, who is my mother's cleaning lady. I spoke with Mrs. Conway on the phone about setting up an interview time and she gave me directions to her house. When I arrived, the first thing she did was show me the photographs of her family members and tell me a little about each of them. In her description, she talked mainly about how each of them looked, what things she thought stood out about them physically. Mrs. Conway is 76 years old and has permed gray hair ("It's thick, feel it!"). She is wearing glasses with pink and green and blue flecks of color on blue frames. She offered me coffee and we began talking about how she decided to go to Photo Phantasies. Her husband had always wanted her to go to PP. Mrs. Conway saw that they were having a special and decided to go. Her husband drove her to the mall and waited for her in the store during the process.

K:	So you went out without make-up on...
Mrs. C.:	Uh huh.
K:	...and you just washed your hair...
Mrs. C.:	Yes, I was petrified that someone might see me without my face on at the mall. Yep, I was walking around the mall without my face.
K:	Ah!!
Mrs. C.:	And you know, they do your hair and your make-up.
K:	So you got right in, and what did they do first? Hair?
Mrs. C.:	They do the make-up, I think. Here, do you want to see the pictures?
K:	Absolutely!

Mrs. C. gets up from the couch and walks into the kitchen. From the other room:

Mrs. C.:	Do you know Michael? (Her son.)
K:	Yes, I love Mike. In fact Robin (her future daughter-in-law) told me that Mike has offered to give her and Joel $2,000 if they would elope to Las Vegas instead of having a wedding. That sounds like Mike...
Mrs. C.:	Oh, yes (still in the other room)
K:	That sounds just like him.

Mrs. C. returns to the living room and hands me two wallet size photos of the same PP. In the photographs, she is wearing a satiny pink drape around her shoulders, pearl earrings and a pearl necklace. Her make-up and hair looks much the same as it does today in her house.

K:	Ah. These are gor-geee-ous!
Mrs. C.:	Thanks. (She giggles.)
K:	Oh, my word!
Mrs. C.:	Boy, I'll tell you, they're expensive.
K:	That's kind of what I thought, too.
Mrs. C.:	They are. Let me tell you, you don't get them for $14.95 like the ad promises.
K:	That's sort of the trick. That price might get you in there, but that doesn't get you anything. Sure, you could walk away without ordering anything, but...
Mrs. C.:	Well, they snap a picture of everything that you have on, everything they put on you, and then they show you the pictures on one of those screens.
K:	One of those video screens?
Mrs. C.:	A video screen. They put all these things on you. Finally after they tried a bunch of I asked for something to be put on me that is pastel."
K:	Where they doing you up in glitter?
Mrs. C.:	Everything. Cowgirl, hats...
K:	Cowgirl?
Mrs. C.:	...gloves, but...it wasn't me.
K:	So you didn't get to pick your clothes?
Mrs. C.:	No, I only asked for something soft and feminine and pastel.
K:	And these are absolutely perfect. How about the jewelry? Did you do
Mrs. C.:	No, they did that.
K:	Are these the only ones that you bought?
Mrs. C.:	I bought eight so the kids could each have one.
K:	So you didn't but any with the dangly stuff?
Mrs. C.:	No, I just went for that one cause...It's me, more me.
K:	Yeh, that's what you want.
Mrs. C.:	It's me.

A copy of my transcript from a conversation with Mrs. Conway. This was the only time I was able to use a tape recorder when gathering information. I like re-reading this. It reminds me of how affirming I am about her pictures. It shows a real genuine connection to her.

A transcript of a conversation with a customer

Composing An Image: After

-describe store

-contrast with descrip. of office

-Ginny mixed me

    - selling v

    - artists

    - create

    - custom

    - phone

Playing Your Part

-describe sales vic

-describe employm

{ -describe thank

{ -describe staff m

Putting On Your

    -interview

    -me

---

map of pp

make-over pic.

Vogue cover

Talking with customers. M/F managers.

Bright star stores.

Ads in paper-rigorous test taking

Process, references, 90 days prob.

All in white.

Extensive training now-prob. in the

past

"On-board" since Feb. 6. Ast. buyer

for Yonkers, worked at MH- more

than selling underwear. Wanted to

give something back to society.

Worked at Science center Shop-

Turned it around.

Christmas w/5 kids-3 step and

marriage.

-How the phone is answered.

-Party atmosphere.

"Not hype."

Artists.

My eye color is my best feature

Mother-daughter. Look at features.

Ancestral pictures.

"I see my mother"-grateful to

age that way. She's beautiful.

One of my many organizational attempts done throughout the "writing up" process. I've included this as a reminder of how a researcher shapes her text.

Not even two months, yet she acts so confident, knowledgeable

What? making people feel better about themselves?

This is a treat, special occasion
Oh really? what about the handout on the closest door which seemed to suggest that compliments sell.

I blush. Feel embarrassed and flattered. "I could do such good things w/those eyes."

emphasis on photos as keepsake

That's a selling pt. in their eyes. How Ginny felt when she saw her pictures.

Pages from Karen's fieldnotes

A collage of fashion words

Karen's Portfolio Reflection

A Pose on "Strike a Pose"

Karen Downing

When I think back over this research process, I'm reminded of something Professor Richard Horwitz said when he spoke to our class. About selecting subjects for ethnography, Horwitz advised, "Think about an experience that is really moving to you, an experience that brings out strong conflicting emotions, possibly within yourself, possibly in relation to yourself and others." That, in a pithy quote, is just what Photo Phantasies is for me.

When I started this project, I was very smug and haughty about PP. I scoffed at the notion, and I scoffed at the women who swallowed the absurd "model for a day" rhetoric PP featured in their ads. I was out to prove myself right. I had a heck of a time gaining access to the kind of information I thought I both wanted and needed. From the beginning, I felt off balance and not in control when dealing with Ginny James, the manager of the PP store at the Forum West Mall. But as the research process went on, I learned that the story I was getting—restricted access and all—was indeed a story, and a very compelling one at that. I was amazed by the conflicting messages embedded in the PP dogma, like saying "customer service" when they actually mean "things we need to do to increase sales." I could laugh at the videos, roll my eyes at some of the things the receptionist said about being an artist, and sit in the corner at the staff in-service meeting furiously scribbling away in my journal. But as soon as I started talking with women, women who either wanted to go to PP or who had experienced PP, I was surprised by my reaction. Not only could I understand their desire to go; I found myself championing their desires and validating their experiences after very brief conversations with them. When I stepped back from my initial stance, I began to see PP as a way for women to treat themselves. Not *my* way, but *a* way. I started thinking about the things I do to treat myself—haircuts and a gym membership and new exercise clothes—and had to admit to the level of vanity and indulgence inherent in my own choices.

The PP topic was so full of metaphors. Early on, it became easy for me to see how the metaphors could shape my text. And not surprisingly, the metaphors I came up with seemed applicable to the paradoxes within myself as well as within PP. So the outsider was an insider, and before I knew it, the lines started intersecting all over the place, just like the metaphors. That's probably because the culture of PP could be viewed as a microcosm for a much larger female culture, something I'm naturally a part of, like it or not.

If I had more time with this project, there are other areas I'd want to explore. I would do more readings and interviews on the subject of beauty. What little reading I did made me all the more curious about other sources and other ideas. I would interview women of diverse backgrounds who had been to PP. That way, I would have a more complete picture than any two interviews provided. Believe it or not, I now feel like I could go for the PP experience. (Easy to say after the project is turned in!) It wasn't until I talked with Robin and Norma that I began to feel I could handle immersing myself that completely in the culture, photo session and all. (Mind you, it would only be for the sake of the project!) Finally, I would want more time to simply "look at my fish." Because my research took a while, I found I had very little time to let all of this soak in. Consequently, my final few pages of my piece, which I view as very important, feel tacked on and not as insightful as I would like. In truth, though, PP touches on some issues I could spend a lifetime sorting out and still never be satisfied with the insight I have.

⋯⋯

In this chapter, we've shared several ways to record your spatial gaze: mapping space, writing a visual snapshot, finding a focal point, looking for power dynamics at your fieldsite that might reveal relationships of colonization. Capturing how people view and use their surroundings allows us not only to create a study but also to understand the cultural implications of what's going on there. To discover implications and generate hunches about how people use their space in one or two short visits, you must look closely, record what you see, and then look again.

Recording by writing is not the only way to capture what happens within a space or even what it looks like. Maps, photographs, videos, and sketches—yours or someone else's—can act as fieldnotes and provide you with information that you might not be able to collect otherwise. If you look at a picture long enough, it will reveal data that you can add to your analysis.

For example, Jennifer Hemmingsen's photograph of the carved, hundred-year-old cigar store Indian illustrates the stereotype she's attempting to describe within the culture of Pendleton itself and within American culture. Emily Wemmer's complete essay was full of visual data: reproductions of brochures, sketches of horses, and diagrams of the horse auction barn. The two maps she created (see pp. 189–90) provide data for her analysis and help her readers understand the fieldsite. The visuals in Karen Downing's research portfolio act as data for her, and her portfolio reflection on page 215 shows how the items worked in her overall analysis.

Look at space in as many ways as you can: the implications that you capture will teach you about how the culture operates in your fieldsite. With a careful critique of your written and visual data, you can begin to move from simple recording to thoughtful interpretation and analysis.

Map Your Space

FIRST   Write about your first impressions of the place you are visiting (or researching), and continue to ask the questions that will help you confirm your hunches, analyze the main themes of your experience, and see the landscape from your own and insiders' perspectives.

SECOND   Ask yourself how you feel in the new space. Remember, you are the main instrument of your inquiry. You record and sketch this cultural landscape. Your informants are insiders and will give you their own perspectives. Feeling alone and alien in an unfamiliar place can lead you to new perspectives—about your research site and about yourself.

THIRD   Write about how you know you are an outsider and not an insider there. What small and large behaviors set you apart and mark you as an outsider to the people who inhabit the landscape? Like Jennifer Hemmingsen and Joelle Hann did, take photographs of your surroundings, and analyze their details. Just as Emily Wemmer and Karen Downing did, draw maps and diagrams of your research site to determine the focal points of activity in this space.

5

Researching People: The Collaborative Listener

Portraying people depends on careful listening and observing. In this chapter you will learn to:

- use details to describe people
- gather information from informants
- transcribe others' conversation
- borrow elements of fiction writing

Researching people means stepping in to the worldviews of others. When we talk with people in the field or study the stuff of their lives—their stories, artifacts, and surroundings—we enter their perspectives by partly stepping out of our own.

In an informal way, you are always gathering data about people's backgrounds and perspectives—their worldviews. "So where are you from?" "How do you like it here?" "Did you know anyone when you first came here?" Not only do you ask questions about people's backgrounds, but you also notice their artifacts and adornments—the things with which they represent themselves: T-shirts, jewelry, particular kinds of shoes or hairstyles. The speculations and questions we form about others cause us to make hypotheses about the people we meet. We may ask questions, or we may just listen. But unless we listen closely, we'll never understand others from their perspectives. We need to know what it's like for *that* person in *this* place.

> *Ethnography is interaction, collaboration. What it demands is not hypotheses, which may unnaturally close study down, obscuring the integrity of the other, but the ability to converse intimately.*
>
> —HENRY GLASSIE

Even in an informal conversation, we conduct a kind of ethnographic interview. Good interviewing is collaboration between you and your informant, not very different from a friendly talk. Listening to your relatives share stories at a wedding, pouring over a photo album with your grandmother, and gossiping about old times at a school reunion are all instances in which you can gather data through collaborative listening. You've experienced your local media interviewing sports heroes and newsworthy citizens, and you know famous television and radio interviewers such as Oprah, Barbara Walters, and Charlie Rose. Your fieldworking interviews might employ the same skills: establishing rapport, letting your informant digress from your questions, as well as carefully listening and navigating the conversation process.

This chapter will help you strengthen the everyday skills of listening, questioning, and researching people who interest you. You'll experience interactive ways to conduct interviews and **oral histories**. You'll look for and discover meaning in your informants' everyday cultural artifacts. You'll gather, analyze, write, and reflect on **family stories**. And you'll read some examples of how other fieldworkers have researched and written about people's lives.

The Interview: Learning How to Ask

Fieldworkers listen to and record stories from the point of view of the informant—not their own. Letting people speak for themselves by telling about their lives seems an easy enough principle to follow. But in fact, there are some important strategies for both asking questions and listening to responses. Those strategies are part of interviewing—learning to ask and learning to listen.

Interviewing involves an ironic contradiction: you must be both structured and flexible at the same time. While it's critical to prepare for an interview with a list of planned questions to guide your talk, it is equally important to follow your informant's lead. Sometimes the best interviews come from a comment, a story, an artifact, or a phrase you couldn't have anticipated. The energy that drives a good interview—for both you and your informant—comes from expecting the unexpected.

Expecting the Unexpected   It's happened to both of us as interviewers. As part of a two-year project, Elizabeth conducted in-depth interviews with Anna, a college student who was a dancer. Anna identified with the modern dancers at the university and also was interested in animal rights, organic foods, and ecological causes. She wore a necklace that Elizabeth thought served as a spiritual talisman or represented a political affiliation. When she asked Anna about it, she learned that the necklace actually held the key to Anna's apartment—a much less dramatic answer than Elizabeth anticipated. Anna claimed that she didn't trust herself to keep her key anywhere but around her neck, and that information provided a clue to her temperament that Elizabeth wouldn't have known if she hadn't asked and had persisted in her own speculations.

In a shorter project, Bonnie interviewed Ken, a school superintendent, over a period of eight months. As Ken discussed his beliefs about education, Bonnie connected his ideas with the writings of progressivist philosopher John Dewey. At the time, she was reading educational philosophy herself and was greatly influenced by Dewey's ideas. To her, Ken seemed to be a contemporary incarnation of Dewey. Eventually, toward the end of their interviews, Bonnie asked

Ken which of Dewey's works had been the most important to him. "Dewey?" he asked. "John Dewey? Never exactly got around to reading him."

No matter how hard we try to lay aside our assumptions when we interview others, we always carry them with us. Rather than ignore our hunches, we need to form questions around them, follow them through, and see where they will lead us. Asking Anna about her necklace, a personal artifact, led Elizabeth to new understandings about Anna's self-concept and habits that later became important in her analysis of Anna's literacy. Bonnie's admiration for Dewey had little to do directly with Ken's educational philosophy, but her follow-up questions centered on the scholars who did shape Ken's theories. It is our job to reveal our informant's perspectives and experiences rather than our own. And so our questions must allow us to learn something new, something that our informant knows and we don't. We must learn how to ask.

Asking

Asking involves collaborative listening. When we interview, we are not extracting information the way a dentist pulls a tooth, but we make meaning together like two dancers, one leading and one following. Interview questions range between closed and open.

Closed Questions *Closed questions* are like those we answer on application forms or in magazines: How many years of schooling have you had? Do you rent your apartment? Do you own a car? Do you have any distinguishing birthmarks? Do you use bar or liquid soap? Do you drink sweetened or unsweetened tea, caffeinated or decaffeinated coffee? Some closed questions are essential for gathering background data: Where did you grow up? How many siblings did you have? What was your favorite subject in school? But these questions often yield single phrases as answers and can shut down further talk. Closed questions can start an awkward volley of single questions and abbreviated answers.

To avoid asking too many closed questions, you'll need to prepare ahead of time by doing informal research about your informants and the topics they represent. For example, if you are interviewing a woman in the air force, you may want to read something about the history of women in aviation. You might also consult an expert in the field or telephone government offices to request informational materials so that you avoid asking questions that you could answer for yourself, like "How many years have women been allowed to fly planes in the U.S. Air Force?" When you are able to do background research, your knowledge of the topic and the informant's background will demonstrate your level of interest, put the informant at ease, and create a more comfortable interview situation.

Open Questions *Open questions*, by contrast, help elicit your informant's perspective and allow for a more conversational exchange. Because there is no single answer to open-ended questions, you will need to listen, respond, and follow the informant's lead. Because there is no single answer, you can allow yourself to engage in a lively, authentic response. In other words, simply being interested will make you a good field interviewer. Here are some very general open questions—sometimes called *experiential* and *descriptive*—that encourage the informant to share experiences or to describe them from his or her own point of view.

Open Questions for Your Informant

- Tell me more about the time when…
- Describe the people who were most important to…
- Describe the first time you…
- Tell me about the person who taught you about…
- What stands out for you when you remember…
- Tell me the story behind that interesting item you have.
- Describe a typical day in your life.
- How would you describe yourself to yourself?
- How would you describe yourself to others?

When thinking of questions to ask an informant, make your informant your teacher. You want to learn about his or her expertise, knowledge, beliefs, and worldview.

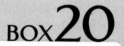
BOX 20

Using a Cultural Artifact in an Interview

PURPOSE

This exercise mirrors the process of conducting interviews over time with an informant. It emphasizes working with the informant's perspective, making extensive and accurate observations, speculating and theorizing, confirming and disconfirming ideas, writing up notes, listening well, sharing ideas collaboratively, and reflecting on your data.

To introduce interviewing in our courses, we use an artifact exchange. This exercise allows people to investigate the meaning of an object from another person's point of view.

Choose a partner from among your colleagues. You will act as both interviewer and informant. Select an interesting artifact that your partner is either wearing or carrying: a key chain, a piece of jewelry, an item of clothing. Both partners should be sure the artifact is one the owner feels comfortable talking about. If, for example, the interviewer says, "Tell me about that pin you are wearing," but the informant knows that her watch has more meaning or her bookbag holds a story, the interviewer should follow her lead. Once you've each chosen an artifact, try the following process. Begin by writing observational and personal notes as a form of background research before interviewing:

1. *Take observational notes.* Take quiet time to inspect, describe, and take notes on your informant's artifact. Pay attention to its form and speculate about its function. Where do you think it comes from? What is it used for?

2. *Take personal notes.* What does it remind you of? What do you already know about things similar to it? How does it connect to your own experience? What are your hunches about the artifact? In other words, what assumptions do you have about it? (For example, you may be taking notes on someone's ring and find yourself speculating about how much it costs and whether the owner of the artifact is wealthy.) It is important here to identify your assumptions and not mask them.

3. *Interview the informant.* Ask questions and take notes on the story behind the artifact. What people are involved in it? Why is it important to them? How does the owner use it? Value it? What's the cultural background behind it? After recording your informant's responses, read your observational notes to each other to verify or clarify the information.

4. *Theorize.* Think of a metaphor that describes the object. How does the artifact reflect something you know about the informant? Could you find background material about the artifact? Where would you look? How does the artifact relate to history or culture? If, for example, your informant wears earrings made of spoons, you might research spoon making, spoon collecting, or the introduction of the spoon in polite society. Maybe this person had a famous cook in the family, played the spoons as a folk instrument, or used these as baby spoons in childhood.

5. *Write.* In several paragraphs about the observations, the interview, and your theories, create a written account of the artifact and its relationship to your informant. Give a draft to your informant for a response.

6. *Exchange.* The informant writes a response to your written account, detailing what was interesting and surprising. At this point, the informant can point out what you didn't notice, say, or ask that might be important to a further understanding of the artifact. You will want to exchange your responses again, explaining what you learned from the first exchange.

7. *Reflect.* Write about what you learned about yourself as an interviewer. What are your strengths? Your weaknesses? What assumptions or preconceptions did you find that you had that interfered with your interviewing skills? How might you change this?

8. *Change roles and repeat this process.*

BOX**20** continued

Lini Ge's Watch

Although we've done this exercise with many people—students, teachers, and researchers—we're always surprised at the flood of cultural information that comes from the pages people fill during their interviews. We both enjoy practicing interviewing with artifacts, so we almost always participate in the process. Here's an interview Bonnie did with her student Lini Ge:

> When Lini handed me her watch, my first reaction was "Oh, she's a swimmer or some other kind of an athlete." I noticed it was made out of a black, supple, strong, rubbery, plastic kind of material. It's very colorful and it says "sports watch" in yellow and "water resistant" in purple on the strap.
>
> There are three elliptical openings on either side of the strap, about three inches on each side, suggesting, too, another kind of practical water resistance. "It's an ugly belt," she tells me. "Do you call it a belt?" "Oh, *strap*," I answer; "it looks lke a belt; it has a black buckle, but I guess because you wear it on your wrist you call it a strap," and I realize it's yet another American synonym that would make no sense to a native speaker of another language. It is, basically, a belt. Lini has owned it since her aunt in Beijing gave it to her almost a decade ago, and she had to replace the strap when the original one broke. She liked that strap better; it was black leather. I noticed that the new strap has nine holes. When I had been a tourist in China, I learned the spiritual and historical importance of the number 9. Lini laughed when I asked her about that and said she'd never even bothered to count how many holes her watch strap had. I realize it's the company's way to accommodate many sizes of wrists.
>
> But truth to tell, such complicated watches scare me. I grew up on the old-fashioned wind-up watch with a traditional face, and although I do love battery power, I still prefer a round two-hand dial. My daughter changes all of my digital clocks twice a year because I find it so frustrating. But obviously, since Lini is a member of the high-tech generation, all of the buttons and features would not be a problem for her. The mechanism and face are practical and complex, too, a slightly exaggerated square—about 1" × 1.3"—with many color-coded features, inside and outside of a thin red border.
>
> She keeps the watch set to twenty-four-hour time, the convention used in China (it is 18:20:54 when I observe it; 6:20 p.m. in American convention). But it's really not. "I keep it about five minutes fast," she tells me. "I don't want to miss my bus, and I'm always running behind." A critical skill for any student.
>
> Lini has Lupus, I remember, a chronic illness. She also has problems with her kidneys. Disease has changed the course of her life and studies. The more I observed the watch before I talked with her, the more I realized that a major function for her would be that she could keep track of her blood pressure—conveniently on her wrist while also telling the time. Outside the border, there are four buttons, two on each side. On the left, there is "adjust" and "mode," for keeping time. On the right, a black button is labeled "bp start" and a yellow one labeled "restart." On the upper portion of the face, aside the CASIO company logo, are the words "Blood Pressure Monitor" and BP-120 (a model number, but ironically, the number of healthy blood pressure). A yellow panel offers the day, the date, and a small red heart. The time is displayed digitally: hour, minutes, and seconds. On the lower portion are the words "systolic"

and "diastolic," as well as what appears to be a sensor light on one side and a panel that proclaims "pls" and "ekg." Aha. Medical terms about blood pressure.

I am intrigued that it's a Japanese watch with English language labels, owned by a Chinese woman who got it as a gift from an aunt who doesn't speak English. It is a symbol of our global economy, our multinational world. I assumed wrongly that Lini must have bought it in the United States. "Oh, a Chinese person would buy this watch this way," Lini told me. "Casio is a famous brand, and it's more convenient to use these terms." Her friends in China were fascinated by the watch's special features, although Lini admits it isn't that convenient for its medical value. She quickly discovered that the blood pressure features will only work with fresh batteries. But her friends enjoyed taking their heartbeats and blood pressure with it. She hasn't yet shared it with her U.S. friends. I want to buy her some fresh batteries and check to see if it works for me!

In interviews, researchers sometimes use cultural artifacts to enter into the informant's perspective. We might start by talking about something in our informant's environment: a framed snapshot, a CD or DVD collection, an interesting or unusual object in the room—anything that will encourage comfortable conversation. When we invite informants to tell stories about their artifacts, we learn about the artifacts themselves (Lini Ge's watch) and, indirectly, about other aspects of their world that they might not think to talk about. Artifacts, like stories, can mediate between individuals and their cultures.

Learning How to Listen

Although most people think that the key to a good interview is asking a set of good questions, we and our students have found that the real key to interviewing is being a good listener. Think about your favorite television or radio talk show personalities. What do they do to make their informants comfortable and keep conversation flowing? Think about someone you know whom you've always considered a good listener. Why does that person make you feel that way?

Good listeners guide the direction of thoughts; they don't interrupt or move conversation back to themselves. Good listeners use their body language to let informants understand that their informants' words are important to them, not allowing their eyes to wander, not fiddling, not checking their watches or their phones. They encourage response with verbal acknowledgments and follow-up questions, with embellishments and examples.

To be a good listener as a field interviewer, you must also have structured plans with focused questions. And you must be willing to change them as the conversation moves in different directions. With open questions, background research, and genuine interest in your informant, you'll find yourself holding a collaborative conversation from which you'll both learn. It is the process, not the preplanned information, that makes an interview successful.

Etiquette for Conducting an Interview

In addition to preparing yourself with guiding questions and good listening habits, here are some basic rules of etiquette for conducting a successful interview. Always keep in mind that you are using someone's time.

- Arrange for the interview at your informant's convenience. Your interview should fit into that person's schedule, not vice versa. Put his or her needs first.

- Explain your project in plain language that your informant will understand. Don't bore or scare them with insider expressions such as "ethnographic" or "fieldsite research."

- Agree on a quiet place to talk. Avoid places like cafés that have a lot of ambient noise.

- Arrive on time and be prepared. Make sure your equipment works (pens, batteries, recording devices). Have your questions and notepad ready.

- Dress appropriately for the setting and for your informant. You'd wear something different to interview a lifeguard on the beach than your grandmother in her living room.

- Don't try to squeeze too much into a short time. Be sensitive to social cues and, if necessary, arrange for an additional interview.

- Thank your informant and follow up with a thank-you note, e-mail, or, if appropriate, a token of gratitude.

A Successful Interview

Paul Russ conducted interviews with five AIDS survivors for an ethnographic film, *Healing without a Cure: Stories of People Living with AIDS*, sponsored by a local health agency. He developed a list of open and closed questions to prepare for and guide his interviewing process. He knew that closed questions would provide him with similar baseline data for all of his informants. For this reason, he formulated some questions that had one specific answer:

Paul's Closed Questions

- "How many months have you lived with your diagnosis?"
- "When did you first request a 'buddy' from the health service?"
- "Does your family know about your diagnosis?"

But the overall goal of his project was to capture how individuals coped with their diagnoses daily, drawing on their own unique resources. He wanted to avoid creating a stereotypical profile of a "day in the life of a person living with AIDS" since he knew that no one AIDS patient's way of coping could represent all other patients' coping styles. Paul constructed open questions to allow his informants to speak from their lived experiences.

Paul's Open Questions

- "What did you already know about AIDS when you were diagnosed?"
- "How did others respond to you and your diagnosis?"
- "What has helped you most on a day-to-day basis to live with the virus?"
- "Have people treated you differently since you were diagnosed?"

In the following excerpt from his hundreds of pages of transcripts, Paul talks with Jessie, a man who had been living with his diagnosis for eight years. For Paul, this interview was a struggle because Jessie hadn't talked much with others about AIDS. And because Paul chose to study people whose lives were very fragile, he paid particular attention to the interactive process between himself and his informants. In the following transcript, Paul uses Jessie's dog, Princess, just as another interviewer might have used an artifact to get further information:

P: What was your reaction when you were first diagnosed?

(This is one of the questions Paul posed to each of his five informants. Because he was making a training film for public health volunteers, he wanted to record people's initial reactions on discovering that they had a publicly controversial illness.)

J: My first reaction? How am I going to tell my family. And I put it in my mind that I would not tell anyone until it became noticeable. And I wondered who would take care of me. . . . I knew sometimes AIDS victims go blind. I panicked a little bit, and I started thinking of all the things I have to do to make my life livable. . . . I started thinking about the things I could do to make it go easier. And I started thinking of things I would miss.

P: Like Princess, your dog?

(Paul knew from previous talks that Jessie's dog was an important part of his daily life.)

J: I've had Princess for three years. I had another red dachshund, but she got away. I got Princess as a Christmas gift. . . . She comforts me. She knows when I'm not feeling right. She comes and rubs me. She goes places with me. If I'm in the garden, she's right there. She can't let me out of her sight. Sometimes

I talk to her, late at night, we just lay there. She seems like she understands....I don't think she can live without me. If something happens to me, she'll be so confused. I think she'll be so lonely, she'll go off somewhere and just die....I want to give her to somebody. Maybe an older person, someone I believe will take care of her.

(By talking about his dog, Jessie opened himself up to Paul. By following up on Jessie's comment about "things he'd miss," Paul deepened their interaction and intensified their talk. It was not the dog herself that was important in this exchange but what Princess represented from Jessie's perspective. Paul did not intend to make Jessie talk about his fear of dying, but it happened naturally as he talked about Princess. At this point, Paul found a way to ask another one of the prepared questions that he used with each of his informants. And Jessie's answer brought them back to Princess.)

P: What's your typical day like?

J: My typical day is feeding Princess, letting her out, doing my housework. I like to do my work before noon because I'm addicted to soap operas....I like to work in the yard. I've got a garden. I have some herbs. And I like every now and then to pray. I go to the library. I do a great deal of reading.

(Paul continued to interview Jessie about his spirituality and his reading habits. He brought this interview around to another pre-planned question that he asked of all his AIDS informants.)

P: What advice do you have for the newly diagnosed?

J: Don't panic. You do have a tendency to blow it out of proportion. And find a friend, a real friend, to help you filter out the negative. Ask your doctor questions. Let it out and forgive. Forgive yourself, you're only human. And forgive the person you think gave it to you. Then you will learn that the key to spirituality is to abandon yourself....I don't want a sad funeral. I want music, more music than anything else. I don't want my family to go under because of this disease.

Paul's interviews eventually became a training film for volunteers at the Triad Health Project and area schools that wanted to participate in AIDS support and education. In the film, Paul has the advantage of presenting his data, not just through verbal display but visually as well. As Paul conducts his interviews, we hear his voice and see his informants—their surroundings and artifacts, their gestures and body language, and the tones of voices as they respond to Paul.

BOX 21

Establishing Rapport

PURPOSE

Paul Russ worked hard to establish rapport with his informant. Rapport doesn't happen in one short interview. Interviewing is a collaborative and interactive process in which researchers make themselves knowledgeable about their informants' positions, interests, feelings, and worldviews.

ACTION

In this activity, you will reflect on your relationship with an informant and gain greater understanding of yourself as a researcher. Write a short paper about your subjective attitude toward an informant. Think about whether you've felt tentative or hesitant toward your informant, feelings that you may not want to write about in your final paper but that you acknowledge and understand as part of your researcher self. Use the following list to guide you:

1. Describe your first meeting with your informant. What did you notice about yourself as you began the interview process?

2. Describe any gender, class, race, or age differences that may have affected the way you approached your informant.

3. Discuss ways you tried either to acknowledge or to erase these differences and the extent to which you were successful.

4. Discuss how your rapport changed over time in talking with and understanding your informant and her worldview.

RESPONSE

Paul Russ faced many race and class differences when he interviewed his informants about how they lived with AIDS. The most obvious was health, since his informants were facing disease and he was not. Paul's response describes the many conflicting feelings he had when he interviewed Jessie:

> I picked up Jessie to drive him to the Health Project office for the interview. At first, we didn't conduct the interviews at his house. I'm not sure if he was uncomfortable about me seeing the inside of his house, if he didn't want the neighbors seeing a tall white guy carrying a bunch of camera equipment into his house. Anyway, as Jessie rode in my car, I was incredibly aware of the two different worlds we came from. I had a bad case of white man's guilt. As he sat in my car, I apologized for the dog hair left from taking my two dogs to the vet. He said that it was fine, that he was used to it. Then he mentioned his dog, Princess. It was the first thing we had to talk about. Jessie admitted that he had little family support to cope with AIDS and that Princess was his family. I shared that my dog had had a difficult pregnancy and that I almost lost her. That's when he first opened up to me about his fear of living without Princess or Princess living without him. When it later came up in our interview, it was an obvious opportunity to encourage Jessie to speak personally.

BOX 21 continued

It was essential to establish common ground with him because I felt I had nothing in common with Jessie. Perhaps this was because he did not come from where I came from and, perhaps, because he did not look like me. And while I've never considered myself prejudiced, I realize that we all have prejudices deeply buried inside no matter how intelligent or informed we are. In order to know him with some degree of intimacy, I had to be vulnerable and share myself. I had to address the baggage of race, class, education. I did this with all the informants in my project, and it scared me because being friends with someone who is facing mortality requires an emotional investment. I knew I had to establish a friendship.

While I was making a personal connection with Jessie, I also had professional distance. With everything that came out of Jessie's mouth, I was thinking about how it could be used in the final project. For me, interviewing is very active. It's not passive at all. You have to listen for meaning and listen for what's not being said. I had trouble getting Jessie to speak from the heart. His responses to early questions were pressed. I knew that if I were writing his story for a reader, I could project a much clearer sense of his identity than he gave me on camera. I knew that. But I wasn't writing his story. My mission was to record him telling his story in his own words. So I looked for opportunities to help him reveal himself to me. Princess was one of these opportunities.

Recording and Transcribing

Interviews provide the bones of any fieldwork project. You need your informants' actual words to support your findings. Without informants' voices, you have no perspective to share except your own. When you record and transcribe your interviews, you bring to life the language of the people whose culture you study.

The process of recording and transcribing interviews has been advanced by computers, software, and audio recorders that are small, relatively inexpensive, and easily available. It's no coincidence that interviewing and collecting oral histories have become more popular in recent years with these accessible technologies. With a counting feature to keep track of slices of conversation and a pause button to slow down the transcription process, even the most basic recorder becomes a valuable tool for the interviewer.

Your choice of recording device will partially depend on whether you need a recorder that is lightweight and handheld, high resolution, and low noise, or one that records to a memory card. You may find that an inexpensive recorder will suit your purposes just fine if you want to record one-on-one in a quiet space and transcribe it yourself before integrating the interview into your own text. However, if you plan to record in a noisy setting and make both the audio and written transcription available, you will need a higher-quality recording device.

How you are going to share your work is another consideration. Will you transcribe it into print only, or will you also distribute it as an audio file, podcast, or part of a multimedia presentation? How you will use your interview material will affect what kind of equipment you purchase or rent.

Advances in recording devices and software have cut down the tedium of sorting, classifying, and organizing huge amounts of data. But transcribing is tedious business nonetheless. Three or more hours might be required to transcribe one hour of recording. And editing your audio files (if you choose to do that) will require even more time. However, you learn an enormous amount about your informants and yourself as you listen, replay, and select the sections for your study.

You don't want to record everything you hear, nor do you want to transcribe it all. That's why it's important to prepare ahead—with research, guiding questions, and adequate equipment as well as knowledge of how to use it. The following guidelines will help make your recording and transcribing go smoothly.

- *Obtain your equipment* Before borrowing or purchasing quality equipment, research what's available. A digital counter that helps keep track of time, multidirectional microphones that minimize ambient noise, and functions that record separate tracks are some key features that will facilitate your research. Investigate what's available and appropriate to your research.

- *Prepare your equipment* Dead batteries and full memory cards can ruin your data collection. Always carry extras. Test your recorder before using it by stating your name, the date, the place of the interview, and the full name of your informant, and then playing this information back to yourself. If you use a microphone, check out its range before you begin. Most fieldworkers have stories of losing interviews because of equipment malfunction. Be prepared.

- *Plan to take notes* Consider how you will take fieldnotes during the interview so that you'll capture all the features of the experience and have a backup in case your recording equipment fails. You want to note the environment where the interview takes place, the facial and body language of your informant's responses, and any hesitations or interruptions that take place. Your fieldnotes will help supplement the actual recording. Also consider taking photos that you can use later to jog your memory.

- *Organize your interview time* Be considerate in setting up a time and place for the interview. Ask your informant what's convenient for him or her. Arrive a few minutes early and test your equipment as well as the space so that you don't have any extraneous noise or distractions. Remember to have a timepiece—be it a watch or a phone—so that you can keep track of interview time.

- ***Organize time to listen to your audio***   Begin the labeling process as soon as possible. Key the filename (date, place, and informant's name) into your audio device or download the file from your memory card and label it on your computer. Also write down the filename of each recording in your fieldnotes. After the interview, listen to the recording as soon as you can to keep it fresh in your mind. Take notes as you listen for topics covered, themes that emerge, and possible follow-up questions.

- ***Transcribe the interview***   As soon as you can, begin to transcribe your recording. Don't wait too long, as the initial listening process enhances your memory of the interview and your sense of purpose about the project. Remember that you do not need to transcribe all the material you record—only the sections that are useful to your study. To transcribe, listen directly from the recorder or upload your audio files to your computer. Check with your media lab to see if they have a device sometimes known as a footswitch. If they do, you can attach it to your audio device to stop and start the recording as needed. This can be immensely helpful. Whatever sections you decide to use, transcribe them word for word using parentheses or brackets to indicate pauses, laughing, interruptions, sections you want to leave out, or unintelligible words. For example: [Regina laughs nervously] or [phone rang, maybe match? Or march?—check with Regina] or [unintelligible word].

- ***Bring your informant's language to life***   As a transcriber, you must bring your informant's speech to life as accurately and appropriately as you can. Most researchers agree that a person's grammar should remain as spoken. If an informant says, "I done," for example, it's not appropriate to alter it to "I did." But if when you share the transcript with your informant she chooses to alter it, respect those changes. As well, many characteristics of oral language have no equivalents in print. It is too difficult for either transcriber or reader to attempt to capture dialect in written form. "Pahk the cah in Hahvahd Yahd" is a respelling of a Boston accent, meant to show how it sounds. But to a reader who's never heard it—even to an insider Bostonian who isn't conscious of her accent—the written version of her oral dialect looks artificial and complicates the reading process. Anthropologists and folklorists have long debated how to record oral language and currently discourage the use of spelling as a way to approximate oral language.

  For more on using insider language in your writing, see Chapter 6, page 281.

- ***Share your transcript***   Offer the transcripts to your informant to read for accuracy, but realize that you won't get many takers. Most informants would rather wait for your finished, edited version of the interview. In any case, the informant needs the opportunity to read what you've written. In some instances, the informant may make corrections or ask for deletions. But most of the time, the written interview becomes a kind of gift in exchange for the time spent interviewing.

● ***Edit the audio files*** You may decide to go beyond the written transcript to include your raw audio recording in a Web-based media presentation that will add an extra dimension to your project. To create a usable audio clip, you will need to use software to edit or splice your recordings together. Talk to fellow students or researchers about what they use. If possible, test-drive the editing software in order to understand its full capacities before you purchase it.

You'll also want to consider what medium in which to share your audio clips, as this will affect their length and content. Blogs, multimedia presentations, and podcasts are some of the popular formats at the time of this writing. Be sure to include the URL for your blog, Web site, or podcast in your written work—especially if you plan to publish it—so that your readers can access it and enhance their understanding of your study.

Reminders for Recording and Transcribing

- Set up your interview.

- Familiarize yourself with your recording device.

- Arrive early and evaluate your recording environment.

- Conduct the interview and take notes.

- Arrange sufficient time for listening to and transcribing the interview.

- Consider your final presentation format and its audience.

Fieldworkers must turn interview transcripts into writing, making a kind of verbal film. As interesting as interview transcripts are to the researcher, they are only partial representations of the actual interview process. Folklorist Elliott Oring observes, "Lives are not transcriptions of events. They are artful and enduring symbolic constitutions which demand our engagement and identification. They are to be perceived and understood as wholes" (258). To bring an informant's life to the page, you must use a transcript within your own text, sometimes describing the setting, the informant's physical appearances, particular mannerisms, and language patterns and intonations. The transcript by itself has little meaning until you bring it to life.

Cindie Marshall conducted a semester-long field project at Ralph's Sports Bar, frequented by men and women who ride motorcycles and describe themselves as bikers. In "Ralph's Sports Bar," she combines her skills as a listener, an interviewer, and most of all a writer. In her study, her informants speak in their own voices, but Cindie contextualizes them, offering readers a look into the biker subculture as it exists at Ralph's. As you read Cindie's research study, notice the fieldworking skills she brings together.

Ralph's Sports Bar

Cindie Marshall

The Arrival

Everyone in the bar eyed me suspiciously during my visit. I didn't dress, walk, or talk like the other women. Because of the illegal activity that goes on in the bar, I guessed they were probably wondering if I was an undercover cop. I realized that given the way the groups marked their boundaries, they probably wouldn't be very inviting to a stranger asking a lot of questions about their "culture."

I decided that I would go to the table out front and perhaps there I could find someone to answer my questions. At the very least, I could get some fresh air and think about my approach. When I arrived at the table, there was a woman sitting alone, drinking a beer. She had obviously had a lot to drink. But we talked for a minute, and she was really quite nice. I introduced myself, and she said her name was Teardrop. It was dark outside, so I couldn't see her very well. We talked about the weather, and that led her to tell me that she had moved here from Michigan three years ago and that she came to Ralph's every day.

(Photo: Minshall Strater)

Ralph's Sports Bar

I knew that this was my opportunity to talk to a patron. On a long shot, I asked her if she would like to shoot a game of pool. She agreed, and I was delighted. This was an opportunity to ask questions and be seen with a regular.

Once we were inside, I saw that Teardrop was wearing new Lee jeans, a nice pale yellow sweater, and a heart-shaped brooch. Her hair was brown but was showing signs of graying. She had it neatly pulled back, and her bangs were teased and carefully sprayed in place. It wasn't until she laughed that I noticed she was missing her front teeth, both top and bottom. She had a small dark-green vine tattoo around her wrist. Most of the tattoo was covered by her watch.

As we played pool, I noticed she also had a black tattoo in the shape of a teardrop high on her cheek. When I asked her about her teardrop tattoo, she started really talking to me. She told me that when she was 13, she had been kidnapped by a group of bikers. The biker that kidnapped her had eventually sold her to a fellow biker. This went on for years until finally, three years ago, she got away. The teardrop was there because she couldn't cry anymore.

After hearing Teardrop's story, my admiration for the bikers' "do your own thing" attitude was lost. She had described sheer abuse, and she wore that abuse both on her face, in the shape of a teardrop, and in her smile, which was darkened by missing teeth.

I left the bar to reflect on all that I had seen. I wanted to know why the groups in the bar would come together in a place just to keep themselves segregated. The only way I could get the answers to my questions was to talk to a person who had been in all three groups and had spent a lot of time at the bar: Alice.

Conversation with Alice

Alice's boyfriend, Ralph, owned the bar. She had worked there prior to becoming the receptionist at the law firm at which I worked, and she could probably tell me everything I wanted to know.

Alice agreed to my interview, and I prepared a list of the three groups, outlining what I thought their characteristics were. Alice read my list and we began.

Characteristics of the "Rednecks"

We both agreed that one of the groups we would call "rednecks" for lack of a better term. My list ascribed the following characteristics to this group: they would be lazy; they would value freedom; they would not like or adhere to any rules imposed on them; they would have no self-pride, either in their work or appearance; they would demean women; they would have no materialistic values; they would have no work ethic; and they would have no moral code among themselves—it would be every man for himself.

After reviewing my list, Alice commented that actually, "they are hardworking and take pride in their jobs. Because they like to be able to say 'I do something well.'...Most of them are blue-collar workers—construction workers, electricians,

(Photo: Minshall Strater)

Ralph's Sports Bar parking lot

people who do things with their hands. They're good at what they do to a certain extent. A lot of them do change jobs frequently because of the drinking problem that they have, and I think the majority of them do have drinking problems. . . . They are lazy in the sense that they don't aspire to be anything more than what they are."

We discussed how they treated their women, and Alice was quick to point out "that's the biggest thing that they do. . . . It makes them feel like they are bigger." We had talked prior to the interview about how uncomfortable I was at this bar. It seemed that all the men treated the women with little or no respect.

On the subject of the rednecks' commitment to their fellow rednecks, I felt that it would be every man for himself. I doubted that the rednecks had lasting bonds or would stand up for a buddy in trouble. Alice said that she had "seen where one night two guys would sit there and be buddy-buddy and would fight together side by side. Two weeks later, they would fight each other."

Overall, the only real corrections Alice made to my list of characteristics was that she strongly disagreed with my idea that rednecks were lazy. I asked her later outside the interview how they could all be working yet spending their entire day at Ralph's. She told me those individuals worked third shift and would simply go to work drunk.

Characteristics of the Bikers

I had made a similar list of characteristics for the bikers at Ralph's. I had decided that they, too, would value freedom and not like rules imposed on them. However, they would have a higher moral code among themselves. I guessed that they didn't care what other people thought of them and therefore would not be materialistic. They would likely believe in making their own way and have a higher work ethic than the rednecks. I would categorize them as more the "weekend warrior" type. I also concluded that unlike the rednecks, they were probably ritualistic in the way they meticulously parked their bikes. As for their treatment of women, after talking with Teardrop, my view on that was clear. To the bikers, women were property, and that was all.

Alice started her revision of my list by first telling me that "there are even two different classes of bikers.... There are some bikers that are construction workers, moochers, low lifes. They live from day to day in how they get their money, how they live. They come from a culture of brotherhood and "my buddy." They are more clannish in that, if a guy drives a bike, they will stand beside him no matter what. But also, there are a lot of bikers that come in there that are white-collar workers; they do this on the weekend and like to be someone different. They change their persona and how people perceive them. They put on their leather pants and leather jackets and ride these motorcycles all week-end long and go back to their jobs. There are four or five of them that nobody knows.... They are businessmen who own companies over in High Point... but you would never guess it by the way they look when they are sitting there on the weekends drinking."

When we talked about the stereotypical biker, I asked her if she felt they "treat women the same way the rednecks do." She said no. It was more of a kind of ownership. She said, "'My old lady' and 'my old man,' this is the way they talk. Rednecks are a little more respectful... 'this is my wife' or 'this is my girlfriend.' I think that the 'old lady' and 'old man' can change from week to week. I have seen [bikers] swap women around as if they were pieces of property." Surprisingly enough, she made her point about the way bikers treat women by telling me Teardrop's story.

We talked about the bikers and how they felt about freedom. Alice pointed out, "You will find that most of the bikers will be outside, they will not be inside the bar.... Bikers like the openness and the freedom — that's why they're bikers."

Conclusion

Alice is a reliable source of information on all three groups because she has been very deeply connected to all of them. She truly does cross the line of the cultural boundaries. As she put it, "I've been there. I've been a drinker and down on my luck and slept in my car. I've been just where they are on many occasions...."

My own stereotypes show in my list of characteristics that I mapped out for Alice to review. As for Alice, it is clear that she has stereotyped these groups, too.

After talking with her and visiting the bar, my question still remained: Why would these distinctly different groups of people, each representing a unique culture, come to one small bar, each mapping their turf and intentionally stay-ing separated? Alice felt that the common bond was Ralph. Ralph moved easily between the cultures and was actually a part of each group. She said that he did it much the same as she did, the difference being that Ralph held the role of "leader" or "policer" of each group. It was because of Ralph that the groups could all drink their beer in harmony while at the bar.

I feel that it goes much deeper than that. The one common bond that all of these groups share is love of freedom. The white-collar, part-time biker enjoys the freedom of wearing his leather and riding his Harley on the weekend without anyone knowing. The redneck enjoys the freedom to drink his beer and be totally wild if he wishes. All these people go to Ralph's to escape, to be free of the watchful eyes of a judgmental society. They like the comfort of not worrying what anyone else will think because they know no one will care....

Read Cindie Marshall's full essay at **bedfordstmartins .com/fieldworking**, under Student Essays.

Commentary: With More Time . . .

I would love to have had more time to visit this bar and try to become part of this culture. I am certain that there are errors in my list of characteristics, and I know that these characteristics do not apply to every individual. It would have been interesting to make connections in the bar and test my ideas; to prove or disprove the stereotypes that I have about each group. With that research perhaps it would be more clear where the stereotypes actually come from. I have asked myself that question over and over again while writing this paper. At this point, I cannot clearly say where they come from. I think it is a combination of many sources.

I am still very intrigued with the biker culture. I wish I could have talked with more female bikers to get their ideas on the treatment-of-women issue. Teardrop really changed my attitude.

Before we discuss Cindie Marshall's study, we want to show you some excerpts from her portfolio that illustrate her notetaking and categorizing skills. In some of her interviews, she simply took notes and later checked them with Alice. But she also recorded other conversations with Alice.

As she learned more from her interviews with Alice, Cindie looked carefully at the words in the interview and began to see the patterns in the biker culture that Alice described. Here is a sample from her recorded interview.

Cindie Marshall's Interview Notes

INTERVIEW WITH ALICE

C: Let's go over the category list. You believe the rednecks value their freedom and are hardworking.

A: I think that they are hardworking and take pride in their jobs. Because they like to be able to say, "I do something well." But their whole goal in what I have viewed is that "I work to drink and I drink to work."

C: What kind of work do they do normally?

A: Most of them are blue-collar workers—construction workers, electricians, people who do things with their hands. They're good at what they do to a certain extent. A lot of them do change jobs frequently because of the drinking problem that they have, and I think the majority of them do have drinking problems.

C: We talked about their being lazy, and we concluded that they're lazy in the sense that they don't aspire to be anything more than what they are.

A: Yes. If their daddy taught them how to do construction or to build houses, they don't make goals other than that.

C: And no self-pride in terms of their appearance?

A: Yes.

C: And we talked about how they demean women.

A: Yes, very much so. That's the biggest thing that they do. It makes them feel stronger and feel like better people. It makes them feel like they are bigger.

C: We talked about every man for himself, and you were saying that there were no lasting bonds between the members of this particular culture within the bar.

A: This is true. Because I have seen where one night two guys would sit there and be buddy-buddy and would fight together side by side. Two weeks later, they would fight each other. If the situation changes. The alcohol changes people's personalities, and it varies day to day who is buddy-buddy.

C: The other culture that I saw when I was there is—you have your rednecks and you have your bikers. What is the difference between the bikers and the rednecks?

A: I think that there are even two different classes of bikers.

C: In this bar?

A: In this bar. In the sense that there are some bikers that are construction workers, moochers, low lifes. They live from day to day in how they get their money, how they live. They come from a culture of brotherhood and "my buddy." They are more clannish in that, if a guy drives a bike, they will stand beside him no matter what. But also, there are a lot of bikers that come in there that are white-collar workers; they do this on the weekend and like to be someone different. They change their persona and how people perceive them. They put on their leather pants and leather jackets and ride these motorcycles all weekend long and go back to their jobs. There are four or five of them that nobody knows. They are very honest and they tell you what they do, that they are businessmen who own companies over in High Point and one thing and another. But you would never guess it by the way they look when they are sitting there on the weekends drinking. (*Need to ask her how these guys are treated by the full-time bikers. Do they tell the full-time bikers about their other identity?*)

C: So those particular guys really fit both in among the bikers and the white-collar professionals.

A: Yes.

C: So they are just choosing what culture they want to be in on weekends basically. They could go into the biker thing or the professional white-collar worker thing if they wanted to, just whichever way they wanted to go.

A: Yeah.

One of the strengths of Cindie's study is that she acquires different perspectives about Ralph's Sports Bar, which mirror the three categories of patrons she is attempting to understand. Cindie positions herself at the outset as part of the "white-collar weekend professional" group, admitting her own stereotypes. The second perspective is what Cindie calls the "regular bikers," and her informant Teardrop has belonged to that "regular biker" culture much of her life. The third perspective comes from Alice, Cindie's colleague at the law firm and Ralph's girlfriend, who defends the "redneck" position.

Cindie was fortunate to find Teardrop, who was in many ways an ideal informant. Teardrop frequents Ralph's every day, so she is an insider to the culture. But Teardrop had stepped out of the biker culture long enough to be able to reflect on it. Teardrop was also an ideal informant because Cindie interacted with her informally, gathering data as they shot pool together. Cindie didn't record Teardrop's story but remembered it and wrote it into her fieldnotes. She didn't worry about forgetting Teardrop's story because it was indelible, just like the tattoo that was there "because she couldn't cry anymore." Cindie learned this story from Teardrop as they interacted, each gaining trust for the other. Had Cindie pulled out her tape recorder and tried to interview Teardrop by asking, "So tell me how you got your name?" she probably wouldn't have heard Teardrop's story. The process of interaction and rapport allowed Cindie to acquire good insider data.

Cindie's interview with Alice was entirely different because it was structured and planned. Cindie prepared a list of questions based on her own fieldnote observations of the three categories of patrons at the bar. Because Alice was already a friend from the law firm where Cindie worked, she didn't need to establish rapport.

Both Teardrop's and Alice's perspectives give weight and evidence to Cindie's own field observations, allowing her to confirm and disconfirm her data. As we point out throughout this book, when researchers use multiple data sources (interviews, fieldnotes, artifacts, and library or archival documents), they triangulate their findings. In this semester-long study, Cindie collected and analyzed varied sources (interviews, fieldnotes, and artifacts), and wrote from the perspective of a woman who interviewed other women about a predominantly male subculture.

Because Cindie's final account is smoothly written and her research skills are well integrated, it might not be apparent that she has engaged in many aspects of the fieldworking process. A summary of her many fieldworking strategies reveals, however, that Cindie was able to do all of the following:

- ***Prepare for the field***.

    She gained access through her colleague Alice, an insider at Ralph's.

    She read other research studies and material about fieldworking.

    She drafted a research proposal that explained her interest in the biker subculture.

    She wrote about her assumptions and uncovered her prejudices about bikers and rednecks.

- ***Use the researcher's tools***.

    She established rapport by hanging out at Ralph's and by locating Teardrop, an insider informant.

    She observed, taking detailed fieldnotes about the physical environment.

    She participated in the culture by shooting pool with Teardrop, talking and interacting at the same time.

    She gathered descriptions of many cultural artifacts, taking photos and noting what they implied.

    She interviewed two informants, Alice (formally) and Teardrop (informally), taking fieldnotes on their physical characteristics as well as their stories.

    She transcribed Alice's interview, selecting potential sections to use in her final project.

- ***Interpret the fieldwork***.

    She read her data, proposal, fieldnotes, interview notes, and transcripts, looking for themes and patterns.

    She categorized her data into findings according to the three groups she observed.

    She made meaning collaboratively with her informants:

    > With Alice, she verified her categories and disconfirmed her own cultural stereotypes in her interview.

    > With Teardrop, she reflected on her data, particularly after her interview, and expanded her findings with insights about the treatment of women within the biking culture.

    She reflected on how her data described a subculture.

- ***Present the findings***.

    She acknowledged and wrote about her position as an outsider.

    She used descriptive details in her writing, selecting particular written artifacts that convey the meaning of the culture.

She turned her informants into characters by melding her fieldnotes and her transcripts.

She integrated her informants' voices with her narrative by using direct quotations from her transcripts.

She designed sections with subheadings to guide her reader through the project: "The Arrival," "Conversation with Alice," "Characteristics of the 'Rednecks'," "Characteristics of the Bikers," "Conclusion," and her commentary called "With More Time...."

BOX 22

Analyzing Your Interviewing Skills

PURPOSE

Reviewing and analyzing an excerpt from your transcripts can help you refine your interviewing skills and see ways to improve them. Pausing to look closely at your interviewing and transcribing techniques may smooth the way for the rest of your project.

ACTION

Select and transcribe a short section (no more than a page) from a key interview to share. Play the corresponding portion of the recording as your colleagues read the transcript and listen. Have your colleagues jot down notes and suggestions about your interview so that you can discuss their observations together afterward:

- Has the interviewer established rapport with the informant?
- Who talks more, the informant or the interviewer? Does that seem to work?
- What was the best question the interviewer asked? Why?
- What question might have extended to another question? Why?
- How did the interviewer encourage the informant to be specific?
- Were any of the questions closed?

Try using the line-by-line analysis in a small section, like the following example from Cindie Marshall.

RESPONSE

Here we analyze one of Cindie's transcripts, a portion of her interview with Alice. In this excerpt, both interviewer and informant struggle with what they mean by the word *redneck* and its associated cultural stereotypes. Fieldworkers need to be sensitive to words that have different meanings for insiders in a culture. From her outsider perspective, Cindie knew that the word *redneck* is a loaded term and that it's used differently in different areas of the country. She was eager for Alice to help her clarify what it meant to different groups at Ralph's Sports Bar.

C: You believe the rednecks value their freedom and are hardworking.

(Cindie wants confirmation from Alice about one group of people she has observed frequenting Ralph's Sports Bar. She tries to get Alice to untangle her own perspective about this category of patrons in the bar.)

A: I think that they are hardworking and take pride in their jobs. Because they like to be able to say, "I do something well." But their whole goal in what I have viewed is that "I work to drink and I drink to work."

C: What kind of work do they do normally?

(Cindie follows Alice's lead, asking for more information, trying to find out more about what they each mean when they use the term redneck. *When the researcher recognizes that one word has different meanings among different informants, she ought to try to understand it.)*

A: Most of them are blue-collar workers—construction workers, electricians, people who do things with their hands. They're good at what they do to a certain extent. A lot of them do change jobs frequently because of the drinking problems that they have, and I think the majority of them do have drinking problems.

C: We talked about their being lazy, and we concluded that they're lazy in the sense that they don't aspire to be anything more than what they are.

(Rather than trying to get more information from Alice about biker patrons who "do things with their hands," Cindie introduces her own stereotype—that bikers are lazy, an idea that she and Alice had discussed before. Cindie's question represents her indecision about whether her stereotypes of bikers were true or if they came from movies.)

A: Yes. If their daddy taught them how to do construction or to build houses, they don't make goals other than that.

(Alice tried to move the conversation away from yet another stereotype—that bikers are lazy—by offering her own observation: that bikers seem to have limited career goals. Both interviewer and informant struggle to understand each other's stereotypes.)

C: And no self-pride in terms of their appearance?

(This is a leading question and in the end a closed question. Alice has no choice but to answer yes or no. Later in the interview, Cindie asks a descriptive question that prompts Alice to talk about what bikers actually do like to wear.)

A: Yes.

C: And we talked about how they demean women.

(Cindie raises yet another topic based on earlier conversations with Alice and also based on stereotypes of bikers that, in her later interview with Teardrop, prove to be true.)

A: Yes, very much so. That's the biggest thing that they do. It makes them feel stronger and feel like better people. It makes them feel like they are bigger.

The Informant's Perspective:
An Anthropologist on Mars

Most field interviews in their final form look smooth and polished and don't reveal any fumbling, false starts, missed appointments, muddled communication, and malfunctioning equipment. Because fieldworking takes a long time, once interviewers and informants establish rapport, the early messiness and hesitations of the relationship fade into the background. When they experience troubles with interviewing, most researchers decide not to highlight them. But they talk and write about them a lot. Our favorite interviewer's story comes from the *Foxfire* collection (edited by Eliot "Wig" Wigginton and others). In this excerpt, a high school student named Paul Gillespie (working alongside his teacher, Wigginton) interviews an elderly informant named Aunt Arie at her house in the Appalachian Mountains.

> [W]e walked in on her on Thanksgiving morning. She had her back to the door, and we startled her. There she was trying to carve the eyeballs out of a hog's head. I was almost sick to my stomach, so Wig helped operate on this hog's head while I turned my head and held the microphone of the tape recorder in the general vicinity of the action.
>
> They struggled for at least fifteen minutes, maybe more, and then I witnessed one of the most amazing events of my life. Aunt Arie took an eyeball, went to the back door, and flung it out. When she threw it, the eyeball went up on the tin roof of an adjoining outbuilding, rolled off, snagged on the clothesline, and hung there bobbing like a yo-yo. I had Wig's Pentax, so I took a picture of it, and it appeared in a subsequent issue of the magazine. It was very funny, remarkable. (56)

Oliver Sacks is a doctor who specializes in disorders of the nervous system and uses some fieldworking strategies to understand the perspectives of his patients. Rather than examining them in a hospital setting, Sacks visits his patients in their own contexts to explore their lives "as they live in the real world." In fact, in the preface to his bestselling collection of interviews, *An Anthropologist on Mars: Seven Paradoxical Tales*, he describes his fieldwork as "house calls at the far borders of human experience" (xx).

In one interview, he visits Temple Grandin, a woman with autism who, as a professor of animal science at Colorado State University, studies animal behavior. Sacks wanted to find out about autism from an insider's perspective. After researching autism from a medical point of view, he realized that he needed a person to give it voice, to create a portrait of the autistic person. Grandin told him that in her daily life, she feels like an outsider, like a researcher from another planet who is constantly studying the culture in which she lives to understand it. She provided Sacks with a critical understanding of her autistic worldview—as well as the title for his study—with the comment, "Much of the time I feel like an anthropologist on Mars."

In this essay from *An Anthropologist on Mars*, Sacks makes use of all the interviewing skills we've introduced in this chapter. He presents his information about Temple Grandin, offering details of her home, her own words, and her body language, and giving us especially her squeeze machine — the artifact which makes her so unique. Rather than relying on a question/answer interview format, Sacks holds an ordinary conversation with her as they drive together. By making her comfortable and by being interested in her life, Sacks allows Grandin to tell stories about her past relationship with her "enriched" research pigs — which provides him (and later us, his readers) with important insights about Grandin's personality as well as her neurological disorder.

When he arrives at her house after the ride, he observes the artifacts there — buttons, badges, and the squeeze machine — which offer more information about her private and professional lives, about her worldview. Just as Paul Russ established rapport with his informant by talking about Jessie's dog, Sacks focuses on his informant's unusual apparatus for receiving affection and even tries it out to feel her perspective.

Although Sacks's polished final essay reveals none of the bones of the interview (as we offered with Cindie Marshall's notes on Teardrop), it's a good guess that Sacks took piles of fieldnotes and probably even recorded his conversation. The overall effect is that Sacks allows Grandin's words, her stories, and even her artifacts to guide his account of her story. Because of his careful research and detailed writing, this essay remains her story and not his.

Notice that each of the details he offers is like a puzzle piece, fitting one item at a time into this description.

An Anthropologist on Mars

Oliver Sacks

Early the next morning, a Saturday, Temple picked me up in her four-wheel-drive, a rugged vehicle she drives all over the West to visit farms, ranches, corrals, and meat plants. As we headed for her house, I quizzed her about the work she had done for her Ph.D.; her thesis on the effects of enriched and impoverished environments on the development of pigs' brains. She told me about the great differences that developed between the two groups — how sociable and delightful the "enriched" pigs became, how hyperexcitable and aggressive (and almost "autistic") the "impoverished" ones were by contrast. (She wondered whether impoverishment of experience was not a contributing factor in human autism.) "I got to love my enriched pigs," she said. "I was very attached. I was so attached I couldn't kill them." The animals had to be sacrificed at the end of the experiment so their brains could be examined. She described how the pigs, at the end, trusting her, let her lead them on their last walk, and how she had calmed them, by stroking them and talking to them, while they were killed. She was very distressed at their deaths—"I wept and wept."

She had just finished the story when we arrived at her home—a small two-story town house, some distance from the campus. Downstairs was comfortable, with the usual amenities—a sofa, armchairs, a television, pictures on the wall—but I had the sense that it was rarely used. There was an immense sepia print of her grandfather's farm in Grandin, North Dakota, in 1880; her other grandfather, she told me, had invented the automatic pilot for planes. These two were the progenitors, she feels, of her agricultural and engineering talents. Upstairs was her study, with her typewriter (but no word processor), absolutely bursting with manuscripts and books—books everywhere, spilling out of the study into every room in the house. (My own little house was once described as "a machine for working," and I had a somewhat similar impression of Temple's.) On one wall was a large cowhide with a huge collection of identity badges and caps, from the hundreds of conferences she has lectured at. I was amused to see, side by side, an I.D. from the American Meat Institute and one from the American Psychiatric Association. Temple has published more than a hundred papers, divided between those on animal behavior and facilities management and those on autism. The intimate blending of the two was epitomized by the medley of badges side by side.

Temple Grandin, Ph.D., a gifted animal scientist

(Courtesy of Temple Grandin)

Finally, without diffidence or embarrassment (emotions unknown to her), Temple showed me her bedroom, an austere room with whitewashed walls and a single bed and, next to the bed, a very large, strange-looking object. "What is that?" I asked.

"That's my squeeze machine," Temple replied. "Some people call it my hug machine."

The device had two heavy, slanting wooden sides, perhaps four by three feet each, pleasantly upholstered with a thick, soft padding. They were joined by hinges to a long, narrow bottom board to create a V-shaped, body-sized trough. There was a complex control box at one end, with heavy-duty tubes leading off to another device, in a closet. Temple showed me this as well. "It's an industrial compressor," she said, "the kind they use for filling tires."

"And what does this do?"

"It exerts a firm but comfortable pressure on the body, from the shoulders to the knees," Temple said. "Either a steady pressure or a variable one or a pulsating one, as you wish," she added. "You crawl into it—I'll show you—and turn the compressor on, and you have all the controls in your hand, here, right in front of you."

When I asked her why one should seek to submit oneself to such pressure, she told me. When she was a little girl, she said, she had longed to be hugged but had at the same time been terrified of all contact. When she was hugged, especially by a favorite (but vast) aunt, she felt overwhelmed, overcome by sensation; she had a sense of peacefulness and pleasure, but also of terror and engulfment. She started to have daydreams—she was just five at the time—of a magic machine that could squeeze her powerfully but gently, in a huglike way, and in a way entirely commanded and controlled by her. Years later, as an adolescent, she had seen a picture of a squeeze chute designed to hold or restrain calves and realized that that was it: a little modification to make it suitable for human use, and it could be her magic machine. She had considered other devices—inflatable suits, which could exert an even pressure all over the body—but the squeeze chute, in its simplicity, was quite irresistible.

Being of a practical turn of mind, she soon made her fantasy come true. The early models were crude,

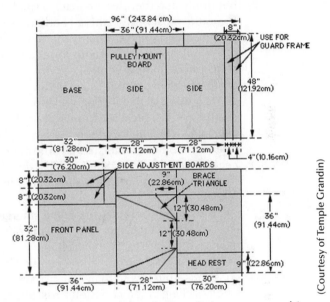

PLYWOOD CUTTING DIAGRAM: MAKE ALL CUTS ON CENTER
USE TWO SHEETS OF 3/4" (19mm) AC   USE THIS LAYOUT SO PLYWOOD GRAIN WILL FACE IN THE RIGHT DIRECTION

(Courtesy of Temple Grandin)

Schematic diagram of Temple Grandin's squeeze machine

with some snags and glitches, but she eventually evolved a totally comfortable, predictable system, capable of administering a "hug" with whatever parameters she desired. Her squeeze machine had worked exactly as she hoped, yielding the very sense of calmness and pleasure she had dreamed of since childhood. She could not have gone through the stormy days of college without her squeeze machine, she said. She could not turn to human beings for solace and comfort, but she could always turn to it. The machine, which she neither exhibited nor concealed but kept openly in her room at college, excited derision and suspicion and was seen by psychiatrists as a "regression" or "fixation"—something that needed to be psychoanalyzed and resolved. With her characteristic stubbornness, tenacity, single-mindedness, and bravery—along with a complete absence of inhibition or hesitation—Temple ignored all these comments and reactions and determined to find a scientific "validation" of her feelings.

Both before and after writing her doctoral thesis, she made a systematic investigation of the effects of deep pressure in autistic people, college students, and animals, and recently a paper of hers on this was published in the *Journal of Child and Adolescent Psychopharmacology*. Today, her squeeze machine, variously modified, is receiving extensive clinical trials. She has also become the world's foremost designer of squeeze chutes for cattle and has published, in the meat-industry and veterinary literature, many articles on the theory and practice of humane restraint and gentle holding.

While telling me this, Temple knelt down, then eased herself, facedown and at full length, into the "V," turned on the compressor (it took a minute for the master cylinder to fill), and twisted the controls. The sides converged, clasping her firmly, and then, as she made a small adjustment, relaxed their grip slightly. It was the most bizarre thing I had ever seen, and yet, for all its oddness, it was moving and simple. Certainly there was no doubt of its effect. Temple's voice, often loud and hard, became softer and gentler as she lay in her machine. "I concentrate on how gently I can do it," she said, and then spoke of the necessity of "totally giving in to it.... I'm getting real relaxed now," she added quietly. "I guess others get this through relation with other people."

It is not just pleasure or relaxation that Temple gets from the machine but, she maintains, a feeling for others. As she lies in her machine, she says, her thoughts often turn to her mother, her favorite aunt, her teachers. She feels their love for her, and hers for them. She feels that the machine opens a door into an otherwise closed emotional world and allows her, almost teaches her, to feel empathy for others.

After twenty minutes or so, she emerged, visibly calmer, emotionally less rigid (she says that a cat can easily sense the difference in her at these times), and asked me if I would care to try the machine.

Indeed, I was curious and scrambled into it, feeling a little foolish and self-conscious—but less so than I might have been, because Temple herself was so wholly lacking in self-consciousness. She turned the compressor on again and filled the master cylinder, and I experimented gingerly with the controls. It was indeed a sweet, calming feeling—one that reminded me of my deep-diving days long ago, when I felt the pressure of the water on my diving suit as a whole-body embrace.

· ·

As you can tell from this essay on Temple Grandin, the process of asking and listening collaboratively allows us to gain the perspective of an "other." Examining our own assumptions and worldviews from the vantage points of others exposes us to our quirks and shortcomings and cultural biases. In the process of understanding others, we come to more fully understand ourselves.

Gathering Family Stories

Yet another way to gather data from an informant is to listen for stories. Temple Grandin's stories and Teardrop's stories came directly out of answers to their interviewer's questions. But sometimes stories that are buried and unconscious offer important information about our lives.

Stories, like artifacts, serve to tell us about our informants' worldviews and function as data in our fieldwork. Informants have entire repertoires of stories based on their childhoods, their interests, their occupations. Our job as researchers is to elicit our informants' stories, record them, and carefully analyze what they mean. Researchers who study verbal art think about stories in these ways:

- Stories preserve a culture's values and beliefs.
- Stories help individuals endure, transform, or reject cultural values for themselves.
- Stories exist because of the interrelationship between tellers and audiences.

The most influential kinship structure is, of course, the family. And stories begin in our families. And to understand someone's culture, we often need to understand the person's family too. Family stories help us do that. Because we first hear them when we're young, family stories influence and shape us. In many cultures, family storytelling sessions are a deliberate way of passing along values. They are often expected events, almost ritualized performances. Judith Ortiz Cofer, in a memoir of her Puerto Rican childhood, writes about how the younger females in her extended family were encouraged to eavesdrop on the adult storytelling ritual:

> At three or four o'clock in the afternoon, the hour of the *café con leche*, the women of my family gathered in Mama's living room to speak of important things and retell family stories meant to be overheard by us young girls, their daughters.... It was on these rockers that my mother, her sisters, and my grandmother sat these afternoons of my childhood to tell their stories, teaching each other, and my cousin and me, what it was like to be a woman, more specifically, a Puerto Rican woman. They talked about life on the island, and life in Los Nueva Yores, their way of referring to the United States from New York City to California: the other place, not home, all the same. They told real-life stories, though, as I later learned, always embellishing them with a little or a lot of dramatic detail. And they told *cuentos*, the morality and cautionary tales told by the women in our family for generations; stories that became part of my subconscious as I grew up in two worlds. (64–65)

These stories from Ortiz Cofer's childhood were not merely afternoon entertainment. Her family's stories recorded history and carried instructions about behaviors, rules, and beliefs. Like the legends, folk tales, and proverbs of specific cultures, family stories reflect the ways of acting and even of viewing the world sanctioned or approved by a family. Ortiz Cofer's relatives conserve cultural traditions of their old country, Puerto Rico, and translate them into the "Los Nueva Yores" culture.

In addition to preserving cultural values, many writers suggest that the act of storytelling is also an act of individual survival. To endure in our families and the culture at large, we must explain our lives to ourselves. First we share our stories, and then we reflect on what they mean. Our own storytelling memories teach us about our personal histories. When you think of a family story, try to decide why it survived, which tellers have different versions, what parts of the story remain the same no matter who tells it, and how you've refashioned it for your own purposes.

Family stories are often transformed in oral retellings, but they clearly change when they are written down. Although they belong to the oral narrative tradition, writing them down helps us analyze their meaning and potential relevance to our own lives.

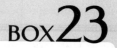

BOX**23**

Writing a Family Story

PURPOSE

We're not always conscious of how our family stories serve us, nor are our informants. But they are worth exploring as a rich source of data when we want to better understand our own lives—and the lives of the people with whom we're working. As scholar Elizabeth Stone, in *Black Sheep and Kissing Cousins: How Our Family Stories Shape Us*, writes,

> What struck me about my own family stories was first, how much under my skin they were; second, once my childhood was over, how little deliberate attention I ever paid to them; and third, how thoroughly invisible they were to anyone else. Going about my daily life, I certainly never told them aloud and never even alluded to them.... Those who say that America is a land of rootless nomads who travel light, uninstructed by memory and family ties, have missed part of the evidence.

ACTION

Recall a family story you've heard many times. It may fall into one of these categories: fortunes gained and lost, heroes, "black sheep," eccentric or oddball relatives, acts of retribution and revenge, or family feuds. After writing the story, analyze its meaning. When is this story most often told, and why? What kinds of warnings or messages does this story convey? For the family? For an outsider? What kind of lesson does the story teach? How does your story reflect your family's values? How has it changed or altered through various retellings? Which family members would have different versions?

Our student Teresa Shorter writes, "My family on my mother's side came from very poor roots. My maternal great-grandparents were farmers who struggled by with 13 children. My paternal great-grandparents raised a dozen children—most were boys who came to violent ends. Their stories are of struggles and poverty. I think this story is told in my family to teach us of our humble beginnings and to help us be aware of how bad it could be. And even though we didn't have a lot of money growing up, my cousins and I always had food to eat, a bed to sleep in, and arms that would hug us—we never had to live in fear. We always knew we were loved." Teresa's story goes like this:

My Grandmother's Wise Stand
Teresa Shorter

My maternal grandfather was named Daniel Hancock. I never knew him—he died when my mother was only nine years old. Of his nine children, she was his favorite—this was almost her undoing.

Daniel Hancock was a mean man. He was a moonshine runner in the hills of southern Virginia. Times were tough and there was never enough to eat. He was a small, dark man who loved to drink, and when he drank he became a monster. He would beat my grandmother and the older children, often coming at them with a knife. They would try to hide when he came home, afraid he would kill one of them one day. They lived a life of fear and want.

One day a few weeks after the birth of the twins Ray and Fay, my grandfather was preparing for another run. He had already been drinking. As he often did, he tried to take my mother riding with him. I think he favored her best because she is so different from him—most of the other children have his Native American looks, but my grandmother at nine had bright blue eyes and whitish-golden hair. She took after my grandmother. Even though my young mother was willing to go "riding," my grandmother convinced her inebriated husband not to take my mother on this run—a run from which he would not return.

Hours later, relatives would be at the door telling my grandmother that Daniel had been killed in a car accident. His car had run off the road around the bend a few miles out. That was the story. However, these were the roads he had run his whole life—drunk and sober. Truth came out later that he was found with his head bashed in from behind. We'll never know if it was a robbery or if someone stepped in to save my grandmother and her children—these were rough times. All I know is that my mom dodged a bullet that day.

Family stories like Teresa's preserve family beliefs through morality lessons with subliminal messages and subconscious instructions. Some family stories act as cautionary tales, or what writer Judith Ortiz Cofer calls *cuentos*, to pass on warnings about behavior to the next generation. Through storytelling, family tales can be transformed and reshaped to make them fit the teller's needs and life circumstances. As they transform family stories, tellers can remain loyal to the family unit but be released from it as well. They can connect us with our families while allowing us our identities as we reshape them to fit our own lives and our own audiences.

One Family Story: The Core and Its Variants

When Donna Niday, a professor at Iowa State University, was a student in Bonnie's class, she decided to study one of her family's stories. It illustrates a significant idea: that different family members tell one story in very different ways, and each way reveals something about the teller. Donna was in her forties at the time, and she was lucky that her mother and sisters were all alive and accessible while she conducted her study. In researching "The Baby on the Roof," Donna expected to get different perspectives from the five Riggs sisters—her own mother and her four aunts who grew up on a farm in the rural Midwest of the 1920s. She began by interviewing her cousins to see what they remembered about the story, which would have been passed down to them by their mothers. Just as she suspected, each of Donna's cousins told the story with different details and points of emphasis. She confirmed the aunts' family reputations: "she was the daring one" or "she was always the chicken."

Donna was realistic enough to know that there would be no "true" version of the tale, but the story would have a stable core, a basic frame, shared among the sisters. She also anticipated that there would be many variants, differences in details according to the tellers. She interviewed each elderly sister in her home, allowing time to look through family photo albums together and to visit before recording the stories. As she listened and recorded, Donna gathered both the core story and its variants.

The oldest sister, Eleanor, who claimed responsibility for the secret family event, told the core story this way, emphasizing herself and the baby:

> I took Mary to the top of the house when Mom went out to work. You know, all four of us took the ladder—went down to the barn and got the big ladder. Mom just said to take care of Mary, and I did. I took her everywhere I went. Mary was six months old. Well, she was born in January. This would be June, I suppose, when we were doing hay. I knew she'd lay wherever you put her. And so there was a flat place there on the roof. There wasn't any danger—I don't think there was ever any danger of her getting away at all. Yeah, we could see them mowing. If Mom had ever looked toward the house, she would have had a heart attack to see her kids up on the roof.

Especially when we were supposed to be looking after the baby. Yeah, well see, I was ten when Mary was born, so I was ten then, a little past ten. I should have known better, but it shows that you can't trust ten-year-olds. I never got punished for that because Mom never did find out.

And so, with Eleanor's version, Donna had the core family story: four sisters spent the day on the roof with their six-month-old baby sister while their mother and father mowed the fields. Each sister provided her own variation. One remembers that the parents were mowing hay; another insists they were cutting oats. Such details would also change the time of the story from June to late summer or early fall. The sisters debate other details. Donna's mother rejects the idea that they got a ladder from the barn, saying they climbed on a chair or rain barrel to reach the lower part of the farmhouse roof, which was accessible from their bedrooms. Another of the sisters tells the story as if she remained on the ground while the others climbed to the roof. When they challenge her version, this sister admits that she probably did follow the others. She confesses jealousy of the new baby: until then, she had been the baby of the family. "They weren't worried about me," she recalls. "They were only worried about Mary, the baby."

Mary's version of the story deviates the most. She claims that she fell off the roof and that her sisters climbed down and put her "right back on." Because Mary's variant has no support from the other sisters, she retreats by saying, "Maybe I just dreamed that, but it seems like I fell off when I was up there. Of course, I wasn't really old enough to remember."

(Photo: Donna Niday)

The Riggs family farmhouse

After recording and transcribing all five versions of this story, Donna proposes that the "baby on the roof" story displays defiance of authority and rebellion against rules for these otherwise compliant farm girls. She also thinks that the story illustrates "pluck and adventure," as no harm was actually done. Donna admits that her mother and aunts would deny that these stories convey any meaning other than "pure entertainment" and confesses that any analysis of the meaning of these stories is her own. She recognizes that each sister embellished the story based on her family reputation, individual temperament, and storytelling ability. Donna's conclusions are consistent with what we know: that a story has a stable core of details but also many variants according to the tellers.

For information on working with family archives, see Chapter 7, page 317.

Discover Core Details in Your Informants' Stories

Use the following questions to uncover the core details of your informants' stories:

- What facts are stable?
- What's the chronology of the story?
- What characters are key?
- What is the central conflict in the story?
- What is the theme?
- Does the story contain a cultural message or lesson?

Donna followed several important steps in gathering her family stories, steps that any fieldworker considers:

- She conducted preliminary research by interviewing the people involved—in this case, her mother and aunts. Had they all told the same story, the project would not have illustrated the core and variants inherent in family stories.

- She interviewed her informants in their own home settings, making all participants comfortable as she recorded and asked questions. She didn't rush her project; she allowed time for scheduling, visiting, interviewing, transcribing, sharing the transcripts, and writing her paper.

- She triangulated her data in two ways. First, by checking the five stories against one another, she could see how one story might verify another or disconfirm it. She shared her work with the sisters as she went along and afterward so that they might confirm, disconfirm, or add to each other's stories.

- She acknowledged the importance of her informants' participation. In this case, as they were her relatives, she presented her essay in a family album complete with photos of the old farmhouse as a gift in return for the time and energy they spent helping her learn how to listen to family stories. This kind of **reciprocity** is crucial to the ethics of fieldworking.

Stories that are passed down within a culture help to shape a culture's self-identity. But it's also true that the variants (each teller's version) of a story can explain even more. Knowing how the variants differ helps us find clues about informants, their worldviews, and how a culture has changed over time. If you are working in a fieldsite, you will want to find any important stories that have come out of a shared event, an important moment, or a special person whom everyone knows.

In your own work, it is important to record each teller's version as audio or video or by careful word-for-word notetaking. Whether you record several versions of one story or several stories about one event, you will need to look for the unchanging core elements as well as the variants' details. After gathering stories, analyze your data. Here are some things to look for.

Discover the Variants in Your Informants' Stories

- Use the following questions to uncover the variants in your informants' stories:

- What are the features that change?

- Why do those features change?

- What do the variants suggest about the tellers?

- What do the variants suggest about their audiences?

You may want to find some features that don't fit the other versions, and those will provide clues about the teller's positions and attitudes toward the story and the cultural themes that the story contains.

Gathering Oral Histories

An oral history is a life story shared collaboratively with a fieldworker, emphasizing the individual's life against the cultural significance of that life. Cindie Marshall uses her interviews to support her research on the biker subculture. But if she were to do an oral history, she would interview Teardrop in depth to record her whole life's story. Teardrop's role as a biker's companion would be a major part of her oral history, but the emphasis would be on Teardrop.

In an oral history, the fieldworker gathers real-life stories about the past experiences of a particular person, family, region, occupation, craft, skill, or topic. The fieldworker records spoken recollections and personal reflections from living people about their past lives, creating a history.

Anthropological fieldworkers who record an entire life's history as well as speculate on the relationship between that life and the culture it represents are called **ethnohistorians**, and their studies span many years. Over ten years' time, folklorist Henry Glassie visited, interviewed, and wrote about one four-square-mile Irish community in *Passing the Time in Balleymenone*. Shirley Brice Heath, a linguist, researched literacy in the Piedmonts of the southeastern United States for her study *Ways with Words*, and spent 14 years gathering data from parents, teachers, and children there. Anthropologist Ruth Behar traveled back and forth between the United States and Mexico for over five years and wrote a life history of Esperanza, a Mexican street peddler, in her book *Translated Woman*.

However, not all oral histories need to be full-length ethnographic studies. There are many national oral history projects, including Save Our Sounds, Story Corps, and the Veterans' Oral History project, all sponsored by the American Folklife Center of the Library of Congress. A quick Internet search reveals a range of local, national, and global projects that all use forms of oral history collection.

Gathering oral history is not new. A successful traditional project in the United States comes from a group of high school students in 1970s rural Georgia. There, teenagers documented the stories, folk arts, and crafts of elderly people in their Appalachian community, writing about moonshine, faith-healing, building log cabins, dressing hogs, and farming practices. With their teacher Eliot Wigginton, they originally published their fieldwork in the high school's *Foxfire* magazine, and later collected these articles into the now classic *Foxfire* anthologies (12 books in total), one of which gives us the eyeball story on p. 244.

In this section, we introduce you to three different varieties of oral histories: one visual, one auditory, and one textual. Our first oral historian, Nancy Hauserman, is a professor of law and ethics in the College of Business at the University of Iowa and an amateur photographer. Nancy has always been interested in the lives of people who are often invisible and ignored. In one study, she spoke to workers at University of Iowa Hospitals and Clinics, a large hospital in Iowa City, recording their perspectives on the value of their work. She also photographed them on the job. As she writes, her project combined her "love of taking photos along with a deep appreciation for the myriad kindness people do for others every day." Nancy's collection, called "Taking Care: A Recognition of Good People Doing Things," is a permanent exhibit on the walls of the hospital and has also been published as a book. Its power, we believe, comes from the artful combination of photographs of ordinary people in their workplace supported by the words of each informant. Their words are ones you might not always have the chance to hear.

We present here two of her seventeen oral history portraits, this one of Allen Reed, a custodian, followed by one of Mona Ibrahim, a dietetic clerk, both of whom talk about how they feel about their jobs.

Taking Care

Nancy Hauserman

Allen Reed, Custodian

I work second shift with the project crew. I pick up already bagged trash and make it disappear. I strip and wax hardwood floors, clean carpet, move furniture before and after meetings, burnish and wax floors. When I'm House Man, I do anything for anyone as needed.

Any requests I get from patients and visitors, if I can take care of it, it's with a positive attitude like "I'm gonna take care of this for ya." In fact I see somebody that's, well, you just know these people are lost. I will walk up and say, "Excuse me I'm Allen Reed. Can I give you some assistance?" They may say, "We're looking for Emergency." I never give directions to Emergency; I always walk them to the Emergency Room, because if you're asking for the Emergency Room, you have other things on your mind. And when some folks say, "Well, you're not going to get in trouble are you?" I tell them, "It's not a problem, anytime you folks need help

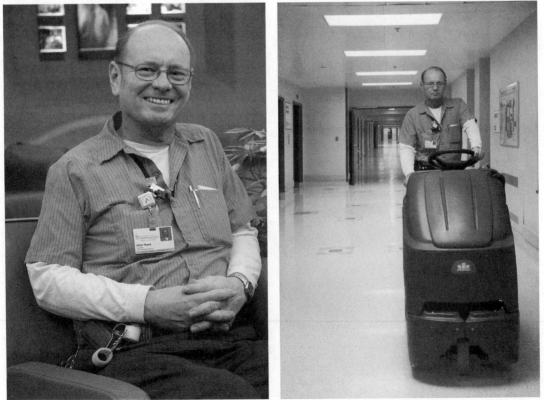

Allen Reed, custodian, University of Iowa Hospitals and Clinics

(Photos: Nancy Hauserman)

that can be my top priority beside what I'm supposed to be doing." So I never take no for an answer; I never say I can't do it, I always look into it, and I'll work on a problem as long as it takes to get it done.

I'm here every day because I enjoy helping people. There's no time that I haven't been able to give directions or take someone where they needed to be or help a patient or a visitor out. It makes you feel like you've accomplished something at the end of the night, especially when I'm House Man and I get a lot of different calls during the night from patients or visitors. It makes a difference.

I always try to say, is this what I would want?

Mona Ibrahim, Dietetic Clerk

I take patient orders on the phone and check to make sure they are ordering according to their diets. If the food isn't on their diet, I try to suggest what they could have instead. I call patients if they don't call in for meals for a while. We use computers now, but for years it was all done by paper.

I think what I do makes it easier sometimes [for patients and families]. When patients are ordering, sometimes the family is not there. They call and ask how

Mona Ibrahim, dietetic clerk

(Photos: Nancy Hauserman)

they should order…they don't know their diet sometimes so we try to tell them what they can have and what they can't. At the same time, sometimes they just like to talk to me on the phone. When speaking to someone for a while and they call you…the way they answer, you can tell that they feel there is someone there that they know.

You think about it as if you were in their place. They can be comforted by someone to speak to.

Recorded—rather than written—oral histories have their own strengths. In them, you can experience a range of linguistic features: people's actual voices, their accents, hesitations, intonations, laughter, and the overall rhythm of their speech. How many times do you wish you could bring back the voice of someone you've lost? An audio interview offers us the ability to do that. As the researcher, you choose among the recorded data about how much or how little of the informant's language you want to include. You also choose what form—electronic or print—you will present it in. No matter what technology you use or whether your recorded oral history ends up as an essay or an mp3 file, you will need to decide how to incorporate your informants' words with your own. Some oral histories present only the informants' words. But note that the editor of those words is usually the researcher. As with other data collections, most oral historians record far more words than they use, whether the final presentation is on paper or in an audio file. It may seem easy to simply record someone else's life story, but the responsibility for arranging, organizing, and editing it is still yours.

One of our favorite examples of auditory oral history is the StoryCorps project. It began in 2003, became associated with the American Folklife Center at the Library of Congress, and is now a regularly featured series on National Public Radio. Dave Isay, the founder of StoryCorps, began with a booth in Grand Central Station in New York. On the day it launched, Studs Terkel, a great oral historian of the twentieth century, proclaimed, "Today we shall begin celebrating the lives of the uncelebrated." Since then, the project has added many permanent and mobile recording studio-booths around the country. You could go to one with your boss or favorite teacher, for example, and spend 45 minutes talking with the assistance of a facilitator. You'd end up with a broadcast-quality CD for yourself—as well as contributing your story to the archive at the American Folklife Center. It is from these CDs that StoryCorps has edited three-minute oral histories and organized them into a range of topics. You can sample them at http://storycorps.org/listen.

We'd like to share one example from Isay's first collection, *Listening Is an Act of Love: A Celebration of American Life from the StoryCorps Project* (2007), recorded in Portland, Maine, between Joyce Butler, 73, and her daughter, Stephanie Butler, 47. In it, Joyce talks about her mother, who was a welder and single mom during World War II.

Listening Is an Act of Love

Joyce Butler, 73, interviewed by her daughter, Stephanie Butler, 47

Joyce Butler: My parents divorced in 1941. In those days divorce was not as common as it is now. A divorced woman was called a "grass widow," and grass widows were scorned. There was a stigma attached, which is why it took such courage for my mother to ask for a divorce from my father. We moved to Maine Avenue in Portland.

Even though my father paid my mother money every month, it wasn't enough. She had to go to work, and she had not finished high school. So she worked in the laundry, and she finally got a job at Montgomery Ward department store on Congress Street. And we kids were more or less on our own. That was not a happy time for me—I missed my mother.

During the war, the shipyard had begun to function in South Portland, and these young women would come into the store, all dressed in these big boots and rough overalls. And they would have checks of six hundred dollars to cash for their shopping. She finally asked, "Where do you work that you make so much money?" They said, "In the shipyard." So my mother went over and tried to get a job. The man who interviewed asked if she wanted to be a welder or a burner, and my mother said, "Which pays the most?" And he said, "A welder." And she said, "That's what I want to do." And he said, "Oh, a mercenary, huh?" And she said, "No. I have four children to take care of."

Her shift was midnight to 6:00 a.m., so she could be home with us during the day. I remember her dressing in that heavy clothing and big boots—men's clothing. Once she fell and hurt her ankle, and they brought her home in the middle of the night, and she was weeping. It was awful.

It was bitter cold in the winter, going into the bowels of those steel ships. They had to wiggle into narrow crawl spaces and lay on their backs and weld overhead. She was very thin in those years, but I remember her neck and her chest, all spotted with burn marks from the sparks. They had to wear special goggles, but even so, sometimes they would have a flash condition in their eyes. She suffered from that, and they had to take her to the hospital once.

After the shipyard closed, she went back to Montgomery Ward and worked all day. And at five o'clock when she got out of Montgomery Ward, she got on a bus and worked in the S. D. Warren Paper Mill from six o'clock until midnight. Came home, got up in the morning, and went back to Montgomery Ward.

Stephanie Butler: Bless her heart.

Joyce: My mother wanted to keep us together as a family. She was determined.

Our final example is of a textually-rendered oral history and comes from the Great Depression. In the United States of the 1930s, writers were among the many unemployed. The government sponsored the Federal Writers' Project, which put writers to work as interviewers. Among them were Claude McKay, Richard Wright, Saul Bellow, Loren Eisley, and Ralph Ellison. This project's goal was to record the life histories of ordinary American people whose stories had never been told: carpenters, cigar makers, dairy people, seamstresses, peddlers, railroad men, textile workers, salesladies, and chicken farmers were among the informants.

One collection of these life histories, *These Are Our Lives* (1939), assembled by R. R. Humphries for the Federal Writers' Project, includes the life story of Lee Lincoln, a man who learns to read and write as an adult. The fieldworker, Jennette Edwards, inserts her own observations and description into the interview while quoting Lee's words directly as she collected them. You can access the excerpt on our Web site. As you read this piece, remember it was written in 1939, when black Americans were called Negroes, when jobs were difficult to get, and $65 a month was a decent living. You may want to think about other cultural assumptions, attitudes, and beliefs that have changed in the past decades.

Read Jennette Edwards's piece, *I Can Read and I Can Write*, at **bedfordstmartins.com/ fieldworking**, under Professional Essays.

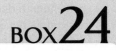

BOX 24

Starting an Oral History

PURPOSE

Many oral histories today are gathered from ordinary people who have lived through extraordinary times and experiences. Contemporary informants can share their life histories and experiences from, for example, the women's movement, the civil rights movement, the Holocaust in Europe, or the end of apartheid in South Africa. Other oral histories can record the everyday life during an occupation that no longer exists. Studs Terkel's collections of occupational stories, *Working*, and of Depression stories, *In Hard Times*, offer examples of short histories from real people whose voices are seldom heard or recorded.

Possible projects for an oral history are limited only by your imagination and access to the people you wish to interview. Many people begin an oral history by interviewing their relatives, friends, or teachers about living through a particular era or a time of personal struggle that resulted in dramatic life changes. Perhaps you know someone who's lived through a major catastrophe (such as an earthquake or a flood) or someone who's been caught personally in a political or social entanglement (like war, bankruptcy, or discrimination). Such people make good subjects for oral history.

BOX 24 continued

Many local and compelling oral history projects can emerge in unexpected places and on unexpected topics. Think about someone you know who has a particular skill, such as cooking ethnic food, whittling wooden figures, weaving, or embroidering, or an unusual hobby such as clogging, playing the bagpipes, or raising llamas. Someone's life-long passion can yield fascinating oral histories. Good subjects for oral histories also hide in places where people spend their time alone—for example, in garages tinkering with engines or in antique shops restoring items others have discarded.

ACTION

If you're interested in pursuing an oral history project, spend some time interviewing someone who fascinates you. As with any other interviewing project, all of the information you record in your fieldnotes may not be what you'll use in a final write-up, but you'll need to record it nonetheless. Your choices of details will help you feature your subject without distracting the reader from the informant's own words. An elaborate oral history takes a great deal of time. We hope that what you'll learn by reading and writing oral history is that it's important to foreground the informant and her words and to background the topic, yourself, and her surroundings.

RESPONSE

Laura Carroll conducted a series of oral history interviews with Mexican women who had emigrated to the southeastern United States. Laura volunteered to teach English as a second language in a public library program, where she met one informant, Luis, who led her to the immigrant women who offered their oral histories. Because of her interest in women's issues, she felt drawn to interviewing women in their new American homes. This excerpt is from her first visit with Estela Núñez.

Estela Núñez, *La Primera Visita*/The First Visit
Laura Carroll

I called Estela, and she invited me to come to her house. After much confusion over her directions, I finally just wrote down her address and looked it up on MapQuest. I brought my friend and consultant, Luis, to our first meeting so he could interpret and also because he's fun to have around in a new social situation. When we arrived at Estela's house, Luis noticed the new truck in the driveway and commented that her husband must be getting paid well. The house was small, new, and suburban, spotless, with new-looking furniture. A "telenovela"—a Spanish-language soap opera—was on the television.

Estela invited us in and introduced us to her three boys, who seemed excited to have guests. The youngest boy, who looked about five, opened his eyes wide when he saw me. In English, he shouted, "You're GIANT!" I laughed.

Estela invited us to the table to eat her *tacos de pollo*. She had made a pot of beans and some spicy red salsa to go with it. The smell and taste transported me to

Mexico. I had to stop eating for a second to let the dense meal settle. "Come, come," Estela's melodic voice exclaimed. Then I remembered how it's done in Mexico. You eat until it's gone.

After listening to Spanish flow at light speed between Estela and Luis, I began to record her story.

Here are a few excerpts from several of Laura's interviews with Estela that eventually became her oral history. Estela says:

"I grew up in the small town of El Rosario in Guanajuato. I went to La Primaria but left in the sixth grade to work at home. Girls and boys often leave school at this age because the family needs their help at home and in the fields. My father died in an accident when my mother was 28 years old, so we were needed at home more than usual. My mother never remarried because she was afraid that a new husband might treat the children badly....

"In the morning, we got up and did *los labores de la casa*. We washed the clothes by hand and brought in milk from the cows. . . . All of the women work inside the house. Some work outside of the house, but very few. It is hard for us to get accustomed to the work life here; it is a big change for us....

"I'm always working, always taking care of the children, always doing house-work. I'm *muy activa*. I like working outside the house. I clean houses three days a week. I don't need to speak English; I already know how to clean. *Poco a poco* I am adjusting to life here. I like it here. I taught myself to drive and went to the DMV without my husband's permission and got my driver's license. I am learning English...."

Estela is also learning how to cook vegetarian. She asked me to go to the store with her to help her find a type of oil she had heard about that is supposed to be healthier than corn oil. I expected her to take me to a supermarket, and I was surprised when we arrived at the local cooperative health-food store where I used to work. She took me by the hand and led me around the store asking me what all of the labels on the food meant. "What is organic?" "What is tofu?" "I've heard of soymilk. What is it?" "I want to be *flaca* like you!" When I answered each question, she got excited and said, "Aaaaaah," and put the item in her basket.

During our last visit, Estela told me that she'd be going to El Rosario with her three children this summer for two months. Her husband would stay here and work, although he's very sad not to be going. I asked her how she's getting there, and she said she'll fly, but she'll have to come back another way because she doesn't have valid immigration papers. She said that she'll find friends to help her. She seemed concerned about the possibility of not being allowed back in the United States, but I could tell that the need to see her mother, whom she had not seen in five years, far outweighed any problems she might have at the border.

When I asked Estela if she likes living in the United States, she replied, "Ah, *sí, es muy bonito, pero extraño mi tierra. Extraño mi Rosario.*"

FieldWriting: Using Character, Setting, and Theme to Create a Portrait

To bring their informants to the page from a pile of data, fieldwriters must pay close attention to informants' personal characteristics and surroundings and write about details that relate to the overall themes they want to highlight. Creating verbal portraits means studying your fieldnotes, selecting your most relevant details, and drafting sentences that portray each informant against a cultural backdrop. In this chapter, the fieldwriters who give us portraits write them on the basis of carefully gathered observations from their fieldnotes and other sources and their own interpretations confirmed by their data.

Details of Character

Choosing the details to describe an interview with an informant is hard work. Fieldwriters must gather and record far more information than they will ever use because during data collection they don't know the themes they'll eventually want to highlight. Written portraits of an informant require noting the same kinds of character details that fiction writers use: physical features, material artifacts, body language, oral language patterns, and personal history. But those details are borne in fieldnotes, interviews, artifacts, and documents.

- *Physical features* (vine-shaped tattoo around wrist; brown hair with gray, neatly pulled back)
- *Material artifacts* (new Lee jeans, pale yellow sweater)
- *Body language* (sitting alone drinking beer, shooting pool)
- *Oral language patterns* (Alice and Christie discuss the bikers' treatment of women)
- *Personal history* (goes to Ralph's every day, moved from Michigan three years ago)

Details of Setting

When fieldwriters paint verbal portraits, they also create a backdrop for their informants. In Chapter 4, we discuss how writers present landscapes or what we call "verbal snapshots." Setting details must be organized from notes about time, place, weather, color, and other sensory impressions at the fieldsite.

To bring her reader into Ralph's, Cindie Marshall moves from exterior to interior. She selects details of texture and space to represent Ralph's Sports Bar outside, focusing first on the parking lot.

As she moves inside, she describes tastes and smells in an atmosphere of smoke, stale beer, cigarette ashes, and body odor. Cindie also listens to the sounds from the jukebox. Her selection of details to present an image of Ralph's, a so-called sports bar, defies her earlier assumptions about such places.

Details of Theme

Fieldwriters must choose details to support the themes they want to highlight. In fieldworking, themes don't emerge directly from lists in fieldnotes, words in transcripts, or library books and collected artifacts, but such sources suggest them. Themes *do come* from active interpretation of your data, as you study it, triangulate it, organize it, reflect on it, and write about it. Themes are bigger than the actual details you record, but those details, as they cluster into categories of data and images from your observations, generate larger interpretations.

For example, in her study of Ralph's Sports Bar, Cindie's themes work off of the contrasts she observed within the subculture in the biker bar. She arrives at Ralph's with a mental image of what a sports bar is like, and immediately that image contrasts with the reality of this biker sports bar. As she spends more time and takes more notes, Cindie sees other contrasting themes within this subculture.

Another set of contrasting themes is that of bikers as a community of independent people who "do their own thing," but Cindie sees that within this subculture, they come together only to be separated: "I also wanted to know why three groups in a bar would come together in a place just to be segregated." Cindie interprets still another contrast when she notices that the biking subculture includes many women. Her fieldnotes report 13 people at the bar, 8 men and 5 women. But this inclusion is deceptive when her informant Teardrop describes her life as a biker woman: "What Teardrop had described was sheer abuse, and she wore that abuse both on her face, in the shape of a teardrop, and in her smile, which was darkened by missing teeth."

Fieldwriting is a skill that requires close observation, careful documentation, and the rendering of data into thick descriptions of informants within their cultural spaces. To be an accurate and sensitive fieldwriter, you'll need to manipulate your multiple data sources, call on your informants' voices, examine your reflective writing, and craft a text so that it will give your reader a sense of participating in the fieldwork you've experienced. As we collect data about people, we must continually look over what we've gathered in terms of ourselves, our informants, and the information's meaning against the larger backdrop of our research. In addition to carefully retelling our informants' stories, we need to ensure that we present the narrative situation fairly, including our own roles in it. In his book *Writing the New Ethnography*, H. L. "Bud" Goodall, whose work you read in Chapter 2, offers some helpful questions for researchers to ask themselves as they write up interviews, oral histories, and storytelling situations (106–7):

1. What is the context, and where are you in this scene? What is the nature of the relationship between you and your informant?

2. What's the meaning behind the recorded words? What influences your informants' and your own fixed positions? Subjective positions? What power relationship exists between you and your informant?

3. What do you hear in the way the informant speaks? What are the gaps? The tones? The rhythms? The emphases (of both you and your informant)? (For more on this idea, see Chapter 6, "Researching Language: The Cultural Translator.")

In the process of collecting data about people, we must continually look over what we've gathered in terms of ourselves, our informants, and its meaning against the backdrop of our research. We bring to our narratives about our informants as much as they bring to the data we've collected about them. In addition to rendering careful verbal portraits, we need to break down the conversational context to ensure that we present it fairly.

BOX 25

Writing a Verbal Portrait

JENNIFER S. COOK, RHODE ISLAND COLLEGE

PURPOSE

Just as a verbal snapshot (Box 17 in Chapter 4) asks you to synthesize data from your field-notes, a verbal portrait asks you to synthesize data from your interviews. It is another way to make sense of your data.

A verbal portrait asks that you use data from your interview to paint a portrait of your participant in a brief piece of writing (500 words) that is rich with description, illustrative quotes (carefully selected), and thoughtful (but spare) commentary.

In crafting your portrait, you are making choices about what to include and exclude, about what to reveal and what to ignore. These kinds of editorial choices are a way for you to interpret your interview data. Additionally, you need to include some evaluation or assessment (analysis) of the person and his or her role in the subculture you are studying. In asking yourself, "What was the essence of this interview?" you also need to ask, "What is the essence of this person?" Both of these questions are central to the kinds of analysis you should include in your verbal portrait.

ACTION

To craft your verbal portrait, you need not only interview data and analysis (an interview transcript you have analyzed) but also a description of your participant. Your job here is to create an image in the minds of your readers. It also helps to have "supporting data"—that is, details about the time of day, the weather, the location of the interview, and a description of the space, as well as other significant details about context. Once you have these essential ingredients, you can begin to sketch a portrait of your participant. Remember that your overarching goal here is to capture the essence of the person, his words, and what he means to the fieldstudy.

Once you have sketched your portrait, share it with a colleague or classmate to see if you have successfully communicated the essence of this person and his role in the subculture. You may ask your reader to keep these questions in mind as she reads.

- What images or details from this piece create the most vivid impressions?
- What "clues" do you get from this piece about the essence of this subculture?
- What clutter can I omit to make this piece stronger or clearer?
- What would you like to know more about? Where can I provide more detail and information?

RESPONSE

Gabby Lopez's fieldwork project, "Head in the Clouds," is a study of young, aspiring fine artists in and around Providence, Rhode Island. As a fine arts major, Gabby wanted to explore the complexities of being a fine artist in a society that, from her perspective, does not value artists or their contributions to the common good. During the course of her fieldwork, Gabby discovered that, though fine artists struggle financially, they find happiness in each other's company and safety in the "art world." This is Gabby's verbal portrait of one of her key participants; it is also the source of the title of the fieldstudy.

Brendan Kennedy sat deep in a chair that more resembled a red, cushioned bowl. His long, thin legs dangled off the front end of the chair; his elbows lay on the side of the chair and his hands rested, laced together, on top of his stomach. He had no problem getting comfortable despite the difficulty of lowering himself into the unstable bowl. His brown, short hair topped his thin, pale frame. He sat patiently, looking around the large room, focusing on the nearby chalkboard wall and the elaborate chalk drawings and vulgarities scribbled on it.

I met Brendan in high school. He was popularly known as the hyperactive boy who openly expressed himself a bit too much. In his later high school years, Brendan started to express himself through art. He joined a few art classes and became involved with Riverzedge Arts Project, where he and I met. He is now a first-year student at the Art Institute of New England; he is 18 years old. More experienced artists might consider him to be fresh meat.

I asked Brendan to visit me so I could ask him a few questions about his aspiration to be a fine artist. Sitting in my red chair, Brendan patiently answered my questions. He seemed to be waiting for things to get interesting; I was worried that I was boring him. Soon enough, Brendan got excited about something: "I'm affected by things that other people aren't," he said. "I understand things differently. I know color, and I can easily see how something is composed when a non-artist probably can't." I asked Brendan how a non-artist might see him and other artists like him. He took a second to think, then confidently, proudly, he said, "Like our heads are in the clouds."

BOX25 continued

Brendan is not the only one to experience this "difference." The very nature of making art is the opposite of the nature of American culture and society today. I am not surprised that artists like Brendan feel a little different, a little separate from society. Artists value slowing down and looking closely, while society teaches us to generalize and judge as quickly as possible. Artists value work that is creative and visionary, while society values work that pays a high salary. Artists value representation and interpretation, while society values the "bottom line." These thoughts drove me to ask Brendan Kennedy his views about feeling different. He replied, succinctly and assuredly, "I'm kind of okay with it…art isn't about making money."

THE RESEARCH PORTFOLIO:
Reflective Documentation

Whether you've chosen to learn to research people by continuing your major fieldwork project or by trying separate short studies, we hope you've seen that the researcher-informant relationship is a symbiotic one. It is full of interaction, collaboration, and mutual teaching and learning. In this chapter, we focus on how people are a dominant source of data in the field—through family stories, remembered histories, responses to questions, the personal artifacts they consider important, and your own observation of them.

The research portfolio is an important place to record, keep track of, and make sense of the skills you've learned, the routines and organization you've used, and your responses to readings that illustrate how other fieldworkers have written about their work. Listing and categorizing your research processes illustrate your progress as a fieldworker. We like to call this charting process "reflective documentation."

For your portfolio, try listing, mapping, outlining, or charting the skills you've learned and the variety and amounts of material you've gathered. You may want to document each of your projects from this chapter separately: family stories, oral histories, and interviews. Or if you are working on a large project, use the questions to document what is relevant to your project. Here is an outline framed around fieldworking strategies. You might choose a few questions under each category, try to work with them all, or document your work in a different way:

I. Prepare for the field.
    A. What did you read to prepare for your fieldwork? Where did you find it?
    B. What did you learn from reading the fieldwork of others?

C. How did you select your informants? How did you prepare before meeting them?

D. How did you gain access to your informants and your fieldsites? Were there any problems? What might you do differently next time?

E. What assumptions did you have going into the field? How did you record them? What did you expect to see, and what did you actually find?

II. Use the researcher's tools.

A. How did you record your fieldnotes? Did you separate observational notes from personal notes? Did you invent your own method for organizing your fieldnotes?

B. What equipment did you use? What would you want at hand if you could do this work again?

C. How did you transcribe your recordings?

D. What interviewing skills did you develop? What skills would you like to work on?

E. What different types of data did you gather? Print sources? Cultural artifacts? Stories and interviews?

III. Interpret your fieldwork.

A. Which initial impressions turned out to be part of your final piece? Which ideas did you discard?

B. What strategies did you develop to categorize your data? Did you use patterns that were linear? Thematic? Chronological? Abstract to concrete? Concrete to abstract?

C. What strategies did you develop to analyze your data? What didn't fit?

D. What is your favorite piece of data — or data source — and why?

IV. Present your findings.

A. What decisions did you make about writing up your fieldwork?

B. How much of your voice is in the final project? How much of your informants' voices?

C. What details did you select to illustrate key points to bring your informants to life?

D. Did you use subheadings to guide your reader in your final paper or some other way to organize your material?

You might decide to use these questions to help you write an essay or commentary about your process as a researcher.

Wherever people interact in the same space, you have an opportunity to look carefully at artifacts, personal histories, traditional stories, and ways of behaving together and alone. But simply describing people as you see them does not produce sufficient data for a fieldstudy. You must use many different ways to gather their perspectives on their experiences—and do so in their voices. As you gather information about others, you'll also need to record your own feelings, responses, and reactions as you learn about them and your understanding deepens and shifts. Eventually, your responsibility is to the informants' voices, perspectives, stories, and histories—as much as it is to your own.

Reflect on Researching People

Try listing the people who are present at your fieldsite. Use the following questions to guide your exploration of how they interact:

FIRST   How many people are there? Have you talked to each of them? What connections and disconnections exist between them? How do they help each other? How do they define their roles within that culture—for themselves and for others? Who defines the roles for them?

SECOND   What artifacts or stories have more than one person discussed with you? How have those artifacts or stories helped explain the culture or those people's places in it? How did each person talk about the artifact or tell the story? How was each story different? What was the same about the stories?

THIRD   Whose oral histories would you like to gather? If you had time for a much longer study about your fieldsite, who else would you interview? What stories or artifacts would you want to understand? Whose personal histories would probably yield interesting information for you?

Whether or not this is your first fieldstudy, the skills of asking and listening—of collaborating in conversation with others—are lifetime skills for personal interactions with family, with friends, with coworkers, and in new cultural contexts. Practicing these skills, reflecting on what you're learning, and writing from other people's perspectives will strengthen your ability to talk, analyze, evaluate, and become a more active and knowledgeable citizen.

6

Researching Language: The Cultural Translator

....

Cultures and subcultures always share
language. In this chapter you will:

- translate conversation into written text
- interpret nonverbal language
- create a glossary for your research
- write dialogue in different ways

....

It is difficult to realize how language both shapes and reflects our culture
because it's so intrinsic to our everyday lives. As N. Scott Momaday reminds
us, listening is a crucial skill that both builds
and binds cultures. This chapter is about listening to language and translating what it has to say
about culture. You'll read, write, and research language and language events—the use of words in
everyday talk. You'll also research more formal
oral "performances": jokes, stories, sayings, and
legends.

*The simple act of listening is crucial to the
concept of language, more crucial even
than reading and writing, and language
in turn is crucial to human society. There
is proof of that, I think, in all the histories
and prehistories of human experience.*

—N. SCOTT MOMADAY

Although some **linguists** claim that there is no thought without language,
we think much of daily life moves along *without* the language of *words*. The
visual and musical arts, dance and athletics, and scientific notation are all
examples of nonverbal languages with which we communicate. Fieldworkers
notice and record a culture's *nonverbal* languages in an attempt to learn more
about the people they study. But they depend on *verbal* language as an intricate
tool for at least three purposes. First, as a tool for the mind, verbal language
brings nonverbal thoughts to the surface of consciousness. Second, for some
fieldworkers, language becomes the topic of their research, illustrating how a
culture shares knowledge through words. Finally, because researchers write,
language provides them with the means to communicate knowledge about
others.

Language can act as a kind of filter, keeping outsiders away from understanding. You've probably felt outside the range of some groups' languages: musicians, nurses, computer technicians, and athletes are just a few examples of groups that talk their own insider language. In the same way, a language can clarify a culture for insiders, reminding them of their membership.

Listening to language will help you move further inside a culture and become intimate with it. You'll introduce yourself to a subculture as you describe its settings, daily events, and behaviors and learn more by examining its histories and artifacts. But when you listen to and record its language, you'll understand the connection of language to a culture's way of being. You serve, in a way, as a cultural translator.

Linking Body Language and Culture

When we think about human expression, we often think first and only of speech. But fieldworkers learn early in their work that verbal communication is only one of several modes that communicate individual and collective meaning about a culture. Early in his study of truckers (see Chapter 1), Rick Zollo realized the significance of body language. Asking questions of Morris, a lease operator of his own rig, Rick sensed he had asked one question too many. In his final project, Rick writes, "The question of time raised Morris's suspicions again, and instead of answering, he fixed me with a hard gaze. Sensing I had crossed some invisible boundary, I thanked him for his time. Obviously, my question related to logbook procedures, and I made a mental note to avoid that type of inquiry."

By being attentive to body language, Rick realized his intrusion and backed off, respecting Morris's need for privacy. At the same time, Rick made mental notes that deepened his understanding of his subject. The sooner and the more sensitively you discover, interpret, and use the nonverbal conventions of the culture you're studying, the more successful you'll be.

Kinesics   With Ray Birdwhistell's 1952 *Introduction to Kinesics*, researchers began to study body communication (**kinesics**)—how individuals express themselves through body position and motion (facial expression, eye contact, posture, and gesture). Of course, we all engage in the study of kinesics informally, particularly in college classrooms, when we notice someone who slumps over her desk, puts her feet on another chair, or refuses to make eye contact with others. Still other researchers extended the study of individual body communication to **proxemics**—how individuals communicate nonverbally when in groups. Members of sports teams are experts at proxemics: they communicate meaning constantly with their bodies as they strategize together throughout a game.

Using Space   If you have ever entered an unfamiliar coffeehouse or bar, you may find yourself startled by how people use that public space to send messages. On airplanes, people signal whether they want to talk to their seat companions or remain silent merely by the way they hold a book or a folder. And an unspoken set of rules governs the use of an automatic cash machine: the person next in line stands at a respectful distance to signal that he cannot see the numbers you enter. If you have ever ventured into a culture to find yourself startled by unfamiliar uses of personal or public space, you know the significant role that body language plays in human expression.

Dress and Adornment   The physical display of our bodies to others signals who we are and who we are in relation to those who "read" us. The body is not just a physical object; it is a social object. For this reason, studying how your informants dress or adorn their bodies and how they use them will tell you much about how they see themselves and their cultures. In Jake's participation with skinheads (Chapter 3), one obvious feature that linked members of this group was their shaved heads. Skinheads, Jake discovered, did not want their membership to be secret or underground.

Capturing Body Language in Fieldnotes

Understanding the language of the body can come about in at least two ways—through observing adornment and behavior. First, you might observe and describe how members of the culture adorn their bodies—features of clothing, accessories, and body decoration (like makeup, tattoos, piercings, and hairstyles). In Chapter 5, Cindie Marshall's informant, Teardrop, used her tattoo to tell her story. Second, you can document body language in fieldnotes (this is better than waltzing up to informants and asking questions that will leave you sorry and them feeling awkward or abused).

One way to build reflexivity into your fieldnotes is to consider your own body in relation to the people you study. What sense do you get of their perceptions of your adornment? What, in terms of body language, is the relationship of self and other? In "Strike a Pose" (Chapter 4), Karen Downing reflected on her own makeup habits as she prepared to meet the manager of Photo Phantasies.

From an initial focus on adornment, you might next begin to consider a person's body as a kinesic form of expression. Reflect on the patterns of movement you observe and the meanings that these patterns communicate to outsiders (in this case, you) and to other members of the culture—the insiders. If Karen had posed for Photo Phantasies herself, she might have added another dimension of feeling about herself in that space.

Finally, you might broaden your study of the body to consider how the people you study share and possess space. In other words, what do you notice about the proxemics of the culture? Your fieldnotes may help you discover why people move and communicate as they do. Perhaps these reasons have something to do with informants' "fixed positions" (gender, race, class, or age); perhaps they do not.

Elizabeth's longest fieldstudy, a book called *Academic Literacies*, shows one of her informants, Nick, a college student, as he stretches himself over three chairs when he works in a writing group with three women. This behavior was a kind of defense against his classmates because he was afraid they would assault his text. And it was a "male thing" to take more space than was allotted to him.

As an interpreter of body language, your job as fieldworker is to discover not just what bodies say but why they say what they do. Another way to elicit information about body language is to ask informants directly. Keep in mind that questions about body language require a good deal of rapport, particularly if your informant (or the culture) views the body as a taboo subject. But if it strikes you that an informant might ponder your questions without taking offense, think about the observations, and ask for an insider's perspective. For instance, Elizabeth, merely by asking Nick, "Why did you need three chairs?" learned a lot about how he felt having three women read drafts of his writing. If your informant is willing to think consciously about his or her adornment, movement, and use of space, you will have a wonderful opportunity to test and revise your thinking.

BOX 26

Observing Body Language

AMIE OHLMANN, UNIVERSITY OF IOWA

PURPOSE

When we "read" people's body language, we observe and record physical features like gestures, facial expressions, body positions, and eye contact. We also notice people's use of their surrounding spaces (how a police officer manipulates the equipment in his car) and even their clothing (how a teenager covers his face with his sweatshirt hood). These observations become clues about how the culture operates from the insider's perspective.

ACTION

Take fieldnotes on body language at your research site, observe your classmates, or choose a piece of visual data (a photo or sketch) and analyze it. How does a person move in this space? What expressions do you see on her face? In what ways is she gesturing? Is he using his body in unusual ways? How does the person interact with others? Write one paragraph in which you describe your observations and then another paragraph of analysis. Share your writing with a research partner; allow the partner to ask questions about what she understands and doesn't understand about what's important in the culture or subculture you've documented.

Willa's nonverbal gestures

RESPONSE

The accompanying photographs represent multiple ways that my infant daughter communicates her feelings. Her nonverbals, particularly her facial expressions and gestures, provide signals to me about what she needs or wants. When she is tired, she rubs her eyes and her busy body stills as the quietness of sleep begins to overtake her. When she is interested in something, she twists her body toward the object of her interest and her hands immediately reach for the toy or baby goat. The need to experience the world is most evident in the use of her hands—from her quickness to grab whatever she wants, like a soft baby goat's ear, or reaching toward me for comfort. In particular, when she is excited, such as in the morning when her little body is recharged for the day, her hands move in wild circles. This photo captures the intensity of her excitement with the halos of movement around her hands. Of course, there are myriad ways that babies use nonverbals to communicate—from varying cries to facial expressions like a scrunched-up face when she doesn't like something, to gestures such as pushing things or people away.

The importance of nonverbals is obvious when it comes to babies. In fact, they seem to inhabit a "culture" all their own while parents are left to decipher their insider language. Of course, nonverbals are babies' only means to communicate. As the mother of a seven-month-old, I have been relying on my ability to "read" my daughter Willa's nonverbals since she was born. Honing my ability to communicate with my daughter is similar to the skills ethnographic researchers must have in order to understand a culture. The images represent frozen moments in time where I had to interpret my daughter's nonverbals. Willa has learned that these gestures, facial expressions, and even babbling sounds are a way to affect her world. As she grows, she will learn the gestures, facial expressions, and vocalics of this culture—from waving "bye-bye" to giving hugs to tell someone she cares about them. Understanding the significance of nonverbals as a means of communication and as a means of conveying culture is crucial to a researcher truly seeking to gain insight into that culture, just as my growth as a mother is contingent on my ability to decipher my daughter's needs and wants through nonverbals.

Linking Words and Culture

Listening to the spoken language of your informant is an important way to learn about a culture. One key word can unlock information about the habits, beliefs, geography, and history of a whole group of people. Your job as a fieldworker is to act as a cultural translator, recording and questioning the meanings of key words, phrases, and ideas that might serve as clues about your informant's culture.

We become cultural translators in situations that we may not realize are important. Sometimes, a parent, a peer, or a teacher may ask us about a word or a slang expression that we've inherited from a particular place or subculture of peers. If you live in the Midwest or in the western United States, for example, you'd ask for a soft drink using the word *pop*. An East Coast person would call the same drink *soda*. And in the Boston area, it's called *tonic*.

As teachers and former teenagers ourselves, we've watched words of approval (or praise or excitement) change over many years. Something good was *hot* or *neat* when we were teenagers, and then it somehow became *cool*, which has lasted for a while. But in the meantime, our students have used *bad*, *awesome*, *wicked*, *rad*, *gnarly*, and *mad*. Language grows and changes over time and across spaces.

One of our favorite researchers is a nineteenth-century ethnographic journalist named Lafcadio Hearn. He was a journalist who listened to language, collected stories, and observed urban life in Cincinnati, New Orleans, New York, and Japan, among other places. We'd like to share one of Hearn's short essays, which he wrote for the newspaper the *New Orleans Item* in January 1881. The essay's title word—*cheek*—is no longer in common use, but toward the end of the nineteenth century it described what we would call *attitude*. Don't be intimidated by the opening sentence and its archaic language. Read on. Remember that the average newspaper reader at that time was comfortable with this style. In fact, it may remind you of older styles of literature or historical documents.

. . . .

Cheek

Lafcadio Hearn

There is a picturesque force of laconic expressiveness about certain American slang-terms which has brought them into familiar use even among persons who ordinarily eschew slang in common conversation. Such a term is "cheek." Cheek comprises in one syllable all that is usually expressed in such words as assurance, self-confidence, impudence and insolence, the significance of cheek, largely depending on the context. For example, if we say that it is necessary to have some cheek in order to get along in the world, we mean self-confidence. But if we observe that a certain person has "more cheek than a brass monkey" or "a government mule," we mean that he is impertinent to an astonishing degree, and has little or no regard for the feelings of his fellow-men. What we propose to consider, however, is what part does cheek play in success. It would be folly to generalize cheek in the person of any one type of cheekiness; for they are multitudinous and varied. But cheek, as the opposite of timid delicacy, may be considered in a general way through its effects.

A timid man, however talented, has a poor chance in a race with a shrewd and cheeky man, of infinitely less ability. The former may catch up in time when the momentum which cheek has given his rival begins to die out; the timid man may be sometimes the winning tortoise. But his tendency to underestimate himself, his comparative ignorance of the world, and his dread of appearing rude or uncultivated—all these causes—in fact, which tend to produce his timidity, are very hurtful to his chances of success in life. The world usually regards timidity an indication of incapability; and there must be some general truth at the bottom of such a tendency. The cheeky man, even after he has been discovered to have too much self-confidence, usually manages to keep ahead. Moreover, he learns rapidly as he goes, and his faith in his own capacity aids him marvellously well. He forces a way for himself while others beg and plead for it. He considers himself as good a man as any other upon the face of the earth; and this democratic spirit enables him to bring himself directly in contact with men from whom the timid shrink with dismay in consequence of their comparative weakness. Moreover he can adapt himself to any society, and familiarize himself with people whom delicate persons dread to meet. He resents an insult quickly, relies much upon his physical vigor and, to use his own expression, "knows how to take care of himself." He compels persons to listen to him who hate to see him, and obliges people who inwardly despise him to respect him outwardly. And if he be really a sharp and shrewd type of this class, when you ask him how he gets along so well in the world, he will answer,—"My dear fellow, it is very simple. I have plenty of cheek; and I know the value of it, and how to use it to the best advantage." But suppose the enquirer goes further, and asks, "What is cheek? what causes it? how can it be acquired?"—then the answer would probably be,—"Cheek is confidence in one's self, courage, impudence, power to adapt

Lafcadio Hearn, 1850–1904

(Library of Congress)

one's self to all circumstances; you may not acquire it, although you may repress your rational timidity in time to a great extent; you must be born with cheek to be cheeky," or words to that effect.

Then, what does cheek in the best sense depend on? It depends upon physical vigor to a great extent. It is the self-confidence inspired by perfect health and natural energy which must be inherited to possess. Broad shoulders and strong muscles, a loud and dominating voice, a big beard, a fearless eye, a carriage that seems to suggest the belief, "I am as good as the next man, and fear no one,"— these will do more to help a man along in life than much learning and wisdom. The race to the strongest!—the survival of the fittest! This is why the world regards timid men with suspicion. There is nothing about them which imposes and forces itself upon the spectator,—no strong physical individuality,—no violent magnetism of voice and eye,—none of that bodily power which compels reluctant attention and imposes a respect like that we give to certain fierce animals we dare not refuse to caress lest they should become angry.

A little illustration from newspaper life. Some years ago a certain newspaper circle in one of the Eastern cities opened to admit a new reporter. He was a man of forty years of age, weighed about two hundred pounds, had a great brown beard, an aquiline face, and large grey eyes. He had had far less experience than any of his comrades, was partly deaf, spoke in a low voice, and was an inferior writer; but it was soon found that he had no equal as a newsgatherer. With the same chances as the rest he obtained news no one could procure, interviewed parties who had refused to see any other newspaper men,—even the cheekiest,—got full particulars of secret sessions of municipal bodies which nobody else could get,—fathomed mysteries which baffled the skill of the most experienced,—and universally secured more attention than his fellows. No one could understand his "good luck" as they called it at first, his "peculiar tract," as they styled it later on. He explained in this way; "You are all young men; I have the air of a middle-aged man; I have a ponderous aspect and a dignified look; I have big whiskers and a big beard. It has been my experience that people always pay more attention to what might be called "heavy-looking men" than to any others; and I rely largely upon that fact." This was not a case of cheek; but only a little illustration of what the physical advantages which self-confidence is generally based upon may accomplish in a calling which demands mental, not physical, superiority.

Lafcadio Hearn offers us a meditation on the word *cheek* that shows how a slang term used over a hundred years ago can offer us insights into an entire culture. As outsiders to his time, we learn from Hearn's precise and sensitive descriptions of cheeky people: they are self-confident, fearless, courageous, adaptable. In fact, we might call Hearn's essay itself "cheeky." A careful inquiry about a single word can teach us much about a culture.

BOX 27

Listening for Words: Creating a Glossary

PURPOSE

Special words, jargon, slang, and the unique uses of everyday language are important clues to understanding a culture or subculture. Knowing what terms insiders use will help you step away from your outsider status, and analyzing the words—and their uses—will assist you in seeing what's important to insiders.

ACTION

Listen for key words in your fieldsite, and create a glossary of insider language. It will be important to get informants' permission to take fieldnotes or record your conversation. As you listen, you may want to repeat what you hear so that your informants can add to, correct, or respond further to the insider language they are sharing with you. Later, you will also need to confirm your list of terms with informants in your fieldsite. Try to collect as much insider language as you can. Do you notice certain everyday words being used in new ways? Are there names for things that are entirely new to you? In this exercise, we want you to sharpen your listening skills to make yourself alert to language at your research site.

Our student, William Harvey Purcell, studied the disability movement among artists. He attended a weekend conference, the Disability Culture Festival, in which he recorded interviews with artists who celebrate their disabilities. He extracted a glossary of disability terms from his interviews and supplemented it with online resources.

To read William's essay, go to Chapter 8, page 371.

RESPONSE

advocate (n): an individual who is not an attorney, but who assists parents and children in their dealings with school districts regarding special education programs.

assistive technology (n): any item or piece of equipment used to maintain or improve the functional capabilities of individuals with disabilities.

cognitive (adj): a reference to a person's reasoning or intellectual capacity.

congenital (adj): existing at or dating from birth.

crip/krip (n): slang for a person with a disability, used only by those who are members of the disability culture.

developmental delay (n): conditions that represent significant lags in the "normal" process of development, which may involve cognitive, physical, communicative, social, emotional, and/or adaptive areas of growth.

disability (n): a physical, sensory, cognitive, or affective impairment that causes a child to need special education (there are significant differences in the definitions of *disability* in IDEA and Section 504).

early intervention (n): an attempt to locate, identify, and evaluate young children with developmental disabilities and delays and the accompanying provision for services to accommodate these situations and facilitate children's development.

BOX 27 continued

genetics (n): the study of heredity, and in particular, genes. Human genetics attempts to understand heredity to predict, diagnose, and treat genetic diseases and conditions.

inclusion (n): a popular philosophical position in education, based on the belief that every student is entitled to an instructional program that meets his or her individual needs and learning characteristics—within a school system.

independent living (n): a belief that individuals with disabilities have the same rights and responsibilities as other citizens in a society—and the educational system needs to prepare and support them as they try to achieve this goal.

individualized educational plan (IEP) (n): Public Law 94-142 mandates that each child who receives special education services must have an IEP, a plan designed, reviewed, and agreed on each year by a team of school administrators, teachers, parents, and other relevant professionals.

individualized family service plan (IFSP or ISP) (n): Public Law 99-457 requires that each family of a disabled person must establish an agreement between family members and professionals to provide the necessary resources to help the individual and her/his family achieve their goals and satisfy their needs.

mainstreaming (n, v): a term used by schools that reflects IDEA's preference to provide education in the "least restrictive environment" for every student.

occupational therapy (n): a service that focuses on the development of a person's fine motor skills and/or the identification of adaptive strategies for accomplishing activities of daily living.

other health impairment (OHI) (n): having limited strength, vitality, or alertness, including heightened awareness of environmental stimuli that results in limited alertness in the educational environment.

"people first" language (n): the idea that citizens must learn to stop using language that sets people apart and devalues them, and instead turn to language that puts people first and the descriptor second (if listed at all).

tab (n): temporarily able-bodied; slang for a person outside the disability culture.

wheeler (n): a person who uses a wheelchair.

After William had gathered and alphabetized his glossary, he asked several of his informants—disability artists—to read and check his list for accuracy and relevance within their subculture. In his full study of the disability world, "Disability Is Beautiful" (Chapter 8), William uses the language from his glossary to bring his informants' world and words to life. In the following section is an example of how another student integrated the language of a subculture into her study.

Using Insider Language in Your Writing

Dina Dwyer studied the insider culture of people who legally own and use guns. Her quest began at a fashion show run by her hairstylist friend. First, she completed a form for the show's master of ceremonies that required her to state her hobbies as she wanted them announced: "I didn't care for the idea of jaunting around a stage in front of hundreds in my new pink hair while the announcer said I enjoyed 'postcard collecting' or 'napping.' So I jotted down something I'd never done: sharp shooting." Her research takes her to sporting goods shops, a gun convention, the police station where she applies for a gun license, and finally a shooting range. In the following section of her study, Dina is with her friend Tommy for her first target practice. Her use of insider language, drawn from her glossary, offers us a vivid insider view:

> I set up my camera and throw sticks to his dog as Tommy unloads the weapons. He lays out three rifles—a .222, a 7 mm, and a .22. We staple a target silhouette of a man to a large cardboard box and place it out at about fifty yards. We get right down to it, shoving cigarette filters in our ears for protection and loading up the .22. "You've seriously never fired a gun before?" Tommy asks me, eyebrow raised.
>
> "Nope," I say as I sit down on the little stool provided by the state parks. Tommy shows me how to line up the barrel with the sights on top of it. He checks to see if the butt of the rifle is snug against my inner shoulder. The rifle feels comfortable as I inhale to make my body tense.
>
> I pull the trigger. Pop! The noise is tiny, and the gun doesn't kick back much at all. Tommy looks through his binoculars; I hit the target. He shows me how to discard the shell and prepare for the next shot. I fire again and again and again.
>
> We try the .222. It's bigger, and so are the bullets. For this one, Tommy has me lean against the four-foot rock hill that marks the beginning of the 100-yard line. This gun is louder but not as loud as the next one I fire—the 7 mm. As I squeeze the trigger on that one, the shock goes through my body. BANG! I look back over at Tommy, who's laughing. "Pretty loud, huh?" he calls. I nod, dazed. I fire this one again after mentally preparing myself. The time it takes to reload, aim, and fire for me is about 15 seconds. I'm taking my time.
>
> The next is a .44 Red Hawk revolver. It's massive. Holding it out to aim at a duck decoy 100 yards away is like holding a bucket of water at arm's length. It kicks back so hard my palm hurts. My arms are sore after just two six-bullet rounds. I can't hit the duck. Tommy can't hit the duck. We get mad at the duck. He suggests we try the 9 mm Glock 17 because it's getting late. We spend the next few minutes loading the bullets into a few magazines. They are modified +2's, which means that they fit 19 bullets instead of 17. The gun is solid black and utilitarian. It means business.

I fire, and it jams. Tommy picks out the lodged shell and tells me to keep it steady. It jams again. I see that the reason it's jamming is because after I pull the trigger, the gun kicks up as the bullet flies out. This jerking causes the shell to become lodged instead of popping out the top as it should. We go through a few magazines, and I jam the damn thing every other bullet. Gradually, I learn to compensate for the up-kick.

As we can see from the above excerpt, Dina integrated the language of sharpshooting into "Bang Ka-Pow Zap: My Semester with Guns," her account of becoming an insider. Her knowledge of the words and her glossary developed over the time she conducted her study.

As Dina shows us, telling the story of your own understanding of insiders' terms and usage as it grows during your fieldwork can become an integral part of your study—and keep your readers informed of your journey as you move closer toward the insiders' culture. A single word can unlock a flood of insider knowledge.

Words as Cultural Artifacts

In this section, we illustrate how knowing one simple fact about a culture's language can, like an artifact, help us conduct an interview that leads to important insights about our informants and ourselves. Our colleague and friend,

For more on interviewing, see Chapter 5, page 220.

Danling Fu, grew up in the People's Republic of China. We knew that Danling had kept pet silkworms as a child and that there are over twenty different words for *silk* in Chinese (denoting purity, shine, thickness, weight, smoothness, and so on). This high number of silk words would lead a fieldworker to investigate more about the cultural significance of silk. We wanted to see how these two facts might show us more about other features of Chinese culture, so we interviewed Danling as a fieldworker would.

As we take you through the process of this interview, we've denoted ourselves "B & E" and Danling "D," and, in italics with parentheses, we provide our own insights and thoughts as the interview proceeds.

B&E: Were you unusual, or do all Chinese children keep pet silkworms? *(We wanted to start with what we knew—that she had a pet silkworm when she was a child.)*

D: Our relationship with worms is like yours with cats and dogs. I grew up in Jiangsu province, a silk-producing place, and all children kept silkworms. Every family does it. The full name we use is "baby silkworms." We care for them, keep them clean, learn to hold them tenderly, and watch the whole life cycle process.

B&E: How do you care for them?
*(Although we were looking for
language—words and stories—
we wanted to give her time to
remember details about keeping
silkworms. We also wanted to hear
more about the process because we
knew that would illustrate more
about the whole culture.)*

A silkworm cocoon

D: In early spring, we put eggs—
thousands of little eggs, laid by
the silk moth the year before—
on little squares of paper in a
shoebox. We put them in the sun
for warmth. Sometimes we start them in school, like American
children grow seeds in paper cups or chick eggs in incubators.
Eventually, a worm hatches—so tiny, so black, smaller than an ant.
As the leaves come out, we feed them to the little worms. Day by
day, we watch them grow bigger, as thick as a little finger, in different shades of white and black.

B&E: Do children compete over how many silkworms they have?
*(We wondered whether Chinese children have rules for ownership,
if they trade or have contests, and if that would suggest anything
more about the culture itself. We weren't prepared for her answer,
because our thinking was so American and based on our sense of
competition.)*

D: Yes, but only because we all want a few to live so we can care for
them. They eat a lot of leaves, and we don't have enough of them.
In cities, families protect their trees because children steal each
other's leaves. Sometimes I would buy extra leaves from farmers
to feed my worms. Each year, if I had a ten percent survival rate, I
would consider it a victory.

B&E: So where does the silk come in? What do you do with the silk?
*(The discussion was beginning to move in a different direction. We
wanted to know about silk; she wanted to talk about keeping pets.
We tried to redirect it.)*

D: Until their last moment of life, they produce silk. These worms are
hard workers, a good image for Chinese people. When they are ready
to build the cocoon in the summer, they become transparent—they
look like the silk itself. And we build little hills for them with straw.
The cocoons are red and pink and yellow—so beautiful on the straw
hills. My mother used them as decorations in the house.

B&E: But then what? How do you get the silk out of the cocoon?
(It was fun to visualize those little straw mountains with the colorful cocoons. But we hoped that she'd describe a very specific cultural practice there.)

D: We put the cocoon in hot water. And then we pull out a silk thread, very carefully. You wouldn't believe how long it is. One cocoon makes one very long silk thread—yards and yards of silk. We wrap it around a bamboo chopstick, and then we have the thread to play with.

B&E: Do you play games with the silk thread? Weave with it?
(The silk thread and bamboo pole sounded like the beginning of a children's game. Would children's games tell us more about the culture? Again we were biased by our own culture and surprised at her answer.)

D: Not really. It's only just a part of watching the whole process and learning about life and production. Life and productivity are the main parts of our culture. Such a little body, so much hard work. It just gives and gives and gives until the moment it dies. You know, we use every part of the process.

B&E: What do you mean by "every part of the process"?
(Her answer takes an interesting direction. Games with silk aren't as important to her as learning about the life cycle and how production is tied to life.)

D: Well, besides the silk, we watch the males and females produce the eggs together. We even use the waste. We dry it and stuff pillows. We eat the cocoon.

B&E: Yuk! Ugh! Are you kidding? You eat the cocoon?
(We laughed as we recognized our own assumptions about acceptable food. The message was still tied to productivity—the Chinese don't want to waste anything).

D: Yep. It's good. We deep-fry the inside. Tastes like a peanut.

B&E: So the silkworm is a pet, but you use so much of it to learn about other things.
(We wanted to see what other insider cultural information might come when we asked what they learned from keeping these pets.)

D: The worm is so soft, so tender. That's why we call it "baby silkworm"; we learn to care for it like a baby. These worms live really clean lives. We change the papers and the boxes. We scrape the leaves and the waste when we feed them. We need cheap pets, you

know, in China. We cannot feed
them our food like you do with
your pets because we don't even
have enough for ourselves.
*(Without realizing it, she offers an
important insight—that Chinese
pets must not threaten human
needs but must offer children a
chance to learn about life.)*

Silkworms feeding on a leaf

B&E: So children learn about the life
cycle with these pets? And you
have all those words about how
silk is made: texture, shininess,
thickness, weight. It's about life
and production, as you said?
*(We wanted to summarize what we had already heard her say, hoping
we'd hear more about how silk and silkworms figure into Chinese
language. We were hoping for more, but we couldn't force it.)*

D: Yes, we have a children's song. It says "Be faithful. Even when you
die, you can still contribute without taking anything. Like a silkworm." The silkworm gives us songs, metaphors, and images of our
culture.
*(Aha, a song! The song holds many of the values she's been describ-
ing: economy, production, collaboration, and the cycle of life. And
she recognizes it as she tells us.)*

B&E: Wow, all those images of production. Bet that worked well during
the Cultural Revolution.
(We knew Danling had been a teenager during the Cultural Revolution.)

D: *(laughs)* Yes, there are a lot of revolutionary songs with silkworms
in them.
*(If it had a song, would a culture that keeps silkworms and has many
words for silk also have other forms of "verbal art"—stories, proverbs, and the like—that revealed its beliefs? She was telling us more
about exactly what we wanted to know. This was exciting data.)*

B&E: Are there any legends or proverbs about silkworms?

D: Well, not proverbs, exactly, but there are many stories. There's an
image-story like "The Tortoise and the Hare." We say that to get
something done with patience and consistency, it's like a silkworm,
eating a leaf bit by bit, little by little. That little mouth eats so quietly, so fast. Overnight it can consume so many leaves.
*(Ah, a relevant saying: to live a productive life takes patience and
consistency. A cultural truth with a silkworm as the main character.)*

B&E: And are there other sayings about the silk itself?

D: A silk thread, when it's in a cocoon, is so long, so intricate, so soft, and so tangled. It is difficult to figure out where the beginning is and where the end is. When we have a complicated problem, we say we are "tangled by a silk thread."
        (And the silk thread even figures into explaining problems—another indicator of its importance in the culture.)

B&E: So there's the silkworm as a pet and so many words about silk. Language and learning and life.
        (She was really remembering, and we didn't want to stop or redirect her line of thought. But we wanted her to know we were interested. So we offered another summary. Her own lovely statement summarizes—from her own perspective—better than we ever could from ours.)

D: With silkworms, we see the whole process. We see how silk comes into our lives—not only how we wear it, but how we live with it.

This interview taught us much about Chinese culture—not only how Chinese wear silk, as Danling put it, but also how they "live with it." Two key words that were far more important in her language than in ours, *silk* and *silkworm*, show the extent to which thought determines language—how a culture creates the words it needs. Our focus on these words unleashed information about Chinese history, metaphors, images, sayings, and songs. Danling's digressions on the care and feeding of pet silkworms revealed the cultural values of hard work, sacrifice, and productivity, not to mention the practice of eating cocoons. Because Danling is bilingual and bicultural, she assisted in our cultural translation.

We want our interview with Danling to serve as a model for you, but we realize that she was able to translate, as many insiders cannot do. Most of us

Unlocking the Language of Your Informant's Culture

- Listen for unusual insider words or phrases from your informant, words that refer to rules, rituals, behaviors, beliefs, or practices.

- Ask questions that invite your informant to explain how insiders use that language.

- Continue with follow-up questions that further reveal the meanings of words, phrases, signs, or language events (songs, sayings, stories) in your informant's culture.

- Record your informant's explanations carefully and check that you've captured their perspectives and not your own.

begin as outsiders who don't know our informants. Outsider status is the point of entry for all fieldworkers, and practice in listening to insider language is a good way to step in.

Ethnopoetics

One way to present a transcript and to analyze it for its themes, rhythms, and language patterns is what folklorists and sociolinguists call **ethnopoetic notation**. Folklorist Dennis Tedlock used it to study and record Navajo speech. It also was adapted by sociolinguist Deborah Tannen, author of the bestseller *You Just Don't Understand: Women and Men in Conversation*, to analyze conversations in everyday living and in the workplace. Ethnopoetic notation is a procedure in which a language researcher turns oral speech into poetic form. Transforming oral speech into poetry allows a closer look, not only at an informant's language but also at the informant's perspective. As you take the words, lay them out on a page, and identify repetitions, pauses, and themes, you capture the rhythms of your informant's everyday speech. Here is an excerpt from Danling's transcript, transformed into poetry on the page:

> In early spring we put eggs, thousands of little eggs
>> laid by the silk moth
>> the year before
>> on little squares of paper
>> in a shoebox.
>
> We put them in the sun for warmth; sometimes we start them in school
>> like American children
>> grow seeds
>>> in paper cups
>> or chicken eggs
>>> in incubators.
>
> Eventually, a worm hatches
>> so tiny
>> so black
>> smaller than an ant.
>
> As the leaves come out, we feed them to the little worms.
>> Day by day,
>> we watch them grow bigger
>> as thick as a little finger
>> in different shades
>>> of white
>>> and black.

This layout of Danling's oral language in poetic form is similar to the oral context in which our conversation took place. The poetic notation allows you to see where she pauses and clusters images together: "so tiny / so black / smaller than an ant." In this poem, her figures of speech also stand out ("as thick as a little finger") and her cultural comparison is clear ("like American children / grow seeds / in paper cups / or chicken eggs / in incubators"). Ethnopoetic notation preserves the integrity of the oral conversation more closely than a written transcript. Although a word-for-word transcribed interview may seem more authentic, in fact, by writing it down we remove language from its oral context entirely. The process of ethnopoetic notation allows the researcher to recapture and study informants' language and thought more closely.

Read a student essay that uses ethnopoetics at **bedfordstmartins.com/ fieldworking**, under Student Essays.

Using Ethnopoetics with Transcripts

Ethnopoetic notation allows you to revive your informant's talk from a flat transcript and understand your data better.

- Reread a section of your transcript (or consult the audio file) in which you think your informant's words reveal something deeper than what lies on the surface of the page.

- Break apart the words and phrases to re-create your informant's oral language in a poetic form. Remember, your goal is not to write a poem, but to illustrate rhythms, repetitions, tensions, insights, and cultural meanings.

- Remember, also, that while you can't change the order of the actual words, you can rearrange the words in different patterns by breaking them at different places.

Noticing Words and Phrases

When you study another culture, you begin to pay attention to the way that specific words and phrases are used by that group. Gathering examples of language use allows you to probe the culture of your informants in further depth, particularly when common words and phrases are used differently or carry different meanings and interpretations. As fieldworkers, both Elizabeth and Bonnie instinctively record language use wherever they are, whether traveling for pleasure or just paying attention to the way that specific cultures operate. For example, Bonnie visited China in 2007, the summer before the Beijing Olympics, a time when China was attempting to appeal to international tourists. She photographed signs that translated Chinese into English. Some of these seem awkward to English speakers, but recording these allowed further insights into what happens when cultures come together and influence one another.

A sign from Bonnie's China trip, 2007

A café sign in China

- "Please take good care of the environmental hygiene"
- "Aristocracy Tour"
- "Buy Bye Cafe"
- "Forbid throwing the rubbish to the bridge arbitrarily"
- "4,636 m above seal level"

Similarly, in her travels in the United States, Elizabeth keeps a little 4×3 purple notebook of "wayside pulpit" announcements. She finds the way that churches use language as public messages is really fascinating and representative of how churches invite newcomers into their communities. The challenge of the wayside messages is to use very concise and catchy phrases. Here are a few examples from her notebook:

- "Everyone will live forever, somewhere"
- "The light of the world knows no power failure"
- "Self-worth beats net worth"
- "One letter is the difference between 'danger' and 'anger'"

As a fieldworker, you will strengthen your research skills by always paying attention to the written phrases and signs that are part of the culture you are studying. Recording these phrases and words provides further evidence of how language binds cultures and subcultures together.

Researching Occupation: Recording Insider Language

Anthropologists, sociologists, and folklorists have always been interested in the language of occupations. They have studied and written about flight attendants, police, bartenders, fishermen, and waitresses. To research insider occupational language, you cannot be merely an observer, but you must become a participant-observer, asking questions. You will notice that a few phrases of occupational language reveal entire sets of rules, rituals, and ways of thinking. Insider language—a word, a term, or a phrase—can trigger whole stories that illustrate the perspective inside a subculture.

In her full-length ethnography called *Dishing It Out: Power and Resistance among Waitresses in a New Jersey Restaurant*, anthropologist Greta Foff Paules includes a list of waitresses' insider terms, including "the floor," "call out," "walk out," and "pulling bus pans." These grassroot expressions are not part of an officially sanctioned language that we would find in a manual, a guidebook, or even a photocopied set of rules for working in a restaurant. It's interesting, though, that occupational terms are stable. Whether you are a waitress in California, Texas, or New Jersey, you'll know that a "station" is a waitress's service area and that to be "stiffed" by a customer means that you've been left no tip.

Occupations that form subcultures, like waitressing, often convey their insider terms through stories, words, and phrases. Occupational folklorists have suggested that the relationship between job terms and a group's cultural worldview is so strong that the terminology literally shapes the perspective of the workers. Most waitresses agree that to be busy feels like being caught "in the weeds" and to be insulted by a customer evokes retaliation against those who "stiff" them. Learning occupational terms and swapping stories shape behaviors and values. In the case of waitresses, stories can serve as reminders of caution against customer disrespect and efficiency in the face of customer demands. The occupational language and stories help initiate new waitresses into the profession and reaffirm seasoned waitresses' experience. Occupational language reflects an insider's perspective.

Researchers in many fields have long been interested in the insider's view of occupations. Chicago radio journalist Studs Terkel, for example, published *Working*, a collection of interviews with workers about their jobs during the mid-twentieth century. More recently, journalist Barbara Ehrenreich depicted people trying to live on poverty-level wages in her acclaimed book *Nickel and Dimed: On (Not) Getting By in America.* Ehrenreich lived for a year on minimum-wage salaries, taking jobs across the United States as a waitress, a hotel maid, a nursing home aide, and a salesperson at Wal-Mart. In the excerpt from *Nickel and Dimed* that we've posted online for you to read, Ehrenreich describes her experiences as a housekeeper in Maine and her employer's training videos, which demonstrated cleaning procedures. The viewing of videotapes about dusting and vacuuming and the language used to describe these acts introduce workers to the company's insider terms and to the attitude it wants its employees to assume toward clients.

Whether you are an insider or an outsider to the subculture you study, whether you conduct a formal interview or collect words, phrases, and stories informally, you can learn much from listening to language. Your goal is to try to describe language from your informant's perspective and analyze what it tells you about the occupation it represents.

BOX 28

Describing Occupational Terms

PURPOSE

Collecting the **verbal art** of a subculture is an important way of understanding it: insiders teach one another how to belong by sharing special terms, proverbs, jokes, sayings, and especially stories. As you spend time in your fieldsite, you may find your informant wanting to explain techniques, rules, rituals, or processes of their occupations—and at those times you'll probably hear much verbal art. Like the researchers who studied waitresses,

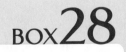

BOX **28** continued

you may hear some good stories. The best way to get a good story, of course, is to hang out long enough to hear one.

ACTION

In your fieldsite, select an occupation or a person who uses specific occupational language. Spend some time watching the work and listening to the workers and their language. Record fieldnotes or tape insider language, if possible. When you've gathered some terms or phrases and unfamiliar usages, arrange to interview an informant. From your informant, find out as much as you can about the history and uses of these occupational terms or phrases. Ask your informant to tell a story that illustrates the term. You may ask, "What do you mean by X?" or "Tell me how Y works" or "How do you use Z?"

RESPONSE

When we use the term *occupation*, we mean the insider language that members of a subculture use during the time they spend together. Nick Kowalczyk studied a group of people who reenact the French and Indian War. He attended the Grand Fête of Chez les Canses, an annual fall event for reenactors. He spent 12 hours at the Fête, interviewed 15 people, snapped photos, pored over scrapbooks and memorabilia, and read Web sites, magazine articles, and books about reenactors of "living history."

Nick's final study is a thick portrait of one reenactor named Dan who regularly reenacts an Osage Indian character named Spotted Dog. Here, Nick describes the scene and explains a new word, *"farby,"* which he'd learned from Dan and the other reenactors, and realizes it applies directly to him.

> *Outsider at "the tavern," December, late in the study*
>
> Dan's friend Blake portrays a Scottish highlander, and he decorates an entire cabin with eighteenth-century items. His other friend Ed runs a business with his wife selling authentically woven haversacks, wool blankets, socks, mittens, and other cloth or leather goods. At sunset, the group retreats to a candle-lit cabin, "the tavern," where they drink, sing eighteenth-century songs, and play an old dice game named Farkle. When I was there, roughly 30 reenactors crammed inside the tavern and grew more festive with each emptied cup. They shouted "Huzzah!" at the end of each a capella song. . . .
>
> I was the only person in street clothes. Earlier in the day, I'd learned the word *farby*, which describes something obviously inauthentic or anachronistic. Allegedly this term stems from "*Far be* it for me to criticize, but your (blank) is incorrect." I was farby head-to-toe: spiked hair, turquoise T-shirt, a cell phone.

Verbal Performance: Curses

Waitress stories fit the category of occupational folklore, as does Nick's account of the reenactors, but they are also what folklorists and anthropologists call "performance events" or examples of "verbal art." Performance events include a wide range of expressive art, from informal to formal: jokes, proverbs and taboos, songs and chants, urban legends, curses and spells, myths and tales, traditional stories, and entire ceremonies complete with storytelling and ritual verbal behaviors (like weddings, initiations, retirements, and seasonal celebrations). These **performances** use spontaneous verbal art; they are unrehearsed, unscripted, and not often staged. This concept of verbal performance comes from folklore and depends on three features: a performer who is an insider to the culture, a recognizable oral performance, and an audience of insiders.

In the same way that a folk object, like the basket we described in Chapter 3, is an expressive art form that blends cultural tradition with individual creativity, so does a verbal performance. A joke, for example, has a traditional core—either of content (the chicken crosses the road) or of form ("Knock, knock!" "Who's there?"). But jokes and stories have **variants**; they change according to the performer's creativity, personal history, and culture ("Oh, I heard a different version of that where I lived").

So the twin laws of folklore—tradition and creativity—are present in our verbal performance events, although we are not consciously aware of them. Telling a joke and gossiping, both verbal performances, are so automatic and integrated into our conversational lives that we don't often stand back to analyze them. But we all know someone who is a good joke teller, and we depend on certain people to give us the latest gossip. We also notice when an outsider "doesn't get" a joke—"You had to be there." Only insiders to a subculture have the cultural knowledge to "get it."

Like a joke or a story, a curse is a kind of verbal performance that exists in many cultures. It is closely connected with other verbal arts: songs and chants, for example. Looking at the curses of a culture helps us understand its taboos, history and geography, values and beliefs. Zora Neale Hurston, an anthropologist working in the 1930s, was one of the first ethnographers to study the folktales and magic practices of her own culture, recounted in her book *Mules and Men*. She used her status as an insider to work her way toward New Orleans to study hoodoo, a uniquely American practice, blended from a mixture of African and Haitian black magic (voodoo) and New Orleans French Catholic religious beliefs. From hoodoo doctor Luke Turner, Hurston learned the process for putting a curse on someone, which involves invoking this curse-prayer:

> To the Man God: O Great One, I have been sorely tried by my enemies and have been blasphemed and lied against. My good thoughts and my honest actions have been turned to bad actions and dishonest ideas. My home has

been disrespected, my children have been cursed and ill-treated. My dear ones have been backbitten and their virtue questioned. O Man God, I beg that this that I ask for my enemies shall come to pass:

That the South wind shall scorch their bodies and make them wither and shall not be tempered to them. That the North wind shall freeze their blood and numb their muscles and that it shall not be tempered to them. That the west wind shall blow away their life's breath and will not leave their hair grow, and that their finger nails shall fall off and their bones shall crumble. That the East wind shall make their minds grow dark, their sight shall fail and their seed dry up so that they shall not multiply.

I ask that their fathers and mothers from their furthest generation will not intercede for them before the great throne, and the wombs of their women shall not bear fruit except for strangers, and that they shall become extinct. I pray that the children who may come shall be weak of mind and paralyzed of limb and that they themselves shall curse them in their turn for ever turning the breath of life into their bodies. I pray that disease and death shall be forever with them and that their worldly goods shall not prosper and that their crops shall not multiply and that their cows, their sheep, and their hogs and all their living beasts shall die of starvation and thirst. I pray that their house shall be unroofed and that the rain, thunder and lightning shall find the innermost recesses of their home and that the foundation shall crumble and the floods tear it asunder. I pray that the sun shall not shed its rays on them in benevolence, but instead it shall beat down on them and burn them and destroy them. I pray that the moon shall not give them peace, but instead shall deride them and decry them and cause their minds to shrivel. I pray that their friends shall betray them and cause them loss of power, of gold and of silver, and that their enemies shall smite them until they beg for mercy which shall not be given them. I pray that their tongues shall forget how to speak in sweet words, and that it shall be paralyzed and that all about them will be desolation, pestilence and death. O Man God, I ask you for all these things because they have dragged me in the dust and destroyed my good name; broken my heart and caused me to curse the day that I was born. So be it. (197–98)

This curse, collected by Hurston, is a good example of verbal performance art. If you read this curse aloud or to a friend, you would understand the full force of its performance features, which link it closely to a wide range of spiritual traditions that invite audience participation.

Curses and spiritual performances, like seances, tarot readings, and fortune telling—even religious sermons—reveal aspects of a culture's belief system. Less formal oral performances like proverbs, jokes, and sayings reveal the everyday rules and rituals that a culture lives by. All cultures and subcultures have sayings, which are often not only entertaining but also didactic—they teach youngsters and newcomers the values and traditions that a culture holds true. Even though there is a traditional core (form or content), verbal art is valued in a culture because its shared oral tradition allows each person to bring creativity to each rendering of the performance.

BOX**29**

Gathering Verbal Performances: Proverbs, Jokes, and Sayings

PURPOSE

Curses, chants, jokes, proverbs, and sayings are all types of verbal art, as are toasts, roasts, poetry slams, and stand-up comedy. Insiders "perform" them for other insiders' benefit to instruct as well as affirm the features of having insider status. In this activity, you will gather examples of verbal art and reflect on them. This is a good time to supplement your knowledge—and your field data—with library or online research. The folklore section in your library holds a treasury of many forms of verbal art—collections of proverbs, jokes, and stories particular to certain cultures and subcultures. You might even want to look in the reference room for two works: Stith Thompson's *Motif-Index of Folk Literature* and Antti Aarne's *The Types of the Folk-Tale: A Classification and Bibliography*. These two valuable reference indices categorize types and themes of folk narratives and other verbal art from around the world and throughout history. Of course, you may be able to collect quite a few pieces of verbal art just by requesting it from the people around you.

ACTION

If you are working on a major project, you may want to relate this exercise to your fieldwork. If not, try it with any subculture that interests you. Begin data collection by choosing a form and a theme: a certain type of joke told about a certain kind of profession, proverbs, childhood chants, or jump-rope rhymes about a certain theme. After you've collected a few examples, categorize them in a list, and try some analysis. Here are a few questions that might help you: What are the common themes? What words reappear in different ways? What do the variations tell you about the unique features of culture from which these words came? What behaviors do they encourage or discourage? If you were an outsider to this culture, what could you learn from these pieces of verbal art?

BOX**29** continued

RESPONSE

Lori Bateman was researching a Swedish American cultural center, and she gathered this cluster of proverbs:

It is better to stumble with your feet than with your tongue.

The one who wants to lie should have a good memory.

Many know much, but nobody knows everything.

Better to ask for directions twice than get lost once.

Lori writes, "These first four proverbs all deal with verbal actions and stress honesty and caution. Sweden is a northern environment, and rural areas are sparsely populated. Attention to honesty and caution would be important survival skills in such a place." And then she adds:

Love is like the dew; it falls on weeds as well as on lilies.

One cannot make soup out of beauty.

"To me, these two proverbs tie together and deal with appearance. Beauty is acknowledged in both proverbs, but the emphasis in the first is that everyone finds a partner, and in the second, that beauty alone will not provide a person with what they need. These proverbs really hit home for me because when I was a child my father would use the English proverb 'Pretty is as pretty does' with me, along with the Swedish 'One cannot make soup out of beauty' to make me focus more on my actions and skills rather than my appearance."

Another category Lori found in her collection of verbal art (which contained prayers and song as well) was a group of proverbs that concerned eating or drinking. Here are a few of those, followed by Lori's analysis:

What fills your heart is revealed by your mouth.

Better without bread than without hope.

Let the food hush your tongue.

When it rains soup, the poor man has no spoon.

What is eaten from the pot never comes to the platter.

Drink and eat, but do not forget God, death, and the judgment.

Where wine goes in, wit goes out.

Lori speculates about this grouping: "I found a few of these proverbs on the back of a cookbook and heard the others at the Swedish cultural center. I thought it was interesting that so many images of eating could supply double meanings for spiritual nourishment and moral behavior. Maybe there are so many proverbs using food imagery because of the Swedish tradition of smorgasbords and the focus on food-centered celebrations. I'll have to ask my informants what they think about that."

Researching Urban Legends

So far in this chapter we've suggested that you collect performance events: everyday stories of a subculture and more ritualized language events (jokes, curses, proverbs) that fall into the category of **lore**. We are just as unconscious of our folklore as we are of our everyday language. The lore we pass along in our culture, like curses, stories, tales, and songs, is much more than mere superstition. Our folklore serves to control our anxieties, explain our deepest fears, and teach us how to go about living in our cultures.

A culture's myths, one form of lore, are never taken as truth, whereas legends and tales have enough truthful elements to serve as what we might consider folk history. We hear American lore without recognizing it: about dead ancestors (your uncle who almost made a fortune), about famous historical figures (George Washington couldn't tell a lie), and cultural heroes (John Henry built the railroad and Rip Van Winkle awoke to a changed world after a 20-year sleep). We retell legends without consciously recognizing the cultural belief systems they symbolize: capitalism, honesty, hard work, progress.

One class of folklore narrative is the *urban legend*, set in contemporary times, including elements that are believable to us. Like other verbal art, urban legends can also be considered cautionary tales for ways of behaving in our modern life. Like all folklore, urban legends travel from one site to another. We have found from our students that a legend told in Des Moines, Iowa, may have a variant in the outer banks of North Carolina. Wherever you grew up, you probably heard about a woman with a ribbon around her neck, a haunted family tombstone, a bloody hook, or rat meat in a fast-food hamburger.

Jan Harold Brunvand, a famous folklorist, has collected examples of urban legends, weird and macabre tales that often feel like truth. We offer you, online, an excerpt from his book *The Vanishing Hitchhiker: American Urban Legends and Their Meanings*, which describes many variants of the urban legend that folklorists call "The Roommate's Death."

> To learn more about researching urban legends and folk tales, visit **bedfordstmartins.com/ fieldworking.**

Being a Cultural Translator

Verbal lore—culturally saturated words (like *silk* for Danling Fu), occupational phrases (like waitresses who are "in the weeds"), audience-directed verbal performance events (such as sharing a joke or casting a spell), and urban legends—reveals how a group uses language and much about a culture's rituals, beliefs, fears, and history. All these language events help the fieldworker translate insider ideas about a culture for outsiders. As you saw in Chapter 5, the most accessible language event for people researching another culture is storytelling, both for what the story is (the core version and different tellers' variants) and for how and to whom the story is told (the context, the conditions, and the audience).

Professional linguists spend their lives studying the intricate differences, connections, politics, and histories of language. You might already know that there are both limitations and strengths to what each language can convey. Whether you study far away in a community that speaks a language other than your primary one or whether you volunteer, work, or study among unfamiliar words, stories, or languages in your own community, learning about language can teach you about a larger culture. Those details reveal important features of a culture.

In the following reading, "A Language Journey," Ofelia Zepeda reflects on her native Tohono O'odham language that she learned as a child. As an insider in her American Indian culture, Zepeda recognizes the poetic quality of this language, which binds speakers together through conversations, songs, prayers, and rituals. She also understands that this language could never be completely translated to outsiders: "It is a beautiful language in so many ways that often it renders itself indescribable." Language and culture are intimately linked and the Tohono O'odham tongue represents a type of wealth that means more than material goods to her family and her people. Zepeda learned English in school and became a poet who writes in English as well as a professional linguist. As you read her piece, think about the cultures you are studying and how you might translate their oral habits and traditions into written texts.

A Language Journey
Ofelia Zepeda

> I don't bother to explain my parents are illiterate in the English language.
> What I really want to tell her is they speak a language much too civil for writing.
> It is a language useful for pulling memory from the depths of the earth.
> It is useful for praying with the earth and sky.
> It is useful for singing songs that pull down the clouds.
> It is useful for calling rain.
> It is useful for speeches and incantations
> that pull sickness from the minds and bodies of believers.
> It is a language too civil for writing.
> It is too civil for writing minor things like my birth.
> This is what I really want to tell her.
> But I don't.[1]

Writing an oral language is like offering someone a drink of water and the only vessel you have is one you make by cupping your hands together. You cup your hands carefully, forcing your fingers tight together, but nonetheless too much of the water seeps in between the fingers. The seal is never good enough. A certain amount of water will spill from the source to the mouth. The thirst will never be satisfied. Or will it? Is what makes it into the cupped hand enough?

I have spent my entire career thinking about moving an oral language to printed page. Mind you, I am not concerned with the symbols we use because I understand as a linguist that any symbol evolves from some arbitrary decision. I began my career in linguistics when the evolution of writing symbols for my first language, Tohono O'odham, was already established. It was established but not yet standardized. My career has spanned the first twenty years of our tribe's movement toward the standardization of these symbols. We continue on that journey now with many jumps and starts. We have a written language that we try to make sense of in this fast-paced society, and we try to fully comprehend that it takes time, a long time, for something like a writing system to make a place in the complex world of language.[2]

The Tohono O'odham language (also known as O'odham) is spoken in southern Arizona and Northern Sonora, Mexico. There are approximately ten to fifteen thousand speakers of O'odham. The language belongs to the Uto-Aztecan family. Languages related to Tohono O'odham extend from as far north as Idaho through the Great Basin, San Diego, and deserts of southern Arizona and south into Mexico to the landscape of once great civilizations.[3] These many related languages, like all indigenous languages of the Americas, are oral and do not have great histories of being written. The languages are spoken, chanted, sung, and presented in oratory and ritualized language. They have many levels of sophistications in their oral forms. The languages are indeed sophisticated at the oral level, not only in their presentation at the word or sentence level but also at the sound level before that. There are amazing sounds still not completely described, and their description and categorization are not solidified in standard sound charts. There are sounds that cause you to push air in ways completely foreign to the English-speaking tongue. Many of these American Indian languages are characterized by having an unusual number of consonantal sounds, whereas others are impoverished but are rich with vocalics. A colleague who works on a Coast Salish language, one so rich with consonants that it boggles the mind of novices, told me that the next time we met he would bring me a gift, a big bag of consonants. I have yet to receive that bag of consonants. Instead, I continue to speak this somewhat quiet language where every utterance seems to be swallowed by the desert sand or quickly dissipated by the summer heat.

My parents, my grandparents, and all the people before them spoke this language, the Tohono O'odham language. And because they all spoke this language and only this language I also spoke this language and only this language, as did my seven siblings. This was the language of the home, it was the language of the poor, rural neighborhood I grew up in, it was the language of our traditional village in what is now Mexico. It was the language of the Tohono O'odham, the "desert people." It is a beautiful language in so many ways that often it renders itself indescribable.

Growing up, I had this language all around me. It was the only language of discourse for many generations, generations going back so far that even memory and oral tellings can't recall. Then the chain broke. My siblings and I were the first generation of our family to attend school. I often wonder what my parents must have thought about us as we each started. I wonder if they worried about what would happen to us once we learned English. Would we change in personality and temperament because of that language? Did they worry about those things? I never asked, and they never offered. Of one thing I am certain: As in all families in which children go to school for the first time, things change. And so they did. I am the first in my family to complete high school and go to college. I am only the second person from my tribe to obtain a Ph.D.

I have been given many gifts because of my education. I have been comfortable for a few years now. I recall telling a friend in jest when I turned fifty that I had been published, been on television and national radio, traveled (by my standards), and, also by my standards, attained wealth. What else is there? These material things have been part of my life for a short time now, but I am still not accustomed to such a life. I know that it can change more quickly than it took to achieve it. It can be precarious sometimes, and I try not to get too comfortable. In this life I have a home in the city of Tucson while my extended family still lives among the rural cotton fields of the town in which we were all born, Stanfield, Arizona, then and now a small, hot, dusty town with a small grocery store, post office, and elementary school surrounded by fields and fields of cotton. Cotton was our livelihood. It is still the livelihood of my brothers. The only claim to fame this place had was that the fields and fields of cotton were owned by the actor John Wayne's brother. John Wayne came to Stanfield for an annual cattle auction, but other than that it was a nondescript farming town.

My parents picked this cotton and hoed weeds in these fields while we worked or played alongside them. I grew up in and around these fields. The O'odham who lived on the reservation had a name for families like mine, *toki oidag amjed* (people of the cotton field), named for the place in which we lived and the type of work we did. Even though other O'odham from the reservation worked in the cotton fields, their stay was always temporary; they had other homes and villages to return to. My family didn't, at least not in the United States. Our home, our village, was on the other side of the Mexican border. Our family was one of several hundred that, not by choice, ended up in a "foreign country." That is why we lived in the "border" town of Stanfield and our parents and the generation after them worked in the fields.

Regardless of this status I somehow knew that even though we were poor, simple laborers we had something special. This thing I later appreciated as wealth, wealth instilled in a language and all the things a language can encompass for a people. We had knowledge that held information important to our identity as a family and as a people. This was knowledge that transformed into various ritualized performances, performances that had been practiced for many generations. I didn't really know this as a child, but I grew up being slowly provided information about it on into adulthood.

While the adults carried out the day-to-day labors of the field they seemed to remain busy mentally. They practiced the mental exercises of filtering their memories of songs, ritual oratory, the images of ceremonial grounds, through their minds. They would run these memories back and forth and back and forth again, much like playing and rewinding a tape of what they knew. They did this so that they would not be the ones to forget first. They nodded their heads to the quiet beat and rhythm of songs they must remember but never sang in such settings as a cotton field. They held that part of the language close, watching each other across the rows of cotton. Catching one another's eye, they would give a brief smile because they knew what was running through the other's mind or being quietly vocalized in each throat. They knew, especially the men, that they would be called on to sing or pray in the one language that was theirs and given to them for this purpose.

How do I know that this is what was going on in their minds while they worked? How do I know that songs were being quietly sung while they did their backbreaking work? I know because at the end of the day, when we sat at our evening meal or sat outside under the stars to begin our rest for the evening, they would talk. They talked and talked into the night, they lay awake unbothered by the long day's labor they had put in. They talked about what was running through their minds while they worked. My uncle would sometimes sing the song he had been quietly vocalizing. He sang it for all of us in our family circle under the stars. They explained things to one another, clarifying for each other, supporting each other's remembrances of certain practices and rituals. This was their talk that would take them far into the night and then finally to sleep. This is what I listened to in the darkness. As a listener, I was only a distant participant; I heard everything but didn't understand everything. I lacked their experience, their knowledge of the ritual life they had been living since adulthood. My time would come. I listened and fell asleep to the rhythm of their comforting voices, their quiet, familiar laughter.

With the morning star on the horizon and the sun not yet even a dim light I would be urged to wake. In the still, darkened morning as I prepared to wake I would hear them talking, talking, talking in the echo of the last of the darkness. They would still be on the same subject that they were when I fell asleep— repeating things over and over.

"My sister, isn't this the way that our father would say it, or was it this way?"

"Yes, you had it right the first time. You have a good memory. You sound just like him."

This talk in the language that happened all around me as a child stayed with me as a young person. It stayed with me even after I learned the English language, which happened when I was around eight. I learned English only after I was put in school, but in that era English was only used in school because no one at home had any use for it. I left English on the school bus that dropped me off by the road and walked home with brothers, sisters, and cousins, all of us shifting comfortably back into our first language. The walk just a few yards to the house transformed us by the time we reached the front door. The ability to transform enabled me to remain a participant of all the things my language had to offer me while growing up. This ability, I later realized, was key to the way that I saw language and the things I chose to write about.

My parents never talked to me about school, and I never said much about it. They knew I had to attend every day, and so they made sure of that. Only in the evening my mother would ask, "Napt hab ju: g eo'ohana?" (Did you do your writing?), meaning, Did you do your homework? Only then would I revert to some degree of using English, mostly some quiet reading and maybe some writing, usually spelling and math problems.

"Napt hab ju: g e-o'ohana?" That question seemed to be a primary connection for my mother with schooling, with the English language, and writing. And, ironically, I did start writing. I started writing poetry when I was an adult, but my earlier work had a fairly practical purpose. It is usually the case that few language materials are available for classes in American Indian languages, so such classes are created along with the material for them. I assigned one of my classes to write poetry in O'odham, and was delighted to see the beautiful forms put down on paper by O'odham students who were also singers and storytellers. We played with the language orally and in print.

From these singers and others like them I learned about the patterns, the repetition, that are part of O'odham song form. More important, I became even more aware of the language and metaphor that is an important level of O'odham songs. I also came to a new appreciation of all the various themes that songs employ. I love listening to a good singer and have concluded that I am not a singer, so I participate in a poor replacement, reading and writing poetry written in O'odham.

I consider myself fortunate in being literate in the O'odham language. In this situation, with such a "new literacy" available to me, I want to promote the aesthetics of the language when I can. I became literate in O'odham after I came to the University of Arizona. When I first arrived, in fact, I tested for language proficiency as a speaker of a language other than English. My tester was a white anthropologist. I was tested for oral proficiency only. I passed. My desire to become literate was purely personal. I wanted to have full access to two books that had been written in O'odham by missionary linguists. I again was taught by a white anthropologist to read and write my language, and my journey with it was under way.

"S-wa'usim i:bhei" (breathing with wetness), "ñ-bijimida g wipismel ñe'e" (I am surrounded by hummingbird songs), and "s-cukma, sikolim him" (blackening, moving, encircling), all of these phrases, fragments, of O'odham songs concern rain in the desert. "Breathing with wetness" is part of a beautiful rain song about the mourning dove, the first animal to taste the ripened saguaro fruit in early summer. The beautiful phrase encompasses all the elements of summer, rain, and renewal for the O'odham. Likewise, "blackening, moving, encircling" metaphorically illustrates the movements of black buzzards in the still, hot summer air. They circle slowly in the distance and then descend. This speaks of the observed behavior of dark thunderclouds in their preparation for rain. There are many more of these songs, there are entire cycles that must be sung in the summer darkness of July and August in order to pull down the clouds or make it rain. The O'odham language is suited for this type of song language. I have tried to pay attention to it all my life. I pull on the words I have heard. I pull on the memories of how people close to me have used these words, and I have made them my own.[4]

I have moved many O'odham words into print, but the printed form cannot replace the soft, laughing talk that I listened to in the darkness of our family circle. It cannot replace the comforting voices that began my days on those so early mornings, moving me from sleep to wakefulness. It cannot replace growing up with a generation of adults who deliberately forced themselves to remember things they saw maybe only once a year, when no one sat next to them to explain things. They observed and began a life of remembering. They used the language in spoken form or in song form, whatever it took to help them remember. They took it as a responsibility, the responsibility of remembering. I was fortunate to have been around them. Being around them taught me many things about language. Some of the things I learned from them appear at the beginning of this essay in a poem that tells of part of my life. The excerpt is specific to the way I have come to understand my language and its role in the humanity of the O'odham people and perhaps the world. It is a language used for doing many important things, some of which I list, and it is "too civil for writing . . . for writing minor things."[5]

Birth Witness
My mother gave birth to me
in an old wooden row house
in the cotton fields.
She remembers it was windy.
Around one in the afternoon.
The tin roof rattled, a piece uplifted
from the wooden frame, quivered and flapped
as she gave birth.
She knew it was March.
A windy afternoon in the cotton fields of Arizona.

She also used to say I was baptized standing up.
"It doesn't count," the woman behind the glass window tells me,
"if you were not baptized the same year you were born
the baptismal certificate cannot be used to verify your birth."

"You need affidavits," she said.
"Your older siblings, you have some don't you?
They have to be old enough to have a memory
of your birth.
Can they vouch for you?"
Who was there to witness my birth?
Who was there with my mother?

Was it my big sister?
Would my mother have let a teenager watch her giving birth?
Was it my father?
I can imagine my father assisting her with her babies.
My aunts?
Who was there when I breathed my first breath?
Took in those dry particles from the cotton fields.
Who knew then that I would need witnesses of my birth?
The stars were there in the sky.
The wind was there.
The sun was there.
The pollen of spring was floating and sensed me being born.
They are silent witnesses.
They do not know of affidavits, they simply know.
"You need records," she said.
"Are there doctor's receipts from when you were a baby?
Didn't your parents have a family Bible, you know,
where births were recorded?
Were there letters?
Announcements of your birth?"

I don't bother to explain my parents are illiterate in the English language.
What I really want to tell her is they speak a language much too civil for
    writing.
It is a language useful for pulling memory from the depths of the earth.
It is useful for praying with the earth and sky.
It is useful for singing songs that pull down the clouds.
It is useful for calling rain.
It is useful for speeches and incantations
that pull sickness from the minds and bodies of believers.
It is a language too civil for writing.
It is too civil for writing minor things like my birth.
This is what I really want to tell her.
But I don't.
Instead I take the forms she hands me.
I begin to account for myself.

Notes

1. This excerpt, from a poem in the collection *Where Clouds Are Formed* (Tucson: University of Arizona Press, 2008), is included in its entirety at the end of this essay.
2. Ofelia Zepeda, *A Tohono O'odham Grammar* (Tucson: University of Arizona Press, 1983).
3. Marianne Mithune, *The Languages of Native North America* (New York: Cambridge University Press, 1999).

4. Ofelia Zepeda, *Ocean Power: Poems from the Desert* (Tucson: University of Arizona Press, 1995).
5. Zepeda, "Where Clouds Are Formed."

Zepeda writes poetry in English in an attempt to capture the comforting sounds, images, feelings, and relationships of her people. In her poem at the end of the essay, "Birth Witness," Zepeda shares how her mother remembers and tells of the silent witnesses to her daughter's birth: the sound of the wind, the smell of spring, and the open sky. While we may not record our informants' words in poetry or ethnopoetic notation, we need to pay attention to the particular rhythms, images, and sounds of our informants' language and describe it for our readers. As we write about our informants' conversations and stories, we need to also record the context surrounding these language events. Context can be as important as the actual words themselves.

FieldWriting: Dialogue on the Page

In the fieldwriting section in Chapter 3, we reviewed how to cite your published and unpublished written data sources accurately for your reader. But we recognize that in doing fieldwork, the researcher has a special responsibility to use informants' words as carefully as any written source material. Fieldwriters choose the most appropriate way to represent oral language on the written page when they capture informants' voices—in recordings, in fieldnotes, and in transcripts and texts.

As fieldwriters, we need to create texts that embrace our informants' diverse voices and also include our own. When we research verbal art, our data are words—the language of our informants. Rather than overwriting or erasing our informants' language, we use their voices to help us tell the fieldwork story.

We must make choices about how best to represent language on the page. Fieldworkers *cannot legitimately make up informants' words,* any more than scholars can legitimately plagiarize someone else's texts. It is critical to represent people's words with accuracy, for their integrity and for our own.

You might choose to present informants' language on the page in one of the following ways:

1. Borrowing techniques from fiction. Our colleague Donna Qualley studied the way waitresses at a Norton's Seafood restaurant talked and worked. She presents the following conversations between waitresses Rae and Erin in the form of fictional conversation. Note the standard conventions for writing conversation in dialogue: indenting each time the speaker shifts, framing each sentence with quotation marks, and using strong verbs like *interjects*, *mumbles*, *begins*, and *laughs* to indicate response.

> "I had this young couple."
>
> "How old?" Erin interjects.
>
> "In their twenties, I would guess. They order two fish and chips and two glasses of water."
>
> "Cheap. I'm surprised they didn't ask to split one meal," Erin mumbles.
>
> "When they are done I put the check on the table and tell them I will be right back to collect it for them. I go into the kitchen and when I come back, there is a ten-dollar bill, a dime, a nickel, and a penny on the table."
>
> "How much is the bill?" I ask.
>
> "Ten fifteen."
>
> "That makes me so mad...," Erin begins.
>
> "But," Rae smiles, "the woman had left her coat on the chair. They were in such a hurry to get out she forgot her coat! I grab the coat, check, and money, and then I see her coming back for her coat...."
>
> "I hope you kept it until they left you a better tip," I laugh.
>
> "I said to this woman, 'Oh, did you come back for your change?'"
>
> "You really said that? How much was the bill again?" Erin asks.
>
> "Ten fifteen, and they left me ten sixteen. Well, this woman turns all red and apologetic and says, 'We didn't have any money—we thought this was a take-out place.' Yeah, right. They knew what they were doing."

2. Quoting within a transcript.   In the following example from Greta Paule's *Dishing It Out: Power and Resistance among Waitresses in a New Jersey Restaurant*, the researcher records a waitress who quotes her friend Kaddie when telling a "stiffing" story in which both waitresses participated:

> This party of two guys comes in and they order thirty to forty dollars' worth of food . . . and they stiff us. Every time. So Kaddie told them, "If you don't tip us, we're not going to wait on you." They said, "We'll tip you." So Kaddie waited on them, and they tipped her. The next night they came in, I waited on them and they didn't tip me. The third time they came in [the manager] put them in my station and I told [the manager] straight up, "I'm not waiting on them." So when they came in the next night . . . [they] said, "Are you going to give us a table?" I said, "You going to tip me? I'm not going to wait on you." (31)

3. Summarizing dialogue.   Sometimes, for variety and conciseness, a fieldwriter summarizes dialogue rather than using direct quotes. Because journalist Barbara Ehrenreich worked undercover, she did not record her conversations. In the following excerpt from her book, she combines summary and direct quotation:

I get pushy with Rosalie, who is new like me and fresh from high school in a rural northern part of the state, about the meagerness of her lunches, which consist solely of Doritos—a half bag from the day before or a freshly purchased small-sized bag. She just didn't have anything in the house, she says (though she lives with her boyfriend and his mother), and she certainly doesn't have any money to buy lunch, as I find out when I offer to fetch her a soda from Quik Mart and she has to admit that she doesn't have eighty-nine cents. I treat her to the soda, wishing I could force her, mommylike, to take milk instead. So how does she hold up for an eight- or even nine-hour day? "Well," she conceded, "I get dizzy sometimes."

When you work with the spoken words of an informant, your goal is to preserve the integrity of the informant's original verbal art and respect it. As with any art form, how you choose to display your informants' language for the reader must be a conscious and carefully considered choice.

THE RESEARCH PORTFOLIO:
Synthesis

As you've worked your way through the exercises in this chapter, you've researched, read, and written a lot. Whether you chose to focus on your main fieldworking project or have done each exercise separately, you've probably piled up a lot of writing—transcripts, lists, short analyses, and written examples of verbal art.

One of the jobs of a research portfolio is to help you synthesize what you have collected and selected. It offers you an opportunity to reflect on what you've learned and on how your research writing fits into the larger picture of your research. It suggests how all this material will help you shape your future goals—both for the project and for yourself as a reader, writer, and researcher.

And if you've tried one or more of the exercises, you have linked your own research project to extended writing about language in a cultural site. You may have

- Classified insider language by exploring the word,
- Clustered, categorized, and analyzed language used in occupational groups,
- Gathered and interpreted a range of verbal art (proverbs, jokes, sayings, chants, and curses), and
- Collected, written, and shared stories.

At this point, for your portfolio, we suggest three ways to synthesize your studies of language and language use: focusing on personal history, on use of language, and on verbal art. You will want to write reflections and share them with your portfolio partner, and you will want to synthesize what all of these exercises, coupled with the readings, have taught you so far.

Personal History

What is your own personal history with verbal art?   In this chapter, we have offered several personal accounts of verbal art, but we have not invited you to think about your own. Here is an opportunity to synthesize with a personal reflection, applying what you've learned about verbal art by looking back at your own history. You may want to focus on one of these questions, or you may instead want to write a traditional story from your own cultural background to put in your portfolio:

- What proverbs or sayings governed your growing-up life?
- What special family language "events" happened in your home? At family celebrations? In the subculture of your workplace, your school, your church, or another subculture to which you belong?
- What kinds of stories were important in your background? Who were the important storytellers? How many different audiences have you been a member of? What has been your own role as a storyteller?

Use of Language

What have you learned about language and language use?   The many forms of verbal art that you have studied and collected offer you an array of ways to look at language use and storytelling. Write a reflective analysis of yourself at this point as a language researcher:

- As you survey all the data, what themes do you see about your process as a researcher? Which themes do you seem particularly interested in? Which themes do you seem to discard?
- How did your expectations match the data you actually assembled? What kinds of assumptions did you make before you began your research on language? What surprised you?
- What language behavior do you want to know more about? How would you go about obtaining more data?
- What have you learned about language and language use that will be important to you as a reader, a writer, and a researcher?

Verbal Art

What do you now know about verbal art for your research project?   If you related all your exercises to your fieldsite, you have done important work toward your final project. As you reread all the data you've collected, which of the exercises will be most useful for describing the language practices of the subculture you are researching? Using these guidelines, write a reflective response about yourself as a language researcher at this cultural site:

- What words, phrases, or insider languages have given you insights into the culture you are studying? How do you serve as a "cultural translator" with your informants?

- What has surprised you most about the language use of the people at your site? What verbal behaviors would you like to know more about? How would you go about getting that data?

- What forms of verbal art (proverbs, jokes, curses, chants, stories, urban legends) have you looked for and found at your site?

- How have your informants reacted to your interest in their use of language? What were they eager to share? What made them nervous? What have you learned from them about researching language?

- What have you learned about yourself as a researcher of language? What are you good at? What kinds of skills do you need to practice?

Most of us learn specifics about culture from participating in activities such as listening to folk songs, watching traditional performances, and recognizing the colors and patterns woven in a culture's textiles. We learn about subcultures and fusions of cultures by focusing our lenses on contemporary daily events, such as a Muslim comedy night in a student union, the media's portrayal of an unusual moment in an American baseball game, and a state fair's butter-sculpture competition. These opportunities are easier to notice and to "translate" than language.

In this chapter, we've considered language as a reflection of culture: proverbs, legends, chants, stories, and even single words reflect the people and places from which they come. When we become fieldworkers and act as cultural translators, we learn to notice the importance of language—in our own and others' cultures and subcultures.

It's curious that we might miss how a culture uses language but would notice its sports or traditional performances. To give language its due, a fieldworker listens, notices, records, and translates linguistic elements. We bring our informants' language to life the way we'd use a snapshot, a CD, or a video. And we must look critically at our choices of translating and writing—including proverbs, traditional stories, single words, specialized glossaries, straight prose interviews, and ethnopoetics. Using someone else's language and another culture's verbal art forms requires respect and an understanding of the many choices we have as cultural translators.

Translate Culture

By now you may feel like a partial insider at your fieldsite. In what ways do you understand its language forms? What do you wish you knew? In what ways will you always be a nonnative speaker?

FIRST   Make a list of the words, phrases, or other verbal art forms that you've heard that might be impenetrable to outsiders. Share this list with two partners—an insider and an outsider. How does each partner describe or identify the meaning behind the terms you've listed?

SECOND   As you review your transcripts and fieldnotes, list words, language fragments, signs, jokes, stories, and other verbal art forms that seem important to you from your informants' point of view. How have you designed your informants' language on the page—as dialogue, drama, or ethnopoetics?

THIRD   Rearrange the words in your list to represent the nuances of language and conversation that you have gathered as data. Let the language speak to you. What stands out for you? What do you need to learn more about? How will your informants react to the way you've recorded their language? In what ways can you serve as a cultural translator?

7

Researching Archives: Locating Culture

Archives offer materials to support your study. In this chapter you will:

- recognize different types of archives and how to use them
- locate potential archives for your project
- understand the Internet as an archive
- consider alternative archives
- organize archived data for your study

As folklorist Robert Cantwell suggests below, culture is elusive—hard to capture and even harder to retain. One way people capture culture is by assembling **archives**—collections of documents and artifacts. An archive can be a shoe box full of mementos from your volleyball career, a room in your town hall showing maps and photographs tracing the town's historical development, or a county's agricultural museum. Simply, an archive contains important "stuff" so that family, ethnic, local, or national cultures and subcultures don't—to paraphrase Cantwell's words—pass secretly, silently, or untended.

An example of one of the largest archives in the United States, the Smithsonian Institution in Washington, DC, describes itself as "the nation's attic." In this attic, as in any archive, you will find stored a dazzling and surprising variety of artifacts, records, correspondence, historical documents, and audiovisual media. The Smithsonian has 10 separate archives, which hold an estimated 50,000 cubic feet of paper documents, 7 million still photographs, and thousands of motion picture films, videos, and audio recordings. He also includes such artifacts as:

> Culture is elusive. It passes secretly, often silently, telepathically . . . ; it ripens, untended, often unconsciously in dreams, suddenly unexpectedly to reveal itself in an expression or a turn of phrase . . . or, at another level, in our musical and pictorial preferences, in the narratives we construct about ourselves and others or to which we turn for understanding. It may arise by accident, from a half-remembered memory, from fingers or hands idling with instruments and tools.
>
> —ROBERT CANTWELL

- The ruby slippers Judy Garland wore in *The Wizard of Oz*
- The Woolworth's lunch counter stools from one early civil rights sit-in
- The first typewriter, from 1870, which weighs 165 pounds
- A 1918 Oldsmobile Model 37

The Internet also allows us access to a treasure trove of public and private archives—photographs, maps, documents, works of art, manuscript collections, corporate archives, church records, and historical society records. These online collections are international and growing constantly. Immediate public access to such information is new in human history and a significant development in research and fieldwork. You can find a museum that specializes in almost any collection of artifacts or archives you can imagine, such as the Google Art Project, where you can see in detail some of the world's greatest art and artifacts, or the Museum of Online Museums, which you can only visit online.

Some of the students you've met in this book have used online archives and museums—from public ones such as the Louvre and the Aerospace Museum to the more specialized resources of the Disability History Museum, the Hair and Beauty Museum, and the Virtual Tattoo Museum. There are lots of other specialized museums and archives, both virtual and actual; there's probably one in your hometown. Here are a few others that we have enjoyed: the Mustard Museum in Mt. Horeb, WI; the Roseville Pottery Museum in Zanesville, OH; the Creationist Museum in Petersburg, KY; the National Cowboy and Western Heritage Museum in Oklahoma City, OK; and the Museum of Puppetry in Storrs, CT.

Representative Artifacts

All cultures and subcultures collect representative artifacts to hand down to group members. To an outsider, those collections may appear to be mere clutter; to an insider, they are the concrete objects of tradition—symbols of the rituals, behaviors, language, and beliefs that teach a culture about itself as it shifts and changes with time. Even when a cultural group is oppressed or exiled from its place of origin, human ingenuity prevails, finding ways to preserve old traditions and apply them in new settings.

Hmong embroidery, for example, stitches the story of the Hmongs' life for 2,000 years in Laos, Thailand, and China, and later in refugee camps as they prepared for relocation in cultures very different from theirs. Since they had no written language, the Hmong developed the concept of the "storycloth" (*pa ndau*) to retain and pass on their history. They used the ancestral traditions of embroidery to record the stories of their past, share their current situation, and anticipate their future lives (see the facing page).

In this chapter, we explore a wide range of archival materials—the stuff of collections—from private family diaries, journals, letters, and scrapbooks to the bigger institutional archives like museum holdings and the very public

Hmong storycloth

archive, the Internet. All archival work, including traditional library research, strengthens fieldwork through triangulation—ways to validate, check, confirm, or disconfirm data. And, of course, accumulating and analyzing multiple data sources can make fieldstudies more persuasive.

To review triangulation, go to the "Reading Electronic Communities" section in Chapter 3, page 141.

While digging around in dusty archives might not seem appealing at first, you will be surprised at how excited you become to see original documents, or touch other pieces of material culture connected to your topic. In the following piece, A. Kendra Greene, once a manager of a museum photo collection and now a graduate student in nonfiction writing, flew across the country at the invitation of an audio-visual archivist at the Ronald Reagan library. Once there, Kendra and her brother shared an unexpected adventure as they searched the photo archives for unpublished pictures of the former president posing with famous people.

Everything, Perfectly, Forever

A. Kendra Greene

Mr. T is the reason I started sending Christmas cards. Well, Mr. T with the help of Nancy Reagan. And, true, it wasn't Mr. T the man himself so much as his appearance with the first lady in one particular photograph. But the point is: that was enough. I saw something in an archive and it changed me.

Everyone walking the archives, those white-washed basement levels of the Ronald Reagan Presidential Library and Museum, is either an employee or a guest escorted by an employee. It is the kind of vast and silent place where you could go half an hour without bumping into anyone at all. The archives themselves are a series of cloisters: papers slipped in mylar sleeves, sleeves packed in boxes, boxes stacked on shelves, with only a tattoo of neatly written alpha-numeric code on the box or the shelf to interrupt a uniform anonymity. I needed a barcode before I could enter the archives, a paper sticker I pressed high on my shirt like a nametag. My brother wore his similarly and we both, once the elevator doors opened, stayed close on the heels of one Ray Wilson, a tall, late-30s man who wore his barcode on the back of a staff ID.

I'd met Ray Wilson shortly after I was hired to manage an art museum collection of 8,000 photographs. Ray was an audio-visual archivist more concerned with historical film and negatives, but our respective employers both thought we'd benefit from a week at the Eastman House in Rochester, New York, so there we were at the Image Permanence Institute taking notes about silvering and foxing and what little could be done about either. Ray Wilson had perhaps been kidding when he suggested from the remote distance of professional courtesy and three thousand miles from home that I should, at some unspecified date, if I was ever in California, come by the archives. But I liked to think he wasn't, and he was in every way cordial when I called six months later to announce my visit.

"Great," Ray said. "So what do you want to see?"

I had only one request. "I want to see the picture you can't talk about."

Archives are different from museum collections. Collections follow a model of making some few select things accessible to a wide audience, while archives are essentially the reverse: a mass of information protected so that an individual researcher might wade about and uncover something of interest. Sure, they both exist for study and enlightenment, but they operate on inverse theories of how to get there.

Archivists, the joke goes, want to preserve everything, perfectly, forever— even if maintaining that level of preservation means none of it will ever be seen again. When I first met Ray Wilson, he was talking to a grey-haired conservator about the gems hidden in their respective collections. I remember they were laughing. I don't know what Ray told her about the photograph he will never discuss, but I will tell you what Ray told me then when I asked: the picture is of a president. It was taken at the White House. Beyond that, Ray mostly told me what the picture isn't. The picture is not, for instance, one of the 8 × 10 reproduction glossies on file by year or subject in the library archives. It was never published. It does not circulate. It has never been requested—and Ray, who had no particular loyalties to the ex-president before he started working at the archive, intends to keep it that way.

When I landed at LAX, my brother was waiting. Gavin was born two months before Carter won in '76, three and a half years before the spring Reagan swept the primaries and I was born. It's because of Gavin I grew up watching *He-Man* and *The A-Team* and reading *Mad Magazine*—and it is surely, somehow, because of those credentials that I invited him to go see a picture that could not be discussed. I tossed my suitcase and my winter coat in the back seat of his car and climbed in front.

"You know," he said as I got in, "I don't really remember much about the Reagan administration."

"Me neither," I said.

"And, frankly, I don't really like libraries."

"That's okay," I nodded. "I think this is going to be different."

The entrance of the Ronald Reagan Library offers two paths. The left doorway enters a sunny gift shop with presidential magnets and presidential coloring books and presidential everything in tiers and racks and gleaming rows. The right doorway is darkened, goes into the museum, and between the two, completely hidden, is the elevator that goes down to the archives.

"Ray said to give you these," the receptionist said when we announced ourselves. We looked down at a pair of museum tickets, looked back up confused. "Have a look around the museum," she instructed us, "and when you're done, I'll call him up from the archives." I assumed it was an act of good hosting, a you've-come-all-this-way bonus, but it felt like a hedge. Maybe Ray didn't think there was enough in the archives to sustain our interest. Maybe he thought some background would do us good. Either way, we did what he said.

We couldn't have been less reverent. "That chair!" I would mock exclaim as we walked through the exhibitions, pulling Gavin's arm, "He sat in *that* chair!" Then, around the next turn, "That pen!" I would squeal, feigning delight. "He signed something with that *pen*!" We went on that way through Air Force One and Christmas Trees of the World and everything else until the circuit brought us back to the lobby, where Ray was waiting, just as he'd promised. He asked if we wanted a drink of water or a bite to eat, and then escorted us to the staff elevator. We tried to be equally polite as he showed us through the stacks and the shelves of the archives.

Not every president gets a library—just the 13 from Herbert Hoover to George W. Bush. It's as if you need a critical mass of papers to get a library, and each administration produces, and proceeds to preserve, more than the last. The Reagan Library, for its part, holds 50 million pages of presidential documents, half a million feet of motion picture film, and tens of thousands of audio and video tapes. Among its 1.6 million photographs are the celebrity and VIP pictures, which take up exactly two tan, four-drawer filing cabinets of manila file folders. Ray stopped our tour there.

"Who do you want to see?" he asked after explaining the contents of the cabinets.

Gavin and I tried to think of famous people from the '80s. All we could come up with was Mikhail Gorbachev, Pee Wee Herman, and Alf.

"Okay," Ray said. "I'll flip through the files, and you tell me when you want to see something." We figured we could do that. "1981 Miss Universe Shawn Weatherly?" Ray said. "Muhammad Ali? Lucille Ball? William F. Buckley?" He read through Walter Cronkite and Wayne Gretzky and Luciano Pavarotti, but we weren't ready to commit. "Frank Sinatra?" he asked with a wink. The wink meant nothing to me or to Gavin, and after a pause Ray went on. "Jimmy Stewart. Mr. T. . . ."

It seemed impossible that Ray had just said *Mr. T*—said it as if there was nothing more natural to come across in the Reagan archives, as if Mr. T had been the vice president or the chief of state. Ray was calling out Mother Teresa and Margaret Thatcher by the time we collected ourselves enough to say, louder than we intended, "Stop!"

"John Travolta?" Ray asked, his finger poised on the folder tab.

"No," we said in unison. "Mr. T!"

There was only one picture in the Mr. T folder, a glossy 8 × 10 with a white border. Mr. T was wearing a Santa suit with the arms ripped off. Nancy Reagan sat

Nancy Reagan with Mr. T

on his knee, her pointy-toed flats dangling above his duct-taped combat boots. There was a Christmas tree behind them, the old-fashioned kind with hundreds of thin white candles at the tips of its boughs, and Nancy Reagan rather absently held at her side what I can only assume she had been hoping Santa T would deliver to a good girl like herself: a two-foot-tall Mr. T doll, grimacing from behind the cellophane cut-out of a cardboard box emblazoned with the A-Team logo and images of its soldier of fortune characters firing automatic weapons. The First Lady and Mr. T both seemed distracted, unprepared for the camera, yet there were Nancy Reagan's lips frozen against Mr. T's forehead in a permanent, passionless peck.

It was stunning. It had overtones of tradition and rebellion and violence and tenderness and abstinence and indulgence and entertainment and grace. It was the lion lying down with the lamb. It was *I pity the fool* and *Just Say No.* It was two members of the Screen Actors' Guild who perhaps had more in common than I'd thought. I turned to my brother, both of us wide-eyed, our open mouths starting to pull into smiles. He hugged me and I hugged back. The picture wasn't just funny and odd and surprising—it was miraculous and ironic and sublime in a way that spoke, if not directly to the season, then at least to everyone in my address book. It was perfect. And we found it whole rooms and firewalls and more rooms away from the picture I had come to see.

The picture I went there for, the picture Ray Wilson will never discuss, is in fact three pictures, proofs on a contact sheet taken in quick succession. Ray showed them to us on the condition that we not reveal their specifics. After we saw them, Gavin and I were escorted out. I should say there is nothing scandalous about these pictures. They are, in fact, endearing. That there even *is* a code of silence— that the sheer mass of a million photographs is not cover enough—is far more interesting than what little the hush conceals. Ray imagines that before the pictures were taken, the president of the United States said to his staff photographer, "Be prepared when I come in that door. I am only going to do this once." I imagine Ray is right. And I imagine what else has been seen only once.

Family Archives

Digging through any archive can be as overwhelming as entering a fieldsite for the first time. Even if it's a small private archive like your grandmother's attic, you have no idea at first how to sort through and make use of it in any systematic way. The way to organize someone else's clutter does not announce itself to you; that process is the job of the fieldworker.

Tradition-bearing archives are part of almost every family's legacy. There is great joy and pleasure in knowing that you have an artifact or an archive of stuff from someone in your own family. Boxes of old photographs, bundles of letters, diaries, journals, daybooks, family Bibles with genealogies and notes, jumbles of mementos, and business ledgers can all open up a family's connection with the cultures that define it.

Meg Buzzi's Family Archive: The Letters of "Rad-Rad"

Our student Meg Buzzi grew up in a large Italian American family in Pittsburgh, Pennsylvania. Meg's grandfather, Raymond Barone, known to his family as "Rad-Rad," left a valuable legacy to his family. Feeling both proud and abandoned when his children left home for college, he began writing family letters as a way of keeping them together. For Raymond, the extended family was his most important community and his way of maintaining the traditions he wanted to pass on. His handwritten letters on yellow legal paper cover a nearly 30-year period. Each letter, about nine to 12 pages long, begins with the salutation "Dear Kiddies," and is addressed to the collective audience of children and grandchildren. Because these letters were an entertaining, literary accounting of family activities, they were often read aloud at family parties and holidays. After Raymond's death, Meg's mother and aunts typed the letters and placed them in two large binders of 500 pages each.

Meg saw these letters as a family archive and used them in a fieldstudy incorporating family research, interviews, history, and her own reflective commentary. The letters were so full of history, politics, and family details that she felt she could spend a lifetime, rather than just a semester, on her study. In the back of her mind, Meg knew that she was searching for a theme or a focus within this mass of paper. When she began telephone and in-person interviews with her relatives—Aunt Monica, her mother, brother, and cousins—she noticed that they each recalled hilarious events that featured Rad-Rad's outrageous humor. She looked back through her own personal journals to connect dates with facts in the letters and found that she too had recorded funny family stories. Then she e-mailed her brother Nathan and her cousins Ben and Bryan, asking them to add their own memories and confirm the details of the letters. As a researcher, Meg knew enough not to take personal letters on their face value alone. Any stories written down privately need confirmation from a broader, more public range of evidence. To get a feel for the times her grandfather wrote about, she familiarized herself with a 30-year period in politics and popular culture by looking at newspapers, magazines, and books. So in addition to the collection of Raymond's personal letters, Meg triangulated these other data sources and in the process discovered the theme of family humor.

In this excerpt called "The Fridge," from her larger study called "Dear Kiddies," Meg incorporates and analyzes three letters. Notice that she draws on the following data sources—her grandfather's 1979 letter about the vegetable drawer and a family photograph of vegetables that she now owns.

The Fridge

When our freezer section is opened, something invariably falls to the floor. . . . Of late things don't just fall straight down; they kind of leap out about 3–4 feet. Actually, the most interesting thing about our "fridge" is the various textures which can be achieved in its various sections. From your crisper sections comes your "no-noise" carrots. . . . It works for celery and radishes too. One week in the CRISPER takes all the noise out. On the other hand, the bottom shelf will put snap, crackle, and pop in cooked spaghetti, put the snap back into cooked green beans and even make stewed prunes crunchy. . . . I believe that "fridges" should be seen and not heard. (1/26/79)

After this excerpt from one of her grandfather's letters, Meg writes:

There is a story about a photograph my grandfather took. It is a picture of rotting vegetables: carrots, onions, tomatoes, and peppers in varying degrees of decay, all carefully arranged on my grandmother's heirloom serving platter. Entitled "Still Life?" this 40″ × 28″ masterpiece hung in his dining room as a constant reminder to my grandmother that her produce-preservation skills were less than acceptable. Currently it graces my dining room wall in a black and gold Baroque-style frame with cream-colored matting. Previous to that, it was I who dared to remove it from the basement bowels it had been condemned to by my grandmother. His aim to satirize her treatment of the vegetable drawer had never been well received.

Meg could not have accomplished her study of her grandfather's humor without the collection of letters that her mother and aunts kept. The boxes you

Still Life?

discover in your own family archives can come in all shapes and sizes—a relative's diary, a scrapbook of pictures and newspaper clippings, a box or drawer full of random-looking odd items.

It is both puzzling and thrilling to find family letters, journals, and artifacts that explain—or complicate—hunches you've always had about traits you've inherited, stories you've overheard, or histories your family has witnessed. Finding personal archives can lead you into further research to confirm and expand the data. Writer Edward Ball used his extended family's personal archives as a starting point for his institutional research. Through deeds, documents, and ledgers he found at the South Carolina Historical Society, Ball continued constructing the story of his family. In his book *Slaves in the Family*, Ball rhapsodizes on the emotions he experiences as he works with old documents:

> Old papers are beautiful things. Coarse, mottled parchment containing business records sometimes has the look of white skin. The pages are veiny, with age spots, the black ink coursing down them like hair. In some places, the ink is as dark as the day it was unbottled, and the paper as blotchy as an English cheek. I read through the Ball papers, beginning with the story of the first Elias Ball, who died in 1751, at 75; his will filled four pages with script. The paper was pierced here and there by holes, signatures of bookworms. A rip had been mended on the second page, and there in the splotch of a dried glue stain, a thumb print appeared.

Ball did research on his own family based on documents that were housed in institutions open to the public. In his book, he hunts down the history of his family, which includes plantation owners in South Carolina and the slaves with whom they had children. While Ball is primarily focused on finding documents about his own family's history, his research also uncovers a whole culture of interracial marriages in the South. In the following excerpt from this nonfiction bestseller, Ball traces his genealogy to a "mixed-blood" namesake born in 1740. Notice how, as archivist, he adopts the stance of a detective toward the records he examines to make this discovery. As you read this short selection from *Slaves in the Family*, try making a mental or a written list of all the types of documents you think Ball needed to consider in his genealogical detective work.

· ·

Slaves in the Family

Edward Ball

In the early 1730s, a young black woman named Dolly came to work in the Comingtee big house. Elias's second wife had three children at the time, and Dolly probably helped with the young ones, cleaned house, and cooked. A little homage to Dolly appears in the published Ball memoir. "Perhaps the name that stands out above the others is 'Dolly,'" wrote one of the Ball women at the beginning of the twentieth century. "We know little about her, but enough to show that she was well thought of in the family. Perhaps she had 'minded' the children, and been a faithful nurse in illness. The ministrations of such humble friends of the family—they were surely no less—have soothed many a bed of suffering; and in death their hands have tenderly performed the last offices."

It seems strange that the name of a slave would evoke sentimental memories in the family of her owners some 150 years after her death. Just as strange is the aside "We know little about her," which seems to contradict the familiarity of the memory.

Dolly was born in 1712, though I cannot say where and I can only fix the year of her birth from a note about her death that states her age. Dolly was evidently more than a good housekeeper. In his will, dictated in 1750, Elias devoted considerable thought to Dolly, whom he called his "Molattoe Wench." As used then, the word "mulatto" described children of black mothers and white fathers. (In Elias's day, the children of one Native and one black parent were called "mustees" by whites.) Since the colonial legislature had already passed a law forbidding sex between white women and enslaved blacks, the white mother of a daughter of color would have been subject to prosecution. Therefore, in all likelihood, Dolly's father was white, her mother black.

It is undeniable that white men on the plantations forced and persuaded black women to have sex with them, and evidence of white-black sex appears in official records from the earliest days. In one case, from 1692, a woman named Jane LaSalle filed a petition with the Grand Council, the highest authority in Charleston. The petition involved her husband, who had left her for a black woman, probably one of the white couple's slaves. The abandoned wife appealed for help, and the Grand Council ordered the husband to return to his spouse, or else pay her a sum of money. The public nature of the case and matter-of-fact way in which it was disposed give reason to believe that interracial sex was a common part of Elias's world.

Because the earliest Ball plantation records date from 1720, and Dolly was born in 1712, it is difficult to say who her parents were. I don't believe her father was Elias Ball. I suspect, from much circumstantial evidence, he bought her as a child and later grew fond of her. During her youth Dolly seems to have gotten unusual attention. At age sixteen, according to plantation accounts, Dolly fell ill and Elias quickly summoned a doctor to the plantation to treat her. The following year, he again called a doctor for Dolly and paid a high fee for the cure. It almost never occurred, on the remote plantations, that a slave was singled out for individual medical care. Physicians were scarce, and doctors had to be enticed with large sums of money to make trips to the country, since they could easily find patients in Charleston. But thanks to Elias, Dolly received house calls, the only black person on Comingtee to warrant such attention.

The pattern of care continued throughout Dolly's young life. On one occasion Elias had special shoes made for her. Beginning in the colonial days, plantation owners hired shoemakers to sew one kind of footwear for themselves and their families and another kind, called Negro shoes, for slaves. Once, Elias hired a shoemaker from the nearby settlement of Goose Creek to sew shoes for his son, and, in the same order, to make similar high-priced footwear for Dolly. There is no evidence that other slaves ever received such treatment.

Dolly was about twenty when she went to work in the Ball house. After a year or two there, she began to have children. Her son Cupid was born April 1735. Because the slave owners often left out the name of the father in records of slave births, I cannot say who Cupid's father was. In all likelihood he was another slave on Comingtee, because Cupid went on to become a field hand, lived his entire life on Ball plantations, and died sometime after 1784.

In the 1730s, Elias and Mary were also having children. Mary gave birth to her last, a son, in 1734; he died as an infant. There is no record of Mary's death, but soon after the birth of her final child, Mary herself passed away and Elias buried her sometime around 1735, ending a marriage of fifteen years. Upon Mary's death, Elias was left with three daughters to look after—Mary, Eleanor, and Sarah—ages two to thirteen. In 1736, he turned sixty. When Elias married Mary Delamare, he had made clear his preference for younger women. Now Dolly, twenty-four, was on hand.

Mary's death seems to have made possible a liaison between Elias and Dolly. On September 16, 1740, Dolly gave birth to her second child, who was given the name Edward. Among the slaves on Comingtee, none carried English forenames. What's more, when Edward grew up, records show that the Ball family paid him respect. Edward was given his freedom and lived among the Balls, who handled his business affairs. When he died, at eighty, his will and other papers went into the Ball family collection. According to probate records, Edward was a mulatto, described in his estate papers as "a free yellow man." If Edward had been able to take the name of the man whom I believe was his father, he would have been called Edward Ball.

A few years later, while still working in the big house, Dolly had another child who received an English name, Catherine. Like her brother Edward, Catherine would also later gain freedom, evidently granted to her by the Balls. The two siblings, Catherine and Edward, were the only people owned by Elias who would ever be freed from slavery.

Around the time Dolly began to have her mulatto children, sex between whites and blacks was a topic of sharp discussion in the local newspaper. The frequency of the editorials suggests that Elias and Dolly's relationship had plenty of precedent. In July 1736, one writer for the *South Carolina Gazette* pleaded with "Certain young Men" of Charleston to hide their relationships with colored women. He called on them to "frequent less with their black Lovers the open Lots and the . . . House on the Green between old Church street and King street." If they did not keep their heads down, he added, other whites might step in "to coole their Courage and to expose them." The writer ended his cranky editorial with an appeal to white men to stay away from women slaves, if only in solidarity with other whites. White women, he maintained, were "full as capable for Service either night or day as any Africain Ladies whatsoever."

When he sat down to write his will, Elias kept young Dolly high in his mind. After declaring that his property would pass to his white children, he added this unusual clause: "I give & Bequeath the Molattoe Wench called Dolly to such of my children as she shall within three months next after my Decease make her Election for her master or mistress." Elias wanted Dolly to be able to decide her fate after he was gone: she was to choose which among Elias's white children would give her a home. It was an incomplete gesture—Dolly could select only her next master or mistress, not freedom—but in this way Elias acknowledged her humanity. The telltale clue is the phrase "within three months next after my Decease." Dolly would have a period of mourning to collect herself before deciding her next step, a graceful interval of grief.

If Dolly and Elias kept up a relationship for several years, was it rape? Or could they have cared for each other? Mockery and danger would have faced the couple on both sides. Not only would Elias have felt ostracized by some whites, but Dolly may have angered some of the other slaves at Comingtee by sleeping with the master. As for the sex itself, could Elias and Dolly both have felt desire? Or did Dolly trade sex (willingly or not) for more lenient treatment? Despite the pitiful circumstances of their attachment, could these two have, somehow, loved each other?

I imagine several of these things may simultaneously have been true.

. . . .

Edward Ball read family histories, plantation records, wills, and business records, as well as newspapers of the times. His primary sources were the oral histories he recorded from his relatives. To confirm (and sometimes disconfirm) parts of the oral histories, Ball relied on an interesting array of public archives—the Afro-American Historical and Genealogical Society in New York, family papers that he found in several states' historical society archives and university libraries, United States census records, warrants and deeds, mortgage records, town papers, genealogies and maps, birth records, statutes, contracts, probate records, estate inventories, wills, medical and death records, and even gravestones. He consulted books on Indian history, American slavery, economic life and rice farming in the southern United States, life in seventeenth- and eighteenth-century Africa, and more specific resources as he needed them in his research.

Not all archival research projects are this complex. Your study won't demand as much time of you but will require you to examine and consider a wide range of sources.

BOX 30

A Box about Boxes

PURPOSE

Sometimes dusty boxes, even boxes that we find in our homes or that belong to people we know, are important sites for archival study. Looking with the eyes of a researcher can shift the way we sort through a collection of stuff, whether it comes from a family member, someone we know (like a teacher or a student), or an anonymous figure whose stuff promises the beginning of a fascinating fieldstudy.

ACTION

Locate a box of archival stuff—a grouping of artifacts or documents that someone has collected, even if the purpose is simply "to keep because it's important." This box could belong to you, a member of your family, or someone else. List the contents of the box. Try organizing or mapping the contents in different patterns—chronologically, by size, by type or shape, by order from beginning to end or from inside to outside. See if there are one or more overall logical shapes to the data, and determine how the organizing patterns would show different themes about the contents of the box.

RESPONSE

David Jakstas, one of our students, comes from a family that owns a hotel on a lake in a small town in Illinois, not far from Chicago. The hotel is old and stately and is known to city weekenders as "the big white building on the lake." It was built in 1884 with 100 rooms, a 240-foot porch, a ballroom, a tower, and a bar. Only the bar exists today for business, though the family is planning to restore both the bar and the hotel. David's uncle, who is planning the restoration, manages a successful marina next to the hotel. For David, the hotel itself is an archive full of information, documents, and artifacts from basement to tower. Already equipped with the family stories he's heard all his life and knowing he could listen to other family versions of them, David's early fieldwork consisted of uncovering archival material from the old hotel, much of which was in the bar. "One particular slot machine," he writes, "sits in a showcase of the bar but was found in one of the storage rooms in the hotel. The sign below the machine reads, 'a switch underneath the machine quickly makes this machine dispense candy instead of money, in case of a police raid.'" Also in the showcase is a hat with this caption: "This hat was worn by Al Capone. It was left by him in the back seat of a cab after leaving the hotel."

David's research led him to wonder what role the hotel had played in the lives of Chicago gangsters, who would "pull off a big heist in the city" and head for the lake-area hotels. His family's stories involve bullet holes in the walls, ghosts in the rafters, boating accidents, and floods. David studied a scrapbook of news articles about the hotel that had been clipped by various family members throughout the hotel's lifetime. He found an original lease, evidence that the hotel had once been a clubhouse for a Board of Trade, several old maps, menus, souvenir programs from celebrations, and news articles with pictures, details, and stories spanning a hundred years of history. David writes: "I did not start with this topic; I literally walked into it one day. My problem was that I had never looked at the place as a place for research. . . . My dad and I went through boxes of things about the hotel in our basement before I talked to anyone at the bar. Although my mom thought we'd trashed the basement, I found plenty of information and a lot of history. I had the main material for my project."

Historical Archives

These days more than ever before, researchers have access to all kinds of information in all kinds of places, which fuels their passion for historical archives, leading to documentary films, radio essays, TV series, books, and new ways to present old histories. *History Detectives* is a **PBS** television show in which scholars (a sociologist, an anthropologist, a museum curator, an appraiser, and a library archivist) examine an interesting artifact and reconstruct the story of the culture that surrounds the object. Another **PBS** show, *Secrets of the Dead*, uses forensic science and teams of researchers to investigate the past and reinterpret the details of history they find by looking at long-buried mysteries.

Perhaps the best-known public fieldworker is Ken Burns, the filmmaker who has given us a detailed look at American cultural history through his numerous documentaries, which include *The Civil War* (1990), *Baseball* (1994), *Jazz* (2001), *Unforgivable Blackness: The Rise and Fall of Jack Johnson* (2004), and *The National Parks: America's Best Idea* (2009). These examples of suspenseful, artful, educational entertainment are also **ethnohistory**. A standard definition of ethnohistory would imply "a study of the development of cultures," but anthropologist James Peacock reminds us that we understand history through the perspectives of the people who lived at the time. Archival historical research allows us to do just that.

You may become fascinated by a topic or an artifact from another time. Even if most of that historical period has vanished, you will be able to retrieve and recreate whole pieces of it. One of our students, Bill Polking, used an institutional archive in his study of a Catholic boarding school for Native American tribes of the Southwest United States. Bill had been a teacher and dorm counselor at the school before it closed its doors in 1998. His project posed a special challenge because the fieldsite he once knew no longer existed. Yet Bill had access to personal and historical archives as well as Internet connections with his former colleagues and students. Bill began the study with his own archives, a few boxes of mementos from his years at this school. He supplemented the study with e-mail interviews with former students and colleagues, as well as a return visit to the site of the school.

Bill worried about how to use the archives he had at his disposal. How would he use his personal journal? What was important about the order of nuns who ran the school? What was the value of the other fieldstudies he'd read? How would he bring the voices from personal e-mails into this study? He needed to find one way to represent his complicated understanding of the school's culture.

Eventually, a visual artifact helped Bill determine his focus—a framed rectangular sign that had hung above the door of the boys' dorm and announced "Nothing but the best for the boys because the boys are the best." This motto became the title and controlling thesis of his fieldwork essay. Using the motto as his thesis helped to guide his awareness of the ethics of his position, the needs and opinions of the former students and colleagues who were his informants, and the tangled cultural issues that arose at this Catholic coed boarding school for Native Americans:

> A small school, down to just over two hundred students by the time it closed, St. Catherine prided itself on its sense of community: "Some seek St. Kate's to escape the hardships at home. We welcome them. Some come here to escape other hardships of life. We welcome them. Some come here because they belong nowhere else. We welcome them, too" (Belin Tsinna-jinnie, boys' dorm student).
>
> "Everyone was like a family here," said day student Nicole Hernandez, and from my beginnings . . . St. Catherine and the boys' dorm in particular were my family, my home. Home in the literal sense, as I lived in the dorm, in a small room next to the ninth graders and (unfortunately) the bathroom. . . .
>
> Others saw the boys' dorm in similar fashion: "Although it was infused with respect for the cultural/tribal traditions from which its students came, the boys' dorm seemed to form an identity, a 'culture,' quite apart from those traditions, and in this way it was able to unite students from diverse backgrounds" (Jenn Guerin, girls' dorm director).
>
> "I believe the main objective of the boys' dorm, aside from introducing a person to a very diverse community and making sure they did well academically, was to create an environment where a sense of brotherhood evolved and a comfortable form of reliance on one another was developed" (Oscencio Tom, boys' dorm student).
>
> "The thing that has stood out in my memory . . . is the respect the boys seemed to show for each other. The fact that we didn't have one fist fight all year is remarkable. . . . Even the tougher kids treated each other with dignity or indifference" (Tom McGrory, boys' dorm staff).
>
> "Nothing but the best for the boys because the boys are the best" (sign made by Jerry Payne, boys' dorm director).
>
> "The boys are spoiled" (numerous girls' dorm students).

Whether you supplement your study with archival research or identify a fieldstudy topic from personal, historical, or online sources, archives can provide the shape, texture, depth, and color that help bring a study to life. Even though institutional archives are organized more formally than family archives, the challenge of the research is still the same—finding a focus. Eventually a visual artifact—a framed rectangular sign—helped Bill figure out his focus.

University Archives

All colleges and universities have archival collections of materials that document the shared histories, academic lives, and memories of their institutions, as well as the specialties they represent and the cultures that surround them. We've both had experiences in our own schools. When Elizabeth was composition director and wanted to know how the writing program had developed over time, she visited the archives in her library and read syllabi, student essays, and course descriptions of writing classes taught since the 1940s. Bonnie discovered the huge Women's Archive at the University of Iowa when she was involved in planning an international meeting on the history of the Nancy Drew mystery series. The original author, unknown for a long time, was Mildred Wirt Benson, an Iowa native and the first female graduate of the Iowa School of Journalism's master's degree program.

Archival collections usually include photographs, material culture, oral histories, scrapbooks, yearbooks, letters, local holdings dating from the school's founding, and records of courses and programs from the school's history. Sometimes they include manuscripts about the area surrounding the institution as well as rare collections that have been donated by patrons. The University of North Carolina at Greensboro was originally a women's college, and the archives include, for example, a collection of documents—uniforms, letters, and oral histories—from women Air Force veterans that was organized by a former librarian. The University of Iowa, Bonnie's school, includes such collections as science fiction fanzines and comic books, medieval illuminated manuscripts, a thousand linear feet of film and TV, and an extensive archive related to Iowa's medical school.

College and university collections provide unique views into the past of an institution and are fascinating to explore. Usually located in the library, the archives often require permission to use, but are open to any student wanting to do research among these materials. Most archives have special staff members who will not only welcome you but also help you sift your way through collections. Check out your own institution's archives; you might be surprised at the treasures you find.

Speaking of treasures, the Internet's material archival grows continually. Here are three examples of huge online archives:

1. The Library of Congress's *American Memory* collections include seven million digital objects from more than a hundred U.S. historical and cultural collections. Included, for instance, is the University of Iowa's *Traveling Culture* site: 30,000 images of brochures advertising Chautauqua performers, from 1902 to 1932. Visit it at: **http://memory.loc.gov/ammem/amhome.html**.

2. The *Making of America,* a joint project of the University of Michigan and Cornell University, creates a digital library of nineteenth-century American social history: 10,000 books and 50,000 magazine articles (over 900,000 pages) with strengths in education, psychology, American history, sociology, religion, and science and technology. Visit it at: **http://quod.lib.umich.edu/m/moagrp/**.

3. The *American Periodical Series* has online texts of more than 1,100 periodicals published between 1740 and 1900, including special interest and general magazines, literary and professional journals, children's and women's magazines, and many other historically significant periodicals. Find it at: **http://www.proquest .com/en-US/catalogs/databases/detail/aps.shtml**.

Archives offer what scholars call primary sources—the actual "stuff" people wrote, read, created, used, and saved at a specific time in a specific place. We hope you think of ways to use archives in your fieldwork and give yourself an opportunity to rummage, online or in boxes, through a few.

Museum Archives

Many of us are unaware of the archival resources we have in our hometowns or nearby cities. Bonnie comes from the Philadelphia area, while Elizabeth grew up in a small Ohio town. Although Bonnie had early contact with rich metropolitan museums and other resources through her art-teacher mother, Elizabeth didn't realize that her Ohio hometown was important, historically or artistically, as a ceramic center until she moved away and found that many people collected Roseville and Zanesville pottery. (Her hometown now has a pottery museum.)

We like to tell the story of a high school student we know in a small town in New Hampshire who was assigned a fieldwork project and complained to his teacher, "There's nothing in this town—nothing to do, nothing to research, no one to talk to. All I'm interested in is basketball."

"Okay," his teacher replied. "Why don't you try to find out about the history of basketball in this town?"

He grumbled all the way to the town archives in the small Historical Society building where he began his research. There he discovered pictures and newspaper clippings about a family basketball team formed at the turn of the twentieth century in New England, just a few decades after basketball was invented in Springfield, Massachusetts. The four boys and one girl were the town's first team and won fame because the sister helped win many contests. Our young researcher was intrigued and traced the local family until he found a living relative. He interviewed this elderly man, one of the original team members, and wrote a compelling study of the team, which became part of the school district's collective fieldproject. Even with a skeptical attitude, this student was able to use archival research to inspire his rediscovery of a local family's sports fame long ago. Sometimes a fieldworker can overlook a small-town archive or even a small institutional archive.

When we visited Ball State University in Muncie, Indiana, we became fascinated with the kinds of archives and talented people who teach us about how the culture of a town is reflected in its history. Although we learned from our Ball State colleagues about Muncie's connection to the manufacturing of Ball jars, it was folklorist Beth Campbell, then curator and exhibits developer at Muncie's cultural center, who guided us through exhibits and shared with us archival research projects she developed for the museum's heritage collection. As a fieldworker, Beth was interested in collecting data about the lives of everyone in the town, from the Ball brothers and their wives to the factory workers. She collected materials to document the class differences in Muncie during the 1920s. She also consulted other sources written at that time—such as diaries, journals, letters, and newspapers—and interviewed town residents about their memories of the Ball family. To our delight, Beth also showed us an exhibition script—the curator's organizational blueprints—for an exhibition on the restoration of the cultural center's gardens, the transcript for an oral history project, and interviews with senior citizens who had worked in the Ball brothers' glass jar factory.

For more on how Beth Campbell worked in Muncie, visit **bedfordstmartins.com/ fieldworking**.

(Photo: Lia Schultz)

A Ball jar

We were happy to learn that radio personality Garrison Keillor devoted a segment of his radio show, *A Prairie Home Companion*, to the Ball jar connections when he visited Muncie. Portions of his Ball jar stories have appeared in his written work as well as on his radio shows since then. You can find them easily online through National Public Radio. To find most radio or television transcripts, you can use educational online resources. As you probably know, most radio and TV news broadcasts, magazine shows, talk shows, and other informative presentations end their programs with information about how to request a transcript of the program.

For a link to the full audio version of Garrison Keillor's piece, go to **bedfordstmartins.com/ fieldworking** and click on Audio Links.

BOX**31**

Sorting through Public Archives

PURPOSE

For the kind of fieldwork we describe in this book, we define *public archive* as a place where collections of public and private records, as well as other historical documents and artifacts, are stored. It can be a town hall, a museum, a library's or business's special collection, a school, a club, or a church. A public archive might be as small as a scrapbook or as large as a building.

The archive's organizational patterns will probably be less than efficient—from files in chronological order to jumbles of papers in large boxes. Looking for his slave and slave owner heritage, Edward Ball reflected as he pored through wills, deeds, ledgers, and town records: "Shut in the vaults of the historical society's pink stucco building, I read as much as I could absorb. One family at a time, the stories surfaced, and in glimpses and parts, I began to piece together what happened." Working your way through a public archive can be frustrating and sometimes daunting; it takes time and patience and offers no quick answers. But as we mention at the beginning of this chapter, you will find that the data begin to come alive as you find what you need.

ACTION

To see how archival material coincides with other sources of data, check out a few public archives related to your topic of interest, your site, or your informants. These archival materials can be any documents or artifacts that are part of a collection; the collection can be either organized or disorganized. List the sources you've looked at, and see what connections or correspondences turn up or what gaps you can perceive. Freewrite about the archives themselves and the ways that they relate to your topic, your site, and your informants. Try to triangulate this information with other material you might find about your topic while browsing the Internet.

Bonnie likes to teach a short "flash research" project in which her class splits duties and works collectively. Over the years, her classes have studied a BYOF ("bring your own food") bar, a performance of Indian dancers, the Iowa marching band's practice sessions over the course of a week, and an environmental consciousness rally. In all of these projects, the students have used archives as they've gathered data to share.

During one fall semester, the article "Play Me, I'm Yours" appeared in a local paper. Everyone had seen two colorfully painted upright pianos perched on the downtown sidewalks, and a few students had stopped to hear the players. One student actually played the piano there herself; another recalled an *NBC Dateline* story about sixty pianos installed on the streets of New York City. With those tidbits, the class's "flash research" (a two-week project) began as they investigated the history of the pianos, the idea of pianos as public art, and even the history of boogie-woogie.

Pianos as Public Art

British artist Luke Jerram began his Play Me, I'm Yours installation of public pianos in 2007 in Birmingham, United Kingdom. Since then, street pianos have made appearances in Sydney, Australia; Barcelona, Spain; New York City; as well as many other cities. Jerram observes that public pianos are about "bringing live art to our urban centers, democratizing the arts, and renewing our civic spirit." Though the project is very new, it's publicly visible. So Bonnie's class found piles of archival information already available. Major TV news networks, Internet blog sites, and major and minor newspapers—from the New York Times to the Iowa City Press Citizen—had covered the installations.

The class began with three main Web sites: **www.streetpianos.com**; **www.lukejerram .com/projects/play_me_im_yours**; and **www.singforhope.org/streetpianos**. Students then found these related archives:

1. *Videos from news organizations:* All of the major news organizations—ABC, NBC, CBS, and CNN—produced stories about the public pianos. The people interviewed in each segment talked about how the pianos were fun, beautiful conversation pieces for people to meet and share music.

2. *Videos from YouTube:* One long look at YouTube offered 201 videos, some captured on cell phones, of people from all over the world playing the street pianos. These amateur clips offer a nice comparison with professionally edited news segments.

3. *Radio broadcasts:* NPR's *All Things Considered* offered "Turning the Public into Performers with 'Street Pianos.'" Since this program depends on only sound, it featured a different "view" of the piano and its surrounding sounds—taxis honking, motors revving, sirens screeching, feet shuffling—illustrating how people paused to enjoy other people and moments that would not have occurred without the pianos as conversation pieces.

4. *Stories and quotations from those playing the pianos:* Each city has its own Web site where people can post stories, pictures, and video related to each piano installation.

BOX**31** continued

Bonnie's class found it a rich archival record. In one video shot in Brooklyn Bridge Park, a young man sets his backpack on the ground and plays John Denver's "Take Me Home, Country Roads." Spontaneously, people of all ages and ethnicities gather and sing along.

5. *Pictures of players:* The three Web sites offer photos that illustrate the joy and spontaneity of audiences, and the beauty of the art in the painted pianos, their music, and the players. Luke Jerram's site includes 22 photos of people playing from all over the world.

6. *News articles:* National and local news coverage was almost all positive (only one editorial claimed the piano was an annoyance). Most newspapers built the concept into their headlines—the *New York Times'* "Piano by the People"—and quoted ordinary people who stopped to play or listen. Ironically, a look at the articles revealed that the street pianos in Iowa City were installed just after an ordinance had banned other kinds of panhandling and street performances.

Students investigated archives related to the piano project; they also shared other data collection: three students took fieldnotes while hanging out near the pianos, one student interviewed the two businessmen who sponsored the project, two students studied public art projects in general, one music student actually played the piano while another student recorded her and interviewed the audience. Another student watched and interviewed a musician who played every Wednesday and attended a local boogie-woogie night concert at a local theater.

Read a detailed account of this project at **bedfordstmartins.com/ fieldworking**, under Student Essays.

As you research, we hope that you'll collect family, historical, and institutional items to create an archive that is specific to your project.

Poet and essayist Naomi Shihab Nye shares the feelings of archival researchers in her prose poem "The Attic and Its Nails." In her attic archive, the narrator tries to decide what fits, what doesn't fit, and how to organize it.

The Attic and Its Nails (poem)

Naomi Shihab Nye

It's hard up there. You dig in a box for whatever the moment requires: a sweater, wreath, the other half of the walky-talky, and find twelve things you forgot about which delay the original search, since now that you found them you have to think about them. Do I want to keep this, bring it downstairs? Of course your life feels very different from the life you had when you packed it up there. Maybe your life has another kind of room in it now, maybe it feels more crowded. Maybe you think looking at this old ceramic cup with the pocked white glaze that you made in college would uplift you in the mornings. Your search takes on an urgent ratlike quality as you rip paper out of boxes, shredding and piling it. Probably by now you've stood up too fast and speared your head on one of the nails that holds the roof shingles down. They're lined up all along the rafters, poking through aimed. Now you have to think about tetanus, rusty nails, the hearty human skull. A little dizzy for awhile, you're too occupied to remember what sent you up into the dark.

To read a full student essay that uses ethnopoetics, go to **bedfordstmartins.com/ fieldworking** and click on Student Essays.

With words like "crowded" and "dizzy" and phrases like "It's hard up there" and the "search takes on an urgent ratlike quality," Nye shows us how we can begin to make sense of the "dark" and the chaos we feel when we first confront archives.

Locating and Using Archival Materials

When you're looking for archives related to your project, consider using:

- the representative artifacts of your chosen culture or subculture as support documentation

- a family's archival collection of letters, diaries, scrapbooks, and photographs

- genealogical documents

- a local or national historical society's archives

- your own university's archives as possible support for your research

- local museums for archival resources or specialized museums online that relate to your topic

Remember that someone else organized these archives and you'll need to develop your own organizational pattern that fits your project.

Organizing Archival Material

When you look at historical documents—old photos, family letters, maps or blueprints, a family's financial records, or an old steamer trunk full of mildewed fabrics and rusty tools—your first job is to organize what you see. There is no one way to do this.

Your decision about how to organize artifacts, archives, fieldnotes, print sources, transcripts, and other data provides a framework for how you might write about your material. But even as you are collecting data, your organizational structure will help you decide what else to collect. One important idea in any historical research, then—whether it is about a family, an institution, a period in history, or even oneself—is that we need to decide how to place our archival material within a time frame.

Framing Time

We can organize materials diachronically (according to many points over a length of time) or synchronically (according to events, environmental features, or artifacts or items that exist at one period of time).

Author and comedian Amy Borkowsky chose a diachronic approach to analyze and write about a boxful of bills. In the introduction to her book *Statements: True Tales of Life, Love, and Credit Card Bills*, she writes as follows:

> Not long ago, I was looking through some boxes in my closet and became nostalgic. I'm talking all-out, mascara-running, nose-blowing nostalgic.
>
> The boxes didn't hold faded photographs.
>
> They didn't contain love letters.
>
> They held twelve years of credit card statements, chronicling virtually every significant event in my life as a single career woman.
>
> While I was too busy to keep a diary, it turned out that American Express had kept one for me.
>
> They've recorded for all eternity the fact that on July 7, 1992, I spent $89.12 at Victoria's Secret—and that on July 17, 1992, I returned the entire purchase, documenting in black and white a relationship that unraveled just before The Lingerie Phase. The $30.25 charge for my first caller ID box forever preserves the memory of my fruitless attempts to avoid my interfering mother, and I can tell just how many late nights I worked at my high-pressure ad job by tracking the charges for Chinese take-out.
>
> This is a collection of true stories about how I, literally, spent my early years living, working, and looking for love in Manhattan when it seemed that the only knight in armor I'd find was the one on the front of my Amex card.

Borkowsky's sometimes poignant and often hilarious analysis is diachronic. By looking at her credit-card purchases and returns over 12 years and triangulating the data with memories, other artifacts, people, and knowledge of her life, she offers a view of her private life and a portrait of a single, contemporary urban woman.

An exciting example of synchronic research is a book by Columbia University professor James Shapiro called *1599: A Year in the Life of William Shakespeare*. Shapiro chronicles one year in Shakespeare's life by looking at as much as he can see:

My interest in this subject dates back fifteen years. At that time, though I was familiar with Shakespeare's plays and taught them regularly, I didn't know enough about the historical moment in which plays like *As You Like It* and *Hamlet* were written and which they engaged. I had no idea, for example, that England braced itself for an invasion in the summer of 1599. . . . I knew less than I should have known about how Shakespeare traveled to and from Stratford or about the bookstalls and playhouses that he frequented in London. . . . My ignorance extended beyond history. Along with other scholars, I didn't fully grasp how extensively Shakespeare revised and what these changes revealed about the kind of writer he was. And my notion of the sources of Shakespeare's inspiration was too bookish. It was one thing to know what Shakespeare was reading, another to know about what sermons he may have heard or what art he viewed in the royal palaces of Whitehall and Richmond where he regularly performed.

This work, then, grew out of frustration with how much I didn't know and frustration with scholars . . . who never quite got around to addressing the question I found most pressing: how, at age thirty-five, Shakespeare went from being an exceptionally talented writer to being one of the greatest who ever lived—put another way: how in the course of little over a year he went from writing *The Merry Wives of Windsor* to writing a play as inspired as *Hamlet*. (xxi–xxii)

Shapiro organizes his 15-chapter book in four chronological sections, one for each season of the year 1599. He uses illustrations, maps, and a fascinating bibliographic essay to look ethnographically at the culture, politics, and even weather conditions of the environment in which Shakespeare spent his pivotal thirty-fifth year, one in which the Globe theater was built and Shakespeare wrote four new plays: *Henry the Fifth*, *Julius Caesar*, *As You Like It*, and a first draft of *Hamlet*. Shapiro's book is a fine example of a synchronic study that carefully draws on one particular moment in time.

Alternative Archives

For many people, attics, basements, garage sale tables, flea markets, backyard sheds, and professional storage containers hold junk. But for collectors and curators of both public and private archives—and for fieldworkers—someone else's junk could be the treasure needed to understand a culture or subculture. We don't often think about the artifacts that people discard, but sometimes they hold important cultural meanings. Researchers who work in schools, for example, find themselves emptying wastebaskets to read through the papers and notes that students or teachers throw away—to find clues to what matters and what doesn't matter within the culture of school.

In "On Dumpster Diving," Lars Eighner describes experiences he had when he was homeless, roaming a college town with his dog, Lizbeth, and devising intricate ways to live off what other people discarded. His essay considers the Dumpster as an unusual, alternative archive that revealed much about the behaviors, rituals, rules, totems, and taboos of the culture in which he was living. As you read this essay, notice the way Eighner uses the Dumpster as an archive and peels away the layers of meaning it holds.

· ·

On Dumpster Diving

Lars Eighner

Long before I began Dumpster diving I was impressed with Dumpsters, enough so that I wrote the Merriam-Webster research service to discover what I could about the word *Dumpster*. I learned from them that it is a proprietary word belonging to the Dempster Dumpster company. Since then I have dutifully capitalized the word, although it was lowercased in almost all the citations Merriam-Webster photocopied for me. Dempster's word is too apt. I have never heard these things called anything but Dumpsters. I do not know anyone who knows the generic name for these objects. From time to time I have heard a wino or hobo give some corrupted credit to the original and call them Dipsy Dumpsters.

I began Dumpster diving about a year before I became homeless.

I prefer the word *scavenging* and use the word *scrounging* when I mean to be obscure. I have heard people, evidently meaning to be polite, use the word *foraging*, but I prefer to reserve that word for gathering nuts and berries and such, which I do also according to the season and the opportunity. *Dumpster diving* seems to me to be a little too cute and, in my case, inaccurate because I lack the athletic ability to lower myself into the Dumpsters as the true divers do, much to their increased profit.

I like the frankness of the word *scavenging*, which I can hardly think of without picturing a big black snail on an aquarium wall. I live from the refuse of others. I am a scavenger. I think it a sound and honorable niche, although if I could I would naturally prefer to live the comfortable consumer life, perhaps—and only perhaps—as a slightly less wasteful consumer, owing to what I have learned as a scavenger.

While Lizbeth and I were still living in the shack on Avenue B as my savings ran out, I put almost all my sporadic income into rent. The necessities of daily life I began to extract from Dumpsters. Yes, we ate from them. Except for jeans, all my clothes came from Dumpsters. Boom boxes, candles, bedding, toilet paper, a virgin male love doll, medicine, books, a typewriter, dishes, furnishings, and change, sometimes amounting to many dollars—I acquired many things from the Dumpsters.

I have learned much as a scavenger. I mean to put some of what I have learned down here, beginning with the practical art of Dumpster diving and proceeding to the abstract.

What is safe to eat?

After all, the finding of objects is becoming something of an urban art. Even respectable employed people will sometimes find something tempting sticking out of a Dumpster or standing beside one. Quite a number of people, not all of them of the bohemian type, are willing to brag that they found this or that piece in the trash. But eating from Dumpsters is what separates the dilettanti from the professionals. Eating safely from the Dumpsters involves three principles: using the senses and common sense to evaluate the condition of the found materials, knowing the Dumpsters of a given area and checking them regularly, and seeking always to answer the question "Why was this discarded?"

Perhaps everyone who has a kitchen and a regular supply of groceries has, at one time or another, made a sandwich and eaten half of it before discovering mold on the bread or got a mouthful of milk before realizing the milk had turned. Nothing of the sort is likely to happen to a Dumpster diver because he is constantly reminded that most food is discarded for a reason. Yet a lot of perfectly good food can be found in Dumpsters.

Canned goods, for example, turn up fairly often in the Dumpsters I frequent. All except the most phobic people would be willing to eat from a can, even if it came from a Dumpster. Canned goods are among the safest of foods to be found in Dumpsters but are not utterly foolproof.

Although very rare with modern canning methods, botulism is a possibility. Most other forms of food poisoning seldom do lasting harm to a healthy person, but botulism is almost certainly fatal and often the first symptom is death. Except for carbonated beverages, all canned goods should contain a slight vacuum and suck air when first punctured. Bulging, rusty, and dented cans and cans that spew when punctured should be avoided, especially when the contents are not very acidic or syrupy.

Heat can break down the botulin, but this requires much more cooking than most people do to canned goods. To the extent that botulism occurs at all, of course, it can occur in cans on pantry shelves as well as in cans from Dumpsters. Need I say that home-canned goods are simply too risky to be recommended.

From time to time one of my companions, aware of the source of my provisions, will ask, "Do you think these crackers are really safe to eat?" For some reason it is most often the crackers they ask about.

This question has always made me angry. Of course I would not offer my companion anything I had doubts about. But more than that, I wonder why he cannot evaluate the condition of the crackers for himself. I have no special knowledge and I have been wrong before. Since he knows where the food comes from, it seems to me he ought to assume some of the responsibility for deciding what he will put in his mouth. For myself I have few qualms about dry foods such as crackers, cookies,

(Photo: Bradford Reed)

Dumpster diving

cereal, chips, and pasta if they are free of visible contaminants and still dry and crisp. Most often such things are found in the original packaging, which is not so much a positive sign as it is the absence of a negative one.

Raw fruits and vegetables with intact skins seem perfectly safe to me, excluding of course the obviously rotten. Many are discarded for minor imperfections that can be pared away. Leafy vegetables, grapes, cauliflower, broccoli, and similar things may be contaminated by liquids and may be impractical to wash.

Candy, especially hard candy, is usually safe if it has not drawn ants. Chocolate is often discarded only because it has become discolored as the cocoa butter de-emulsified. Candying, after all, is one method of food preservation because pathogens do not like very sugary substances.

All of these foods might be found in any Dumpster and can be evaluated with some confidence largely on the basis of appearance. Beyond these are foods that cannot be correctly evaluated without additional information.

I began scavenging by pulling pizzas out of the Dumpster behind a pizza delivery shop. In general, prepared food requires caution, but in this case I knew when the shop closed and went to the Dumpster as soon as the last of the help left.

Such shops often get prank orders; both the orders and the products made to fill them are called *bogus*. Because help seldom stays long at these places, pizzas are often made with the wrong topping, refused on delivery for being cold, or baked incorrectly. The products to be discarded are boxed up because inventory is kept by counting boxes: A boxed pizza can be written off; an unboxed pizza does not exist.

I never placed a bogus order to increase the supply of pizzas and I believe no one else was scavenging in this Dumpster. But the people in the shop became suspicious and began to retain their garbage in the shop overnight. While it lasted I had a steady supply of fresh, sometimes warm pizza. Because I knew the Dumpster I knew the source of the pizza, and because I visited the Dumpster regularly I knew what was fresh and what was yesterday's.

The area I frequent is inhabited by many affluent college students. I am not here by chance; the Dumpsters in this area are very rich. Students throw out many good things, including food. In particular they tend to throw everything out when they move at the end of a semester, before and after breaks, and around midterm, when many of them despair of college. So I find it advantageous to keep an eye on the academic calendar.

Students throw food away around breaks because they do not know whether it has spoiled or will spoil before they return. A typical discard is a half jar of peanut butter. In fact, nonorganic peanut butter does not require refrigeration and is unlikely to spoil in any reasonable time. The student does not know that, and since it is Daddy's money, the student decides not to take a chance. Opened containers require caution and some attention to the question "Why was this discarded?" But in the case of discards from student apartments, the answer may be that the item was thrown out through carelessness, ignorance, or wastefulness. This can sometimes be deduced when the item is found with many others, including some that are obviously perfectly good.

Some students, and others, approach defrosting a freezer by chucking out the whole lot. Not only do the circumstances of such a find tell the story, but also the mass of frozen goods stays cold for a long time and items may be found still frozen or freshly thawed.

Yogurt, cheese, and sour cream are items that are often thrown out while they are still good. Occasionally I find a cheese with a spot of mold, which of course I just pare off, and because it is obvious why such a cheese was discarded, I treat it with less suspicion than an apparently perfect cheese found in similar circumstances. Yogurt is often discarded, still sealed, only because the expiration date on the carton had passed. This is one of my favorite finds because yogurt will keep for several days, even in warm weather.

Students throw out canned goods and staples at the end of semesters and when they give up college at midterm. Drugs, pornography, spirits, and the like are often discarded when parents are expected—Dad's Day, for example. And spirits also turn up after big party weekends, presumably discarded by the newly reformed. Wine and spirits, of course, keep perfectly well even once opened, but the same cannot be said of beer.

My test for carbonated soft drinks is whether they still fizz vigorously. Many juices or other beverages are too acidic or too syrupy to cause much concern, provided they are not visibly contaminated. I have discovered nasty molds in vegetable juices, even when the product was found under its original seal; I recommend that such products be decanted slowly into a clear glass. Liquids always require some care. One hot day I found a large jug of Pat O'Brien's Hurricane mix. The jug had been opened but was still ice cold. I drank three large glasses before it became apparent to me that someone had added rum to the mix, and not a little rum. I never tasted rum, and by the time I began to feel the effects I had already ingested a very large quantity of the beverage. Some divers would have considered this a boon, but being suddenly intoxicated in a public place in the early afternoon is not my idea of a good time.

I have heard of people maliciously contaminating discarded food and even handouts, but mostly I have heard of this from people with vivid imaginations who have had no experience with the Dumpsters themselves. Just before the pizza shop stopped discarding its garbage at night, jalapeños began showing up on most of the thrown-out pizzas. If indeed this was meant to discourage me, it was a wasted effort because I am a native Texan.

For myself, I avoid game, poultry, pork, and egg-based foods, whether I find them raw or cooked. I seldom have the means to cook what I find, but when I do I avail myself of plentiful supplies of beef, which is often in very good condition. I suppose fish becomes disagreeable before it becomes dangerous. Lizbeth is happy to have any such thing that is past its prime and, in fact, does not recognize fish as food until it is quite strong.

Home leftovers, as opposed to surpluses from restaurants, are very often bad. Evidently, especially among students, there is a common type of personality that carefully wraps up even the smallest leftover and shoves it into the back of the refrigerator for six months or so before discarding it. Characteristic of this type are the reused jars and margarine tubs to which the remains are committed. I avoid ethnic foods I am unfamiliar with. If I do not know what it is supposed to look like when it is good, I cannot be certain I will be able to tell if it is bad.

No matter how careful I am I still get dysentery at least once a month, oftener in warm weather. I do not want to paint too romantic a picture. Dumpster diving has serious drawbacks as a way of life.

To read Lars Eighner's full essay, go to **bedfordstmartins.com/ fieldworking** and click on Professional Essays.

In your fieldwork, you may discover alternative archives—like a Dumpster—that reveal the rules, rituals, and behaviors of a particular subculture. Alternative archives interest us because they are unusual, even to insiders. We don't usually think of a Dumpster as a collection of clues about how a college town functions, and we don't think of what's in an old box in the corner of a long-time teacher's classroom or in unused film footage in a movie director's home garage as a type of archive. We begin to think about alternative archives when we observe a fieldsite, listen to informants, and learn where and how they keep their collections and libraries.

BOX32

Alternative Archives

DEIDRE HALL, UNIVERSITY OF NORTH CAROLINA AT GREENSBORO

PURPOSE

Every day we are surrounded by images and scenes that we have to "read" accurately in order to survive and thrive. Often we interpret our surroundings instinctively: researchers tell us that when we encounter a new face, we make "snap" judgments within one-tenth of a second. When we shop for groceries we glance into another customer's cart and make unconscious assumptions about them, their lives, and their habits. If we think of the grocery cart as a kind of alternative archive, we can use it to learn how we "read" ourselves as we read the stuff of others. This exercise asks you to analyze your first impressions about shoppers at a grocery store and how your own positions affect how you see your informants.

ACTION

1. Get ready

Grocery or "big box" stores like Target and Walmart offer plenty of opportunities to talk with shoppers about their purchases. Be sure to bring a cell phone or camera as well as a notebook so you can write about your first impressions, either when you initially see the cart or as soon as you leave the store. Eventually, you'll ask to take a picture of a shopper's cart and speak briefly with the person about what it contains.

2. Approach a shopper

Find a fellow shopper whom you feel comfortable approaching, and explain that you are doing a college project that requires taking photos of carts and talking with people about their shopping habits. You don't need to use their names; you only want to describe the things they buy and how those things represent something about their chosen lifestyles. People are usually eager to talk, particularly about themselves.

- Pick something in the cart and chat about why the person chose it
- Ask how this item says something about the person's household
- Find out one interesting thing the person wants to share about him- or herself
- Offer one interesting thing about yourself

You may find that your subject continues to volunteer additional information—on and off topic. Be a polite listener; you might get information you don't expect. Record the entire response with careful notes for as long as your informant wishes to talk.

BOX 32 continued

3. Write about your experience

- What were your first impressions of the shopper based both on the contents of the shopping cart and on details of his or her appearance? How did you arrive at those conclusions?

- How accurate were those conclusions? What did you find out in conversation that either confirmed or refuted your assumptions?

- What else did you find out from your subject? What additional information, if any, did you gather?

- What kinds of reactions did you have as you talked with your informant?

- How do you think this exercise will influence your definition of the term *archive* in your future research?

RESPONSE

In carrying out this exercise, student Kathryn Auman writes:

> [T]he cart was very diverse, but it had lots of drinks (milk, orange juice, and soft drinks), which I assumed meant they had a large household or family to provide for. I noticed no green vegetables or meats. This made me a little curious about how healthy these people were. They seemed very healthy to me! So I assumed that they

might be vegans, and didn't eat meat at all. I asked the couple what their current occupations are, and they told me they were retired. The woman was a former cafeteria manager, and her husband had been a farmer for sixty years. She said she loved to cook for her family every Saturday at lunch. They preferred home-cooked meals over eating out. I asked them about the lack of green vegetables and meat if they cooked so much. Her husband told me they grew their own vegetables and canned them, so they would have vegetables year round. As a cattle farmer, he had raised his own meat each year, so he knew where his own meat came from. They seemed excited to tell me about how much cheaper it was for them to grow their own vegetables and raise their own meat, rather than to buy it in a store.

My assumptions were very incorrect. The couple was definitely not vegan, and they had no children living with them. They had a large family that visited every weekend. They also shopped for their son and his family because his wife was very sick and could not leave the house. When we analyze people's grocery carts, I guess we are often wrong. I should have known that the couple could not have eaten that much on their own, but I don't often think about people shopping for others. I don't often think about people growing their own vegetables and raising their own cows for meat. I guess my assumptions were right when I thought they were buying for a large family. This grocery cart really did act as an archive and bring out a lot of information about one family's situation.

Electronic Archives: Using the Internet

Like the kind of research you do at your actual fieldsite, conducting research with a Web site requires patience, attention to detail, selectivity, and analysis. Just as you might spend hours sitting and watching your fieldsite, piecing together information as you find it, you ought to spend much time simply sitting and reading information on the Web until you know what focus you need, what data seem appropriate, and how the information will fit with the other parts of your research. You may uncover a wealth of information quickly but will need time to assess it:

- Is what you've found useful to your project?
- Does it answer any questions you or your informants have raised?
- Does it supplement incomplete facts and details about people, places, histories, ideas, and artifacts you've already heard about?
- Are the sources up-to-date?
- What evidence do you have that they're believable?

These questions require your patience, attention to detail, and ability to be selective.

And then you will need to ask questions of analysis—how the details fit into your broader ideas. You will need to decide what fieldsites and Web sites are telling you:

- How can the Web sites enhance your ideas about your fieldsite and about your informants and their culture?
- How does each Web site relate to the others—and to your fieldsite?
- Is the information similar?
- If it's not, how is it different?
- Would one Web site have a different purpose for displaying itself than another?
- And is its information consistent with its purpose?
- How is that consistent with what you know or think already about your fieldsite?

What you find on the Web works in three ways. First, it is a source of basic information to supplement all that you've gathered at your fieldsite, much like library books or journal articles that offer facts, histories, and descriptions about the culture or subculture you're studying. Second, it can offer you potential contact information—telephone numbers or e-mail addresses of possible informants. As Bill Polking discovered from his online chats with former students and colleagues from the Indian school no longer in existence, and Meg Buzzi found in her correspondence with relatives, e-mails from distant but involved people can be an enormously rich source of data. But the third way the Internet works is that the online information itself becomes an artifact that a culture or subculture has produced.

For more on working with electronic sources, see Chapter 1, page 39, and Chapter 3, page 141.

We think, in fact, that these electronic resources blur the traditional boundaries between primary and secondary sources.

When we wrote about Hmong storycloths, for example, in one short paragraph at the beginning of this chapter, we used the Internet to confirm what we'd learned from two Hmong embroiderers, a local folklorist who collects storycloths, a few presentations we've attended, and Hmong students we've known. But we wanted to be sure we had the history right, so we used the word *Hmong* as a keyword in an online search. Instantly, we found a wealth of written material, both published and unpublished, about the Hmong people, traditions, and histories. We found virtual museum exhibits displaying detailed pictures of Hmong crafts, foods, and music traditions; Web sites in which Hmong in various parts of the world can talk with one another in chat rooms; and newsletters with activities and invitations to participate. In a few hours, we had confirmed what we'd learned from informants about story-cloths and felt more confident about writing the paragraph you read at the beginning of this chapter. But we also had found the connected Web sites themselves to be artifacts of the Hmong culture itself, offering us much new knowledge of the culture in the words and choices of the informants who manage the Web sites. This way, we were able to access the Hmong's perspective on their own transplanted American culture.

To do an exercise using the Internet as an archive, go to **bedfordstmartins .com/fieldworking** and click on Internet Fishing.

This all seems familiar, suspiciously, in fact, like the library work you may have done to write a report. And, of course, online research is research.

FieldWriting: Annotated Bibliographies

One useful way to represent the source materials for your fieldwork is to create an *annotated bibliography*, which provides your reader with more information about the published sources you've used than just the basics of author, title, date, and place of publication. Many researchers, writers, and scholars rely on annotated bibliographies to help them sort through masses of material without having to read each and every source. Each bibliographic citation summarizes a large amount of material into just the key concepts of the book, article, or electronic source. To do that well, the researcher must have a good understanding of the original material and its overall importance. Here are some sample entries of annotated sources relevant to ideas of material culture in this chapter:

Ball, Edward. *Slaves in the Family*. New York: Ballantine, 1998.

> This research into the writer's white and black plantation ancestors employs 200-year-old archival documents and oral histories. Ball is a skilled writer who presents a vivid and detailed picture of how the history and devastating legacy of the institution of slavery affected millions of American lives for centuries.

Belanus, Betty J., and Cathy Kerst. "Everyone Eats Bread." *Dry Goods Store*. FieldWorking Online, 2008. Web. 14 Mar. 2008.

> Betty J. Belanus of the Smithsonian Center for Folklife and Cultural Heritage and Cathy Kerst of the Library of Congress's American Folklife Center developed this lesson plan unit for primary schoolers in Wheaton, Maryland. The unit teaches the importance of bread—its forms, its ingredients, and the reasons that people eat it in different cultures.

Eighner, Lars. "On Dumpster Diving." *Travels with Lizbeth: Three Years on the Road and on the Streets*. New York: Ballantine, 1994. 111–25. Print.

> Author Lars Eighner describes experiences he had when he was homeless and roamed a college town with his dog, living on what other people discarded. His essay reveals much about the behaviors, rituals, rules, totems, and taboos of the culture that surrounded the Dumpsters he frequented.

Iowa80truckingmuseum.com. Iowa 80 Group, 2010. Web. 8 Aug. 2010.

> A full description of the new Iowa 80 Trucking Museum, including pictures of vintage trucks, current news, contests, events, educational efforts, directions, and hours for visiting and touring. The Web site also invites visitors to join the museum, donate artifacts, and participate in online events.

Keillor, Garrison. "On Ball Jars." *Mother, Father, Uncle, Aunt: Stories from Lake Wobegon*. Rec. 15 Mar. 1997. High Bridge Audio, 1997. Audiocassette.

> In this radio show taped in Muncie, Indiana, Garrison Keillor muses in historical and humorous ways on the importance of Ball jars. Originally presented before a live audience, Keillor's monologue connects American folk humor about Ball canning jars with other features of living in the Midwest.

Smith, Bruce R. "Shakespeare in an Age of Visual Culture." *Folger Shakespeare Library*. 1998–1999. Web. Oct. 2005.

> Scholar Bruce R. Smith's essay on the Folger Institute's virtual museum Web site discusses the conventions of various media that have interpreted Shakespeare's plays. The essay has four sections—digital media, film and video, stage production, and printed media.

Whether or not you realize it, you have created your own archive as you've collected data for your fieldworking project. When you first gathered that data, you were simply getting stuff that related to the main topic of your project, even though the stuff was originally in another archival context. For instance, if you procured a list of rules for locker-room behavior, the list likely existed within the context of other supporting archival documents about team behavior, sportsmanship, and academic eligibility requirements. But now you've placed it in your archive about locker-room behavior, which also might include transcripts of interviews with coaches and team members, photographs taken in the locker room (with and without people), a sample toiletry kit from one of the athletes, newspaper articles about locker-room talk after wins and losses, architectural specifications and blueprints and color swatches for the projected new locker room, fundraising flyers, and your own fieldnotes and research journal.

Your data archive becomes a large collection—probably in a big cardboard box, a hanging file, a drawer, or a plastic shopping bag. This large collection is not your portfolio, which serves as only a representation of the data you have. As you select for the portfolio, you can see overall themes, patterns, and even gaps. But as you archive what you have (label and date it, move it around, discard some things, and review others), you are organizing it your own way. This selection process is a critical skill for a fieldworker, one that you develop and shift throughout the project. So you have two archives: one is everything you've collected, and the other is a representative selection of what you've collected. In this chapter's Research Portfolio section we discuss the idea of representation and demonstrate how to select portions of your data for your project.

Collecting data is not enough. But archiving, selecting, discarding, and sorting begin to answer some questions: "What does all this stuff mean to me? To a reader who's interested in my topic? To an insider in the culture I'm studying?" As you organize and choose from your archival resources, you are critiquing your materials: Which are the most important? Do I really need all those transcripts, or can one interview say what I want to express? Which photo of the locker room best shows the behavior of the players? Which language uses are specific to these people? What item in the toiletry kit says something important about this subculture? Your critique requires you to stand back, make sense of what you have, and make decisions about selection. This process is not easy; it requires the focus and reflection that fieldworkers develop over time.

THE RESEARCH PORTFOLIO:
Representing the Unflat Stuff

Whether archives belong to families or to local or international institutions, whether they're in dusty boxes or posted on the Internet, it's hard to know how to use them and what references to include as "stuff" in your research portfolio. How do you represent something that was important to your project when it doesn't fit into a paper portfolio? Why should you include what you decide to include? What does each item mean to your overall research project?

Lots of people puzzle over portfolios, wondering how to organize what might appear to someone else as junk. And sometimes the most important "junk" comes in inconvenient sizes and shapes. Perhaps the most provocative question we've ever heard about portfolios came from a high school student: "What do we do with the unflat stuff?" A portfolio, because it usually incorporates only two-dimensional materials, most often cannot include "unflat stuff" like performances, audio or video recordings, an informant's one-of-a-kind artifacts or photos, songs or important sounds, and original documents that are critical parts of your research. Nor can a portfolio house every piece of data you've collected: it would be heavy and unwieldy and wouldn't allow you to arrange and rearrange categories as you continue to work with it. In short, to use the terms we use in Chapter 1, a "portfolio of everything" would simply show the "collection" process—and leave no room for the important processes of selection, reflection, and projection.

A well-designed portfolio is all about representation. It is anything but "flat," even if it fits into a three-ring binder with plastic document covers and stick-on notes. Like a well-designed Web page, it displays the items and connections ("links") you've selected to represent the categories of your research, the data you've collected, and the ways your thinking develops as you look it over, plan more research, and then perhaps recategorize further. A high-tech portfolio using Web technology can—despite a flat, two-dimensional screen—combine even more data than a paper portfolio, show connections and links even better, incorporate sound and motion, and reorganize itself as you shift your understandings and click your mouse.

When you create a portfolio of representative items, you can organize and reorganize, label each item with a sticky note explaining what you think it means, and reflect on what you have selected. As you go through this process, the themes of your project will become clearer. As you discover more connections, as the themes begin to emerge, as you have more items with which to triangulate, you will learn much about your data, yourself in relationship to it, and what you want to share with your readers. Portfolios are wonderful tools for representation and analysis, whether the "stuff" is flat or not.

Anthropologist Don Handleman tells us that a healthy society "re-presents itself to itself." Fieldworkers who use archives as data are engaging in what folklorists call "cultural conservation" when they research, craft, read, and write about their local cultures. Any community's efforts at conservation—whether restoring an old building, sharing citizens' ethnic backgrounds through celebratory festivals, retaining and promoting indigenous language programs, or exhibiting arts and crafts—require careful study and collection of relevant archives. These days, technology assists our local efforts to cooperate with our communities as we all try to conserve culture.

As writers of this book, our work has connected us with projects all over the United States—work by college students, teachers, museum curators, folklorists, and townspeople—that recognize the special and diverse qualities of their communities' cultures and subcultures. Community archives put self-descriptions back into the hands of community members themselves. They depend on fieldworkers who contribute their studies of cultures and subcultures to help larger conservation efforts. If it were not for the curators, the fieldworkers, and students like you, we would not be able to have the outreach, diversity, and historical preservation that our citizens enjoy locally and nationally.

Search the *FieldWorking* Archives

Our publisher, Bedford/St. Martin's, keeps a companion Web site for our book, **bedfordstmartins.com/fieldworking.** We see it as an archive of materials related to fieldwork—our own as well as that of our colleagues and former students.

FIRST   Browse the Web site, where you'll find links to National Public Radio broadcasts, public oral history projects, and more of the work and voices of writers to whom we've introduced you (such as Oliver Sacks and Zora Neale Hurston). You'll also find ethnographic artwork, a list of ethnographic movies, and what we call "field poems" (like Naomi Shihab Nye's in this chapter). Bookmark something that interests you to share with your classmates.

SECOND   Locate a complete version of an essay we've excerpted in this book, such as the Lars Eighner essay on Dumpster diving or a work by another author whose voice interests you. Read the whole piece and contrast it with the shorter version. Whenever possible, you should return to the author's complete version. What does the full essay offer you as a reader?

THIRD   As you browse, keep track of archived resources that might be helpful in your own fieldwork study. This might be another student project or a sample box exercise, both collected from our readers over the years. You may revisit the sections on fieldwriting or ethical issues such as plagiarism by clicking on these links. Prepare to share with your classmates or fieldworkers a section of the Web site that you find particularly useful.

8

FieldWriting: From Down Draft to Up Draft

Writing about your fieldwork is a layered process. In this chapter you will:

- review and evaluate your data
- draft your essay, question it, and "thicken it" with data
- revise your project with a partner
- experiment with ways of representing culture on the page
- apply analytic section headings to your project
- analyze and prepare your research portfolio

At this point in your study, you've probably accumulated stacks of fieldwriting—fieldnotes and journal entries, short observations and descriptions, transcribed interviews, artifacts and documents, responses to readings, and reflections—in your organized, reorganized, and even re-reorganized portfolio. Anthropologists describe the deskwork involved in fieldwork—that period of time when you begin to sort through your data to figure out what you have and what you might still need—as a period of confusion that can be solved only by shaping your data into text. The good news is that you've been writing all along. Researcher Wendy Bishop uses the phrase "writing it down in order to write it up" to describe the process of moving data into text. Those piles of data are evidence that you've "written it down." Now your challenge will be to find an appropriate way to "write it up."

Finding somewhere to stand in a text that is supposed to be at one and the same time an intimate view and a cool assessment is almost as much of a challenge as gaining the view and making the assessment in the first place.

—CLIFFORD GEERTZ

You have many choices for writing up your fieldstudy. How you choose to tell your tale, what parts of the data you choose to include, and what you choose as a theme (a thesis, a focus) are critical for shaping your study toward readers.

To review voice, purpose, and audience, go to "FieldWriting: Point of View and Rhetoric" in Chapter 2, page 63.

In this sense, your data have the power to guide your choices. But your power as a writer lies in your rhetorical decisions as you analyze, question, manipulate, and present your data. These decisions of voice, purpose, and audience are the same decisions all writers make, as we have discussed throughout this book.

As anthropologist Clifford Geertz observes, working out your rhetorical stance in your study is as much of a challenge as working your way into a fieldsite. As you discover "somewhere to stand" in your text, you are negotiating between your "intimate view" (stepping in) of the field experience and your "cool assessment" of it (stepping out). These terms, *stepping in* and *stepping out*, we borrow from Hortense Powdermaker and describe in Chapter 1. As we hope you've noticed in all the fieldstudies you've read, the writer constructs an "I" to accompany the reader through the text. How you construct yourself as part of your study is dependent on the constructed "I" working with all the other voices in your study. This chapter shows you how to shape both your data and your researcher stance as you shape your writing. Writing and analysis take place at the same time. This is not a linear process; in other words, as you reread your data, you'll simultaneously discover theories about what you've seen in the field. Gradually, you'll develop an idea or a theme that will help you draft your draft.

To us, the word **draft** suggests wind blowing through a piece of writing—with little or big holes left to fill as you craft your writing into something your reader will understand. All writers have their own styles of drafting. Just as fieldworkers establish various habits for organizing information during data collection, so do writers develop successful drafting habits. First drafts need to be exploratory, and sometimes we must force them out of a very strange paradox. We write to release ourselves from that stuck-tight, closed-up feeling that we can't write because we don't know the answers to—or the meaning of—what we want to say. We learn more about what we know as we draft. Writing a first draft is not the same as freewriting.

To review freewriting, go to "Exploratory Writing" in Chapter 2, page 57.

Freewriting uncorks your writing process and helps you become fluid, fast, and fluent. *Drafting* frees all the ideas and research about a topic that you've been holding in your mind. With subsequent drafts, you can fill in the holes—for yourself and for your readers. But the trick in getting that first draft written is to "just do it."

From our own experiences we know that even when you're prepared to begin writing, it's difficult. There are myriad and insidious ways to avoid writing. One writer we know spent most of a year vacuuming when she should have been writing. Other writers cook, swim, jog, sharpen pencils, iron, spend hours on the Internet—anything but write. While we wrote this book, in fact, we ate candy, made coffee, took breaks and naps, and talked to our friends and families on the phone.

Even professional writers procrastinate. Our colleague Don Murray gathered quotes from writers about their writing processes and habits and described his own writing processes to students and teachers. In his book *Shoptalk:*

Learning to Write with Writers, Murray says: "The single quality that distinguishes the unpublished writer from the published is not talent but work habits."

This chapter highlights the writing processes of drafting and revising. It's time to share your data, talk about it with partners, and find support from others to create your own version of your research story about the culture you've studied. Remember, in ethnographic writing, no two research essays could possibly be the same. You need to tell *your* researched story, which you've created from your personal data stash.

You may find it helpful to consult the FieldWriting section in each chapter to review the writing skills connected to each chapter's theme and to revisit the writing that you've already completed. All or some of the writing you've done so far, including box exercise material, may find its way into your final essay. See what's in your portfolio, look through your transcripts, reread your fieldnotes, and play around with your organizational patterns.

FieldWriting in *FieldWorking*

To review the FieldWriting section in each chapter, go to:

Drafting Drafts

It's time to write a first draft. Spread out your notebooks, your data, sticky notes, highlighters, scissors, file boxes, and research portfolio. Prepare to let the data speak to you as you sift through what you have. You may decide, for example, in a first sweep through your data that you'll be able to use a memorable quote from a transcript, a key image from your field descriptions, or a reflective piece you've written about your own positioning. It's reassuring to highlight your notes, attach sticky notes to what you have, spread out your printouts or consult your bookmarked Web sites, and somehow find the data you might use. Check your research journal for notes you have written about your own thoughts as they've come up, along with your comments on the artifacts you've assembled in your portfolio. This initial sweep should also help you locate gaps and missing spots that call for further information and perhaps even further research. Evaluating your raw material is not just a mechanical process. Selecting the best snippets of language and describing and reflecting on your data require time and thought.

In your first draft, you will combine many data sources into sections, so it is important to think carefully about different ways you might organize. Some people lay their data on the floor and move pages around. Some use the categories they've arranged in their portfolios. Others experiment using color-coded hanging file folders to review, organize, and change the patterns of their data. Of course, you can cluster and shift data into files on a computer using keywords as guides. Whichever methods you use, try to be flexible so you can order and reorder your disparate data as the themes emerge in your mind. This is an intellectually challenging process. Fieldworkers always accumulate too much data, far more than they can use, and must learn to let go of the data that doesn't work, fit the focus, triangulate with other data, or enrich the study. Selecting appropriate data is perhaps the most complicated part of creating a first draft.

Anne Lamott is a professional writer whose book *Bird by Bird: Some Instructions on Writing and Life* considers not only writing but the writer's habits of mind. Her book title comes from a family story. When her brother, at age 10, became overwhelmed while writing a report on birds, her writer father's comforting line was "Bird by bird, Buddy. Just take it bird by bird."

· ·

Shitty First Drafts

Anne Lamott

Now, practically even better news than that of short assignments is the idea of shitty first drafts. All good writers write them. This is how they end up with good second drafts and terrific third drafts. People tend to look at successful writers, writers who are getting their books published and maybe even doing well financially, and think that they sit down at their desks every morning feeling like a million dollars, feeling great about who they are and how much talent they have and what a great story they have to tell; that they take in a few deep breaths, push back their sleeves, roll their necks a few times to get all the cricks out, and dive in, typing fully formed passages as fast as a court reporter. But this is just the fantasy of the uninitiated. I know some very great writers, writers you love who write beautifully and have made a great deal of money, and not *one* of them sits down routinely feeling wildly enthusiastic and confident. Not one of them writes elegant first drafts. All right, one of them does, but we do not like her very much. We do not think that she has a rich inner life or that God likes her or can even stand her.

(Although when I mentioned this to my priest friend Tom, he said you can safely assume you've created God in your own image when it turns out that God hates all the same people you do.)

Very few writers really know what they are doing until they've done it. Nor do they go about their business feeling dewy and thrilled. They do not type a few stiff warm-up sentences and then find themselves bounding along like huskies across the snow. One writer I know tells me that he sits down every morning and says to himself nicely, "It's not like you don't have a choice, because you do—you can either type or kill yourself." We all often feel like we are pulling teeth, even those writers whose prose ends up being the most natural and fluid. The right words and sentences just do not come pouring out like ticker tape most of the time. Now, Muriel Spark is said to have felt that she was taking dictation from God every morning—sitting there, one supposes, plugged into a Dictaphone, typing away, humming. But this is a very hostile and aggressive position. One might hope for bad things to rain down on a person like this.

For me and most of the other writers I know, writing is not rapturous. In fact, the only way I can get anything written at all is to write really, really shitty first drafts.

The first draft is the child's draft, where you let it all pour out and then let it romp all over the place, knowing that no one is going to see it and that you can shape it later. You just let this childlike part of you channel whatever voices and visions come through and onto the page. If one of the characters wants to say, "Well, so what, Mr. Poopy Pants?," you let her. No one is going to see it. If the kid wants to get into really sentimental, weepy, emotional territory, you let him. Just get it all down on paper, because there may be something great in those six crazy pages that you would never have gotten to by more rational, grown-up means. There may be something in the very last line of the very last paragraph on page six that you just love, that is so beautiful or wild that you now know what you're supposed to be writing about, more or less, or in what direction you might go—but there was no way to get to this without first getting through the first five and a half pages.

I used to write food reviews for *California* magazine before it folded. (My writing food reviews had nothing to do with the magazine folding, although every single review did cause a couple of canceled subscriptions. Some readers took umbrage at my comparing mounds of vegetable puree with various ex-presidents' brains.) These reviews always took two days to write. First I'd go to a restaurant several times with a few opinionated, articulate friends in tow. I'd sit there writing down everything anyone said that was at all interesting or funny. Then on the following Monday I'd sit down at my desk with my notes, and try to write the review. Even after I'd been doing this for years, panic would set in. I'd try to write a lead, but instead I'd write a couple of dreadful sentences, xx them out, try again, xx everything out, and then feel despair and worry settle on my chest like an x-ray apron. It's over, I'd think, calmly. I'm not going to be able to get the magic to work this time. I'm ruined. I'm through. I'm toast. Maybe, I'd think, I can get my old job back as a clerk-typist. But probably not. I'd get up and study my teeth in the mirror for a while. Then I'd stop, remember to breathe, make a few phone calls, hit the kitchen and chow down. Eventually I'd go back and sit down at my desk, and sigh for the next ten minutes. Finally I would pick up my one-inch picture frame, stare into it as if for the answer, and every time the answer would come: all I had to do was to write a really shitty first draft of, say, the opening paragraph. And no one was going to see it.

So I'd start writing without reining myself in. It was almost just typing, just making my fingers move. And the writing would be *terrible*. I'd write a lead paragraph that was a whole page, even though the entire review could only be three pages long, and then I'd start writing up descriptions of the food, one dish at a time, bird by bird, and the critics would be sitting on my shoulders, commenting like cartoon characters. They'd be pretending to snore, or rolling their eyes at my overwrought descriptions, no matter how hard I tried to tone those descriptions down, no matter how conscious I was of what a friend said to me gently in my early days of restaurant reviewing. "Annie," she said, "it is just a piece of *chicken*. It is just a bit of *cake*."

But because by then I had been writing for so long, I would eventually let myself trust the process—sort of, more or less. I'd write a first draft that was maybe twice as long as it should be, with a self-indulgent and boring beginning, stupefying descriptions of the meal, lots of quotes from my black-humored friends that made them sound more like the Manson girls than food lovers, and no ending to speak of. The whole thing would be so long and incoherent and hideous that for the rest of the day I'd obsess about getting creamed by a car before I could write a decent second draft. I'd worry that people would read what I'd written and believe that the accident had really been a suicide, that I had panicked because my talent was waning and my mind was shot.

The next day, though, I'd sit down, go through it all with a colored pen, take out everything I possibly could, find a new lead somewhere on the second page, figure out a kicky place to end it, and then write a second draft. It always turned out fine, sometimes even funny and weird and helpful. I'd go over it one more time and mail it in.

Then, a month later, when it was time for another review, the whole process would start again, complete with the fears that people would find my first draft before I could rewrite it.

Almost all good writing begins with terrible first efforts. You need to start somewhere. Start by getting something—anything—down on paper. A friend of mine says that the first draft is the down draft—you just get it down. The second draft is the up draft—you fix it up. You try to say what you have to say more accurately. And the third draft is the dental draft, where you check every tooth, to see if it's loose or cramped or decayed, or even, God help us, healthy.

What I've learned to do when I sit down to work on a shitty first draft is to quiet the voices in my head. First there's the vinegar-lipped Reader Lady, who says primly, "Well, *that's* not very interesting, is it?" And there's the emaciated German male who writes these Orwellian memos detailing your thought crimes. And there are your parents, agonizing over your lack of loyalty and discretion; and there's William Burroughs, dozing off or shooting up because he finds you as bold and articulate as a houseplant; and so on. And there are also the dogs: let's not forget the dogs, the dogs in their pen who will surely hurtle and snarl their way out if you ever *stop* writing, because writing is, for some of us, the latch that keeps the door of the pen closed, keeps those crazy ravenous dogs contained.

Quieting these voices is at least half the battle I fight daily. But this is better than it used to be. It used to be 87 percent. Left to its own devices, my mind spends much of its time having conversations with people who aren't there. I walk along defending myself to people, or exchanging repartee with them, or rationalizing my behavior, or seducing them with gossip, or pretending I'm on their TV talk show or whatever. I speed or run an aging yellow light or don't come to a full stop, and one nanosecond later am explaining to imaginary cops exactly why I had to do what I did, or insisting that I did not in fact do it.

I happened to mention this to a hypnotist I saw many years ago, and he looked at me very nicely. At first I thought he was feeling around on the floor for the silent alarm button, but then he gave me the following exercise, which I still use to this day.

Close your eyes and get quiet for a minute, until the chatter starts up. Then isolate one of the voices and imagine the person speaking as a mouse. Pick it up by the tail and drop it into a mason jar. Then isolate another voice, pick it up by the tail, drop it in the jar. And so on. Drop in any high-maintenance parental units, drop in any contractors, lawyers, colleagues, children, anyone who is whining in your head. Then put the lid on, and watch all these mouse people clawing at the glass, jabbering away, trying to make you feel like shit because you won't do what they want—won't give them more money, won't be more successful, won't see them more often. Then imagine that there is a volume-control button on the bottle. Turn it all the way up for a minute, and listen to the stream of angry, neglected, guilt-mongering voices. Then turn it all the way down and watch the frantic mice lunge at the glass, trying to get to you. Leave it down, and get back to your shitty first draft.

A writer friend of mine suggests opening the jar and shooting them all in the head. But I think he's a little angry, and I'm sure nothing like this would ever occur to you.

•••

For many writers, there's reassurance in allowing yourself to write a messy first draft, knowing that each subsequent draft will refine what's already there. We like Lamott's father's advice to her brother, and we hope you too will be able to allow yourself to take your writing "bird by bird," one section, one draft, at a time.

As you draft and redraft, adding and subtracting pieces of data and discovering new connections, you should not bother to make your writing look perfect. Revising is *not* editing. The term **revision** implies a reseeing and reimagining of the original material. Both editing and revising can take place during the drafting process, but revising always involves making substantial changes, not just fine-tuning a sentence or two. To revise means to rewrite with an eye toward emerging ideas, themes, and voice. And then it means to draft again.

Eventually, of course, comes what Anne Lamott calls in the preceding piece the "dental draft," in which the writer must polish and edit carefully to meet the expectations and conventions appropriate for the intended audience. This dental draft is the last stage of manuscript preparation. The process of working a dental draft is quite separate from the process of revision. Your instructor probably has a policy (what Lamott might call a dental policy) that describes the conventions a piece of writing must follow in its final form. And you may find useful suggestions for the final polishing stage in the many good handbooks and online resources that are available.

For help from an online handbook, visit **bedfordstmartins.com/ fieldworking** and search under Further Research and Writing Resources.

Questioning Your Draft

Once you've written a first draft, whether it's "shitty" or not, you have something to work with that's not just piles of paper and sticky notes. This phase is a little like interviewing your draft, using guiding questions about your fieldwork material and your relationship to it. Just as interviewing requires both preparation and openness, questioning your draft also requires that you give it both structure and room for discovery.

In this section, we look back at questions you've been asking all along— about your fieldnotes and your fieldworking process—and we present some new questions that focus more tightly on the fieldwriting process. These questions are meant to support you in all the active and recursive processes of questioning, drafting, requestioning, and redrafting.

In Chapter 2, we presented three key questions for you to use regularly as you take fieldnotes and gather data:

1. **What surprised me? (to track your assumptions)**
2. **What intrigued me? (to track your positions)**
3. **What disturbed me? (to track your tensions)**

Answering these three questions can help you understand your shifting assumptions, and tracking your changing research positions helps you construct your researcher's voice to guide your reader through your study. Analyzing your tensions as they appear and sometimes disappear allows you to develop a relationship with your reader by being honest about what disturbs you—and how you come to understand this through the course of your study.

What Surprised Me?

- **A. Kendra Greene** was surprised to learn that archives have secrets (see Chapter 7). She knew there are always unknowns because the amount of material in a large archive is so vast. But what she hadn't thought about was that the archivists themselves are gatekeepers. The archivist, Ray, didn't know where everything was (there was a lot, and some of it he hadn't seen himself), but he felt loyal to the dead president's memory.

- **Rick Zollo's** surprise was in the truckers' logbook. (See Chapter 1 for Rick's study.) As Rick talked to Dan and other truckers about their jobs, they pointed him to the logbook and its restrictions on their lives. He began to see that his assumption that truckers lived an unfettered life was not entirely true. The logbook showed that they were subject to government restrictions, fines, and scrutiny from the police and the U.S. Department of Transportation.

- When **Ivana Nikolic** (see Chapter 1) first volunteered at Ramsey House, she expected it to be "saturated with religion" since it was a church-sponsored facility for the homeless. Her assumptions about the shelter, however, proved wrong. While religion was important to the shelter, Ramsey House proved mainly just "a place to hang your hat" for this displaced population.

- **Karen Downing's** study (see Chapter 4) uncovered many assumptions for her as she encountered other peoples' perspectives on the beauty culture: Ginny, the manager of Photo Phantasies, sees her work as important ("giving back to society"). Darlene, the checker at the supermarket, sees glamour photos as both "an indulgence and a treat."

- **Cindie Marshall** (see Chapter 5) was surprised to find that she felt more comfortable talking with Teardrop than the bikers she set out to study, who turned out to be less stereotypical and more varied than she'd initially assumed.

What Intrigued Me?

- Even though she had flown across the country to find one specific photo, **Kendra** had to tour the museum before she entered the archive. But seeing the museum grounded Kendra's experience and deepened her knowledge of Reagan and his times. She came to see that "there's a kind of sacred value in taking care of stuff, no matter what stuff it is. Collections and archives are really different. An archivist's priority is preservation, conservation, keeping things. But collections put a greater value on use. There's no value if people don't get to see the collection." As a manager of collections herself, Kendra had motives that were different from Ray's. Until her visit, she hadn't understood the distinction, and this was intriguing to her.

- For **Rick**, the comparison between cowboys and truckers was something that attracted him at the beginning and helped him develop a metaphor to guide him through his study. Since he'd always been intrigued by "the open road," his position as a closet cowboy helped him connect with the trucker culture.

- **Ivana** began her volunteer experiences at Ramsey House because she was drawn to the homeless people she saw on the streets of the town where she and her family had relocated. Her own position as a former refugee led her to identify with this population, whom she felt must be "insecure, lost, scared, and lonely," just as she had been when she and her family were refugees from war-torn Bosnia.

- **Karen** was intrigued by the glossy photos on the wall, the wardrobe selections (metal-studded denim jackets and gold lamé blouses), the horse (which provided her with a focus for her study), the business side of Photo Phantasies and how programmed it was, and the idea that "putting on a face" could be empowering. As a middle-class woman and teacher, her position emerged as she found herself fascinated by the details of this culture's business and fashion underlife.

What Disturbed Me?

- **Kendra** was disturbed that she had to promise not to reveal the specifics of the picture she traveled to see. And even though she still thinks it's harmless—and in fact it improved her opinion of President Reagan—she must assume that Ray, the archivist, had his reasons for requiring her promise. Kendra finds it hard to figure out the balance between the rules of the archive and her own questions about how telling others about the photo could do harm. This puzzle offered Kendra an important tension as she wrote about her visit to the archive.

- Over time, **Rick** was disturbed to find out how political the trucking industry is and how truckers face many of the same kinds of constraints in their work as office workers do.

- **Ivana** was disturbed that her work at Ramsey House made her relive her own homeless experiences as a refugee with her family. The homeless shelter became a reflection of a difficult time in her life that she had buried. When the images of eight years as a refugee reemerged, she was both disturbed and surprised by how strongly—and permanently—she had been affected by those terrifying experiences.

- **Karen** felt tension mount throughout her study as she began to track her own feminist stance—that a woman should have control over her own body—when she started to realize that the beauty culture, too, allowed that same control.

- **Cindie** was disturbed that the artifacts she observed implied illegal activities at Ralph's Sports Bar: drugs, stolen goods, and gambling. She was further disturbed by Teardrop's story, which exposed the brutality of some bikers and their abuse of women.

Thickening Your Draft

Anthropologist Clifford Geertz, whose quote introduces this chapter, borrowed the term "thick description" from philosopher Gilbert Ryle to explain the process of compiling layers of data to reveal evidence of your having "been there" in the field as you re-create and re-present your experience for a reader. He explains this data-texturing process in a well-known essay called "Thick Description: Toward an Interpretive Theory of Culture."

In that essay, he distinguishes between "thick" and "thin" description by making an analogy to the difference between two physically indistinguishable facial movements, the wink and the blink. In our culture, these movements carry markedly different implications. Thickening your draft helps you write with a fieldworker's lens. "Right down at the factual base, the hard rock, insofar as there is any," writes Geertz in his essay on thick description, "we are already explicating: and worse, explicating explications" (9).

The process of creating thick description reflects the process of triangulation, which we've discussed at various points in this book. Triangulating data is the heart of the fieldworking process, distinguishing it from library research or observational reportage. You must consider all the data in this process, even data that do not fit neatly into your plan. And since this triangulation process is intimately connected to writing your text, as our colleague Thomas Newkirk says, "the scholarship is in the *rendering*." You may want to use another triad of questions to turn your draft (your choices from "the scholarship") into a thick multilayered text ("the rendering"):

1. **What's going on here?**
2. **Where's the culture?**
3. **What's the story?**

First, "What's going on here?" asks descriptive questions of your data—about informants' rituals and routines, about how people and places interact. "Where's the culture?" refers to descriptions of language practices, place observations, background research, and artifacts you've gathered in the field to understand the group and its history. The final question, "What's the story?," includes a description of what we like to call *twin tales*—your informants' perspectives and your own perspective on the research process.

As you read through the following student drafts, notice how each researcher—
Yolanda, Heather, and Pappi—has compiled and layered specific data for the
writing.

What's Going On Here?

Yolanda Majors studied the culture of a hair salon and published her study in
a collection of essays. As a middle-class African American student, she entered
her fieldsite with many assumptions, positions, and tensions. She collected data
over several months and tried out several different approaches in her drafts.

Yolanda's challenge as a writer was to present a complex fieldsite—a hair
salon that describes itself as "multicultural" and that caters to both black and
white customers in a small, predominantly white city. Yolanda felt ambivalent
about this salon from the outset; she hadn't wanted to have a different hair
experience from the one she'd had since childhood. As a writer, she realized she
needed to show this tension in her descriptions of the places and people at her
fieldsite. In this section from one draft she called "Black Hair Don't Lie Flat,"
she shows how the white and black beauty cultures sit side by side as she contrasts names of beauty products, magazines, lighting, and furniture.

Notice that she quotes from her fieldnotes, letting the reader see her shock
at finding a white hairdresser for herself.

> Before I could enter the salon, three framed posters of white models with
> some serious attitude wearing bright business suits greet me. I pause for a
> moment to take in these advertisements of female ideal before rolling my
> eyes at the posters and givin' the doorknob a strong yank. Inside the wait-
> ing area I am greeted by the motion bells of the door and two floor shelves
> stocked with plastic bottles of this, that, and the other.
>
> "Hello?" Moving beneath a tracked spotlight, I make my way toward
> the L-shaped showcase in black lacquer, functioning as the receptionist
> desk minus the receptionist and doubling as a display case for a field
> of beauty products. Aveda, Tressa, Ecoly, brand names with top-dollar
> advertising in *Mademoiselle* and *Glamour* magazines. I couldn't say that
> this place was representing the repertoire of products in my bathroom
> cabinet—Dark and Lovely, African Royale, Cream of Nature—or of the
> black beauty shops and Korean-owned and -operated beauty-supply stores
> in the heart of my downtown.
>
> "May I help you?" The "black-white girl" appeared from the back of the
> store, entering my experience like she owned part of it.
>
> "Yes, I have an appointment with Darlene. My name is Yolanda." In
> an attempt to locate the best fly-girl-diva voice I had, I ended up sounding
> defensive.
>
> "Ah right, have a seat, I'll tell her you're here." She looked at me with a
> raised eyebrow as if I were crazy, yet managed to give me a smirk of a smile.

"The WG (white girl) greeted me. Her hair was laid in golden black-girl spirals, and I think that she's wearing the same jeans and sweat shirt she had on the other day. Maybe it's a uniform. If it is, someone should tell her that it's not representing the wannabe chic decor in here" (from my fieldnotes).

As I scribbled these first thoughts down in my field journal, I realized that my hand was trembling with embarrassment.

In a different draft, Yolanda shifts her stance to focus on a more reflective theme. Here is an excerpt in which she describes the same place and the same event and yet focuses on different details. She moves in for a close-up using the salon's mirrors as a metaphor to illustrate the black and white tension. You'll see more subtle nuances as she writes herself into the scene through the metaphor of the mirrors:

As I followed Darlene through a wide, doorless entryway, separating the front reception area of the salon from an adjacent room, I looked around hoping to find something familiar. . . . Taking a seat I was literally face to face with a reflection of myself, as I sat in Darlene's chair facing the large, black-framed glass. At first I thought it was unusual to have a mirror facing me directly. In all of my encounters with hair salons, mirrors have always been placed on either the side or in the back of the client's view. It made me uncomfortable at first, yet as I gazed into the picture in the glass, a picture of Darlene, her hands, my "nappy" head, our "talk" being pulled together in that mirror, I felt completely connected to the world around me, as if I too were a thread in this cultural cloth.

While Yolanda's two drafts are quite different, neither of them represents "better" or "worse" writing. Both drafts illustrate how one writer experiments with choices—of descriptive details, of how people and places interact, and of how the researcher fits into the scene.

Where's the Culture?

When you ask the question "Where's the culture?" you are inquiring about the language and artifacts as well as the rituals and behaviors that help the group define its own culture to itself as well as to you. While this question overlaps with "What's going on here?" it focuses on more intricate details of the subculture that become apparent only after repeated visits to the fieldsite, deeper investigations, and accumulations of data. Only the actual informants in the culture can provide answers to this question.

Heather Kiger studied the subculture of bull riding and came to see over a period of time that the performance nature of this sport was much like her own experience with dance. "We are performers who love what we do and have our own fans and supporters who enjoy watching us," she writes. Initially, Heather did not feel this connection to the culture she studied; it took many drafts for her to understand bull riding enough to relate it to dancing.

In the first of six drafts, Heather places herself on center stage, where she makes an ethnographic inventory of the artifacts and the rituals of bull riding. As you read the following excerpt, you can almost imagine what her fieldnotes contained:

> To the left of the pen is an area that has a white sign with red letters that says "Contestants Only." I see several contestants in the area, and most of them have women with them, probably wives or girlfriends, so I walk inside the gate. They all have bags with them, so I peek inside one and see that it contains gloves, a rope, a pair of jeans, a thick vest, a pair of cowboy boots, spurs, and a bottle of Tylenol. The contestants all have on jeans, tennis shoes or cowboy boots, a T-shirt, and a cowboy hat. They all have short hair, clean-shaven faces, and look to range in age from nineteen to twenty-six.
>
> I walk over to a section of bleachers next to the announcer's station, which is a low wooden platform with an overhead covering. Behind me is a very small white building with windows, and I can see trophies inside. On the platform are large speakers on each side, and the announcer is on a stool in the center holding a microphone. He is trying to get people to sign up for a game called bull bingo and an event called steer wrestling.

Heather has accomplished a difficult challenge in writing up fieldwork; she's written the first layer of details for herself, with herself as the main character looking at the culture. But in a later draft, she becomes able to shift her perspective away from herself to a multilayered description of one insider in the culture, along with the artifacts and rituals that represent the whole culture of bull riders:

> It is a Wednesday night, and he is riding down the road singing as loud as he can along with Skinnard on the radio, and his cowboy hat is lying undisturbed on the dashboard. He has left all his troubles back at home, and riding is the only goal on his mind. His bag is packed and is in the back of the truck. When he gets to Creek Junction, his mind turns away from Skinnard and on to the main event of the night. He gets his bag and heads for the designated area. The audience is just starting to arrive, and Little Texas is blasting from the speakers, "You've got to kick a little." The concession stand is open and already packed with hungry fans.
>
> Before he unpacks his bag, he roams the bullpens and hopes he draws a good one. He goes back to his bag and begins unpacking it by putting his chaps, vest, and rope around the fence. He takes his jeans out and goes to the bathroom to change. When he comes back, he is ready to rosin up his rope, the most important piece of equipment. He slips on his glove

and brushes off the remaining dust and grit from the last bull ride, crumbles rosin in this gloved hand, and applies it to the bull rope. This helps him continue to have a good grip on the rope during the extremely bumpy ride. Boots and spurs are the next items to come out of the bag, and then he puts on his long-sleeved buttoned-up shirt. A few of his buddies have arrived, and they start up a bull-riding conversation while moving over to the guy who has the bulls' names to see which one he will ride tonight. His bull is Unforgiven. After they have gone, he returns to his bag, kneels, and begins praying that the ride will be a safe one and that he will walk away uninjured. The last items he puts on before the ride are his chaps and protective vest. The vest serves as the only real protection from the bull. He continues preparing for his ride by stretching out and warming up his legs and arms as a precaution against injury.

In this later draft, Heather has thickened her description to be more than a list. This time, she places her reader inside the bull-rider's culture, bringing it to life through one bull-rider's actions as he prepares for a ride. In answering the question "Where's the culture?" Heather collected descriptions of language practices, observations of her site, and artifacts she gathered about the subculture of bull riders.

What's the Story?

Every fieldstudy has twin tales to tell. One story is about what the culture means through the perspective of informants. The other is the story about how you, the outsider, conducted the research.

Documentaries about "the making of the movie" offer an insider's look at how a finished film came about, and your story of your fieldwork offers your readers the same perspective. An important but difficult job of fieldwriting is to allow informants to tell a tale about their lives—and find a way to include yourself as the fieldworker telling the tale.

Pappi Tomas did a fieldstudy of an Irish tailor, Chipper, who owns a small shop. After Pappi gathered data on Chipper, he found himself overwhelmed with the piles of information he'd accumulated. Pappi's informal writing shows his anxiety about being respectful to Chipper's words as his own data "balloons." He's understanding the delicate balance between his own researcher's tale and Chipper the tailor's story:

Oh, but I had so much to work from. My jottings ballooned. My cassette tapes—which I began using after the first interview—suggested to me that there was too much gold pouring from Chipper's mouth to hold in my measly brainpan. They ballooned, too. And soon my "underground scribblings" contained several different drafts of the same material, plus recordings transcribed long after the fact, so that I was incorporating them into the drafting as I made my way through the essay—like laying a brick road and driving over it at the same time. . . .

When it came to drafting, I had good days and bad days as always. I began with "To find out what sort of tailor Chipper is, you might begin with the walls," which from the start felt like the beginning of the essay. Yet somewhere midway, after I'd shared a draft in process, I was seriously unsure of how to enter this subject. Should it flow narratively? Was this impressionistic beginning forceful enough?

Even now I'm not sure if the voice I settled on is right for the material, or if I settled on a voice at all. . . . You see, I didn't want a journalistic piece. . . . I wanted to build a little poetry if I could into the story of Chipper, which of course did not need the likes of me to give it poetry. Chipper himself speaks a poetry all his own.

In his final essay, you'll notice how carefully Pappi integrates his data sources with his own voice and Chipper's. He transcribes and quotes carefully from his recorded interviews, including his rendering of Chipper's speech to show that "Chipper himself speaks a poetry all his own." One of the ways Pappi achieves a seamlessness in his writing is to use "you" (the second-person pronoun) to invite his readers into his text and into Chipper's shop. He decided to use this rhetorical device after many drafts. In this excerpt subtitled "The Cutter around the Corner," Pappi crafts his voice by using twin tales:

"In the old days," Chipper begins, "there were no electrical machines. They were all just treadle." He talks to me now. "I have to turn me back on you now," he says, from the old green sewing machine, which sits in its table under a window against the wall. A "flat machine," he calls it, though it is anything but flat, with a long arching arm to accommodate bulky folds of fabric. A century-old Singer machine, its kind, in the trade, is used as much now as ever. "Of course, whenever I went to England, you know, when I was a greenhorn, you know—never saw a power machine. Scared the bloody hell out a' me. I thought it was goin' to run up me arm, you know. And I didn't want to let meself down, you know, that I didn't know anything about a power machine."

A long time ago that was, and hard to imagine, when you watch him thread that machine—around and through and down, up, down. As smooth as wrapping thread around a spool; watch him slide the garment under the needle, lean forward in short, heavy bursts of drumming stitch, and watch him hold a conversation with you, greet a customer just come in, nudging, slanting, easing, spreading the folds through all the while. When you see all this, it is indeed a stretch of fancy to see him sitting there, decades ago, a greenhorn in Ireland, poised with belly aflutter.

Likewise a stretch it is when you watch him mark trousers with shaved chalk and ruler or watch him, number two thimble (thirteen on the American scale) in place, poke the needle through, yank to the side, then, like a firefly, dart up and out, pulling the thread taut, ready for the next stitch. These are the moments of consummate skill that I admire, that I yearn (as we all do, those of us who admire the practiced artist) to experience myself in some craft, be it shaping the curve of a sentence or molding the slope of a collar.

As we noted earlier in this chapter, many writers admit to the difficulty of disciplining themselves as they write, revise, write again, revise, write again, revise, and more. Over the course of his visits to the tailor shop, Pappi went through the process of layering his data into his drafts. He changed his mind a lot, learned much about tailoring, and deepened his understanding about Chipper.

In all these excerpts from students' fieldwork, the three questions ("What's going on here?" "Where's the culture?" and "What's the story?") guided the writers' assembly of data. You also may have noticed their struggles to find a place to stand in the text, to construct a voice that would do justice to their data and to themselves as researchers. Their multiple drafts show you that there is no one way to present data, that all writers need to play around to discover a voice that works for them every time they do a writing project.

By now you know that you, as the researcher, are *not* the only character in your fieldwork story. Fieldwriting is multivocal, and you are responsible for other voices as well as your own. Like Yolanda, Heather, and Pappi, you'll want to pay attention to the issue of voice as you draft and redraft. Good fieldwriting allows informants to speak for themselves alongside the writer's cultural interpretations.

BOX33

Listening to the Voices in Your Draft

DAVID SEITZ, WRIGHT STATE UNIVERSITY, DAYTON, OHIO

PURPOSE

Ethnographic writers strive to maintain the individual voices from the fieldsite. As **participant-observers**, their own voices often shift between a cultural insider's and academic researcher's voice. When ethnographic writers use secondary research, they do not want the voices of their sources to overpower either their informants' views or their own. Your final writing should allow these various voices equal opportunity to interpret their **worldviews**. This difficult balance is much easier to develop when you first visibly highlight the voices in your complete first draft.

BOX**33** continued

Highlighting voices helps you hear them more clearly, making sure each remains distinct in terms of language use, what each communicates about the culture of the group, and the contexts for their statements. This activity may also help you better understand the way you represent your relationship with the informants in your fieldsite.

ACTIVITY

Highlight in different colors each of the following kinds of voices you can find in your present draft. After highlighting, use the questions about each kind of voice to reflect on your writing choices and strategies. Write a two- or three-paragraph response based on these reflections, and share your insights with a partner.

1. *Each voice from the fieldsite:* How do the similarities and differences in their voices show unity and tensions in the group or social structures?

2. *Your voice as cultural interpreter:* How does your voice compare to those you are researching? Do you speak in more than one voice in your draft? When are you speaking as insider? As outsider?

3. *Voices of secondary print and electronic sources:* Do they overpower the voices from the fieldsite or your own interpretations?

In your response, try to write about how you would want to revise based on your listening closely to these multiple voices.

RESPONSE

Angela Shaffer studied three young women who worked at a midsize natural history museum. The women operated the front desk and gift shop area, daily greeting customers of all ages, answering questions, selling gifts, and dealing with problem guests. Angela came to understand how the three employees worked together to create a group personality while calling on their individual strengths. Through their humor, informal games, and mutual support, they displayed their beliefs about work, friendship, and even their coworkers and supervisors. Angela wrote a reflective response to this exercise:

> I found that I showed well the group dynamics of Laura, Allie, and Leigh when I described their talk and actions. It appeared they were just goofing off at work, but they were actually creating the open work atmosphere they wanted for their future careers—relaxed when possible, efficient when necessary. I opened my draft with their zip code game (where they try to guess the zip codes of incoming customers as an indication of their social class) to demonstrate their creativity and need to break the monotony using their intelligence.
>
> Nevertheless, I could have developed more their individual voices, styles of talk, and humor along with my descriptions. I did, however, draw a scene with dialogue of Allie and Laura showing how they talk with each other compared with their talk with customers. In this moment, Allie and Laura teased each other about their intelligence as they worked over their daily crosswords but shifted to a more distant tone with customers in between their own conversation, never missing a beat between the two.

I now can see several places where I could have let my informants' voices help interpret their actions that I only described for them. In one area I describe Allie and Laura teasing Leigh, the youngest of the three, about her enthusiasm for waiting on customers. I need to show through Leigh's voice how wild she can get about that. Also, I contrast Allie's voice as she's dealing with irate customers with and without her coworkers to back her up. Although I show the difference in Allie's tone in each situation, I could also include Allie's voice interpreting her different approaches. Similarly, when I examined how they present a unified front when faced with their bosses' expectations and their coworkers' slacking off, I could have let them give their views about it.

Doing this exercise showed me the importance of separating my voice from those of my informants and all the institutional voices that surround the museum gift shop.

Representing Culture in Your Fieldwriting

Taking a stand on the page involves making lots of narrative choices. How do you decide to combine your data? How will you integrate your informants' voices and perspectives with your own? How will you portray yourself, the others, their culture and yours, and the twin tales you're telling? And, above all, how will you keep your reader interested in reading your words about where you've been, what you've seen, and what you've thought about it all? The answers to these questions will rely on your own artistic choices as well as your experiments with words.

We've developed three lists that encompass some of the most effective writing strategies available to fieldworkers, strategies that will bring life to your work—and bring your work to life. Table 8-1 identifies these experiential, rhetorical, and aesthetic strategies.

TABLE 8-1   Selected Strategies for Cultural Representation

Experiential	*Rhetorical*	*Aesthetic*
Fieldnotes	Positionality	Metaphor and simile
Double-entry notes	Voice of the researcher	Sensory image
Research journals	Voice of the "other"	Concrete image
Interview transcripts	Point of view	Ethnopoetic notation
Photos and artifacts	Analytic section heads	Spatial gaze
Notes on readings and other background sources	(subheads) Analytic titles	

Experiential Strategies

You have many layers of data: fieldnotes, double-entry notes, notes from your background reading, and other fieldwork records like tapes and transcripts, photos and artifacts. We like to call this mass of field material **experiential**— firsthand accounts of your experience at specific times and in specific places. In your fieldwriting, you'll use this material to convince readers that *you were there*—that you saw the places, heard the people, and tried to interpret what they were doing.

Rhetorical Strategies

Another way to represent yourself and your informants originates with the **rhetorical choices** you make as a writer—choices of voice, purpose, and audience.

To review rhetorical concepts, go to "FieldWriting: Point of View and Rhetoric" in Chapter 2, page 63.

As a fieldworker crafts a final written text using informants' words, background information, field experiences, and observations, she asks questions that help shape a rhetorical stance. These questions can help the fieldwriter determine her purpose and voice and think about the needs of her audience:

1. Whose views of this culture am I representing—mine, my informants', or background information? What is the balance among these sources?

2. How do I organize data? How can I include my informants' perspective or worldview? Through my own? Or through some theme from my data?

3. How am I representing my informants? What data do I use to re-create an informant on the page? Have I given my reader enough details to visualize or "hear" my informant?

4. What sense of place am I offering? What details of setting do I use to organize and locate what I saw? What data do I use to re-create this place? Will my readers feel as if they've been there with me?

5. What assumptions, positions, and tensions do I bring to my interpretations? Where did they come from? Will my reader know enough about me to understand them?

6. Would I offer my reader the same information if I presented it a different way? Could I shift point of view and tell a similar story?

A fieldwriter's answers to these questions can help guide the writing process. Creative options give us much rhetorical power as writers. Table 8-1 (p. 369) offers a sample of rhetorical choices, many of which we've already discussed in this book. Not every strategy is useful for every study. Each setting, each culture, and each person suggest different rhetorical decisions about the chronology or the shape of the narrative. What fieldworkers actually experience governs the shape of the written text.

Aesthetic Strategies

Finally, the third column in Table 8-1 suggests that like good fiction or poetry, a well-written fieldstudy needs artful design to allow the reader in. Throughout this book, we've pointed out writers' conscious uses of **aesthetic** features. For example, in Chapter 1, Ivana Nikolic describes both the sounds and smells she encounters outside and inside of Ramsey House. In Chapter 4, Maggie McKnight contrasts the light of midwestern winters against the fragrance of English breakfast tea and eggs on garlic toast with prosciutto. In Chapter 6, Danling Fu uses simile when she describes silkworms as pets: "Our relationship with worms is like yours with cats and dogs." Her description of the worms themselves draws on imagery and simile: "thick as a little finger," "smaller than an ant," and "tastes like a peanut."

Crafting a Text

In this section, we'd like to show how all these strategies come together in drafting a text. Our example comes from Elizabeth's student William Harvey Purcell. William studied "the disability arts and rights movement." You've already seen his glossary of disability terms in Box 27 (Chapter 6). As he conducted his research, William traveled from North Carolina to Iowa City to interview an informant. Not only did he find his informant there—musician Jim Whalen—but he also investigated Iowa's disability culture, including Bonnie's colleague, writer and professor Steve Kuusisto, a scholar in disability studies, and also Bonnie's own two disabled adult children and their friends. In this excerpt, William uses some of the formal experiential, rhetorical, and aesthetic writing strategies we've introduced.

· ·

Disability Is Beautiful

William Harvey Purcell

Is disability beautiful? Is it, really? I set out to investigate the cultural landscape of the disability rights and arts movement by attending the Southeastern Disability Culture Festival in Asheville, NC, which is a day to celebrate the poetry, dance, photography, painting, music, film, comedy, theater, lecture, video production, and songs of people experiencing disability. I wanted to challenge expectations, assumptions, and perceptions by showing realties not often seen or completely accepted by society. It seems few people link disability and the arts.

Wanting to Not Be Normal

I started this process as a miner. Like most researchers, I began with an axe, dynamite, and a wheelbarrow, hoping to find jewels and haul them back for "oohs" and "ahhs." Then, as any good miner would, I'd sit down and polish the stones before comparing them to others for sorting, classification, and display. However, during my journey, I discovered that this process is not about mining. It is about traveling together; not about bringing back jewels, but unlearning, relearning, and coming to new understandings about what jewels are; not about wielding an axe, but holding up a mirror; not about exploding, but listening. I was not a miner after all. I was a traveler trying to make sense of a journey with my fellow travelers.

I discovered that understanding what it means to be a person experiencing disability is a journey each of us must undertake if we ever hope to redefine and reshape the world we all inhabit. I discovered that I'm intricately tied to disability culture, not only through the birth of my son who has Down syndrome, but also through family, friends, coworkers, and the more than 60 million people with disabilities in America. I discovered that, yes, disability is beautiful. Yes, I am a part of disability culture. How did I come to these conclusions?

I Don't Want to Be Normal
I don't want to be normal
If I gotta be like you
Follow social rules
Made up by fools
I've got better things to do
I don't need to be special
And my name it isn't Ed
You can pretend
Right down to the end
I'd rather be real instead
My body it may be broken
But my heart it is quite whole
I use half my mind and I try to be kind
And I never will sell my soul
I don't want to be normal
If I gotta be like you

— Jim Whalen, © 2007

I knew Jim Whalen was blind, but it was still hard to believe sometimes. During the Southeastern Disability Culture Festival in Asheville, NC, Jim played an hour-long set of country/rock solo guitar mixed with social satire lyrics. After the standing ovation, I watched him unplug his black-and-white electric guitar from his amp and leave the stage, nodding and waving to the crowd. I knew then that I wanted to interview him.

I continued to relax with my five-year-old son, Liam, before the next performance. I thought it had been a lot to ask of a boy that young. We were at the end of a long day and I could tell that Liam was about to ask a big question. He scrunched up his eyes and leaned in close. I feared what he would ask. How could I answer?

What did he think about the songs Jim just performed about not being normal? What was he thinking about all these people with disabilities: all these wheelchairs, tons of them, rolling to and fro; the woman sitting on the other end of our row who kept taking off her prosthetic foot to scratch at the stump; the white artificial voice box peering out from under another woman's chin; the array of walking braces in institutional silver, sparkling purple, and cherry red; the cacophony of slurred speech, moans, excited yelps, and the hum of electric chairs engaging and disengaging? Liam cuddled up to me while his mother fed his brother, Kenyon. I worried. We had told him this was a festival but didn't really explain the disability part. He had good role models for acceptance and for celebration of diversity. He has a brother with Down syndrome.

Liam leaned in and asked, "Can we come back again tomorrow?"

Experiencing Disabilities

The first time I saw Jim Whalen up close, I wasn't sure I had the right person. Hearing my footsteps on the cold, slick tile, Jim turned, looked me in the eye, and smiled.

"Jim?" I asked.

"That's me," he responded. I explained my project of doing interviews of artists with disabilities at this festival. "Let's get this interview done before my second set." Jim, in the Hawaiian shirt, turned and led the way toward the main hall.

Even though I had just seen him perform, I thought, "Is this guy really blind?" Later, of course, I learned that, yes, in a purely medical sense, Jim is blind.

With the tape recorder between us, I began by asking him about his disability, his blindness. Jim replied at great length. "I'm legally blind, or illegally blind. I don't know what illegally blind is—I guess if you took some illegal substance and blinded yourself. My blindness was from birth. I have lesions on my retina. They've never gone as far as saying it happened because of too much oxygen at birth, but I was a little over four weeks premature and that would be consistent with that. I was small—a little under 4 pounds. And I lost weight. So, I think at one point, I was 2 pounds and something. I survived it. I was born in Mercy Hospital, which is ironic. The nurse, right away, when I was first born, within the first few hours, gave me the rites. They baptized me and did the whole thing. I was anointed. And since it was a Catholic hospital, then they administered last rites."

I prodded him for more information on what it was like to be blind. How much of the world I see does he experience? Jim described his sight. "My vision? It is like looking through a kaleidoscope. I am looking right at your face right now, or I believe I am looking right at your face, or pretty close to right at your face. What I see there are sort of psychedelic, light flashes—yellows, whites, purples. The psychedelic spot is more of a volleyball size."

What kind of schooling had Jim experienced? "One day my mom said, 'Maybe it would be best if you went to the school for the blind in Vinton.' Vinton was a residential program for blind kids. And she said to me, 'I feel bad that you are not a normal kid.' And the thought that struck me—and I can remember the exact place I was standing and the exact stance I was standing in. I just said it, 'This is normal for me. I'm perfectly okay with this. It's normal for me.' That had a profound effect on me from that day on."

Jim made me wonder how other people might understand the perspective of those with disabilities and especially about this slogan written in blue across his T-shirt: "Disability Is Beautiful."

He continued: "I've started, on many occasions, moving from the term 'people with disabilities' to 'people experiencing disability.' It's a more inclusive term. It also allows you to think in terms of the family who experiences that disability as well. Using the word *experiencing* suggests that it has a meaning within the life of a person. That disability has a meaning that we have to pay attention to. It is more important for you or my kids or for anybody to understand the meaning of my disability than to understand the physical nature of it. The medical model would say, 'Jim has a disability.' My vision is this and what I can't do is that. What I can't do is drive a car. What I can't do is see. . . . I really believe that the idea of forcing a different kind of thought process regarding disability is the key to much of what disability in our society is hung up on. Disability is beautiful. If beauty is among the range of thoughts that you need to connect with disability, more power to it. I think any concept that broadens the spectrum of your thinking about labels is good. Disability is beautiful."

Creating a Creative Space

I continued to be fascinated with Jim's worldview and traveled from North Carolina to his home in Iowa City to interview him about being part of the disability culture and, in particular, about expressing that culture through art. Jim's two-story house looked like the others in the neighborhood. They stood tightly packed in deep lots with small front yards and a ribbon of sidewalk connecting one to the other, often with garages in the back. Jim greeted me wearing a dark blue T-shirt and black jeans held up with a set of black suspenders. His work boots were dirty. He had a thin layer of stubble on his face and the wind blew his hair into a wild bird-nest shape. He could have just gotten off work from the steel mill, the barge, the automotive factory, or the hog farm.

When Jim listens to you, he looks you in the eye. When he really gets into a story, he looks to the side or he looks up. When really intent, he looks down. At first I thought he wasn't paying attention, but I soon realized it was the exact opposite. The more Jim lost eye contact, the more into the story he was. He later explained to me that "eye contact" is just an illusion he keeps to make people feel comfortable. When he looks you in the eye, he is not really seeing you. When he rises up nodding with eyes closed, perhaps crossing his arms, perhaps turning his head left or right, you know he is really into your story or really into telling his.

The kitchen and dining room of his house blended together with a wide counter-top in the middle, covered with stacks of mail, a box of envelopes, a Hannah

Montana notebook, an old hat, an MP3 player, spare nickels, pennies, an old watch, and various kids' meal-type toys. On the dining room side was Jim's creative nook. Flanked on either side by glass-door hutches, one displaying his wife's collection of snow globes and the other filled with stacks of china and glassware, Jim's creative nook was about five by four feet. Two dusty acoustic guitars sat abandoned in Jim's nook, one needing to be restrung. The guitars rested atop boxes full of vinyl albums, stacks of books, and unemptied plastic bags from a recent shopping trip. Dividing the boundary of Jim's creative space from the dining room was a stack of stereo equipment: two CD players, four cassette decks, two turntables, an equalizer, and a receiver. Two large speakers rested on either side of the stack, and jewel cases—empty and full—were scattered about. A snake pit of black, brown, purple, and blue cords led out into the middle of Jim's space where a plain folding chair sat. To one side was his amp; to the other were two guitar stands, one with Jim's electric guitar and the other with his daughter's blue bass guitar. Foot pedals formed a semi-circle in front of the chair, where a microphone stand rose up. A print of Eric Enstrom's photograph *Grace* hung on the wall behind Jim's chair. Only inches from this classic American painting was a framed print of Sponge-Bob Square Pants.

Singing an Ode to the Pity Merchant

It's snake oil wrapped in pity
But you dress it up so pretty
And you make it smell like honey
But it still sells for blood money

You keep us on the edges
'Till it's time to ask for pledges
And you really wish that we were gone
Till there's another telethon

When you can
Sell her limp leg to the firefighters
Sell my blind eyes to the banker's wife
You can pocket a cool grand or two
And all it costs is my shot at a life

Now you pity merchants should be proud
In the daylight we see your face in our crowd
But at night you slither for your tainted salaries
And banish us from your social galleries
And you never sell our skills to your boss
Or never think not dating me's a loss
'Cause you're prejudiced and man I've seen it
You never say we're welcome and really mean it

Now listen to me children
A storm it is a buildin'

And I don't want to alarm ya
But it's about to rain bad karma
And I wonder if the pity merchant knows
That there's a bell and for whom it tolls
When the lightning strikes and the thunder rolls?

God help you if it's your own son
Or it is your daughter
That you traded for some pity and
Left out for the slaughter
Because soon we'll all be rallied
And your sins will all be tallied
And forgiveness won't be found
When the truth spills on the ground
And righteousness sees the light of day
And the sword of justice swings this way

Cause we are not just parts and pieces
And we're going to take control
And we won't be sold with pity
We are whole, as we are . . .
We are whole . . . we are whole.

—Jim Whalen, © 2007

Jim and I are talking about his creative process, about how he writes songs like "Ode to the Pity Merchant." Jim smiles and motions in the air with his hands as he tells about his creative process of songwriting, "When I write the germinal idea for a song, I sit in a chair in my dining room—a folding chair—and sing the lyrics and play the sounds and think in my head. And I may play for an hour and write nothing, but it's a process of ideas and music running around each other until they catch up. After playing for about an hour, a song will finish itself. . . . Like 'Ode to the Pity Merchant'—one doesn't think of caregivers or someone like a 'pity merchant,' but if that pity doesn't sell, that person loses their work. 'Ode to the Pity Merchant,' of course, can't be a happy tune. I start maybe with an A minor chord, because that's not a happy chord, and just start rolling some things from my head and that's how the process sort of comes. My music is very daily experience-oriented. I try to reach out and say, 'I heard what you said' with my songs. And that's how it comes. It's hard work."

Hearing Forks and Spoons

As we continued to talk about Jim's music and his abilities, I began to forget he was blind. I might hold up a finger to nonverbally say "wait a minute," and amazingly he responded. I asked, "How'd you do that?" He said, "I heard it." Jim discussed his extraordinary hearing as well as his hopes for others to learn from the divergent and creative thinking of those experiencing disability. Jim shares, "I enjoy the fact that, because I use my hearing for so many things, so many learning experiences, that the range of sounds I recognize is tremendous. I think that's a cool thing. Is it important that I can recognize the sound of a handful of spoons versus a handful of forks? No. I'm never going to make a million dollars saying, 'Here, rattle those. I can tell you what's in there.' In a way, that's cool. The thing I have to do now is transfer that into situations where I'm helping other folks learn."

Negotiating and Reframing Disability

After a few days of sitting across the table, Jim really opened up in a way that honored me. We both shared intimate stories. For me, one moment of connection showed what my entire ethnographic research process was about. "But the thing is," Jim explained, "the thing I miss most is seeing the expressions on the face of my kids. I mean, I kind of imagine them, but it would be good to . . . you know. . . ." I had not heard Jim at a loss for words, but for a moment Jim was silent.

Part of being in a disability culture is negotiating and reframing, letting go of false expectations for my own son. It is likely that Kenyon won't get a driver's license, won't go to college, and won't have children. He will have to work hard to live independently. As parents, we will have to fight for his inclusion in school. We will have to deal with a society that sometimes mocks those with disabilities. Those issues to me are the relatively easy ones to deal with. My personal issues are the harder ones to reframe. Jim made me wonder: when I think of Kenyon and his disability, what do I miss most? What I miss most is speech. Kenyon doesn't communicate with words. Sometimes when he and I are alone at home I will look him in the face and repeat the sentence over and over, "I love you, I love you, I love you . . . ," hoping he will respond. I know he loves me; he communicates that to me in many ways. And it is my personal negotiation of Kenyon's disability to move beyond asking something of him that is only important to me. My interview with Jim made me understand that disability can be beautiful.

• •

William's dilemma as a researcher was that over time he had collected mounds of different kinds of data about the disability arts subculture (including the portrait of Jim). He prepared a documentary video as well as a master's thesis. But his data included journal entries, interview notes and transcripts, observations and fieldnotes, photographs, songs, poems, artwork, brochures, artifacts, video and audio recordings, and background material on disability rights.

As he surveyed his data, William asked himself, "What do I want my readers to learn about this subculture?" Jim's T-shirt, which announced "Disability Is Beautiful," became the title of William's essay. And so, his decision about how to share his data with his readers came from what he had learned about the subculture itself in the very language of his informant.

William's Experiential Strategies

To tell his own researcher's story, William chose data that would show the reader how he interviewed informants from the disability arts community—specifically, in this excerpt, Jim Whalen. His interest in Jim took William on a very long road trip from the concert in North Carolina to Jim's home in Iowa, and we experience that with him. We also experience William's position as a parent of two young sons, one of whom has Down syndrome. William shares his worries and pride with us as he describes his family's delight in the concert. To help readers believe in the research, it's important that researchers disclose the kinds of relationships they form with their informants. In William's case here, he even tells us that he wishes his son Kenyon could speak to him. Depicting the actual fieldwork in process develops the researcher's narrative voice and allows the reader to participate in the story.

William's Rhetorical Strategies

William organized his writing around an argument for the disability arts culture—that people labeled as "disabled" can be artists. He writes that "few people link disability and the arts." He carries his argument, a traditional rhetorical strategy, by choosing data to support his argument—for instance, Jim Whalen's songs and the description of the audience.

William also uses subheadings as a rhetorical strategy. These headings signal important themes in his text and help readers understand his analysis:

- Wanting to Not Be Normal
- Experiencing Disabilities
- Creating a Creative Space
- Hearing Forks and Spoons
- Negotiating and Reframing Disability

William used other rhetorical strategies in his larger study. For example, he included voices of many informants from the disability culture to achieve a balance between "self" and "other" and support his arguments.

William's Aesthetic Strategies

Writers cannot tell feelings to their readers; they must show the feelings instead. Well-chosen imagery and careful use of aesthetic or poetic devices are not extraneous details. Rather, they can sensitize a reader toward a point of view, an argument, or an idea. For the purposes of fieldwriting, researchers draw on the same aesthetic strategies that all writers use to elicit strong emotional responses from their readers.

William learned from Elizabeth's class that "a metaphor can be an ethnographer's best friend." And so he describes beginning his research process as a miner using an axe: He thought he'd be "polishing stones" and sorting them (as in gathering interviews and putting them on display like geologic specimens). But instead, he unearths a new metaphor—not about bringing back jewel specimens, but coming to understand what the jewels are. As he tries to make sense of his research journey, he begins to see himself as a fellow traveler rather than a miner. As readers, we follow his metaphorical thinking along the way.

Another aesthetic strategy William uses is one that poets use: repetition of a strong and personal image. When we first see Kenyon, his mother is feeding him at the concert, while William cuddles with his other son, Liam. This is the image through which we learn that Kenyon has Down Syndrome. We don't return to the image until the end of William's essay, after we've met Jim, read his songs, and considered a lot of information about the disability arts culture. In his final conversation with Jim, William returns to the image of Kenyon as he meditates on the special, loving communication he shares with his son.

When you make choices about writing your fieldwork essay, much of your drafting process involves imagining what a reader needs to know. Imagining your readers as you revise is often a difficult task. Fieldwork studies, we think, are interesting to actual audiences both inside and outside the cultures you study.

FieldWriting: Analytic Section Headings

One of the best things about writing fieldstudies is that they can and should be completed in sections. As you organize your data, certain parts of the study will stand out as potential sections: topics such as "Entering the Field," "Interviewing Informants," "Understanding Culture," and "Looking at Artifacts" can become your way of organizing information. But once you start writing, you'll see that you can refine your text into sections with specific and interesting headings. These headers describe what is in each section but also provide the reader with a type of thematic analysis. The art of organizing fieldstudies engages your mind with significant features and themes, and this is what you want to convey to your audience when writing your section headers. These headers might be key words of the culture, the actual words of your informants, themes from the fieldsite, or descriptive words about the artifacts you find there. On the next page, we list some of the headers William used in his study of the disability arts culture.

When you organize your study with carefully selected subheadings, you are actually making an outline and providing the reader with an analysis of your data at the same time. These headers convey the themes of your study, and you construct them from recurring patterns in the data, from key moments in the interviews, and from a distillation of the observations you have made. List your headings, and scan them to see if they represent the themes and key ideas of the study you are presenting. When a section stands out as not matching the flow of the others, it will provide you with a clue about what is working best and what sections might need more work.

In one of our favorite full-length ethnographic studies, *Translated Woman: Crossing the Border with Esperanza's Story*, researcher Ruth Behar makes wonderful use of analytic section headings. In this ethnographic oral history, Behar crosses the border from the United States to Mexico to interview Esperanza, a street peddler whom she studied for many years. Behar uses headers to provide a thematic outline of her study of Esperanza, a complex and multifaceted woman who experienced many hardships.

The first part of Behar's study is called "Coraje/Rage," evoking the double voice of Spanish and English that the book employs and giving the reader a clue that subsequent headings will be connected to this theme of rage. One of the things Esperanza recognized as she shared her oral history with Behar was the reflexive understanding that her own mother suffered the abuse and sadness that Esperanza would herself experience throughout life. The subheads of this section of the book are

1. The Mother in the Daughter
2. The Cross of the White Wedding Dress
3. The Rage of a Woman
4. The Daughter in the Mother
5. *Con el perdón suyo, comadre, no vaya a ser que el diablo tenga cuernos:* "With Your Pardon, Comrade, Doesn't the Devil Have Horns?"
6. *Mi hija, amárrate las faldas:* "My Daughter, Tie Up Your Skirts"

Working with analytic headings, as Behar does, provides an interesting way to understand your material and to preview the content of each section for your reader in an artistic way. You may want to review some of the headings in the ethnographic studies we have included in this book to see which ones you feel do more than just summarize what the section will be about. Here, for example, are Rick Zollo's headers from "Friday Night at Iowa 80" (Chapter 1): A Modern Trucking Village, Truck Stop Restaurant, The Arcade, Iowa 80 Employees, Talking to Truckers, Town Meeting around the Cash Register, Truck Yard at Night, Old-Timer at the Fuel Center, Conclusion. Note how vivid most of his headers are, with the exception of the final one, Conclusion. Try to make your headers do more analysis than Introduction or Conclusion. Play around with possibilities in shaping an artistic and analytic set of headers for your study.

Revising for a Reader

As we've mentioned so many times in *FieldWorking*, whether a researcher can successfully bring the lives of different cultures onto a page depends very much on how well that fieldworker writes. We agree with writer E. M. Forster's comment, "How do I know what I think until I see what I say?" Research leads to writing, writing leads to reflection and revision of thought—which leads you then into more sharpened research, new reflections, and then more writing. As we've shown in this chapter, detailing your experience with your site, layering and blending your personal tale with the tales of the members of your chosen subculture, and offering your writing to an audience require revision. You reach your goal through many thoughtful drafts.

We want to share with you a voice whose work has guided our work as long as we've been writing teachers, as well as guided us throughout this chapter. Don Murray was a composition scholar who writes about both risk-taking and rewards involved in the revision process. His attention to revision has helped student and professional writers and writing teachers for the past four decades. Here's a short piece he calls "Some Notes on Revision," which he first presented in a writing class.

· ·

Some Notes on Revision

Donald M. Murray

- Revision is not failure but opportunity. It is an essential part of the process of thinking that produces a series of drafts that clarify and communicate significant meaning to a reader. Writing is not thought reported but the act of thinking itself.

- Revision begins before the first draft when writers talk to themselves, make notes, begin to draft in their head and on the screen.

- Find the edge. Revision is first of all a search for the central tension, the knot, the conflict, the intersection, the questions, the news, the contradiction, the surprise that will involve the reader in the draft.

- Do not look first for error. Look for what works, develop the strengths. Ironically, the strengths of the draft are often found in the failures, in the places where the writing is new, awkward, not yet clear because the writer has not written it before.

- Start as near the end as possible. No background information before the draft really begins. Weave in background material when the reader needs it. Often we write our way toward the subject. It is scaffolding similar to the staging we construct to put up a building. It should be taken down before the text is shown to a reader.

- Revision is fun because of the surprise. The draft teaches us and we are surprised by what we didn't know we knew.
- There is a logical sequence to revision:

Message	What do I have to say?
Order	How can I say it?
Develop	What does the reader need to know?
Voice	What is the voice of the draft?

- Write for yourself, *then* your reader.
- Write and edit out loud. Listen to your voice and tune it to the meaning, purpose, and audience of the draft.
- Enter the work. Work within the evolving draft, taking instruction from the evolving work. Enjoy the gift of concentration.
- Cut what can be cut. Everything must advance the evolving meaning.
- Develop. Answer the reader's questions in the order they will be asked with specific, accurate information.
- When do you stop revising? On deadline or when there are no more surprises as you read and edit the draft.
- The effect on the writer of revision—re-seeing, re-feeling, re-thinking—is powerful.

As we've suggested, there is no formula for revision. How to revise depends on the demands of each draft you've written. So Murray's notes are just that, musings about the process from his perspective and that of other writers.

Murray never saw revision as a failure or punishment. One of Elizabeth's students, a reluctant reviser, described his negative attitude toward rewriting this way: "If you bang a nail in once, why would you want to take it out and bang it back in again?" Murray was eager to remove that nail and examine it before he pounds it back in. Revision, he taught us, is a way to gain energy and insight about your topic—far before you commit it to a final polished piece of writing.

When you make choices about writing your fieldwork essay, much of your drafting process involves imagining what a reader needs to know. Your experiential, rhetorical, and aesthetic choices relate to a sense of your audience. Imagining your readers as you revise is often a difficult task. Fieldwork offers you a chance to write for a real reader rather than just to get a grade. Fieldwork studies are interesting to readers both inside and outside of the cultures you study. Yet it remains true that all writers need responses and all writing needs revision.

BOX34

Sharing Data: Partners in Revision

PURPOSE

We believe that all researchers should find collaborative partners. These are people who can help you question and talk through your thinking and the next stage of your project. At different places in this book, especially in the boxes and Research Portfolio sections, we've indicated different ways to use talk to clarify, expand, and reflect on fieldwork projects:

- Meet with portfolio partners to talk over fieldnotes, transcripts, and other data,
- Come together in small groups to share drafts in progress and portfolios as they illustrate your processes,
- Participate in artifact exchanges to understand the cultural objects gathered from the research site,
- Exchange paired reading responses to share ideas about readings and background research, and
- Do collaborative exercises to learn with another fieldworker about the research process.

Conversation, even casual talk, has the power to generate both further thinking and further text.

ACTION

Meet with your research partner, and share some data together. Try choosing something you're feeling unclear or uncertain about. Read your partner's freewriting, look at his or her fieldnotes or artifacts, and have a conversation. After talking, write again, this time about your own data.

RESPONSE

Bonnie Sunstein and Elizabeth Chiseri-Strater

Our commitment to being writing partners and; collaborators ought to be obvious by now. Not only have we coauthored two books; we've written professional articles, taught courses, and given speeches together over the years. But most important, we are to each other what our teacher Don Murray called the "writer's other self." Even though we live and work many miles apart, we've developed the ability to be each other's research assistant, someone on whom we rely to talk us through the data gathering, writing, and revising processes. We're also one another's "first reader" at the drafting stages. We urge you to find such a person for yourself.

Bonnie's current project has too much data. She and three colleagues have been following two groups of high school students—one in rural Iowa and another in urban Massachusetts—who are writing to each other about geometry in their lives. She's collected over 300 e-mails between the two geometry teachers, 86 student versions of

BOX34 continued

10 different assignments, hours of taped conversations, and fieldnotes from both classrooms and their surrounding environments.

Elizabeth asks her, "Okay, what surprised you? What is your most startling piece of data?"

Bonnie, overwhelmed with the boxes of stuff she'd collected, replied, "Well, we gave the students cameras. Their assignment was to take pictures of 'the made and natural environment' and to write about it." She showed Elizabeth a pile of examples. "It's amazing, but I don't know what I see!"

Elizabeth said, "These pictures and this writing give those kids new perspectives on their landscapes—and on the landscapes of others—that will shape the way they see 'the other' for the rest of their lives. This project is about far more than geometry or writing; it's about perception and reordering the way the mind looks and thinks about shapes and patterns. But also how other minds might think differently. Hey, Bon, this is really ethnographic!"

Without ever having worked on the project itself, Elizabeth's fresh eyes offered Bonnie a framework for the main themes that will help her sort her data.

Elizabeth is starting a study of a local day center for the homeless. Her initial visits to the center showed how collaborative this nonprofit agency was, since many of the formerly homeless clients had become staff members. She interviewed clients (called "guests"), staff members (some formerly homeless, some not), visiting volunteer nurses, social workers, the director, board members, parolees given volunteer community service assignments, and church representatives who prepare lunches. She mapped each room and made sure her fieldnotes show what goes on and when in each space: laundry room, computer room, kitchen, reception office, "intake" room, and "day" room (where guests hang out).

Bonnie looked at Elizabeth's notes and said, "Egad! Who's this description going to be for? Who's your audience? What in the world are the politics involved in this operation? Whom do you want to convince—of what? Do you want a grant? Do you want to write a government report? Do you want your university to give you a leave of absence to write a book? Whom do you want to care about the homeless in your town? You'd better decide that before you collect much more data."

Bonnie's fresh eyes helped Elizabeth see that she really did have a personal agenda when she chose this topic. She wanted to convince people that there should be no involuntary homeless population in her town. She recognized that although she was using rigorous ethnographic methods in her data gathering and her field of view, her purpose was to convince a general audience about a serious social reality.

Our ongoing conversations—and honest reactions—helped bring clarity to our individual studies. We returned to our projects with the fresh insights we'd shared. We revised our big ideas and saw the little details differently. This kind of talk allows you to revise in small ways, as you look at one detail of data against another, as well as in the more global ways that your project deserves.

THE RESEARCH PORTFOLIO:
One-Page Analysis and Annotated Table of Contents

You may think at this point that your portfolio resembles a souvenir of your research project. It's helped you sort through important data and see the array of materials you've used. We hope it's assisted you, too, with your analysis. By capturing your process as you go, we hope your portfolio has offered you insights as you've put more things in, taken things out, and sorted through what's there.

Students sometimes wonder (cynically, as opposed to naïvely, at this point, we hope) about the difference between a scrapbook and a portfolio. A scrapbook, as some of us like to say, is a "pasted down" moment in time. But a portfolio is its opposite: it is a shifting document of your multiple processes of learning, constantly changing as you continue to learn about your research site.

You and your teacher may appreciate what the portfolio's done for your project but perhaps observe some deeper dilemmas: "Okay, okay, we love portfolios but can't afford a utility vehicle to haul them around." "The more attached I get to my portfolio, the less I want to turn it in. And I might not get it back." "If I ever want to make a Web page about my research site, I'd use most of what's in my portfolio, and now I won't have it because I turned it in." "I don't want a grade on this portfolio. It shows the process of my work, not the product."

Your research portfolio has been a critical part of your fieldwork project—your research assistant, in a way. Although you've shared it with groups and classroom colleagues and even with the people at your research site, you'd hope your teacher could look at every page of your research portfolio, each time it's changed. But you also know that's an unrealistic expectation for yourself and for your teacher.

The most important strategy we've developed for portfolios is a simple double strategy. Several times each semester, our students submit these two items:

- *An annotated table of contents:* The annotated table of contents is a list of the artifacts in the portfolio at that time. It also includes short sentences or phrases that explain each item. Organizing and reorganizing your portfolio, you've probably begun to see how the items cluster into units. You might organize them chronologically at first or according to type of data. But as you begin to analyze your data, you'll most likely decide that you want to reorganize your portfolio according to the themes that will eventually be the subheadings of your written study (for more on subheadings, see pp. 379–80).

- *A one-page analysis of the portfolio's current contents:* This one-page analysis is sometimes called a "portfolio letter," "one-pager," or "reflective commentary." It offers you an opportunity to explore your current ideas about the overall themes in your research—connections between items, between sites and informants, between past and present, between yourself and the people you've met, and between your current materials and the writing or organizational goals you still want to meet.

These two documents summarize what's in your portfolio so that you can get a clearer picture of your research and its progress. Of course, like much in our lives, there's no substitute for the real thing; the strategy is merely to take a snapshot of the rich and textured living research you've experienced. These snapshots of your portfolio allow your teacher and your research partners to view and record your emerging body of work several times during a research semester.

In this section, we offer you a two-part sample—a table of contents and a reflective analysis of those contents—from Pappi Tomas's fieldwork project. While these snapshots lack the colors, textures, and "unflat" surprises of a real portfolio or research Web site, they are a good way to see the essence of port-folios, peruse researchers' works, and learn a lot about fieldworkers.

Portfolio Table of Contents for "The Cutter around the Corner"
Pappi Tomas

1. Map of the shop
2. Photo of the walls
3. Explorations of my subjective positions exercise: age, my vision of the tailor, my identity as a university student and how it would mesh with him in the shop
4. Jottings notebook/fieldnotes: photocopied samples
5. Sample fieldnotes written up
6. Underground scribblings notebook: whole
7. Article from local magazine
8. A book, *Michael Joe: A Novel of Irish Life*, by William C. Murray, one of Chipper's favorite writers, which I decided to read for the local color, the feel of an Irish village
9. Drafting notebook: in which I drafted when I wasn't using a computer when I had an idea for a passage wherever I was

Portfolio Commentary: "Like Laying a Brick Road and Driving over It at the Same Time"
Pappi Tomas

I am glad I approached the research for this project using a portfolio as an organizing tool. I have to say, though, that the portfolio, physical object that it was, did not help me so much as the various notebooks I designated for this or that purpose. But the portfolio helped me organize big ideas and investigate hunches, getting themes to come out. And I guess that was a bigger help than I realized while I was keeping the notebooks straight. The hardest thing was trying to focus myself thematically. I didn't want a this, then this, then this kind of patchwork fieldwork, though that is exactly what I started with.

First the walls of the tailor shop, then the tables, then Chipper's face, Chipper's walk, Chipper's talk. I did have some ideas from the start (that is, from the start of the drafting process)—ideas of what themes I saw and what would make for an interesting essay. I wanted to present Chipper and his shop in a way that would appeal to a range of readers. I'm not sure I succeeded. Still, I think I stuck to my plan, which included a section on the shop itself and an outline of Chipper's history; one on Ireland, one on tailoring history, one on the disappearance of custom tailoring, and finally, one on the community surrounding Chipper's shop. I ended with that because I felt in the end it was the theme that impressed itself on me most intensely. Hence the title, "The Cutter around the Corner."

But maybe I should go back and begin with the process itself because out of the process came most of the problems that frustrated me later in drafting. Right away I settled on the double-entry notebook method. In one, I kept my fieldnotes, dated and punctuated here and there with questions I planned to ask during my next interview. In the other, I reflected on my fieldnotes, recorded unexpected thoughts that occurred to me when I was not intending to think about this project, tried my hand at drafts, test phrases, images, and so on. I called this second notebook my Underground Scribblings, and it was most valuable to me along the way. In it, I think I was feeling my way into the voice, the style, the syntax, and so forth that I would use later.

One of the earliest artifacts that came into my hands was the two-page profile of Chipper from a magazine, a local archive. It was an affectionate piece about a local character and tradition. For me, it served as a kind of yardstick, an internal compass for the sort of piece I wanted to write. I wanted to build a little poetry if I could into Chipper's story, which didn't really need me to give it poetry. Chipper himself speaks a poetry all his own, and the extent to which I use his words shows how fond I am of them. I did try to pay attention to meter, to rhythm, so that a kind of mood would establish itself and carry through.

Okay, but my portfolio shows that I had so much to work from. My scribblings ballooned. My audio recordings—which I began using after the first interview—ballooned too. There was too much gold pouring out of Chipper's mouth to hold in my brainpan. And soon my Underground Scribblings contained drafts of the same material, transcripts of recordings and I was incorporating them into my writing—like laying a brick road and driving over it at the same time. I couldn't find the time to visit, jot, scribble, record, transcribe, write up fieldnotes, and reflect for every session I had with Chipper. Not with my other studies. . . . But I can see what I'd do differently in the future. . . .

When it came to drafting the final essay, I had good days and bad days. I began with "To find out what sort of tailor Chipper is, you might begin with the walls," which from the start felt like the right beginning . . . I had that written right away . . . had to make moment-by-moment decisions of what to leave out, what pieces served to best illustrate the themes I had chosen, and what information felt simply too valuable to leave out. That's where the portfolio and all its representative items came in. . . . I wanted to represent as much of Chipper as I could in a limited frame. "Of course, as I told him," Chipper says, "I says, well, you had a good subject." I would agree with this.

A Final Comment: Paying Attention to Writing

Whether they're classified as ethnography, creative nonfiction, narrative journalism, or another descriptive term, contemporary fieldstudies are written in a very different style from much of the academic writing we usually read in university courses. A fieldstudy that is as compelling as a novel seems smooth and colorful; we feel as if we're right there with the researcher, entering the culture. Like a good novel or an exciting magazine article, what brings us along as readers are both the details of the research and the attention the researcher pays to writing. And, as writer Susan Sontag suggests, attention to writing begins with our attention to the world around us: "Do stuff. Be clenched, curious. Not waiting for inspiration's shove or society's kiss on your forehead. Pay attention. It's all about paying attention. Attention is vitality. It connects you with others. It makes you eager. Stay eager."

Even a century ago, ethnographic researchers used their own perspectives to bring culture to a reader. The fieldwriter's roots lie in classical anthropology and the other social sciences. To get their fieldwork published, ethnographers sometimes defend their research to the scientific community by writing about their work as physical scientists would. Much interesting anthropology and social science, therefore, uses a distant, scientific style that has what some call an "author-evacuated" voice. Readers of this scientific style of writing don't get much sense of who the researcher is and why he chose to write about what he saw.

Anthropologists have always noticed—and acknowledged—the tension between their artistry as writers and accuracy as social scientists. Gregory Bateson discussed this in his notebook, *Naven*, in 1958: "If it were possible adequately to present the whole of a culture, stressing every aspect as it is stressed in the culture itself, no single detail would appear bizarre or strange or arbitrary to the reader, but the details would all appear natural and reasonable as they do to the natives who have lived all their lives within the culture. Such an exposition may be attempted by either of two methods, by either scientific or artistic techniques" (cited in Goodall 89).

The writers whose work we most admire, whether they call themselves field-workers, anthropologists, journalists, or nonfiction writers, are able to balance both scientific accuracy and artistic sensibility. Although Bateson was a classic anthropologist of another era, John D'Agata, a contemporary writer, echoes the same idea as he introduces a collection of nonfiction: "Do we read nonfiction in order to receive information, or do we read it to experience art? It's not very clear sometimes . . ." (2).

Fieldworkers, journalistic researchers, and nonfiction writers have discussed questions about voice and style for many years. Like the choices that a director makes along with the writers, actors, photographers, musicians, and sound artists in a film, a research writer must choose, use, filter, distill, and discard from the data of real time and lived life. Writing is a *representation* of the context we are recording, not a recording of the reality itself.

The fieldsite and the informants can help us choose a style to present what we see. When we pay attention to how we write about our fieldwork, we begin to understand the array of choices that writers can make, to make decisions based on what we've learned from our informants, and to think carefully about how we want to represent ourselves and the culture we've studied to our readers.

Our colleague H. L. "Bud" Goodall, offers the kind of advice professors enjoy giving to students. From his many years of teaching and conducting ethnographic research, he reminds us that authors are accountable for what they have written:

> We are accountable to readers, to disciplines, to institutions, and to each other for the quality and contribution of the stories we create. We are accountable to our subjects and to their cultures for making good on the promises we made to them in exchange for their experiences, their stories, their lessons, and their lives. We are accountable to the families and friends who support and nurture us, for not only the products of our work, but moreover the kind of person it makes us into while we are at it, and as a consequence of it. And, finally, we must continuously be accountable to ourselves. (170)

As you move your way through your fieldwork, you will shuttle often between research and writing, and each process will enable the other. Research always involves searching for and finding answers to questions, and fieldwork is no different in that respect. As philosopher Roland Barthes writes, "Research is the name we give to the activity of writing . . . whatever it searches for, it must not forget its nature as language" (198). Attention to language is critical when we write about the lives of others and bring their cultures to the page. As you work with your informants' words and with your own, as you retrieve them from your notes and layer them into text for your reader, you will engage in the rigors and joys of writing and researching. We think it's a stimulating process.

Now it's time for us to step out of this chapter—and our book—so that you can step back into your own fieldwriting project. We hope our advice and experiences have been interesting to you and that we've introduced you to students, colleagues, teachers, and writers whose fieldwork and writing will inform and invigorate your own. The best of luck to you from both of us.

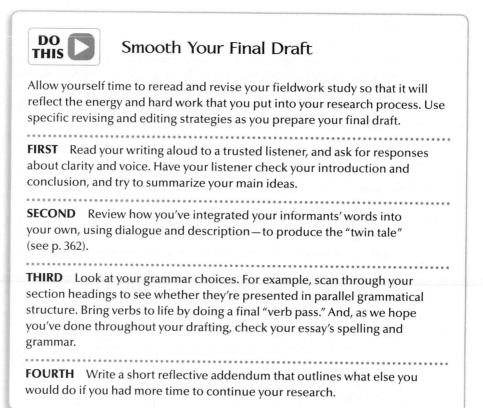

DO THIS ▶

Smooth Your Final Draft

Allow yourself time to reread and revise your fieldwork study so that it will reflect the energy and hard work that you put into your research process. Use specific revising and editing strategies as you prepare your final draft.

FIRST   Read your writing aloud to a trusted listener, and ask for responses about clarity and voice. Have your listener check your introduction and conclusion, and try to summarize your main ideas.

SECOND   Review how you've integrated your informants' words into your own, using dialogue and description—to produce the "twin tale" (see p. 362).

THIRD   Look at your grammar choices. For example, scan through your section headings to see whether they're presented in parallel grammatical structure. Bring verbs to life by doing a final "verb pass." And, as we hope you've done throughout your drafting, check your essay's spelling and grammar.

FOURTH   Write a short reflective addendum that outlines what else you would do if you had more time to continue your research.

MLA Documentation Guidelines

In-Text Citations

1. Author not named in your text

Racial identity is not shaped by skin color alone; rather, "everything from skin color to family attitudes to national politics helps shape how we interpret who we are" (Chideya 55).

2. Author named in a signal phrase

Myerhoff claims that "cultures are, after all, collective, untidy assemblages, authenticated by belief and agreement" (10).

3. Two or three authors

Eldred and Mortensen argue that American women in the early 1800s developed a political language to assuage tensions over slavery and regionalism (184).

OR

The authors argue that American women in the early 1800s developed a political language to assuage tensions over slavery and regionalism (Eldred and Mortensen 184).

4. Four or more authors

Private philanthropy served as a major institutional structure in ancient Greek society, underwriting everything from the welfare of the Greek poor to international relations (Hunt, Martin, Rosenwein, Hsia, and Smith 141).

OR

Private philanthropy served as a major institutional structure in ancient Greek society, underwriting everything from the welfare of the Greek poor to international relations (Hunt et al. 141).

5. Organization as author

Physical activity has been shown to protect against certain forms of cancer "either by balancing caloric intake with energy expenditure or by other mechanisms" (Amer. Cancer Soc. 43).

6. **Unknown author**

Railroad maps in the 1850s often "took liberties with locations of stations and other features" to increase property values ("Mapping Tracks" 1).

7. **Author of two or more works**

One author describes the simplistic images that most children have of Native Americans and shows readers that "the dominant images seem to change little from those most Americans acquire as children" (Lassiter, *Power* 22).

8. **Two or more authors with the same last name**

The writer points to an important conflict of interest when she writes, "Nevada has long been the place where Americans go to do things they can't do at home" (R. Mead 74).

9. **Multivolume work**

Jefferson Davis, a hero of the Mexican War, had "considered his primary talent — or, as he termed it, his 'capacity' — to be military" (2: 3).

10. **Literary work**

After awakening from his drugged sleep, Demetrius immediately asks the disbelieving Helena, "To what, my love, shall I compare thine eyne?" (*MND* 3.2.137).

11. **Work in an anthology**

Cite the author of the work, not the editor of the anthology. Be sure that the author appears alphabetically in the list of works cited.

Contemporary legal definitions of victimhood, Martha Nussbaum argues, can be traced back to Greek tragic plays and "the portrayal of human beings as victims" (361).

12. **Sacred text**

When Moses asks God, "But who am I . . . that I should bring the Israelites out of Egypt," we see for the first time one of God's chosen people question what is asked of them (*Oxford Study Bible,* Exod. 3.11).

13. **Indirect source**

E. M. Forster points to the necessary relationship between language and knowledge when he asks, "How do I know what I think until I see what I say?" (qtd. in Murray 101).

14. **Two or more sources in the same citation**

Educators have suggested that portfolios are the best means we have of assessing students' long-term development and should take the place of standardized tests in public schools as they have in alternative schools (Johnson 24; Sedey 165).

15. **Entire work or a work with no page or paragraph numbers**

In "The Lady or the Tiger," Patricia Williams argues that we are all imitating each other all the time.

OR

In "The Lady or the Tiger," the author argues that we are all imitating each other all the time (Williams).

16. **Electronic or nonprint source**

After living in New York City's East Harlem for five years, anthropologist Philippe Bourgois "constructs a densely textured documentary that affords unparalleled insight into the culture of the street" (Kamiya 3).

Give the page number whenever possible. Do not provide paragraph or section numbers unless they are given in the source itself. If no pages are given, use the abbreviation *n. pag.* If no author is named, format the citation as shown in item 5 or 6 above.

Explanatory and Bibliographic Notes

1. **Superscript number in text**

Tompkins argues that the incorporation of personal experience in school life leads to a stronger sense of commitment and connection among students.[1]

2. **Note**

1. Tompkins, an English professor, may not be aware that several people in the field of education have already made this argument, including Mike Rose, Jerome Bruner, and a number of feminist scholars such as Nel Noddings and JoAnne Pagano.

MLA Style for a List of Works Cited*

Books

1. **One author**

Fried, Seth. *The Great Frustration.* New York: Soft Skull, 2011. Print.

*In standard MLA style, turnovers indent a half-inch or five characters.

2. **Two or three authors**

Blitz, Michael, and Louise Krasniewicz. *Why Arnold Matters: The Rise of a Cultural Icon*. New York: Basic, 2004. Print.

3. **Four or more authors**

Belenky, Mary Field, Blythe Clinchy, Nancy Goldberger, and Jill Tarule. *Women's Ways of Knowing: The Development of Self, Voice, and Mind*. New York: Basic, 1986. Print.

OR

Belenky, Mary Field, et al. *Women's Ways of Knowing: The Development of Self, Voice, and Mind*. New York: Basic, 1986. Print.

4. **Organization as author**

Holocaust Educators Network. *Atrocities from the Past Become Lessons for the Future*. New York: Memorial Library, 2010. Print.

5. **Unknown author**

The Old Farmer's Almanac 2006. Dublin, NH: Yankee, 2005. Print.

6. **Two or more books by the same author(s)**

Diamond, Jared M. *Collapse: How Societies Choose to Fail or Survive*. London: Allen Lane, 2005. Print.

---. *Guns, Germs, and Steel: The Fates of Human Societies*. New York: Norton, 1999. Print.

7. **Editor(s)**

Nicholas, Liza, Elaine M. Bapis, and Thomas J. Harvey, eds. *Imagining the Big Open: Nature, Identity, and Play in the New West*. Salt Lake City: U of Utah P, 2003. Print.

8. **Author and editor**

Shakespeare, William. *The Winter's Tale*. Ed. John Pitcher. London: Arden Shakespeare, 2010. Print.

9. **Work in an anthology or chapter in a book with an editor**

Pocius, Gerald L. "Art." *Eight Words for the Study of Expressive Culture*. Ed. Burt Feintuch. Urbana: U of Illinois P, 2003. Print.

10. **Two or more items from the same anthology**

Ehrenreich, Barbara, and Arlie Russell Hochschild, eds. *Global Woman: Nannies, Maids, and Sex Workers in the New Economy.* New York: Metropolitan, 2004. Print.

Gamburd, Michele. "Breadwinner No More." Ehrenreich and Hochschild 190–206.

Zarembka, Joy M. "America's Dirty Work: Migrant Maids and Modern-Day Slavery." Ehrenreich and Hochschild 142-53.

11. **Translation**

Stoczkowski, Wiktor. *Explaining Human Origins: Myth, Imagination, and Conjecture.* Trans. Mary Turton. New York: Cambridge UP, 2002. Print.

12. **Edition other than the first**

Sunstein, Bonnie S., and Elizabeth Chiseri-Strater. *FieldWorking: Reading and Writing Research.* 4th ed. New York: Bedford/St. Martin's, 2012. Print.

13. **One volume of a multivolume work**

Clark, Cynthia L. *The American Economy: A Historical Encyclopedia.* Vol. 2. Santa Barbara: ABC-CLIO, 2011. Print. 2 vols.

14. **Preface, foreword, introduction, or afterword**

Lewis, Herbert S. Afterword. *Anthropology and Modern Life.* By Franz Boas. New Brunswick, NJ: Transaction, 2004. 247-324. Print.

15. **Article in a reference work**

Daphony, James. "Louis Armstrong." *The New Grove Dictionary of Music.* London: Macmillan, 1980. Print.

OR

"Folklore." *Webster's New College Dictionary.* 4th ed. 2009. Print.

16. **Book that is part of a series**

Allmendinger, Blake. *Imagining the African American West.* Lincoln: U of Nebraska P, 2005. Print. Race and Ethnicity in the Amer. West 2.

17. **Republication**

Robinson, Marilynne. *Housekeeping.* 1980. New York: Picador, 2004. Print.

18. Government publication

United States. Cong. House. Subcommittee on National Security, Emerging
Threats, and International Relations of the Committee on Government
Reform. *Assessing Anthrax Detection Methods*. 109th Cong., 1st sess.
Washington: GPO, 2005. Print.

19. Pamphlet

Seafood Watch: National Seafood Guide. Monterey: Monterey Bay Aquarium
Foundation, 2005. Print.

20. Published proceedings of a conference

Zimmermann, Michael F., ed. *The Art Historian: National Traditions and
Institutional Practices*. Proc. of Clark Conference. 3-4 May 2002.
Williamstown, MA: Sterling and Francine Clark Art Inst. Distr. New Haven:
Yale UP, 2003. Print.

21. Title within a title

Bloom, Harold, ed. *Joseph Conrad's* Heart of Darkness: *Modern Critical
Interpretations*. New York: Chelsea, 2008. Print.

22. Sacred book

The New Oxford Annotated Bible: New Revised Standard Version. New York:
Oxford UP, 2010. Print.

Periodicals

1. Article in a journal

Williams-Davies, John. "'Now Our History Is Your History': The Challenge of
Relevance for Open-Air Museums." *Folk Life-Journal of Ethnological Studies*
47.1 (2009): 115-23. Print.

2. Article in a monthly magazine

Keillor, Garrison. "In Search of Lake Wobegon." *National Geographic* Dec. 2000:
86-109. Print.

3. Article in a weekly magazine

Begley, Sharon. "Can You Build a Better Brain?" *Newsweek* 10 & 17 Jan. 2011:
40-45. Print.

4. **Article in a newspaper**

Morelli, Brian. "Writing for Survival." *Iowa City Press Citizen* 3 Dec. 2010: A1. Print.

5. **Editorial or letter to the editor**

Krugman, Paul. "John and Jerry." Editorial. *New York Times* 3 Apr. 2006: A17. Print.

6. **Unsigned article**

"Survivor Begins Campus Life: Tsunami Aftermath." *Bangkok Post* 29 Apr. 2005: A3. Print.

7. **Review**

Hacker, Andrew. "The Big College Try." Rev. of *Beer and Circus: How Big-Time College Sports Is Crippling Undergraduate Education,* by Murray Sperber. *New York Review of Books* 12 Apr. 2001: 50-52. Print.

8. **Article with a title within the title**

Barron, James. "Public Lives: 'Titanic,' 'Titanic' Everywhere." *New York Times* 21 July 1998: D4. Print.

Electronic Sources

1. **CD-ROM, periodically revised**

National Center for Chronic Disease and Prevention. "Youth Behavior Risk Survey." *Youth 99* Vers. 2 (1999). CD-ROM. *Youth Risk Behavior Surveillance System*. CDC. 2000.

2. **Single-issue CD-ROM, diskette, or magnetic tape**

Freedman's Bank Records. Salt Lake City: Church of Latter-Day Saints, 2001. CD-ROM.

3. **Multidisc CD-ROM**

The Encyclopedia Britannica 2001 Edition. Chicago: Encyclopedia Britannica, 2001. CD-ROM. 2 discs.

4. **Document from an Internet site**

"Colonial Missouri." *The Missouri Site of USGenWeb*. RootsWeb, 2004. Web. 5 Jan. 2011.

5. **Entire Internet site**

   Fish, Lydia, ed. *The Vietnam Veterans Oral History and Folklore Project*. Buffalo State College, 2000. Web. 23 Oct. 2000.

6. **Professional or personal Web site**

   Dederick, Emma I. *Music in Usenet Newsgroups*. Indiana U School of Music, 5 Mar. 2000. Web. 17 Oct. 2000.

   Welch, Gillian. Home page. Gillian Welch, 2006. Web. 8 Feb. 2006.

7. **Home page for a class**

   Neeley, Michael. "Anthropology and the Human Experience." Course home page. Jan.-May 2006. Dept. of Anthropology, Montana State U. Web. 8 Feb. 2006.

8. **Online book**

   James, Henry. *Daisy Miller*. New York: Scribner's, 1909. *The Henry James Scholar's Guide to Web Sites*. Web. 14 May 2011.

9. **Online graphic, video, or audio source**

   Hultstrand, Fred. *Ole Myrvik Wedding, Milton, North Dakota, 1894*. Fargo. *American Memory*. Web. 12 Feb. 2010.

10. **Article in an online periodical**

    Engber, Daniel. "The Great 3-D Debate." *Slate*. Washington Post.Newsweek Interactive, 27 Aug. 2010. Web. 5 Jan. 2011.

11. **Online government publication**

    United States. Dept. of the Interior. Natl. Park Service. *Redwood National and State Parks*. Natl. Park Service, 21 Dec. 2010. Web. 5 Jan. 2011.

12. **Work from an online database**

    Ramamurthy, Prit. "Why Are Men Doing Floral Sex Work? Gender, Cultural Reproduction, and the Feminization of Agriculture." *Signs* 35.2 (2010): n. pag. *JSTOR*. Web. 14 Feb. 2011.

13. **Posting to a discussion group**

    Smyth, Gina. "Did They Tie Jim Up?" *College of Humanities Discussion Board*. Ohio State U, 2 Feb. 1998. Web. 15 Apr. 1998.

14. E-mail message

Hann, Joelle. "FieldWorking Web Site." Message to the author. 22 Dec. 2010. E-mail.

15. Entry in an online reference work

"Communion." *OED Online*. Oxford UP, 2009. Web. 15 Jan. 2010.

Other Sources

1. Unpublished dissertation

Friedman, Teri. "The Experience of Being a Female Police Officer." Diss. New York U, 1989. Print.

2. Published dissertation

Lehner, Luis. *Gravitational Radiation from Black Hole Spacetimes (General Relativity)*. Diss. U of Pittsburgh, 1998. Ann Arbor: UMI, 1998. Print.

3. Article from a microform

Scalon, Leslie. "Black Churches Offered Refuge and Dignity during Slave Era." *Louisville Courier-Journal* 20 Nov. 1996. Microform. *NewsBank: Social Relations* (1996): fiche 76, grids A12-13.

4. Interview

Sampras, Pete. Interview by Charlie Rose. *Charlie Rose*. PBS. WNET, New York. 19 Dec. 1996. Television.

Thompson, Jenna. Personal interview. 7 Jan. 1999.

5. Letter

Paul, Sherman. Letter to the author. 21 Feb. 2001. TS.

6. Film, video, or DVD

Reviving Ophelia: Saving the Selves of Girls. Dir. Mary Pipher. Prod. Tom Gardner and Sut Shally. Media Education Foundation, 1998. Video.
Somewhere. Dir. Sofia Coppola. Perf. Stephen Dorff and Elle Fanning. Focus Features, 2010. Film.

7. Television or radio program

Keillor, Garrison. "Ball Jars." *A Prairie Home Companion*. Amer. Public Radio. Minnesota Public Radio, St. Paul, 1997. Radio.

"Meadowlands." *The Sopranos*. Dir. David Chase. Prod. David Chase. *HBO on Demand*. HBO, 31 Jan. 1999. Web. 12 Jan. 2005.

8. Sound recording

Mahler, Gustav. Symphony nos. 1 and 5. Cond. Leonard Bernstein. Vienna Philharmonic Orchestra. Deutsche Grammophon, 2001. CD.

Springsteen, Bruce. "Hungry Heart." *Bruce Springsteen's Greatest Hits*. Sony/ Columbia, 1995. CD.

9. Work of art

Guyther, Anthony. *Fish Scales*. N.d. Mixed-media collage. Private collection, Vineyard Haven.

10. Lecture or speech

Sunstein, Bonnie, Aimee Mapes, and Lissa Munley. "Vygotsky and a Place to Mess Up: Linking the Overprepared and the Underprepared." In *The Realities of Teacher Research in Dangerous Times: Why Is It So Hard to Do When It Feels So Right?* Conference on College Composition and Communication. New Orleans. Mar. 2008. Conference presentation.

11. Performance

Inherit the Wind. By Jerome Lawrence and Robert E. Lee. Dir. Edward Stern. Repertory Theatre, St. Louis. 11 Oct. 2000. Performance.

12. Map or chart

New York City. Map. Skokie: Rand, 1997. Print.

13. Cartoon

Stevens, Mick. "Fred's Fix-It Shop." Cartoon. *New Yorker* 10 Jan. 2011: 44. Print.

14. Advertisement

Bose. Advertisement. *Time Magazine*. Jan. 2011: 66. Print.

APA Documentation Guidelines

In-Text Citations

1. Author named in a signal phrase

Ackerman (1991) has argued that physical beauty plays a significant role in our life experiences.

Because 70% of our sensory receptors are located in the eyes, Ackerman (1991) argues, "it is mainly through seeing the world that we appraise and understand it" (p. 230).

2. Author named in parentheses

Fieldwork has been described as "house calls at the far borders of human experience" and work that reaches to understand all spectrums of social life and existence (Sacks, 1995, p. xx).

3. Two or more citations of the same work in the same paragraph

After the first mention, you may omit the year. For example,

Ackerman (1991) has argued that physical beauty plays a significant role in our life experiences. However, Ackerman does not agree that physical beauty determines everything.

4. Two authors

Cole and Cole (1993) claim that we know relatively little about human genotypes because of the ethical dilemmas involved in conducting scientific studies of human genetic expression.

Studies of human genetic expression require scientists to expose organisms of the same genotype to a range of environments, some of which may be unfavorable and unsafe (Cole & Cole, 1993).

5. Three to five authors

Battin, Fisher, Moore, and Silvers (1989) point to the discrepancy between beauty and economic value when they argue that art thieves steal the most valuable works of art they can, not necessarily their favorites.

After the first mention, you may refer to the authors as Battin et al.

6. **Six or more authors**

As Gorenstein et al. (1975) show, the Plateau Indians and those of the Northwest Coast were closely connected until ecological conditions altered their natural resources and, in turn, their cultural practices.

7. **Organization as author**

For most of the year this region of Australia is dry, but during the annual monsoon season—between January and March—thunderstorms sweep the land (National Geographic Society, 1998).

8. **Unknown author**

In a North Carolina subdivision that had previously been an apple orchard, soil showed traces of DDT, lead, and arsenic from the pesticides the orchard used ("Apple Orchard," 2000).

Cite only the first few words of the title in a citation. If you're citing the title of a book, as opposed to an article, the title should appear in italics.

9. **Two or more authors with the same last name**

J. Page (2001) shows how forensic anthropologists can determine much about fossils and skeletal remains just through their sense of touch.

10. **Two or more sources within the same parentheses**

List sources by different authors in alphabetical order by author's last name, and separate with semicolons: (Baumeister, 2001; Kline, 2001). List works by the same author in chronological order, separated by commas: (Kline, 1998, 2001).

11. **Specific parts of a source**

Nielson et al. (1983, chap. 25) argue that religious movements developed in periods of cultural and social disintegration have most often occurred in nonliterate societies colonized by European nations and the United States. Always give page numbers for quotations.

12. **E-mail and other personal communication**

E. Cleary (personal communication, November 4, 1999) supported her previous claims that the spots on the leaves indicated a high level of pollutants in the area.

13. **Web site**

To cite an entire Web site, include its address in parentheses in your text. If you do this, you do not need to include it in your list of references. To cite part of a text found on the Web, include the chapter or figure, as appropriate. To document a quotation, include the page or paragraph numbers if they are available.

In her online letter, Mary Foley (2001, para. 4) argues that nurses are leaving acute-care settings and opting for jobs that "don't require them to work up to 12 hours a day . . . and don't impose unsafe working conditions."

Content Notes

1. Superscript numeral in text

The number of family members who had attended college was an important factor in considering them for the HESOP program.[1]

2. Footnote

1. Program organizers Michael Fulton and Regina Kardos developed the standards for entry into the program.

APA Style for a List of References

Books

1. One author

Kramer, J. (1975). *Trucker: Portrait of the last American cowboy.* New York, NY: McGraw-Hill.

2. Two or more authors

Blommaert, J., & Jie, D. (2010). *Ethnographic fieldwork: A beginner's guide.* Bristol, UK: Multilingual Matters.

3. Organization as author

National Geographic Society. (2003). *Guide to the national parks of the United States* (4th ed.). Washington, DC: Author.

4. Unknown author

McGraw-Hill dictionary of scientific and technical terms (7th ed.). (2011). New York, NY: McGraw-Hill.

5. Editor

Oliver, M., & Atwan, R. (Eds.). (2009). *The best American essays of 2009.* Boston, MA: Houghton Mifflin Harcourt.

6. **Selection in a book with an editor**

   Leach, Amy. (2009). You be the moon. In M. Oliver & R. Atwan (Eds.), *The best American essays of 2009* (pp. 67–72). Boston, MA: Houghton Mifflin Harcourt.

7. **Translation**

   Montaigne, M. (2003). *Michel de Montaigne: The essays, a selection* (M. A. Screech, Trans.). New York, NY: Penguin.

8. **Edition other than the first**

   Mead, M. (1969). *Social organization of Manua* (2nd ed.). Honolulu, HI: Bishop Museum Press.

9. **One volume of a multivolume work**

   Kuper, A., & Kuper, J. (Eds.). (2004). *The social science encyclopedia* (Vol. 2). New York, NY: Routledge.

10. **Article in a reference work**

    Watkins, C. (1993). Indo-European and the Indo-Europeans. In *The American Heritage college dictionary* (3rd ed., pp. 1573–1579). New York, NY: Houghton Mifflin.

11. **Republication**

    Bell, A. G. (1974). *The Bell telephone.* New York, NY: Arno Press. (Original work published 1908)

12. **Government document**

    National Institutes of Health. (1999). *Native outreach: A report to American Indian, Alaska native and native Hawaiian communities* (NIH Publication No. 98–4341). Bethesda, MD: Author.

    Patient safety: Instilling hospitals with a culture of continuous improvement: Hearing before the Subcommittee on Investigations of the Committee on Governmental Affairs, United States Senate, 108th Cong. 1 (2003).

13. **Two or more works by the same author(s)**

    Geertz, C. (1973). *The interpretation of cultures.* New York, NY: Basic Books.

    Geertz, C. (1983). *Local knowledge: Further essays in interpretive anthropology.* New York, NY: Basic Books.

Periodicals

1. Article in a journal paginated by volume

Fernsten, L. A. (2008). Writer identity and ESL learners. *Journal of Adolescent & Adult Literacy, 52*(1), 44–52.

2. Article in a journal paginated by issue

Miner, H. (1956). Body ritual among the Nacirema. *American Anthropologist, 58*(3), 9–12.

3. Article in a magazine

Perry, A. (2011, January 11). Can Sudan split without falling apart? *Time Magazine*, 42–49.

4. Article in a newspaper

Goldstein, M. (2011, January 3). I'm too tall in heels [Love letters]. *The Boston Globe*, p. E2.

5. Editorial or letter to the editor

Stevenson, J. (2011, January 5). Lost and found New York [Op-Ed]. *The New York Times*, p. A23.

6. Unsigned article

Harper's index. (2001, March). *Harper's Magazine, 302,* 15.

7. Review

Paulos, J. A. (2001, Winter). [Review of the book *98.6: Where mathematics comes from*]. *The American Scholar, 70,* 151–152.

8. Published interview

Clinton, W. (2000, December 28). [Interview with J. Wenner]. *Rolling Stone,* 84–128.

9. Two or more works by the same author in the same year

Hoy, P. C. (1992a). *Instinct for survival: Essays.* Athens, GA: University of Georgia Press.
Hoy, P. C. (1992b). *Reading and writing essays: The imaginative tasks.* New York, NY: McGraw-Hill.

Electronic Sources

1.   Internet article based on a print source

Perl, S. (2010, December). A simple invitation. *On Austrian soil: Teaching those I was taught to hate.* State University of New York Press. Retrieved from http://www.thememoriallibrary.org

2.   Article from an online journal

Spufford, F. (2010, October). I wanted both. *A public space, 1*(11). Retrieved from http://www.apublicspace.org

3.   Article in a newspaper, electronic version available by search

Bajaj, V. (2011, 5 January). Microlenders, honored with Nobel, are struggling. *The New York Times.* Retrieved from http://www.nytimes.com

4.   Article from an electronic database or subscription service

Gmelch, G., & San Antonio, P. M. (2001, June). Baseball wives: Gender and the work of baseball. *Journal of Contemporary Ethnography, 30*(3), 335–356. Retrieved from http://www.gale.cengage.com/onefile

5.   Stand-alone document on the Web (no date)

Ashliman, D. (n.d.). *Aging and death in folklore.* Retrieved from http://www.pitt.edu/~dash/aging.html

6.   Document from a university program or department Web site

Norris, J. (2010, December 10). *Health care access for poor in South Africa still lags behind.* Retrieved from University of California, San Francisco, Science Cafe website: http://ucsf.edu/science-cafe

7.   Chapter or section of an online document

Anton, P., Silberglitt, R., & Schneider, J. (n.d.). Technology trends. In *The global technology revolution: Bio/nano/materials trends and their synergies with information technology by 2015* (chap. 2). Retrieved from http://www.rand.org/pubs/monograph_reports

8.   Online posting

Lackey, N. (1995, January 20). From Clare to here. [Electronic mailing list message]. Retrieved from http://www.rahul.net/frankf/Nancy/archives/95130.html

9. **Newsgroup message**

> Sand, P. (1996, April 20) Java disabled by default in Linux Netscape.
> [Newsgroup message]. Retrieved from news://keokuk.unh.edu

10. **E-mail message**

The APA's publication manual discourages including e-mail in a list of references and suggests citing e-mail only in text. For example, if you wanted to reference information given to you in an e-mail, you would cite the author in the text in parentheses like this: (M. Lee, personal communication, February 5, 2011).

11. **Software or computer program**

> Chem Office 2001 [Computer software]. (2000). Cambridge, MA: CambridgeSoft.

Other Sources

1. **Technical or research reports and working papers**

> National Council Panel to Evaluate Alternative Census Methods. (1993).
> *A census that mirrors America: Interim report.* Washington, DC: National
> Academy Press.

Include the report number, if given, after the title and in parentheses.

2. **Paper presented at a meeting or symposium, unpublished**

> Tesch, R. (1987, April). *Comparing the most widely used methods of qualitative*
> *analysis: What do they have in common?* Paper presented at the American
> Educational Research Association Annual Convention, San Francisco, CA.

3. **Dissertation, unpublished**

> Steinmetz, A. (1988). *The role of the microcomputer in the social and*
> *psychological world of an adolescent male.* (Unpublished doctoral
> dissertation). New York University, New York, NY.

4. **Poster session**

> Harris, L. M. (1995, June). *Race, ethnicity and poverty status of popula-*
> *tions living near cement plants and commercial incinerators.* Poster
> session presented at the International Congress of Hazardous Waste,
> Atlanta, GA.

5. **Film, video, or DVD**

    Kaufman, C. (Director). (2008). *Synecdoche, New York* [Motion picture]. Los
    Angeles, CA: Sony Pictures Classics.

6. **Television program, single episode**

    Steele, S. (Writer), & Lennon, T. (Director). (2000). Jefferson's blood [Television
    series episode]. In D. Fanning (Executive producer), *Frontline*. New York,
    NY: Public Broadcasting Service.

7. **Recording**

    Williams, H. (1948). I can't get you off of my mind [Recorded by B. Dylan]. On
    Timeless [CD]. Nashville, TN: Lost Highway Records. (2001)

Aarne, Antti. *The Types of the Folk-Tale: A Classification and Bibliography*. New York: Franklin, 1971. Print.

Ackerman, Diane. *A Natural History of the Senses*. New York: Vintage, 1991. Print.

Alanen, Arnold R., and Robert Z. Melnick, eds. *Preserving Cultural Landscapes in America*. Baltimore: Johns Hopkins UP, 2000. Print.

Allen, Barbara, and William Lynwood Montell. *From Memory to History: Using Oral Sources in Local Historical Research*. Nashville: American Association for State and Local History, 1981. Print.

Anderson, Jay. *Time Machines: The World of Living History*. Nashville: American Association for State and Local History, 1984. Print.

Anzaldua, Gloria. *Borderlands: La Frontiera—The New Mestiza*. San Francisco: Spinsters, 1987. Print.

Aristotle. *Ars Rhetorica*. Ed. W. D. Ross. Oxford: Clarendon, 1959. Print.

Barthes, Roland. "Writers, Intellectuals, Teachers." *Image-Music-Text*. Trans. Stephen Heath. New York: Hill, 1977. Print.

Bateson, Gregory. *Naven*. 2nd ed. Palo Alto, CA: Stanford UP, 1958. Print.

Behar, Ruth. *Translated Woman: Crossing the Border with Esperanza's Story*. Boston: Beacon, 1993. Print.

———. *The Vulnerable Observer: Anthropology That Breaks Your Heart*. Boston: Beacon, 1996. Print.

Benedict, Ruth. *Patterns of Culture*. New York: New American, 1953. Print.

Berger, John. *Ways of Seeing*. New York: Penguin, 1972. Print.

Berger, Peter L., and Thomas Luckman. *The Social Construction of Reality*. New York: Anchor, 1967. Print.

Berlinski, Mischa. *Fieldwork*. New York: Picador, 2007. Print.

Berthoff, Ann. *Forming, Thinking, Writing*. 2nd ed. Portsmouth, NH: Boynton, 1988. Print.

Birdwhistell, Ray. *Introduction to Kinesics*. Louisville: U of Kentucky P, 1952. Print.

Bishop, Wendy. *Ethnographic Writing Research: Writing It Down, Writing It Up, and Reading It*. Portsmouth, NH: Boynton, 1999. Print.

Blommaert, Jan, and Dong Jie. *Ethnographic Fieldwork: A Beginner's Guide*. Bristol, UK: Multilingual Matters, 2010. Print.

Bloodworth, Bertha E., and Alton C. Morris. *Places in the Sun: The History and Romance of Florida Place-Names*. Gainesville: UP of Florida, 1978. Print.

Bloom, Stephen, and Peter Feldstein. *The Oxford Project*. New York: Welcome, 2010. Print.

Bohannan, Laura. "Shakespeare in the Bush." *Natural History* 75.7 (1966): 28–33. Print.

Bohannan, Paul, and Dirk van der Elst. *Asking and Listening: Ethnography as Personal Adaptation*. Prospect Heights, IL: Waveland, 1998. Print.

Borkowsky, Amy. *Statements: True Tales of Life, Love, and Credit Card Bills*. New York: Penguin, 2005. Print.

Botchner, Arthur, and Carolyn Ellis, eds. *Ethnographically Speaking: Autoethnography, Literature, and Aesthetics*. Walnut Creek: Sage, 2002. Print.

Bowen, Eleanor Smith. *Return to Laughter*. New York: Anchor, 1964. Print.

Boynton, Robert, ed. *The New New Journalism: Conversations with America's Best Nonfiction Writers and Their Craft*. New York: Vintage, 2005. Print.

Bronner, Simon, ed. *Lafcadio Hearn's America: Ethnographic Sketches and Editorials*. Lexington: UP of Kentucky, 2004. Print.

Brooks, Philip Coolidge. *Research in Archives: The Use of Unpublished Primary Sources.* Chicago: U of Chicago P, 1969. Print.

Brown, Stephen Gilbert, and Sidney Dobrin, eds. *Ethnography Unbound: From Theory Shock to Critical Praxis.* Albany: SUNY P, 2004. Print.

Brundage, W. Fitzhugh, ed. *Where These Memories Grow: History, Memory, and Southern Identity.* Chapel Hill: U of North Carolina P, 2000. Print.

Brunvand, Jan Harald. *The Vanishing Hitchhiker: American Urban Legends and Their Meanings.* New York: Norton, 1981. Print.

Cantwell, Robert. *Ethnomimesis: Folklore and the Representation of Culture.* Chapel Hill: U of North Carolina P, 1993. Print.

Chiseri-Strater, Elizabeth. *Academic Literacies: The Public and the Private Discourse of University Students.* Portsmouth, NH: Boynton, 1991. Print.

Chiseri-Strater, Elizabeth, and Bonnie Stone Sunstein. *What Works? A Practical Guide for Teacher Research.* Portsmouth, NH: Heinemann, 2006. Print.

Clayton, Bruce. *Praying for Base Hits: An American Boyhood.* Columbia: U of Missouri P, 1998. Print.

Cofer, Judith Ortiz. "A Partial Remembrance of a Puerto Rican Childhood." *Silent Dancing.* Houston: Arte Publico, 1990. Print.

Coffey, Amanda Jane. *The Ethnographic Self: Fieldwork and the Representation of Identity.* London: Sage, 1999. Print.

Collins, Paul. *Banvard's Folly: Thirteen Tales of People Who Didn't Change the World.* New York: Picador, 2001. Print.

Conover, Ted. *Newjack: Guarding Sing-Sing.* New York: Vintage, 2001. Print.

Cotter, Holland. "On Sontag: Essayist as Metaphor and Muse." *New York Times* 18 Aug. 2006. Print.

Covington, Dennis. *Salvation on Sand Mountain: Snake Handling and Redemption in Southern Appalachia.* New York: Penguin, 1994. Print.

Cushman, Ellen. *The Struggle and the Tools: Oral and Literate in an Inner City Community.* Albany: SUNY P, 1998. Print.

D'Agata, John. *The Lost Origins of the Essay.* Minneapolis: Graywolf, 2009. Print.

Didion, Joan. "On Keeping a Notebook." *Slouching toward Bethlehem.* New York: Farrar, 1968. Print.

Ehrenreich, Barbara. *Nickel and Dimed: On (Not) Getting By in America.* New York: Holt, 2001. Print.

Elbow, Peter. *Writing without Teachers.* New York: Oxford UP, 1998. Print.

———. *Writing with Power: Techniques for Mastering the Writing Process.* New York: Oxford UP, 1981. Print.

Ellis, Carolyn. *The Ethnographic I: A Methodological Novel about Autoethnography.* New York: AltaMira, 2004. Print.

Emerson, Robert M., Rachel I. Fretz, and Linda L. Shaw. *Writing Ethnographic Fieldnotes.* Chicago: U of Chicago P, 1995. Print.

Faubion, James D., and George E. Marcus. *Fieldwork Is Not What It Used to Be: Learning Anthropology's Method in a Time of Transition.* Ithaca: Cornell UP, 2009. Print.

Federal Writers' Project. *These Are Our Lives.* Durham: U of North Carolina P, 1939. Print.

Feintuch, Burt. *Eight Words for the Study of Expressive Culture.* Urbana: U of Illinois P, 2003. Print.

———. *In the Blood: Cape Breton Conversations on Culture.* Logan, UT: Utah State UP, 2010. Print.

Fishman, Andrea. *Amish Literacy: What and How It Means.* Portsmouth, NH: Heinemann, 1988. Print.

Fiske, John. *Understanding Popular Culture.* Boston: Unwin, 1989. Print.

FitzGerald, Frances. *Cities on a Hill: A Journey through Contemporary American Cultures.* New York: Simon, 1986. Print.

Fletcher, Ralph. *What a Writer Needs.* Portsmouth, NH: Heinemann, 1993. Print.

Freire, Paulo. *Literacy: Reading the Word and the World.* South Hadley, MA: Bergin, 1988. Print.

Galman, Sally Campbell. *Shane: The Lone Ethnographer: A Beginner's Guide to*

Ethnography. New York: AltaMira, 2007. Print.

Geertz, Clifford. *The Interpretation of Cultures.* New York: Basic, 1973. Print.

———. *Local Knowledge: Further Essays in Interpretive Anthropology.* New York: Basic, 1983. Print.

———. "Thick Description: Toward an Interpretive Theory of Culture." *The Interpretation of Cultures.* New York: Basic, 1973. Print.

———. *Works and Lives: The Anthropologist as Author.* Palo Alto: Stanford UP, 1988. Print.

Glassie, Henry. *Passing the Time in Balleymenone: Culture and History of an Ulster Community.* Philadelphia: U of Pennsylvania P, 1982. Print.

Gleason, Norma, ed. *Proverbs from around the World.* New York: Citadel, 1992. Print.

Goffman, Erving. *Behavior in Public Places.* New York: Free, 1963. Print.

———. *The Presentation of Self in Everyday Life.* Garden City, NY: Anchor, 1959. Print.

Goodall, H. L. *Writing the New Ethnography.* Walnut Creek, CA: AltaMira, 2000. Print.

Goodall, Lloyd. *Divine Signs: Connecting Spirit to Community.* Carbondale: Southern Illinois UP, 1996. Print.

Goodenough, Ward. *Culture, Language, and Society.* Menlo Park, CA: Benjamin, 1981. Print.

Gottlieb, Alma, and Philip Graham. *Parallel Worlds: An Anthropologist and a Writer Encounter Africa.* Chicago: U of Chicago P, 1993. Print.

Graves, Donald, and Bonnie S. Sunstein. *Portfolio Portraits.* Portsmouth, NH: Heinemann, 1992. Print.

Hall, Edward. *The Silent Language.* Garden City, NY: Doubleday, 1959. Print.

Hamper, Ben. *Rivethead: Tales from the Assembly Line.* New York: Warner, 1987. Print.

Harrington, Walt. *Intimate Journalism: The Art and Craft of Reporting Everyday Life.* Thousand Oaks, CA: Sage, 1997. Print.

———. "What Journalism Can Offer Ethnography." *Qualitative Inquiry* 9.1 (2003): 90–104. Print.

Heath, Shirley Brice. *Ways with Words: Language, Life, and Work in Communities and Classrooms.* Cambridge: Cambridge UP, 1983. Print.

Hebdidge, Dick. *Subculture: The Meaning of Style.* New York: Methuen, 1984. Print.

Horwitz, Richard P. *The Strip: An American Place.* Lincoln: U of Nebraska P, 1985. Print.

Howard, Jane. *Margaret Mead: A Life.* New York: Ballantine, 1984. Print.

Humphries, R. R., ed. *These Are Our Lives.* Chapel Hill: U of North Carolina P, 1939. Print.

Hurston, Zora Neale. *Mules and Men.* New York: Harper, 1989. Print.

Isay, Dave. *Listening Is an Act of Love.* New York: Penguin, 2007. Print.

Ives, Edward. *The Tape-Recorded Interview: A Manual for Fieldworkers in Folklore and Oral History.* Knoxville: U of Tennessee P, 1980. Print.

Iyer, Pico. *Sun after Dark: Flights into the Foreign.* New York: Vintage, 2004. Print.

Jackson, Bruce. *Fieldwork.* Chicago: U of Illinois P, 1987. Print.

Jackson, Jean. "I Am a Fieldnote: Fieldnotes as a Symbol of Professional Identity." *Fieldnotes: The Making of Anthropology.* Ed. Roger Sanjek. Ithaca: Cornell UP, 1990. Print.

Kammen, Carol. *On Doing Local History: Reflections on What Local Historians Do, Why, and What It Means.* Walnut Creek, CA: AltaMira, 1995. Print.

Keillor, Garrison. "Ball Jars." *Mother, Father, Uncle, Aunt: Stories from Lake Wobegon.* Rec. 15 Mar. 1997. HighBridge Audio, 1997. Audiocassette.

Kerrane, Kevin, and Ben Yagoda, eds. *The Art of Fact: A Historical Anthology of Literary Journalism.* New York: Simon, 1998. Print.

Kincaid, Jamaica. "On Seeing England for the First Time." *Harper's* Aug. 1991: 13–16. Print.

King, Stephen. *On Writing: A Memoir of the Craft.* New York: Scribner, 2000. Print.

Kingston, Maxine Hong. *The Woman Warrior: Memoirs of a Girlhood among Ghosts.* New York: Vintage, 1977. Print.

Kozinets, Robert V. *Netnography: Doing Ethnographic Research Online*. Los Angeles: Sage, 2010. Print.

Lado, Robert. "How to Compare Two Cultures." *Encountering Cultures: Reading and Writing in a Changing World*. Ed. Richard Holeton. Englewood Cliffs, NJ: Blair, 1992. Print.

Lamott, Anne. *Bird by Bird: Some Instructions on Writing and Life*. New York: Pantheon, 1994. Print.

Lassiter, Luke E. *The Chicago Guide to Collaborative Ethnography*. Chicago: U of Chicago P, 2005. Print.

———. *The Power of Kiowa Song*. Tucson: U of Arizona P, 1988. Print.

Lassiter, Luke E., Hurley Goodall, Elizabeth Campbell, and Michelle Natasya Johnson. *The Other Side of Middletown: Exploring Muncie's African American Community*. Walnut Creek, CA: Altamira, 2004. Print.

Lurie, Alison. *Imaginary Friends*. New York: Avon, 1991. Print.

———. *The Language of Clothes*. New York: Random, 1981. Print.

Lynch, Thomas. *The Undertaking: Life Studies from the Dismal Trade*. New York: Penguin, 1998. Print.

Mahoney, James. *Local History: A Guide for Research and Writing*. Washington, DC: National Education Association, 1981. Print.

Marshall, Paule. *The Chosen Place, the Timeless People*. New York: Vintage, 1992. Print.

Mead, Margaret. *Letters from the Field: 1925–1975*. New York: Harper, 1977. Print.

Miner, Horace. "Body Ritual among the Nacirema." *American Anthropologist* 58.3 (1956): 503–07. Print.

Minh-ha, Trinh. *Women Native Other: Writing Postcoloniality and Feminism*. Bloomington: Indiana UP, 1989. Print.

Moffatt, Michael. *Coming of Age in New Jersey: College and American Culture*. New Brunswick: Rutgers UP, 1989. Print.

Momaday, N. Scott. *House Made of Dawn*. New York: Harper, 1966. Print.

———. *The Way to Rainy Mountain*. Albuquerque: U of New Mexico P, 1969. Print.

Moore, Alexander. "Walt Disney World: Bounded Ritual Space and the Playful Pilgrimage Center." *Anthropological Quarterly* 53.4 (1980): 207–18. Print.

Moore, Lorrie. "How to Become a Writer." *Self-Help: Stories*. New York: Knopf, 1985. Print.

Morris, Desmond. "Territorial Behavior." *Manwatching: A Field Guide to Human Behavior*. New York: Abrams, 1977. Print.

Mortensen, Peter, and G. Kirsch. *Ethics and Representation in Qualitative Studies of Literacy*. Urbana: NCTE, 1996. Print.

Murray, Donald. *The Craft of Revision*. 2nd ed. New York: Harcourt, 1995. Print.

———. "Notes on Revision." Letter to the authors. 15 Feb. 1995. TS.

———. *Shoptalk: Learning to Write with Writers*. Portsmouth, NH: Boynton, 1990. Print.

———. "Where Do You Find Your Stories?" *Presence of Mind: Writing and the Domain beyond the Cognitive*. Ed. Alice Brand and Richard Graves. Portsmouth, NH: Boynton, 1994. Print.

Myerhoff, Barbara. *Number Our Days*. New York: Simon, 1978. Print.

Naipaul, V. S. *A Turn in the South*. New York: Knopf, 1989. Print.

Nathan, Rebecca. *My Freshman Year: What a Professor Learned by Becoming a Student*. Ithaca: Cornell UP, 2005. Print.

Naylor, Gloria. *Mama Day*. New York: Vintage, 1988. Print.

Newkirk, Thomas. *The Presentation of Self in Student Writing*. Portsmouth, NH: Boynton, 1997. Print.

Oakley, J., and H. Callaway. *Anthropology and Autobiography*. London: Routledge, 1992. Print.

Oring, Elliott. "Generating Lives: The Construction of an Autobiography." *Journal of Folklore Research* 24.3 (1987): 241–62. Print.

Paola, Suzanne, and Brenda Miller. *Tell It Slant: Writing and Shaping Creative Nonfiction*. New York: McGraw, 2003. Print.

Paules, Greta Foff. *Dishing It Out: Power and Resistance among Waitresses in a New*

Jersey Restaurant. Philadelphia: Temple UP, 1991. Print.

Peacock, James. *The Anthropological Lens: Harsh Light, Soft Focus*. Cambridge: Cambridge UP, 1986. Print.

Perl, Sondra. *On Austrian Soil: Teaching Those I Was Taught to Hate*. Albany: SUNY P, 2005. Print.

Pham, Andrew X. *Catfish and Mandala*. New York: Picador, 2003. Print.

Powdermaker, Hortense. *Stranger and Friend: The Way of an Anthropologist*. New York: Norton, 1966. Print.

Prown, Jules David, and Kenneth Haltman. *American Artifacts: Essays in Material Culture*. East Lansing: Michigan State UP, 2000. Print.

Qualley, Donna. *Turns of Thought*. Portsmouth, NH: Boynton, 1997. Print.

Rafkin, Louise. *Other People's Dirt: A Housecleaner's Curious Adventures*. New York: Penguin, 1999. Print.

Robben, Anoniusk, and Jeffrey Sluka, eds. *Ethnographic Fieldwork: An Anthropological Reader*. Malden, MA: Blackwell, 2007. Print.

Rosaldo, Renato. *Culture and Truth: The Remaking of Social Analysis*. Boston: Beacon, 1989. Print.

Rose, Dan. *Black American Street Life: South Philadelphia, 1969–1971*. Philadelphia: U of Pennsylvania P, 1987. Print.

———. *Living the Ethnographic Life*. Thousand Oaks, CA: Sage, 1990. Print.

Rose, Mike. *Lives on the Boundary: The Struggles and Achievements of America's Underprepared*. New York: Free, 1989. Print.

———. *The Mind at Work: Valuing the Intelligence of the American Worker*. New York: Penguin, 2004. Print.

Rosenblatt, Louise. *Literature as Exploration*. 5th ed. New York: Modern Language Association, 1995. Print.

Rosengarten, Theodore. *All God's Dangers and the Life of Nat Shaw*. New York: Harper, 1966. Print.

Russ, Paul, dir. *Healing without a Cure: Stories of People Living with AIDS*. TRIAD Health Project, 1994. Film.

Sacks, Oliver. *An Anthropologist on Mars: Seven Paradoxical Tales*. New York: Knopf, 1995. Print.

Sanjek, Roger. *Fieldnotes: The Makings of Anthropology*. Ithaca: Cornell UP, 1990. Print.

Santino, Jack. "Miles of Smiles, Years of Struggle: The Negotiation of Black Occupational Identity through Personal Experience Narrative." *Journal of American Folklore* 96.382 (1983): 393–410. Print.

Scanlan, Christopher. *Reporting and Writing: Basics for the Twenty-first Century*. Fort Worth, TX: Harcourt, 2000. Print.

Schwartz, Mimi, and Sondra Perl. *Writing True: The Art and Craft of Creative Nonfiction*. Boston: Houghton, 2005. Print.

Scudder, Samuel. "In the Library with Agassiz." *Every Saturday* 4 Apr. 1874. Print.

Shapiro, Ann-Louise, ed. *Producing the Past: Making Histories inside and outside the Academy*. Middletown, CT: Wesleyan UP, 1997. Print.

Shostak, Marjorie. *The Life and Words of a !Kung Woman*. New York: Vintage, 1981. Print.

Sierstad, Asne. *The Bookseller of Kabul*. Trans. Ingrid Christophersen. New York: Little, 2003. Print.

Sims, Norman, and Mark Kramer, eds. *Literary Journalism*. New York: Ballantine, 1995. Print.

Singer, Mark. *Character Studies: Encounters with the Curiously Obsessed*. New York: Houghton, 2005. Print.

Spradley, James P. *The Ethnographic Interview*. Fort Worth, TX: Holt, 1979. Print.

Spradley, James P., and Brenda Mann. *The Cocktail Waitress: Women's Work in a Male World*. New York: Wiley, 1975. Print.

Stack, Carol B. *All Our Kin: Strategies for Survival in a Black Community*. New York: Harper, 1974. Print.

Stocking, Kathleen. *Letters from the Leelanau: Essays of People and Place*. Ann Arbor: U of Michigan P, 1990. Print.

Stoller, Paul. *The Taste of Ethnographic Things: The Senses in Anthropology*. Philadelphia: U of Pennsylvania P, 1989. Print.

Stone, Elizabeth. *Black Sheep and Kissing Cousins: How Our Family Stories Shape Us.* New York: Times, 1988. Print.

Sullivan, Robert. *Rats: Observations on the History and Habitat of the City's Most Unwanted Inhabitants.* New York: Bloomsbury, 2004. Print.

Sunstein, Bonnie S. *Composing a Culture: Inside a Summer Writing Program with High School Teachers.* Portsmouth, NH: Boynton, 1994. Print.

Sunstein, Bonnie, and Jonathan H. Lovell. *The Portfolio Standard: How Students Can Show Us What They Know and Are Able to Do.* Portsmouth, NH: Heinemann, 2000. Print.

Syring, David. *Places in the World a Person Could Walk: Family, Stories, Home, and Place in the Texas Hill Country.* Austin: U of Texas P, 2000. Print.

Tannen, Deborah. *You Just Don't Understand: Women and Men in Conversation.* New York: Morrow, 1990. Print.

Tedlock, Dennis. *The Spoken Word and the Work of Interpretation.* Philadelphia: U of Pennsylvania P, 1983. Print.

Terkel, Studs. *In Hard Times: An Oral History of the Great Depression.* New York: Pantheon, 1970. Print.

———. *Working: People Talk about What They Do All Day and How They Feel about What They Do.* New York: Pantheon, 1974. Print.

Thomas, Lewis. "Notes on Punctuation." *The Medusa and the Snail.* New York: Viking, 1979. Print.

Thompson, Stith. *Motif-Index of Folk Literature.* Bloomington: Indiana UP, 1965. Print.

Toth, Jennifer. *The Mole People: Life in the Tunnels of New York City.* Chicago: Chicago Review, 1993. Print.

Turner, Patricia. *I Heard It through the Grapevine: Rumor in African-American Culture.* Berkeley: U of California P, 1993. Print.

Ulrich, Laurel Thatcher. *American Homespun: Objects and Stories in the Creation of an American Myth.* New York: Vintage, 2002. Print.

VanderStaay, Steve. *Street Lives: An Oral History of Homeless Americans.* Philadelphia: New Society, 1992. Print.

Van Maanen, John. *Representation in Ethnography.* Thousand Oaks, CA: Sage, 1995. Print.

Walker, Alice. "Everyday Use." *In Love and Trouble: Stories of Black Women.* New York: Harcourt, 1967. Print.

Weitzman, David. *Underfoot: An Everyday Guide to Exploring the American Past.* New York: Scribner, 1976. Print.

Whyte, William Foote. *Street Corner Society: The Social Structure of an Italian Slum.* 4th ed. Chicago: U of Chicago P, 1993. Print.

Wigginton, Eliot, et al., eds. *Foxfire: Twenty-five Years.* New York: Doubleday, 1991. Print.

Williams, Raymond. *The Sociology of Culture.* New York: Schocken, 1982. Print.

Williams, Terry Tempest. *Refuge: An Unnatural History of Family and Place.* New York: Vintage, 1992. Print.

Wolcott, Harry. *The Art of Fieldwork.* Walnut Creek, CA: AltaMira, 1995. Print.

———. *Ethnography: A Way of Seeing.* Walnut Creek, CA: AltaMira, 1999. Print.

———. *Sneaky Kid and Its Aftermath: Ethics and Intimacy in Fieldwork.* Walnut Creek, CA: AltaMira, 2002. Print.

———. *Writing Up Qualitative Research.* 2nd ed. Thousand Oaks, CA: Sage, 2001. Print.

Wolf, Margery. *A Thrice-Told Tale: Feminism, Postmodernism, and Ethnographic Responsibility.* Stanford: Stanford UP, 1992. Print.

Zinsser, William. *Inventing the Truth: The Art and Craft of Memoir.* 2nd ed. New York: Houghton, 1995. Print.

Zipes, Jack. *Don't Bet on the Prince: Contemporary Feminist Fairy Tales in North America and England.* New York: Routledge, 1987. Print.

Glossary

aesthetics The perceived artistic beauty, style, or good taste of an object, as in the visual arts, literature, or performing arts. *Aesthetics* also can refer more broadly to pleasing or artistically beautiful appearances of things, from hairstyles and poetry to athletics.

analysis A close and critical look at a subject, text, or situation. Analysis involves scrutinizing data for further understanding by asking questions (such as, "What do the parts say about the whole?").

archive A physical or electronic place where collections of public and private records, other historical documents, and sometimes artifacts are stored.

artifact A material object that belongs to and represents a culture.

assumption An untested attitude or theory about unfamiliar people, places, or ideas, often based on your own experiences.

authority An expert within a field, usually someone who has done reliable research and has presented well-organized data.

chat room An online forum or space for synchronous (that is, real-time) discussions.

collecting The act of gathering data; in fieldwork, the continuous process of gathering and organizing data in your portfolio.

colonization The takeover of less powerful people by more powerful people who demand conformity to their group's ideas and values, as in a territory ruled or annexed by another country.

construction In writing, the building of a text with a variety of sources, including your own words as well as those of others.

Ethnographic writing is constructed from many text sources, including fieldnotes, descriptions of artifacts, glossaries of vocabulary, informants' words, archival sources, and reflective commentary.

culture The behaviors, patterns, rules, and rituals of a group of people who have contact with one another and share common languages.

data All the information—as represented in both written and material artifacts—that a researcher uses as evidence.

diachronic Relating to a cultural system as it changes between points in time; relating to historical change.

dialect A regional variation in language, such as English spoken in Tidewater Virginia, Downeast Maine, or South Texas.

directory A site that delivers Web content that has been collected and indexed by a human being. Also called a *subject guide*.

double-entry notes Fieldnotes that are divided into at least two columns: one column lists the fieldworker's observations of the fieldsite, and at least one other column lists the fieldworker's personal reflections about the site and informants. Making such distinctions allows the fieldworker to become aware of the differences between verifiable, tangible facts about the chosen fieldsite and his or her thoughts and feelings about those facts.

double voiced fieldnotes Writing that results from the combination of your own field experiences and those of your informants. In this book, we also refer to this strategy as the *twin tale* of the research experience.

dominate To control, govern, or rule.

draft A text that is not yet in its final form. Writers may make many drafts of any piece of their writing. The final draft usually signals the end of a writing project, but some writers continue to revise their work even after publication.

electronic archive A set of electronic files stored on a publicly accessible server, available for download by way of a file transfer protocol (FTP) program.

electronic (online) communities To count as an actual "community" online, participants interact over long periods of time, spend substantial time together online, share insider language, and identify themselves as a coherent group.

emic Relating to the perspective of an insider in a culture.

ethnocentrism The acceptance of one's own culture and values as natural and superior to other cultures and values.

ethnography The study of people in cultures; also the text that is written based on that study.

ethnohistorian An ethnographer who conducts oral and written life histories.

ethnohistory The study of people, cultures, and customs from the past through examination of historical records, collections of artifacts, interviews, and archived documentary materials.

ethnopoetic notation A procedure for the analysis of transcripts in which a language researcher turns oral speech into poetic form.

ethos A rhetorical term borrowed from Aristotle (see Chapter 2) that refers to the use of the speaker's or writer's voice in speech, writing, or other media to produce trust and belief in that speaker's persona.

etic Relating to the perspective of an outsider to a culture.

expanded fieldnotes Comments and reflections made by the researcher after he or she has left the research site.

experiential writing strategies The forms of exploratory writing—journal writing, freewriting, and notetaking—that reflect the researcher's own feelings and observations in the field.

family stories The narratives shared in extended families about other family members that convey messages about behaviors, rules of conduct, or shared values.

fieldnotes The observations written by a researcher at a research site, during an interview, and throughout the data-collection process.

fieldwork The process of living and studying among people in their own context, with their permission and cooperation. Fieldworking involves gathering, interpreting, and validating data via notetaking, interviewing, collecting material artifacts, and other methods.

fieldwriting A study based on data gathered during field research; also the process of drafting such a study.

focal point A central place in the fieldsite where ideas, artifacts, or people converge. A focal point can sometimes provide a guide for writing fieldstudies.

freewriting The spontaneous writing done to release or free the mind from concerns about grammar, punctuation, or other sentence-level distractions. Freewriting is done without stopping and without editing.

genre The classification of an artistic form (such as painting, music, or film). Travel writing, for example, is a genre of nonfiction. Reportage is a genre of news story.

human subjects review board An administrative department at a university that processes researchers' proposals for conducting studies with people as their subjects. This board protects human subjects from inappropriate or unethical projects and helps researchers to anticipate problems they may encounter when working with people.

informant A person who shares information about the meanings of his or her culture with a researcher; also referred to as a *consultant*, a *subject*, or *"the other."*

informed consent The agreement between a researcher and a human participant (informant, consultant, or collaborator) that gives the researcher permission to use the participant's observations, interviews, comments, and artifacts. Sometimes a researcher must also obtain such an agreement to enter a fieldsite and conduct a study there.

insider/outsider The dialectical stance of involvement (insider) or detachment (outsider) that a researcher adopts toward the informants in the culture studied.

intersubjectivity The connection or involvement between separate minds or consciousnesses; in fieldwork, the result of a process of collecting and connecting many different perspectives on one piece of data. In photography, this might translate into taking many pictures of the same object from different angles.

kinesics The study of how individuals express themselves through body position and motion (facial expression, eye contact, posture, and gesture).

linguist A person who studies language and language behaviors.

link A piece of text or an image that has been programmed to allow the user to jump from one Web site to another by clicking on it; also called *hotlink* and *hyperlink*.

logos A rhetorical term borrowed from Aristotle (see Chapter 2) that refers to how information is presented in a coherent way to persuade an audience. Logic is one key means of persuasion among other narrative strategies.

lore The implicit rituals, beliefs, language, stories, or traditional behaviors that surround a culture or subculture.

marginalization The process of pushing nonmainstream people toward the edges of society to prevent their access to power.

material culture The artifacts that represent meaning, history, and values for a group. These artifacts can be tools, printed or written materials, musical instruments, foods, toys, jewelry, ceremonial objects, or clothes.

metacognition Knowledge about one's own knowing. This broad knowledge is sometimes gained by assessing and evaluating one's learning process.

objectivity In social science research, considered a distanced and unbiased perspective.

oral history Stories recorded during interviews with people about their life experiences, crafts, skills, or occupations.

parody A work that imitates the style or voice of an author or other artist for comic effect.

participant-observer A researcher who has become involved in the daily life of a culture in addition to observing it.

pathos A rhetorical term borrowed from Aristotle (see Chapter 2) that refers to all the ways a speaker or writer is sensitive to the presence of an audience and invites their identification with them.

perception The taking in of information, observing, or understanding by means of the senses.

performance The interaction between a performer and audience members who understand many of the cultural values and behaviors represented in the act.

perspective A point of view; an angle of vision (the "spatial gaze," the "ethnographic ear").

plagiarism The deliberate act of representing someone else's ideas or words as your own.

portfolio A collection of material artifacts that demonstrates a learning process and includes a reflective analysis. A portfolio can be used to evaluate progress in a field-study and can be cited as source material.

positioning The researcher's stance toward the place and people being studied.

proxemics The study of how groups of individuals communicate nonverbally while maintaining spatial separation and responding to cultural and environmental influences.

rapport A feeling of connection and trust established between people.

reciprocity A mutual exchange of favors and rights. Fieldworkers usually give something to informants in exchange for their contributions to a project.

reflection The act of considering thoughtfully; looking back to gain insight.

reflexivity The process of self-scrutiny that results from studying others. To be reflexive demands both an "other" and some self-conscious awareness. Without the aid of an "other," and some self-conscious awareness, the process is only reflective.

representation In writing, the use of words to symbolize ideas. In ethnography, a researcher's use of language to describe another person, place, or artifact is a highly charged area of discussion because description is always subjective.

revision The process of reseeing or reimagining a text by changing many aspects of it. For most writers, the real craft of composing takes place in the process of revision.

rhetoric The shaping of language for different purposes and audiences. The three key elements of rhetoric—speaker or writer (*ethos*), content (*logos*), and audience (*pathos*)—shape all written and oral messages. Often defined as "the art of persuasion," rhetoric has a long Western tradition that began with the classical Greek teachings of Plato, Aristotle, and the Sophists.

rhetorical choices The writer's selection of voice, purpose, and audience.

subculture A group of people who share common language, rituals, and behaviors.

subjectivity Feelings and attitudes toward a given subject or topic, as opposed to objective, factual evidence.

synchronic Relating to a cultural system as it exists during one point in time.

thesis The controlling idea of an essay. A thesis does not have to appear as a sentence in the text but must be clear to the writer and the reader. *Thesis* also refers to an extended original study about a subject (such as a master's thesis).

transcript The written, word-for-word text of an interview or other spoken event.

triangulation The process of verifying data using multiple sources of information. For researchers, triangulation means not simply obtaining three pieces of evidence from three perspectives but ways that data are validated, cross-checked, or disconfirmed.

underlife Activities that generally go unrecognized by mainstream authorities. The underlife of a classroom might be student behavior (such as passing notes, whispering, sleeping, and so on) that goes unnoticed by teachers.

variant An alteration from the traditional core of a folk art, according to a performer's or artisan's specific history, cultural understanding, and personal creativity.

verbal art Language behaviors within a culture or subculture, ranging from informal everyday events (grunts, shouts, taunts, jokes, gossip, and stories) to more highly ritualized forms (proverbs and taboos, songs and chants, urban legends, curses and spells, myths and tales, and traditional stories and ceremonies).

worldview The perspective or point of view of any particular culture or individual.

Credits

Edward Ball. From *Slaves in the Family* by Edward Ball. Copyright © 1998 by Edward Ball. Reprinted by permission of Farrar, Straus and Giroux, LLC.

Laura Bohannan. "Shakespeare in the Bush." From *Natural History*, August/September 1966.

Joan Didion. "On Keeping a Notebook." From *Slouching toward Bethlehem* by Joan Didion. Copyright © 1966, 1968, renewed 1996 by Joan Didion. Reprinted by permission of Farrar, Straus and Giroux, LLC.

Jennette Edwards. "I Can Read and I Can Write" (online only). From *These Are Our Lives* by the Federal Writers' Project, Regional Staff. Copyright © 1939 by the University of North Carolina Press, renewed 1967. Reprinted by permission of the publisher.

Lars Eighner. "Dumpster Diving." From *Travels with Lizbeth* by Lars Eighner. Copyright © 1993 by Lars Eighner. Reprinted by permission of St. Martin's Press, LLC.

Peter Elbow. "Freewriting." From *Writing with Power: Techniques for Mastering the Writing Process* by Peter Elbow. Copyright © 1981. Reprinted by permission of Oxford University Press.

Henry Glassie. From *Passing the Time in Ballymenone*. Copyright © 1995. Reprinted by permission of Indiana University Press.

H. L. "Bud" Goodall. From *New Ethnography*. Copyright © 2009 by Alta Mira. Reprinted by permission.

Lafcadio Hearn. "Cheek." From *Lafcadio Hearn's America*, edited by Simon Bronner. Copyright © 2002 by University Press of Kentucky. Reprinted by permission.

Zora Neale Hurston. "To the Man God." From *Mules and Men* by Zora Neale Hurston. Copyright © 1935 by Zora Neale Hurston, renewed 1963 by John C. Hurston and Joel Hurston.

David Isay. "Joyce Butler." From *Listening Is an Act of Love*, edited by David Isay. Copyright © 2007 by Sound Portraits Productions, Inc. Reprinted by permission of the Penguin Press, a division of Penguin Group (USA) Inc.

Jamaica Kincaid. "On Seeing England for the First Time." Copyright © 1991 by Jamaica Kincaid. Reprinted by permission of the Wylie Agency.

Anne Lamott. "Shitty First Drafts." From *Bird by Bird* by Anne Lamott. Copyright © 1994 by Anne Lamott. Reprinted by permission of Pantheon Books, a division of Random House, Inc.

Barbara Myerhoff. "So What Do You Want from Us Here?" From *Number Our Days* by Barbara Myerhoff. Copyright © 1978 by Barbara Myerhoff. Reprinted by permission of Dutton, a division of Penguin Group (USA) Inc.

Gloria Naylor. From *Mama Day* by Gloria Naylor. Copyright © 1988 by Gloria Naylor. Reprinted by permission of Houghton Mifflin Harcourt Publishing Company.

Art Credits

Index